TOYOTA | SIENNA
1998-09 REPAIR MANUAL
Deleted

CHILTON'S

Covers all U.S. and Canadian models of Toyota Sienna

Does not include information specific to all-wheel drive models

by Jay Storer

CHILTON *Automotive Books*

PUBLISHED BY **HAYNES NORTH AMERICA**, Inc.

Manufactured in USA
© 2003, 2010 Haynes North America, Inc.
ISBN-13: 978-1-56392-905-2
ISBN: 1-56392-905-8
Library of Congress Control No. 2010943143

Haynes Publishing Group
Sparkford Nr Yeovil
Somerset BA22 7JJ England

Haynes North America, Inc
861 Lawrence Drive
Newbury Park
California 91320 USA

ABCDE
FGHIJ
KLMNO
P

12N3

Contents

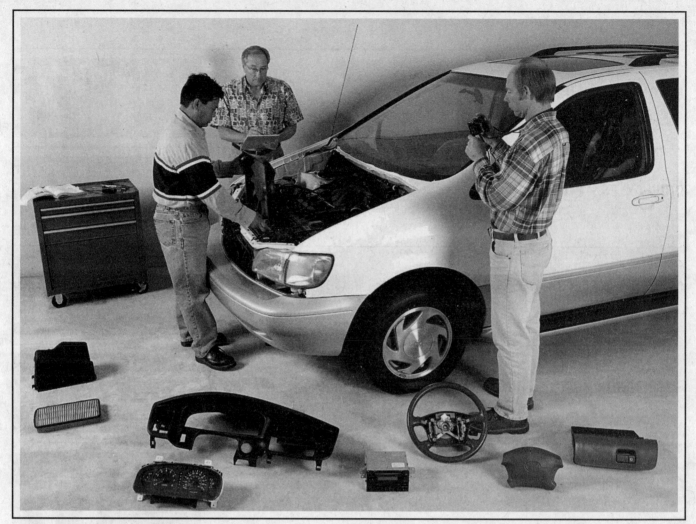

1998 Toyota Sienna

ACKNOWLEDGMENTS

We are grateful for the help and cooperation of the Toyota Motor Corporation. for their assistance with technical information and certain illustrations.

While every attempt is made to ensure that the information in this manual is correct, no liability can be accepted by the authors or publishers for loss, damage or injury caused by any errors in, or omissions from, the information given.

About this manual

ITS PURPOSE

The purpose of this manual is to help you get the best value from your vehicle. It can do so in several ways. It can help you decide what work must be done, even if you choose to have it done by a dealer service department or a repair shop; it provides information and procedures for routine maintenance and servicing; and it offers diagnostic and repair procedures to follow when trouble occurs.

We hope you use the manual to tackle the work yourself. For many simpler jobs, doing it yourself may be quicker than arranging an appointment to get the vehicle into a shop and making the trips to leave it and pick it up. More importantly, a lot of money can be saved by avoiding the expense the shop must pass on to you to cover its labor and overhead costs. An added benefit is the sense of satisfaction and accomplishment that you feel after doing the job yourself.

USING THE MANUAL

The manual is divided into Chapters. Each Chapter is divided into numbered Sections. Each Section consists of consecutively numbered paragraphs.

At the beginning of each numbered Section you will be referred to any illustrations which apply to the procedures in that Section. The reference numbers used in illustration captions pinpoint the pertinent Section and the Step within that Section. That is, illustration 3.2 means the illustration refers to Section 3 and Step (or paragraph) 2 within that Section.

Procedures, once described in the text, are not normally repeated. When it's necessary to refer to another Chapter, the reference will be given as Chapter and Section number. Cross references given without use of the word "Chapter" apply to Sections and/or paragraphs in the same Chapter. For example, "see Section 8" means in the same Chapter.

References to the left or right side of the vehicle assume you are sitting in the driver's seat, facing forward.

Even though we have prepared this manual with extreme care, neither the publisher nor the author can accept responsibility for any errors in, or omissions from, the information given.

➡NOTE

A *Note* provides information necessary to properly complete a procedure or information which will make the procedure easier to understand.

❊ CAUTION

A *Caution* provides a special procedure or special steps which must be taken while completing the procedure where the Caution is found. Not heeding a Caution can result in damage to the assembly being worked on.

❊ WARNING

A *Warning* provides a special procedure or special steps which must be taken while completing the procedure where the Warning is found. Not heeding a Warning can result in personal injury.

Introduction to the Toyota Sienna

This manual covers the Toyota Sienna van. The Sienna has been produced in both "four-door" and "five-door" models. All models have a sliding side-door on the right side, while "five-door" models have an additional sliding door on the left side.

The transversely mounted V6 engines used in these models are equipped with electronic port fuel injection.

The engine drives the front wheels through a four-speed automatic transaxle via independent driveaxles.

Independent suspension, featuring coil spring/strut damper units, is used on the front, while the rear suspension uses a beam-type axle with separate shocks and coil springs. The power-assisted rack-and-pinion steering unit is mounted behind the engine.

Front brakes are disc type. Rear brakes may be either drums or disc. Power assist is standard and anti-lock brakes are available on all models.

Vehicle identification numbers

Modifications are a continuing and unpublicized process in vehicle manufacturing. Since spare parts manuals and lists are compiled on a numerical basis, the individual vehicle numbers are essential to correctly identify the component required.

VEHICLE IDENTIFICATION NUMBER (VIN)

This very important identification number is stamped on a plate attached to the dashboard inside the windshield on the driver's side of the vehicle (see illustration). It can also be found on the certification label located on the driver's side door post. The VIN also appears on the Vehicle Certificate of Title and Registration. It contains information such as where and when the vehicle was manufactured, the model year and the body style.

On the models covered by this manual the model year codes are:

W	1998
X	1999
Y	2000
1	2001
2	2002
3	2003
4	2004
5	2005
6	2006
7	2007
8	2008
9	2009

CERTIFICATION LABEL

The certification label is attached to the end of the driver's door post (see illustration). The plate contains the name of the manufacturer, the month and year of production, the Gross Vehicle Weight Rating (GVWR), the Gross Axle Weight Rating (GAWR) and the certification statement.

ENGINE IDENTIFICATION NUMBERS

The engine serial number can be found on the front side of the engine (see illustration).

The Vehicle Identification Number (VIN) is located on a plate on top of the dash (visible through the windshield)

The vehicle certification label is located at the rear of the driver's door

The V6 engine serial number is located on the front side of the block under the exhaust manifold

Buying parts

Replacement parts are available from many sources, which generally fall into one of two categories - authorized dealer parts departments and independent retail auto parts stores. Our advice concerning these parts is as follows:

Retail auto parts stores: Good auto parts stores will stock frequently needed components which wear out relatively fast, such as clutch components, exhaust systems, brake parts, tune-up parts, etc. These stores often supply new or reconditioned parts on an exchange basis, which can save a considerable amount of money. Discount auto parts stores are often very good places to buy materials and parts needed for general vehicle maintenance such as oil, grease, filters, spark plugs, belts, touch-up paint, bulbs, etc. They also usually sell tools and general accessories, have convenient hours, charge lower prices and can often be found not far from home.

Authorized dealer parts department: This is the best source for parts which are unique to the vehicle and not generally available elsewhere (such as major engine parts, transmission parts, trim pieces, etc.).

Warranty information: If the vehicle is still covered under warranty, be sure that any replacement parts purchased - regardless of the source - do not invalidate the warranty!

To be sure of obtaining the correct parts, have engine and chassis numbers available and, if possible, take the old parts along for positive identification.

MAINTENANCE TECHNIQUES

There are a number of techniques involved in maintenance and repair that will be referred to throughout this manual. Application of these techniques will enable the home mechanic to be more efficient, better organized and capable of performing the various tasks properly, which will ensure that the repair job is thorough and complete.

Fasteners

Fasteners are nuts, bolts, studs and screws used to hold two or more parts together. There are a few things to keep in mind when working with fasteners. Almost all of them use a locking device of some type, either a lockwasher, locknut, locking tab or thread adhesive. All threaded fasteners should be clean and straight, with undamaged threads and undamaged corners on the hex head where the wrench fits. Develop the habit of replacing all damaged nuts and bolts with new ones. Special locknuts with nylon or fiber inserts can only be used once. If they are removed, they lose their locking ability and must be replaced with new ones.

Rusted nuts and bolts should be treated with a penetrating fluid to ease removal and prevent breakage. Some mechanics use turpentine in a spout-type oil can, which works quite well. After applying the rust penetrant, let it work for a few minutes before trying to loosen the nut or bolt. Badly rusted fasteners may have to be chiseled or sawed off or removed with a special nut breaker, available at tool stores.

If a bolt or stud breaks off in an assembly, it can be drilled and removed with a special tool commonly available for this purpose. Most automotive machine shops can perform this task, as well as other repair procedures, such as the repair of threaded holes that have been stripped out.

Flat washers and lockwashers, when removed from an assembly, should always be replaced exactly as removed. Replace any damaged washers with new ones. Never use a lockwasher on any soft metal surface (such as aluminum), thin sheet metal or plastic.

Fastener sizes

For a number of reasons, automobile manufacturers are making wider and wider use of metric fasteners. Therefore, it is important to be able to tell the difference between standard (sometimes called U.S. or SAE) and metric hardware, since they cannot be interchanged.

All bolts, whether standard or metric, are sized according to diameter, thread pitch and length. For example, a standard 1/2 - 13 x 1 bolt is 1/2 inch in diameter, has 13 threads per inch and is 1 inch long. An M12 - 1.75 x 25 metric bolt is 12 mm in diameter, has a thread pitch of 1.75 mm (the distance between threads) and is 25 mm long. The two bolts are nearly identical, and easily confused, but they are not interchangeable.

In addition to the differences in diameter, thread pitch and length, metric and standard bolts can also be distinguished by examining the bolt heads. To begin with, the distance across the flats on a standard bolt head is measured in inches, while the same dimension on a metric bolt is sized in millimeters (the same is true for nuts). As a result, a standard wrench should not be used on a metric bolt and a metric wrench should not be used on a standard bolt. Also, most standard bolts have slashes radiating out from the center of the head to denote the grade or strength of the bolt, which is an indication of the amount of torque that can be applied to it. The greater the number of slashes, the greater the strength of the bolt. Grades 0 through 5 are commonly used on automobiles. Metric bolts have a property class (grade) number, rather than a slash, molded into their heads to indicate bolt strength. In this case, the higher the number, the stronger the bolt. Property class numbers 8.8, 9.8 and 10.9 are commonly used on automobiles.

Strength markings can also be used to distinguish standard hex nuts from metric hex nuts. Many standard nuts have dots stamped into one side, while metric nuts are marked with a number. The greater the number of dots, or the higher the number, the greater the strength of the nut.

Metric studs are also marked on their ends according to property class (grade). Larger studs are numbered (the same as metric bolts), while smaller studs carry a geometric code to denote grade.

It should be noted that many fasteners, especially Grades 0 through 2, have no distinguishing marks on them. When such is the case, the only way to determine whether it is standard or metric is to measure the thread pitch or compare it to a known fastener of the same size.

Standard fasteners are often referred to as SAE, as opposed to metric. However, it should be noted that SAE technically refers to a non-metric fine thread fastener only. Coarse thread non-metric fasteners are referred to as USS sizes.

Since fasteners of the same size (both standard and metric) may have different strength ratings, be sure to reinstall any bolts, studs or nuts removed from your vehicle in their original locations. Also, when replacing a fastener with a new one, make sure that the new one has a strength rating equal to or greater than the original.

Tightening sequences and procedures

Most threaded fasteners should be tightened to a specific torque value (torque is the twisting force applied to a threaded component such as a nut or bolt). Overtightening the fastener can weaken it and cause it to break, while undertightening can cause it to eventually come loose. Bolts, screws and studs, depending on the material they are made of and their thread diameters, have specific torque values, many of which are noted in the Specifications at the end of each Chapter. Be sure to follow the torque recommendations closely. For fasteners not assigned a specific torque, a general torque value chart is presented here as a guide. These torque values are for dry (unlubricated) fasteners threaded into steel or cast iron (not aluminum). As was previously mentioned, the size and grade of a fastener determine the amount of torque that can safely be applied to it. The figures listed here are approximate for Grade 2 and Grade 3 fasteners. Higher grades can tolerate higher torque values.

Fasteners laid out in a pattern, such as cylinder head bolts, oil pan bolts, differential cover bolts, etc., must be loosened or tightened in sequence to avoid warping the component. This sequence will normally be shown in the appropriate Chapter. If a specific pattern is not given, the following procedures can be used to prevent warping.

Initially, the bolts or nuts should be assembled finger-tight only. Next, they should be tightened one full turn each, in a criss-cross or diagonal pattern. After each one has been tightened one full turn, return to the first one and tighten them all one-half turn, following the same

Grade 1 or 2   Grade 5   Grade 8

Bolt strength marking (standard/SAE/USS; bottom - metric)

Grade	Identification
Hex Nut Grade 5	3 Dots
Hex Nut Grade 8	6 Dots

Standard hex nut
strength markings

Grade	Identification
Hex Nut Property Class 9	Arabic 9
Hex Nut Property Class 10	Arabic 10

Metric hex nut
strength markings

Class 10.9   Class 9.8   Class 8.8

Metric stud strength markings

00-1

pattern. Finally, tighten each of them one-quarter turn at a time until each fastener has been tightened to the proper torque. To loosen and remove the fasteners, the procedure would be reversed.

Component disassembly

Component disassembly should be done with care and purpose to help ensure that the parts go back together properly. Always keep track of the sequence in which parts are removed. Make note of special characteristics or marks on parts that can be installed more than one way, such as a grooved thrust washer on a shaft. It is a good idea to lay the disassembled parts out on a clean surface in the order that they were removed. It may also be helpful to make sketches or take instant photos of components before removal.

When removing fasteners from a component, keep track of their locations. Sometimes threading a bolt back in a part, or putting the washers and nut back on a stud, can prevent mix-ups later. If nuts and bolts cannot be returned to their original locations, they should be kept in a compartmented box or a series of small boxes. A cupcake or muffin tin is ideal for this purpose, since each cavity can hold the bolts and nuts from a particular area (i.e. oil pan bolts, valve cover bolts, engine

Metric thread sizes

	Ft-lbs	Nm
M-6	6 to 9	9 to 12
M-8	14 to 21	19 to 28
M-10	28 to 40	38 to 54
M-12	50 to 71	68 to 96
M-14	80 to 140	109 to 154

Pipe thread sizes

1/8	5 to 8	7 to 10
1/4	12 to 18	17 to 24
3/8	22 to 33	30 to 44
1/2	25 to 35	34 to 47

U.S. thread sizes

1/4 - 20	6 to 9	9 to 12
5/16 - 18	12 to 18	17 to 24
5/16 - 24	14 to 20	19 to 27
3/8 - 16	22 to 32	30 to 43
3/8 - 24	27 to 38	37 to 51
7/16 - 14	40 to 55	55 to 74
7/16 - 20	40 to 60	55 to 81
1/2 - 13	55 to 80	75 to 108

00-2

Standard (SAE and USS) bolt dimensions/grade marks

G   Grade marks (bolt strength)
L   Length (in inches)
T   Thread pitch (number of threads per inch)
D   Nominal diameter (in inches)

Metric bolt dimensions/grade marks

P   Property class (bolt strength)
L   Length (in millimeters)
T   Thread pitch (distance between threads in millimeters)
D   Diameter

mount bolts, etc.). A pan of this type is especially helpful when working on assemblies with very small parts, such as the carburetor, alternator, valve train or interior dash and trim pieces. The cavities can be marked with paint or tape to identify the contents.

Whenever wiring looms, harnesses or connectors are separated, it is a good idea to identify the two halves with numbered pieces of masking tape so they can be easily reconnected.

Gasket sealing surfaces

Throughout any vehicle, gaskets are used to seal the mating surfaces between two parts and keep lubricants, fluids, vacuum or pressure contained in an assembly.

Many times these gaskets are coated with a liquid or paste-type gasket sealing compound before assembly. Age, heat and pressure can sometimes cause the two parts to stick together so tightly that they are

Micrometer set

Dial indicator set

very difficult to separate. Often, the assembly can be loosened by striking it with a soft-face hammer near the mating surfaces. A regular hammer can be used if a block of wood is placed between the hammer and the part. Do not hammer on cast parts or parts that could be easily damaged. With any particularly stubborn part, always recheck to make sure that every fastener has been removed.

Avoid using a screwdriver or bar to pry apart an assembly, as they can easily mar the gasket sealing surfaces of the parts, which must remain smooth. If prying is absolutely necessary, use an old broom handle, but keep in mind that extra clean up will be necessary if the wood splinters.

After the parts are separated, the old gasket must be carefully scraped off and the gasket surfaces cleaned. Stubborn gasket material can be soaked with rust penetrant or treated with a special chemical to soften it so it can be easily scraped off.

✳✳ CAUTION:

Never use gasket removal solutions or caustic chemicals on plastic or other composite components.

A scraper can be fashioned from a piece of copper tubing by flattening and sharpening one end. Copper is recommended because it is usually softer than the surfaces to be scraped, which reduces the chance of gouging the part. Some gaskets can be removed with a wire brush, but regardless of the method used, the mating surfaces must be left clean and smooth. If for some reason the gasket surface is gouged, then a gasket sealer thick enough to fill scratches will have to be used during reassembly of the components. For most applications, a non-drying (or semi-drying) gasket sealer should be used.

Hose removal tips

✳✳ WARNING:

If the vehicle is equipped with air conditioning, do not disconnect any of the A/C hoses without first having the system depressurized by a dealer service department or a service station.

Hose removal precautions closely parallel gasket removal precautions. Avoid scratching or gouging the surface that the hose mates against or the connection may leak. This is especially true for radiator hoses. Because of various chemical reactions, the rubber in hoses can

bond itself to the metal spigot that the hose fits over. To remove a hose, first loosen the hose clamps that secure it to the spigot. Then, with slip-joint pliers, grab the hose at the clamp and rotate it around the spigot. Work it back and forth until it is completely free, then pull it off. Silicone or other lubricants will ease removal if they can be applied between the hose and the outside of the spigot. Apply the same lubricant to the inside of the hose and the outside of the spigot to simplify installation.

As a last resort (and if the hose is to be replaced with a new one anyway), the rubber can be slit with a knife and the hose peeled from the spigot. If this must be done, be careful that the metal connection is not damaged.

If a hose clamp is broken or damaged, do not reuse it. Wire-type clamps usually weaken with age, so it is a good idea to replace them with screw-type clamps whenever a hose is removed.

TOOLS

A selection of good tools is a basic requirement for anyone who plans to maintain and repair his or her own vehicle. For the owner who has few tools, the initial investment might seem high, but when compared to the spiraling costs of professional auto maintenance and repair, it is a wise one.

To help the owner decide which tools are needed to perform the tasks detailed in this manual, the following tool lists are offered: *Maintenance and minor repair, Repair/overhaul* and *Special.*

The newcomer to practical mechanics should start off with the *maintenance and minor repair* tool kit, which is adequate for the simpler jobs performed on a vehicle. Then, as confidence and experience grow, the owner can tackle more difficult tasks, buying additional tools as they are needed. Eventually the basic kit will be expanded into the *repair and overhaul* tool set. Over a period of time, the experienced do-it-yourselfer will assemble a tool set complete enough for most repair and overhaul procedures and will add tools from the special category when it is felt that the expense is justified by the frequency of use.

Maintenance and minor repair tool kit

The tools in this list should be considered the minimum required for performance of routine maintenance, servicing and minor repair work. We recommend the purchase of combination wrenches (box-end and open-end combined in one wrench). While more expensive than open end wrenches, they offer the advantages of both types of wrench.

Combination wrench set (1/4-inch to 1 inch or 6 mm to 19 mm)

Adjustable wrench, 8 inch
Spark plug wrench with rubber insert
Spark plug gap adjusting tool
Feeler gauge set
Brake bleeder wrench
Standard screwdriver (5/16-inch x 6 inch)
Phillips screwdriver (No. 2 x 6 inch)
Combination pliers - 6 inch

Hacksaw and assortment of blades
Tire pressure gauge
Grease gun
Oil can
Fine emery cloth
Wire brush
Battery post and cable cleaning tool
Oil filter wrench

Dial caliper

Hand-operated vacuum pump

Fuel pressure gauge set

Compression gauge with spark plug hole adapter

Damper/steering wheel puller

General purpose puller

Hydraulic lifter removal tool

Funnel (medium size)
Safety goggles
Jackstands (2)
Drain pan

➡**Note: If basic tune-ups are going to be part of routine mainte-nance, it will be necessary to purchase a good quality strobo-scopic timing light and combination tachometer/dwell meter. Although they are included in the list of special tools, it is men-tioned here because they are absolutely necessary for tuning most vehicles properly.**

Repair and overhaul tool set

These tools are essential for anyone who plans to perform major repairs and are in addition to those in the maintenance and minor repair tool kit. Included is a comprehensive set of sockets which, though expensive, are invaluable because of their versatility, especially when various extensions and drives are available. We recommend the 1/2-inch drive over the 3/8-inch drive. Although the larger drive is bulky and more expensive, it has the capacity of accepting a very wide range of large sockets. Ideally, however, the mechanic should have a 3/8-inch drive set and a 1/2-inch drive set.

Valve spring compressor

Valve spring compressor

Ridge reamer

Piston ring groove cleaning tool

Ring removal/installation tool

Ring compressor

Cylinder hone

Brake hold-down spring tool

Torque angle gauge

Socket set(s)
Reversible ratchet
Extension - 10 inch
Universal joint
Torque wrench (same size drive as sockets)
Ball peen hammer - 8 ounce
Soft-face hammer (plastic/rubber)
Standard screwdriver (1/4-inch x 6 inch)
Standard screwdriver (stubby - 5/16-inch)
Phillips screwdriver (No. 3 x 8 inch)
Phillips screwdriver (stubby - No. 2)
Pliers - vise grip
Pliers - lineman's
Pliers - needle nose
Pliers - snap-ring (internal and external)
Cold chisel - 1/2-inch
Scribe
Scraper (made from flattened copper tubing)
Centerpunch
Pin punches (1/16, 1/8, 3/16-inch)
Steel rule/straightedge - 12 inch
Allen wrench set (1/8 to 3/8-inch or 4 mm to 10 mm)
A selection of files
Wire brush (large)
Jackstands (second set)
Jack (scissor or hydraulic type)

➡Note: Another tool which is often useful is an electric drill
with a chuck capacity of 3/8-inch and a set of good quality drill
bits.

Special tools

The tools in this list include those which are not used regularly, are
expensive to buy, or which need to be used in accordance with their
manufacturer's instructions. Unless these tools will be used frequently,
it is not very economical to purchase many of them. A consideration
would be to split the cost and use between yourself and a friend or
friends. In addition, most of these tools can be obtained from a tool
rental shop on a temporary basis.

This list primarily contains only those tools and instruments widely
available to the public, and not those special tools produced by the
vehicle manufacturer for distribution to dealer service departments.
Occasionally, references to the manufacturer's special tools are included
in the text of this manual. Generally, an alternative method of doing the

Clutch plate alignment tool

job without the special tool is offered. However, sometimes there is no
alternative to their use. Where this is the case, and the tool cannot be
purchased or borrowed, the work should be turned over to the dealer
service department or an automotive repair shop.

Valve spring compressor
Piston ring groove cleaning tool
Piston ring compressor
Piston ring installation tool
Cylinder compression gauge
Cylinder ridge reamer
Cylinder surfacing hone
Cylinder bore gauge
Micrometers and/or dial calipers
Hydraulic lifter removal tool
Balljoint separator
Universal-type puller
Impact screwdriver
Dial indicator set
Stroboscopic timing light (inductive pick-up)
Hand operated vacuum/pressure pump
Tachometer/dwell meter
Universal electrical multimeter
Cable hoist
Brake spring removal and installation tools
Floor jack

Tap and die set

Buying tools

For the do-it-yourselfer who is just starting to get involved in vehicle maintenance and repair, there are a number of options available when purchasing tools. If maintenance and minor repair is the extent of the work to be done, the purchase of individual tools is satisfactory. If, on the other hand, extensive work is planned, it would be a good idea to purchase a modest tool set from one of the large retail chain stores. A set can usually be bought at a substantial savings over the individual tool prices, and they often come with a tool box. As additional tools are needed, add-on sets, individual tools and a larger tool box can be purchased to expand the tool selection. Building a tool set gradually allows the cost of the tools to be spread over a longer period of time and gives the mechanic the freedom to choose only those tools that will actually be used.

Tool stores will often be the only source of some of the special tools that are needed, but regardless of where tools are bought, try to avoid cheap ones, especially when buying screwdrivers and sockets, because they won't last very long. The expense involved in replacing cheap tools will eventually be greater than the initial cost of quality tools.

Care and maintenance of tools

Good tools are expensive, so it makes sense to treat them with respect. Keep them clean and in usable condition and store them properly when not in use. Always wipe off any dirt, grease or metal chips before putting them away. Never leave tools lying around in the work area. Upon completion of a job, always check closely under the hood for tools that may have been left there so they won't get lost during a test drive.

Some tools, such as screwdrivers, pliers, wrenches and sockets, can be hung on a panel mounted on the garage or workshop wall, while others should be kept in a tool box or tray. Measuring instruments, gauges, meters, etc. must be carefully stored where they cannot be damaged by weather or impact from other tools.

When tools are used with care and stored properly, they will last a very long time. Even with the best of care, though, tools will wear out if used frequently. When a tool is damaged or worn out, replace it. Subsequent jobs will be safer and more enjoyable if you do.

HOW TO REPAIR DAMAGED THREADS

Sometimes, the internal threads of a nut or bolt hole can become stripped, usually from overtightening. Stripping threads is an all-too-common occurrence, especially when working with aluminum parts, because aluminum is so soft that it easily strips out.

Usually, external or internal threads are only partially stripped. After they've been cleaned up with a tap or die, they'll still work. Sometimes, however, threads are badly damaged. When this happens, you've got three choices:

1) *Drill and tap the hole to the next suitable oversize and install a larger diameter bolt, screw or stud.*

2) *Drill and tap the hole to accept a threaded plug, then drill and tap the plug to the original screw size. You can also buy a plug already threaded to the original size. Then you simply drill a hole to the specified size, then run the threaded plug into the hole with a bolt and jam nut. Once the plug is fully seated, remove the jam nut and bolt.*

3) *The third method uses a patented thread repair kit like Heli-Coil or Slimsert. These easy-to-use kits are designed to repair damaged threads in straight-through holes and blind holes. Both are available as kits which can handle a variety of sizes and thread patterns. Drill the hole, then tap it with the special included tap. Install the Heli-Coil and the hole is back to its original diameter and thread pitch.*

Regardless of which method you use, be sure to proceed calmly and carefully. A little impatience or carelessness during one of these relatively simple procedures can ruin your whole day's work and cost you a bundle if you wreck an expensive part.

WORKING FACILITIES

Not to be overlooked when discussing tools is the workshop. If anything more than routine maintenance is to be carried out, some sort of suitable work area is essential.

It is understood, and appreciated, that many home mechanics do not have a good workshop or garage available, and end up removing an engine or doing major repairs outside. It is recommended, however, that the overhaul or repair be completed under the cover of a roof.

A clean, flat workbench or table of comfortable working height is an absolute necessity. The workbench should be equipped with a vise that has a jaw opening of at least four inches.

As mentioned previously, some clean, dry storage space is also required for tools, as well as the lubricants, fluids, cleaning solvents, etc. which soon become necessary.

Sometimes waste oil and fluids, drained from the engine or cooling system during normal maintenance or repairs, present a disposal problem. To avoid pouring them on the ground or into a sewage system, pour the used fluids into large containers, seal them with caps and take them to an authorized disposal site or recycling center. Plastic jugs, such as old antifreeze containers, are ideal for this purpose.

Always keep a supply of old newspapers and clean rags available. Old towels are excellent for mopping up spills. Many mechanics use rolls of paper towels for most work because they are readily available and disposable. To help keep the area under the vehicle clean, a large cardboard box can be cut open and flattened to protect the garage or shop floor.

Whenever working over a painted surface, such as when leaning over a fender to service something under the hood, always cover it with an old blanket or bedspread to protect the finish. Vinyl covered pads, made especially for this purpose, are available at auto parts stores.

Jacking and towing

JACKING

The jack supplied with the vehicle should only be used for raising the vehicle for changing a tire or placing jackstands under the frame.

✳✳ WARNING:

Never crawl under the vehicle or start the engine when the jack is being used as the only means of support.

All vehicles are supplied with a scissors-type jack. When jacking the vehicle, it should be engaged with the seam notch, between the two dimples (see illustration).

The vehicle should be on level ground with the wheels blocked and the transmission in Park. Pry off the hub cap (if equipped) using the tapered end of the lug wrench. Loosen the lug nuts one-half turn and leave them in place until the wheel is raised off the ground.

Place the jack under the side of the vehicle in the indicated position. Use the supplied wrench to turn the jackscrew clockwise until the wheel is raised off the ground. Remove the lug nuts, pull off the wheel and install the spare.

With the beveled side in, install the lug nuts and tighten them until snug. Lower the vehicle by turning the jackscrew counterclockwise. Remove the jack and tighten the nuts in a diagonal pattern to the torque listed in the Chapter 1 Specifications. If a torque wrench is not available, have the torque checked by a service station as soon as possible. Install the hubcap by placing it in position and using the heel of your hand or a rubber mallet to seat it.

TOWING

As a general rule, the vehicle should be towed with the front (drive) wheels off the ground or, preferably, on a flat bed car carrier. If the front wheels can't be raised or a carrier isn't available, place them on a dolly. The ignition key must be in the ACC position, since the steering lock mechanism isn't strong enough to hold the front wheels straight while towing.

In emergency situations the vehicle can be towed from the front with all four wheels on the ground, provided that speeds don't exceed 25 mph and the distance is not over 15 miles. Before towing, check the transaxle fluid level (see Chapter 1). If the level is below the HOT mark on the dipstick, add fluid.

Towing equipment specifically designed for this purpose should be used and should be attached to the main structural members of the vehicle, not the bumper or brackets.

Safety is a major consideration when towing and all applicable state and local laws must be obeyed. A safety chain system must be used for all towing.

While towing, the parking brake must be released and the transmission must be in Neutral. The steering must be unlocked (ignition switch in the Off position). Remember that power steering and power brakes will not work with the engine off.

TRACTION CONTROL

On models equipped with Traction-Control system, push in the TRAC switch (on the dashboard or floor console, depending on model) anytime the vehicle is on a "rolling road" tester such as a speedometer test machine or chassis dynamometer. The TRAC OFF indicator light should illuminate when the system is turned off.

The jack fits over the rocker panel flange, between the two notches (there are two jacking points on each side of the vehicle)

Booster battery (jump) starting

Observe the following precautions when using a booster battery to start a vehicle:

a) *Before connecting the booster battery, make sure the ignition switch is in the Off position.*

b) *Turn off the lights, heater and other electrical loads.*

c) *Your eyes should be shielded. Safety goggles are a good idea.*

d) *Make sure the booster battery is the same voltage as the dead one in the vehicle.*

e) *The two vehicles MUST NOT TOUCH each other.*

f) *Make sure the transmission is in Park.*

g) *If the booster battery is not a maintenance-free type, remove the vent caps and lay a cloth over the vent holes.*

Connect the red jumper cable to the positive (+) terminals of each battery.

Connect one end of the black cable to the negative (-) terminal of the booster battery. The other end of this cable should be connected to a good ground on the engine block (see illustration). Make sure the cable will not come into contact with the fan, drivebelts or other moving parts of the engine.

Start the engine using the booster battery, then, with the engine running at idle speed, disconnect the jumper cables in the reverse order of connection

Make the booster battery cable connections in the numerical order shown (note that the negative cable of the booster battery is NOT attached to the negative terminal of the dead battery)

CONVERSION FACTORS

LENGTH (distance)

Inches (in)	X	25.4	= Millimeters (mm)	X 0.0394	= Inches (in)
Feet (ft)	X	0.305	= Meters (m)	X 3.281	= Feet (ft)
Miles	X	1.609	= Kilometers (km)	X 0.621	= Miles

VOLUME (capacity)

Cubic inches (cu in; in^3)	X	16.387	= Cubic centimeters (cc; cm^3)	X 0.061	= Cubic inches (cu in; in^3)
Imperial pints (Imp pt)	X	0.568	= Liters (l)	X 1.76	= Imperial pints (Imp pt)
Imperial quarts (Imp qt)	X	1.137	= Liters (l)	X 0.88	= Imperial quarts (Imp qt)
Imperial quarts (Imp qt)	X	1.201	= US quarts (US qt)	X 0.833	= Imperial quarts (Imp qt)
US quarts (US qt)	X	0.946	= Liters (l)	X 1.057	= US quarts (US qt)
Imperial gallons (Imp gal)	X	4.546	= Liters (l)	X 0.22	= Imperial gallons (Imp gal)
Imperial gallons (Imp gal)	X	1.201	= US gallons (US gal)	X 0.833	= Imperial gallons (Imp gal)
US gallons (US gal)	X	3.785	= Liters (l)	X 0.264	= US gallons (US gal)

MASS (weight)

Ounces (oz)	X	28.35	= Grams (g)	X 0.035	= Ounces (oz)
Pounds (lb)	X	0.454	= Kilograms (kg)	X 2.205	= Pounds (lb)

FORCE

Ounces-force (ozf; oz)	X	0.278	= Newtons (N)	X 3.6	= Ounces-force (ozf; oz)
Pounds-force (lbf; lb)	X	4.448	= Newtons (N)	X 0.225	= Pounds-force (lbf; lb)
Newtons (N)	X	0.1	= Kilograms-force (kgf; kg)	X 9.81	= Newtons (N)

PRESSURE

Pounds-force per square inch (psi; lbf/in^2; lb/in^2)	X	0.070	= Kilograms-force per square centimeter (kgf/cm^2; kg/cm^2)	X 14.223	= Pounds-force per square inch (psi; lbf/in^2; lb/in^2)
Pounds-force per square inch (psi; lbf/in^2; lb/in^2)	X	0.068	= Atmospheres (atm)	X 14.696	= Pounds-force per square inch (psi; lbf/in^2; lb/in^2)
Pounds-force per square inch (psi; lbf/in^2; lb/in^2)	X	0.069	= Bars	X 14.5	= Pounds-force per square inch (psi; lbf/in^2; lb/in^2)
Pounds-force per square inch (psi; lbf/in^2; lb/in^2)	X	6.895	= Kilopascals (kPa)	X 0.145	= Pounds-force per square inch (psi; lbf/in^2; lb/in^2)
Kilopascals (kPa)	X	0.01	= Kilograms-force per square centimeter (kgf/cm^2; kg/cm^2)	X 98.1	= Kilopascals (kPa)

TORQUE (moment of force)

Pounds-force inches (lbf in; lb in)	X	1.152	= Kilograms-force centimeter (kgf cm; kg cm)	X 0.868	= Pounds-force inches (lbf in; lb in)
Pounds-force inches (lbf in; lb in)	X	0.113	= Newton meters (Nm)	X 8.85	= Pounds-force inches (lbf in; lb in)
Pounds-force inches (lbf in; lb in)	X	0.083	= Pounds-force feet (lbf ft; lb ft)	X 12	= Pounds-force inches (lbf in; lb in)
Pounds-force feet (lbf ft; lb ft)	X	0.138	= Kilograms-force meters (kgf m; kg m)	X 7.233	= Pounds-force feet (lbf ft; lb ft)
Pounds-force feet (lbf ft; lb ft)	X	1.356	= Newton meters (Nm)	X 0.738	= Pounds-force feet (lbf ft; lb ft)
Newton meters (Nm)	X	0.102	= Kilograms-force meters (kgf m; kg m)	X 9.804	= Newton meters (Nm)

VACUUM

Inches mercury (in. Hg)	X	3.377	= Kilopascals (kPa)	X 0.2961	= Inches mercury
Inches mercury (in. Hg)	X	25.4	= Millimeters mercury (mm Hg)	X 0.0394	= Inches mercury

POWER

Horsepower (hp)	X	745.7	= Watts (W)	X 0.0013	= Horsepower (hp)

VELOCITY (speed)

Miles per hour (miles/hr; mph)	X	1.609	= Kilometers per hour (km/hr; kph)	X 0.621	= Miles per hour (miles/hr; mph)

FUEL CONSUMPTION *

Miles per gallon, Imperial (mpg)	X	0.354	= Kilometers per liter (km/l)	X 2.825	= Miles per gallon, Imperial (mpg)
Miles per gallon, US (mpg)	X	0.425	= Kilometers per liter (km/l)	X 2.352	= Miles per gallon, US (mpg)

TEMPERATURE

Degrees Fahrenheit = (°C x 1.8) + 32

Degrees Celsius (Degrees Centigrade; °C) = (°F - 32) x 0.56

*It is common practice to convert from miles per gallon (mpg) to liters/100 kilometers (l/100km), where mpg (Imperial) x l/100 km = 282 and mpg (US) x l/100 km = 235

FRACTION/DECIMAL/MILLIMETER EQUIVALENTS

DECIMALS TO MILLIMETERS

Decimal	mm	Decimal	mm
0.001	0.0254	0.500	12.7000
0.002	0.0508	0.510	12.9540
0.003	0.0762	0.520	13.2080
0.004	0.1016	0.530	13.4620
0.005	0.1270	0.540	13.7160
0.006	0.1524	0.550	13.9700
0.007	0.1778	0.560	14.2240
0.008	0.2032	0.570	14.4780
0.009	0.2286	0.580	14.7320
		0.590	14.9860
0.010	0.2540		
0.020	0.5080		
0.030	0.7620		
0.040	1.0160	0.600	15.2400
0.050	1.2700	0.610	15.4940
0.060	1.5240	0.620	15.7480
0.070	1.7780	0.630	16.0020
0.080	2.0320	0.640	16.2560
0.090	2.2860	0.650	16.5100
		0.660	16.7640
0.100	2.5400	0.670	17.0180
0.110	2.7940	0.680	17.2720
0.120	3.0480	0.690	17.5260
0.130	3.3020		
0.140	3.5560		
0.150	3.8100		
0.160	4.0640	0.700	17.7800
0.170	4.3180	0.710	18.0340
0.180	4.5720	0.720	18.2880
0.190	4.8260	0.730	18.5420
		0.740	18.7960
0.200	5.0800	0.750	19.0500
0.210	5.3340	0.760	19.3040
0.220	5.5880	0.770	19.5580
0.230	5.8420	0.780	19.8120
0.240	6.0960	0.790	20.0660
0.250	6.3500		
0.260	6.6040		
0.270	6.8580	0.800	20.3200
0.280	7.1120	0.810	20.5740
0.290	7.3660	0.820	21.8280
		0.830	21.0820
0.300	7.6200	0.840	21.3360
0.310	7.8740	0.850	21.5900
0.320	8.1280	0.860	21.8440
0.330	8.3820	0.870	22.0980
0.340	8.6360	0.880	22.3520
0.350	8.8900	0.890	22.6060
0.360	9.1440		
0.370	9.3980		
0.380	9.6520		
0.390	9.9060	0.900	22.8600
0.400	10.1600	0.910	23.1140
0.410	10.4140	0.920	23.3680
0.420	10.6680	0.930	23.6220
0.430	10.9220	0.940	23.8760
0.440	11.1760	0.950	24.1300
0.450	11.4300	0.960	24.3840
0.460	11.6840	0.970	24.6380
0.470	11.9380	0.980	24.8920
0.480	12.1920	0.990	25.1460
0.490	12.4460	1.000	25.4000

FRACTIONS TO DECIMALS TO MILLIMETERS

Fraction	Decimal	mm	Fraction	Decimal	mm
1/64	0.0156	0.3969	33/64	0.5156	13.0969
1/32	0.0312	0.7938	17/32	0.5312	13.4938
3/64	0.0469	1.1906	35/64	0.5469	13.8906
1/16	0.0625	1.5875	9/16	0.5625	14.2875
5/64	0.0781	1.9844	37/64	0.5781	14.6844
3/32	0.0938	2.3812	19/32	0.5938	15.0812
7/64	0.1094	2.7781	39/64	0.6094	15.4781
1/8	0.1250	3.1750	5/8	0.6250	15.8750
9/64	0.1406	3.5719	41/64	0.6406	16.2719
5/32	0.1562	3.9688	21/32	0.6562	16.6688
11/64	0.1719	4.3656	43/64	0.6719	17.0656
3/16	0.1875	4.7625	11/16	0.6875	17.4625
13/64	0.2031	5.1594	45/64	0.7031	17.8594
7/32	0.2188	5.5562	23/32	0.7188	18.2562
15/64	0.2344	5.9531	47/64	0.7344	18.6531
1/4	0.2500	6.3500	3/4	0.7500	19.0500
17/64	0.2656	6.7469	49/64	0.7656	19.4469
9/32	0.2812	7.1438	25/32	0.7812	19.8438
19/64	0.2969	7.5406	51/64	0.7969	20.2406
5/16	0.3125	7.9375	13/16	0.8125	20.6375
21/64	0.3281	8.3344	53/64	0.8281	21.0344
11/32	0.3438	8.7312	27/32	0.8438	21.4312
23/64	0.3594	9.1281	55/64	0.8594	21.8281
3/8	0.3750	9.5250	7/8	0.8750	22.2250
25/64	0.3906	9.9219	57/64	0.8906	22.6219
13/32	0.4062	10.3188	29/32	0.9062	23.0188
27/64	0.4219	10.7156	59/64	0.9219	23.4156
7/16	0.4375	11.1125	15/16	0.9375	23.8125
29/64	0.4531	11.5094	61/64	0.9531	24.2094
15/32	0.4688	11.9062	31/32	0.9688	24.6062
31/64	0.4844	12.3031	63/64	0.9844	25.0031
1/2	0.5000	12.7000	1	1.0000	25.4000

Automotive chemicals and lubricants

A number of automotive chemicals and lubricants are available for use during vehicle maintenance and repair. They include a wide variety of products ranging from cleaning solvents and degreasers to lubricants and protective sprays for rubber, plastic and vinyl.

CLEANERS

Carburetor cleaner and choke cleaner is a strong solvent for gum, varnish and carbon. Most carburetor cleaners leave a dry-type lubricant film which will not harden or gum up. Because of this film it is not recommended for use on electrical components.

Brake system cleaner is used to remove brake dust, grease and brake fluid from the brake system, where clean surfaces are absolutely necessary. It leaves no residue and often eliminates brake squeal caused by contaminants.

Electrical cleaner removes oxidation, corrosion and carbon deposits from electrical contacts, restoring full current flow. It can also be used to clean spark plugs, carburetor jets, voltage regulators and other parts where an oil-free surface is desired.

Demoisturants remove water and moisture from electrical components such as alternators, voltage regulators, electrical connectors and fuse blocks. They are non-conductive and non-corrosive.

Degreasers are heavy-duty solvents used to remove grease from the outside of the engine and from chassis components. They can be sprayed or brushed on and, depending on the type, are rinsed off either with water or solvent.

LUBRICANTS

Motor oil is the lubricant formulated for use in engines. It normally contains a wide variety of additives to prevent corrosion and reduce foaming and wear. Motor oil comes in various weights (viscosity ratings) from 0 to 50. The recommended weight of the oil depends on the season, temperature and the demands on the engine. Light oil is used in cold climates and under light load conditions. Heavy oil is used in hot climates and where high loads are encountered. Multi-viscosity oils are designed to have characteristics of both light and heavy oils and are available in a number of weights from 0W-20 to 20W-50.

Gear oil is designed to be used in differentials, manual transmissions and other areas where high-temperature lubrication is required.

Chassis and wheel bearing grease is a heavy grease used where increased loads and friction are encountered, such as for wheel bearings, balljoints, tie-rod ends and universal joints.

High-temperature wheel bearing grease is designed to withstand the extreme temperatures encountered by wheel bearings in disc brake equipped vehicles. It usually contains molybdenum disulfide (moly), which is a dry-type lubricant.

White grease is a heavy grease for metal-to-metal applications where water is a problem. White grease stays soft under both low and high temperatures (usually from -100 to +190-degrees F), and will not wash off or dilute in the presence of water.

Assembly lube is a special extreme pressure lubricant, usually containing moly, used to lubricate high-load parts (such as main and rod bearings and cam lobes) for initial start-up of a new engine. The assembly lube lubricates the parts without being squeezed out or washed away until the engine oiling system begins to function.

Silicone lubricants are used to protect rubber, plastic, vinyl and nylon parts.

Graphite lubricants are used where oils cannot be used due to contamination problems, such as in locks. The dry graphite will lubricate metal parts while remaining uncontaminated by dirt, water, oil or acids. It is electrically conductive and will not foul electrical contacts in locks such as the ignition switch.

Moly penetrants loosen and lubricate frozen, rusted and corroded fasteners and prevent future rusting or freezing.

Heat-sink grease is a special electrically non-conductive grease that is used for mounting electronic ignition modules where it is essential that heat is transferred away from the module.

SEALANTS

RTV sealant is one of the most widely used gasket compounds. Made from silicone, RTV is air curing, it seals, bonds, waterproofs, fills surface irregularities, remains flexible, doesn't shrink, is relatively easy to remove, and is used as a supplementary sealer with almost all low and medium temperature gaskets.

Anaerobic sealant is much like RTV in that it can be used either to seal gaskets or to form gaskets by itself. It remains flexible, is solvent resistant and fills surface imperfections. The difference between an anaerobic sealant and an RTV-type sealant is in the curing. RTV cures when exposed to air, while an anaerobic sealant cures only in the absence of air. This means that an anaerobic sealant cures only after the assembly of parts, sealing them together.

Thread and pipe sealant is used for sealing hydraulic and pneumatic fittings and vacuum lines. It is usually made from a Teflon compound, and comes in a spray, a paint-on liquid and as a wrap-around tape.

CHEMICALS

Anti-seize compound prevents seizing, galling, cold welding, rust and corrosion in fasteners. High-temperature anti-seize, usually made with copper and graphite lubricants, is used for exhaust system and exhaust manifold bolts.

Anaerobic locking compounds are used to keep fasteners from vibrating or working loose and cure only after installation, in the absence of air. Medium strength locking compound is used for small nuts, bolts and screws that may be removed later. High-strength locking compound is for large nuts, bolts and studs which aren't removed on a regular basis.

Oil additives range from viscosity index improvers to chemical treatments that claim to reduce internal engine friction. It should be noted that most oil manufacturers caution against using additives with their oils.

Gas additives perform several functions, depending on their chemical makeup. They usually contain solvents that help dissolve gum and varnish that build up on carburetor, fuel injection and intake parts. They also serve to break down carbon deposits that form on the inside surfaces of the combustion chambers. Some additives contain upper cylinder lubricants for valves and piston rings, and others contain chemicals to remove condensation from the gas tank.

MISCELLANEOUS

Brake fluid is specially formulated hydraulic fluid that can withstand the heat and pressure encountered in brake systems. Care must be taken so this fluid does not come in contact with painted surfaces or plastics. An opened container should always be resealed to prevent contamination by water or dirt.

Weatherstrip adhesive is used to bond weatherstripping around doors, windows and trunk lids. It is sometimes used to attach trim pieces.

Undercoating is a petroleum-based, tar-like substance that is designed to protect metal surfaces on the underside of the vehicle from corrosion. It also acts as a sound-deadening agent by insulating the bottom of the vehicle.

Waxes and polishes are used to help protect painted and plated surfaces from the weather. Different types of paint may require the use of different types of wax and polish. Some polishes utilize a chemical or abrasive cleaner to help remove the top layer of oxidized (dull) paint on older vehicles. In recent years many non-wax polishes that contain a wide variety of chemicals such as polymers and silicones have been introduced. These non-wax polishes are usually easier to apply and last longer than conventional waxes and polishes.

Safety first!

Regardless of how enthusiastic you may be about getting on with the job at hand, take the time to ensure that your safety is not jeopardized. A moment's lack of attention can result in an accident, as can failure to observe certain simple safety precautions. The possibility of an accident will always exist, and the following points should not be considered a comprehensive list of all dangers. Rather, they are intended to make you aware of the risks and to encourage a safety conscious approach to all work you carry out on your vehicle.

ESSENTIAL DOS AND DON'TS

DON'T rely on a jack when working under the vehicle. Always use approved jackstands to support the weight of the vehicle and place them under the recommended lift or support points.

DON'T attempt to loosen extremely tight fasteners (i.e. wheel lug nuts) while the vehicle is on a jack - it may fall.

DON'T start the engine without first making sure that the transmission is in Neutral (or Park where applicable) and the parking brake is set.

DON'T remove the radiator cap from a hot cooling system - let it cool or cover it with a cloth and release the pressure gradually.

DON'T attempt to drain the engine oil until you are sure it has cooled to the point that it will not burn you.

DON'T touch any part of the engine or exhaust system until it has cooled sufficiently to avoid burns.

DON'T siphon toxic liquids such as gasoline, antifreeze and brake fluid by mouth, or allow them to remain on your skin.

DON'T inhale brake lining dust - it is potentially hazardous (see Asbestos below).

DON'T allow spilled oil or grease to remain on the floor - wipe it up before someone slips on it.

DON'T use loose fitting wrenches or other tools which may slip and cause injury.

DON'T push on wrenches when loosening or tightening nuts or bolts. Always try to pull the wrench toward you. If the situation calls for pushing the wrench away, push with an open hand to avoid scraped knuckles if the wrench should slip.

DON'T attempt to lift a heavy component alone - get someone to help you.

DON'T rush or take unsafe shortcuts to finish a job.

DON'T allow children or animals in or around the vehicle while you are working on it.

DO wear eye protection when using power tools such as a drill, sander, bench grinder, etc. and when working under a vehicle.

DO keep loose clothing and long hair well out of the way of moving parts.

DO make sure that any hoist used has a safe working load rating adequate for the job.

DO get someone to check on you periodically when working alone on a vehicle.

DO carry out work in a logical sequence and make sure that everything is correctly assembled and tightened.

DO keep chemicals and fluids tightly capped and out of the reach of children and pets.

DO remember that your vehicle's safety affects that of yourself and others. If in doubt on any point, get professional advice.

STEERING, SUSPENSION AND BRAKES

These systems are essential to driving safety, so make sure you have a qualified shop or individual check your work. Also, compressed suspension springs can cause injury if released suddenly - be sure to use a spring compressor.

AIRBAGS

Airbags are explosive devices that can CAUSE injury if they deploy while you're working on the vehicle. Follow the manufacturer's instructions to disable the airbag whenever you're working in the vicinity of airbag components.

ASBESTOS

Certain friction, insulating, sealing, and other products - such as brake linings, brake bands, clutch linings, torque converters, gaskets, etc. - may contain asbestos or other hazardous friction material. Extreme care must be taken to avoid inhalation of dust from such products, since it is hazardous to health. If in doubt, assume that they do contain asbestos.

FIRE

Remember at all times that gasoline is highly flammable. Never smoke or have any kind of open flame around when working on a vehicle. But the risk does not end there. A spark caused by an electrical short circuit, by two metal surfaces contacting each other, or even by static electricity built up in your body under certain conditions, can ignite gasoline vapors, which in a confined space are highly explosive. Do not, under any circumstances, use gasoline for cleaning parts. Use an approved safety solvent.

Always disconnect the battery ground (-) cable at the battery before working on any part of the fuel system or electrical system. Never risk spilling fuel on a hot engine or exhaust component. It is strongly recommended that a fire extinguisher suitable for use on fuel and electrical fires be kept handy in the garage or workshop at all times. Never try to extinguish a fuel or electrical fire with water.

FUMES

Certain fumes are highly toxic and can quickly cause unconsciousness and even death if inhaled to any extent. Gasoline vapor falls into this category, as do the vapors from some cleaning solvents. Any draining or pouring of such volatile fluids should be done in a well ventilated area.

When using cleaning fluids and solvents, read the instructions on the container carefully. Never use materials from unmarked containers.

Never run the engine in an enclosed space, such as a garage. Exhaust fumes contain carbon monoxide, which is extremely poisonous. If you need to run the engine, always do so in the open air, or at least have the rear of the vehicle outside the work area.

THE BATTERY

Never create a spark or allow a bare light bulb near a battery. They normally give off a certain amount of hydrogen gas, which is highly explosive.

Always disconnect the battery ground (-) cable at the battery before working on the fuel or electrical systems.

If possible, loosen the filler caps or cover when charging the battery from an external source (this does not apply to sealed or maintenance-free batteries). Do not charge at an excessive rate or the battery may burst.

Take care when adding water to a non maintenance-free battery and when carrying a battery. The electrolyte, even when diluted, is very corrosive and should not be allowed to contact clothing or skin.

Always wear eye protection when cleaning the battery to prevent the caustic deposits from entering your eyes.

HOUSEHOLD CURRENT

When using an electric power tool, inspection light, etc., which operates on household current, always make sure that the tool is correctly connected to its plug and that, where necessary, it is properly grounded. Do not use such items in damp conditions and, again, do not create a spark or apply excessive heat in the vicinity of fuel or fuel vapor.

SECONDARY IGNITION SYSTEM VOLTAGE

A severe electric shock can result from touching certain parts of the ignition system (such as the spark plug wires) when the engine is running or being cranked, particularly if components are damp or the insulation is defective. In the case of an electronic ignition system, the secondary system voltage is much higher and could prove fatal.

HYDROFLUORIC ACID

This extremely corrosive acid is formed when certain types of synthetic rubber, found in some O-rings, oil seals, fuel hoses, etc. are exposed to temperatures above 750-degrees F (400-degrees C). The rubber changes into a charred or sticky substance containing the acid. *Once formed, the acid remains dangerous for years. If it gets onto the skin, it may be necessary to amputate the limb concerned.*

When dealing with a vehicle which has suffered a fire, or with components salvaged from such a vehicle, wear protective gloves and discard them after use.

Troubleshooting

CONTENTS

This section provides an easy reference guide to the more common problems which may occur during the operation of your vehicle. Various symptoms and their possible causes are grouped under headings denoting components or systems, such as Engine, Cooling system, etc. They also refer to the Chapter and/or Section that deals with the problem.

Remember that successful troubleshooting isn't a mysterious art practiced only by professional mechanics. It's simply the result of knowledge combined with an intelligent, systematic approach to a problem. Always use a process of elimination, starting with the simplest solution and working through to the most complex - and never overlook the obvious. Anyone can run the gas tank dry or leave the lights on overnight, so don't assume that you're exempt from such oversights.

Finally, always establish a clear idea why a problem has occurred and take steps to ensure that it doesn't happen again. If the electrical system fails because of a poor connection, check all other connections in the system to make sure they don't fail as well. If a particular fuse continues to blow, find out why - don't just go on replacing fuses. Remember, faiiure of a small component can often be indicative of potential failure or incorrect functioning of a more important component or system.

ENGINE AND PERFORMANCE

1 Engine will not rotate when attempting to start

1 Battery terminal connections loose or corroded (Chapter 1).
2 Battery discharged or faulty (Chapter 1).
3 Automatic transaxle not completely engaged in Park (Chapter 7).
4 Broken, loose or disconnected wiring in the starting circuit (Chapters 5 and 12).
5 Starter motor pinion jammed in flywheel ring gear (Chapter 5).
6 Starter solenoid faulty (Chapter 5).
7 Starter motor faulty (Chapter 5).
8 Ignition switch faulty (Chapter 12).
9 Neutral start switch faulty (Chapter 7).
10 Starter pinion or driveplate teeth worn or broken (Chapter 5).

2 Engine rotates but will not start

1 Fuel tank empty.
2 Battery discharged (engine rotates slowly) (Chapter 5).
3 Battery terminal connections loose or corroded (Chapter 1).
4 Leaking fuel injector(s), fuel pump, pressure regulator, etc. (Chapter 4).
5 Fuel not reaching fuel injection system (Chapter 4).
6 Ignition components damp or damaged (Chapter 5).
7 Worn, faulty or incorrectly gapped spark plugs (Chapter 1).
8 Broken, loose or disconnected wiring in the starting circuit (Chapter 5).
9 Broken, loose or disconnected wires at the ignition coil(s) or faulty coil(s) (Chapter 5).

3 Engine hard to start when cold

1 Battery discharged or low (Chapter 1).
2 Fuel system malfunctioning (Chapter 4).
3 Emissions or engine control system malfunctioning (Chapter 6).

4 Engine hard to start when hot

1 Air filter clogged (Chapter 1).
2 Fuel not reaching the fuel injection system (Chapter 4).
3 Corroded battery connections, especially ground (Chapter 1).
4 Emissions or engine control system malfunctioning (Chapter 6).

5 Starter motor noisy or excessively rough in engagement

1 Pinion or driveplate gear teeth worn or broken (Chapter 5).
2 Starter motor mounting bolts loose or missing (Chapter 5).

6 Engine starts but stops immediately

1 Loose or faulty electrical connections at coil pack or alternator (Chapter 5).
2 Insufficient fuel reaching the fuel injectors (Chapter 4).
3 Vacuum leak at the gasket between the intake manifold/plenum and throttle body (Chapters 1 and 4).
4 Restricted exhaust system (most likely the catalytic converter) (Chapters 4 and 6).

7 Oil puddle under engine

1 Oil pan gasket and/or oil pan drain bolt seal leaking (Chapters 1 and 2).
2 Oil pressure sending unit leaking (Chapter 2).
3 Valve cover gaskets leaking (Chapter 2).
4 Engine oil seals leaking (Chapter 2).
5 Timing chain cover sealant or sealing flange leaking (Chapter 2).

8 Engine lopes while idling or idles erratically

1 Vacuum leakage (Chapter 4).
2 Leaking EGR valve or plugged PCV valve (Chapters 1 and 6).
3 Air filter clogged (Chapter 1).
4 Fuel pump not delivering sufficient fuel to the fuel injection system (Chapter 4).
5 Leaking head gasket (Chapter 2).
6 Timing chain worn (Chapter 2).
7 Camshaft lobes worn (Chapter 2).

9 Engine misses at idle speed

1 Spark plugs worn or not gapped properly (Chapter 1).
2 Faulty spark plug wires (Chapter 1).
3 Vacuum leaks (Chapters 1 and 4).
4 Incorrect ignition timing (Chapter 5).
5 Uneven or low compression (Chapter 2C).

10 Engine misses throughout driving speed range

1 Fuel filter clogged and/or impurities in the fuel system (Chapters 1 and 4).
2 Low fuel output at the injector (Chapter 4).
3 Faulty or incorrectly gapped spark plugs (Chapter 1).
4 Incorrect ignition timing (Chapter 5).
5 Leaking spark plug wires (Chapter 1).
6 Faulty emission system components (Chapter 6).
7 Low or uneven cylinder compression pressures (Chapter 2).
8 Weak or faulty ignition system (Chapter 5).
9 Vacuum leak in fuel injection system, intake manifold or vacuum hoses (Chapter 4).

11 Engine stumbles on acceleration

1 Spark plugs fouled (Chapter 1).
2 Fuel injection system needs adjustment or repair (Chapter 4).
3 Fuel filter clogged (Chapter 1).
4 Incorrect ignition timing (Chapter 5).
5 Intake manifold air leak (Chapter 4).

12 Engine surges while holding accelerator steady

1 Intake air leak (Chapter 4).
2 Fuel pump faulty (Chapter 4).
3 Loose fuel injector harness connections (Chapter 4).
4 Defective ECM (Chapter 6).

13 Engine stalls

1 Idle speed incorrect (Chapters 1 and 4).
2 Fuel filter clogged and/or water and impurities in the fuel system (Chapters 1 and 4).
3 Ignition components damp or damaged (Chapter 5).
4 Faulty emissions system components (Chapter 6).

5 Faulty or incorrectly gapped spark plugs (Chapter 1).
6 Faulty spark plug wires (Chapter 1).
7 Vacuum leak in the intake manifold or vacuum hoses (Chapter 4).

14 Engine lacks power

1 Incorrect ignition timing (Chapter 5).
2 Faulty or incorrectly gapped spark plugs (Chapter 1).
3 Fuel injection system malfunctioning (Chapter 4).
4 Faulty coil(s) (Chapter 5).
5 Brakes binding (Chapter 1).
6 Automatic transaxle fluid level incorrect (Chapter 1).
7 Fuel filter clogged and/or impurities in the fuel system (Chapter 1).
8 Emission control system not functioning properly (Chapter 6).
9 Low or uneven cylinder compression pressures (Chapter 2).
10 Restricted exhaust system (most likely the catalytic converter (Chapters 4 and 6).

15 Engine backfires

1 Emissions system not functioning properly (Chapter 6).
2 Ignition timing incorrect (Chapter 5).
3 Faulty secondary ignition system (Chapter 5).
4 Fuel injection system malfunctioning (Chapter 4).
5 Vacuum leak at fuel injectors, intake manifold or vacuum hoses (Chapter 4).
6 Valves sticking (Chapter 2).

16 Pinging or knocking engine sounds during acceleration or uphill

1 Incorrect grade of fuel.
2 Ignition timing incorrect (Chapter 5).
3 Fuel injection system malfunctioning Chapter 4).
4 Improper or damaged spark plugs or wires (Chapter 1).
5 Worn or damaged ignition components (Chapter 5).
6 Faulty emissions system (Chapter 6).
7 Vacuum leak (Chapter 4).

17 Engine runs with oil pressure light on

1 Low oil level (Chapter 1).
2 Short in wiring circuit (Chapter 12).
3 Faulty oil pressure sender (Chapter 2).
4 Oil viscosity too low or oil diluted.
5 Worn engine bearings and/or oil pump (Chapter 2).

18 Engine diesels (continues to run) after switching off

1 Excessive engine operating temperature (Chapter 3).
2 Excessive carbon deposits on valves and pistons.

ENGINE ELECTRICAL SYSTEM

19 Battery will not hold a charge

1 Alternator drivebelt defective or not adjusted properly (Chapter 1).
2 Battery terminals loose or corroded (Chapter 1).
3 Alternator not charging properly (Chapter 5).
4 Loose, broken or faulty wiring in the charging circuit (Chapter 5).
5 Short in vehicle wiring (Chapters 5 and 12).
6 Internally defective battery (Chapters 1 and 5).

20 Voltage warning light fails to go out

1 Faulty alternator or charging circuit (Chapter 5).
2 Alternator drivebelt defective or out of adjustment (Chapter 1).
3 Alternator voltage regulator inoperative (Chapter 5).

21 Voltage warning light fails to come on when key is turned on

1 Warning light bulb defective (Chapter 12).
2 Fault in the printed circuit, dash wiring or bulb holder (Chapter 12).

FUEL SYSTEM

22 Excessive fuel consumption

1 Dirty or clogged air filter element (Chapter 1).
2 Incorrectly set ignition timing (Chapter 5).
3 Emissions system not functioning properly (Chapter 6).
4 Fuel injection system malfunctioning (Chapter 4).
5 Low tire pressure or incorrect tire size (Chapter 1).

23 Fuel leakage and/or fuel odor

1 Leak in a fuel feed or vent line (Chapter 4).
2 Tank overfilled.
3 Evaporative emissions control canister defective (Chapters 1 and 6).
4 Fuel injector seals faulty (Chapter 4).

COOLING SYSTEM

24 Overheating

1 Insufficient coolant in system (Chapter 1).
2 Water pump drivebelt defective or out of adjustment (Chapter 1).
3 Radiator core blocked or grille restricted (Chapter 3).
4 Thermostat faulty (Chapter 3).
5 Electric cooling fan blades broken or cracked (Chapter 3).
6 Radiator cap not maintaining proper pressure (Chapter 3).
7 Ignition timing incorrect (Chapter 5).

25 Overcooling

Incorrect (opening temperature too low) or faulty thermostat (Chapter 3).

26 External coolant leakage

1 Deteriorated/damaged hoses or loose clamps (Chapters 1 and 3).
2 Water pump seal defective (Chapters 1 and 3).
3 Leakage from radiator core or header tank (Chapter 3).
4 Engine drain or water jacket core plugs leaking (Chapter 2).

27 Internal coolant leakage

1 Leaking cylinder head gasket (Chapter 2).
2 Cracked cylinder bore or cylinder head (Chapter 2).

28 Coolant loss

1   Too much coolant in system (Chapter 1).
2   Coolant boiling away because of overheating (Chapter 3).
3   Internal or external leakage (Chapter 3).
4   Faulty radiator cap (Chapter 3).

29 Poor coolant circulation

1   Inoperative water pump (Chapter 3).
2   Restriction in cooling system (Chapters 1 and 3).
3   Water pump drivebelt defective or out of adjustment (Chapter 1).
4   Thermostat sticking (Chapter 3).

AUTOMATIC TRANSAXLE

➡Note: Due to the complexity of the automatic transaxle, it's difficult for the home mechanic to properly diagnose and service this component. For problems other than the following, the vehicle should be taken to a dealer service department or a transmission shop.

30 Fluid leakage

1   Automatic transmission fluid is a deep red color. Fluid leaks should not be confused with engine oil, which can easily be blown by airflow to the transaxle.
2   To pinpoint a leak, first remove all built-up dirt and grime from the transaxle housing with degreasing agents and/or steam cleaning. Drive the vehicle at low speeds so air flow will not blow the leak far from its source. Raise the vehicle and determine where the leak is coming from. Common areas of leakage are:

   a) Fluid pan (Chapter 1)
   b) Filler pipe (Chapter 7)
   c) Fluid cooler lines (Chapter 7)
   d) Vehicle Speed Sensor (Chapter 6)

31 Transaxle fluid brown or has a burned smell

Transaxle overheated. Change fluid (Chapter 1).

32 General shift mechanism problems

1   Chapter 7 deals with checking and adjusting the shift linkage on automatic transaxles. Common problems which may be attributed to a poorly adjusted linkage are:

   a) Engine starting in gears other than Park or Neutral.
   b) Indicator on shifter pointing to a gear other than the one actually being used.
   c) Vehicle moves when in Park.

2   Refer to Chapter 7 for the shift linkage adjustment procedure.

33 Transaxle will not downshift with accelerator pedal pressed to the floor

Throttle Valve (T.V.) cable out of adjustment (Chapter 7).

34 Engine will start in gears other than Park or Neutral

Park/Neutral Position switch malfunctioning (Chapter 7).

35 Transaxle slips, shifts roughly, is noisy or has no drive in forward or reverse gears

There are many probable causes for the above problems, but the home mechanic should be concerned with only one possibility - fluid level. Before taking the vehicle to a repair shop, check the level and condition of the fluid as described in Chapter 1.

Correct the fluid level as necessary or change the fluid and filter if needed. If the problem persists, have a professional diagnose the probable cause.

DRIVEAXLES

36 Clicking noise in turns

Worn or damaged outer CV joint. Check for cut or damaged boots (Chapter 1). Repair as necessary (Chapter 8).

37 Knock or clunk when accelerating after coasting

Worn or damaged CV joint. Check for cut or damaged boots (Chapter 1). Repair as necessary (Chapter 8).

38 Shudder or vibration during acceleration

1   Worn or damaged CV joints. Repair or replace as necessary (Chapter 8).
2   Sticking inner joint assembly. Correct or replace as necessary (Chapter 8).

BRAKES

➡Note: Before assuming that a brake problem exists, make sure . . .

   a) The tires are in good condition and properly inflated (Chapter 1).
   b) The front end alignment is correct (Chapter 10).
   c) The vehicle isn't loaded with weight in an unequal manner.

39 Vehicle pulls to one side during braking

1   Incorrect tire pressures (Chapter 1).
2   Front end out of alignment (have the front end aligned).
3   Unmatched tires on same axle.
4   Restricted brake lines or hoses (Chapter 9).
5   Sticking caliper or wheel cylinder piston (Chapter 9).
6   Loose suspension parts (Chapter 10).
7   Contaminated brake pad or shoe material (Chapter 9).

40 Noise (grinding high-pitched squeal) when the brakes are applied

1   Disc brake pads worn out. The noise comes from the wear sensor rubbing against the disc. Replace pads with new ones immediately (Chapter 9).
2   Drum brake shoes worn out. Replace the shoes immediately (Chapter 9).

41 Brake roughness or chatter (pedal pulsates)

1   Excessive brake disc lateral runout or brake drum out-of-round (Chapter 9).

2 Parallelism of disc not within specifications (Chapter 9).
3 Uneven pad wear caused by caliper not sliding due to improper clearance or dirt (Chapter 9).
4 Defective brake disc (Chapter 9).

42 Excessive pedal effort required to stop vehicle

1 Malfunctioning power brake booster (Chapter 9).
2 Partial system failure (Chapter 9).
3 Excessively worn pads (Chapter 9).
4 One or more caliper or wheel cylinder pistons seized or sticking (Chapter 9).
5 Brake pads contaminated with oil or grease (Chapter 9).
6 New pads or shoes installed and not yet seated. It will take a while for the new material to seat.

43 Excessive brake pedal travel

1 Partial brake system failure (Chapter 9).
2 Insufficient fluid in master cylinder (Chapters 1 and 9).
3 Air trapped in system (Chapter 9).
4 Faulty master cylinder (Chapter 9).

44 D ragging brakes

1 Master cylinder pistons not returning correctly (Chapter 9).
2 Restricted brakes lines or hoses (Chapters 1 and 9).
3 Incorrect parking brake adjustment (Chapter 9).
4 Defective brake calipers (Chapter 9).

45 Grabbing or uneven braking action

1 Malfunction of proportioning valve (Chapter 9).
2 Malfunction of power brake booster unit (Chapter 9).
3 Binding brake pedal mechanism (Chapter 9).
4 Contaminated brake linings (Chapter 9).

46 Brake pedal feels spongy when depressed

1 Air in hydraulic lines (Chapter 9).
2 Master cylinder mounting bolts loose (Chapter 9).
3 Master cylinder defective (Chapter 9).

47 Brake pedal travels to the floor with little resistance

Little or no fluid in the master cylinder reservoir caused by leaking caliper, or loose, damaged or disconnected brake lines (Chapter 9).

48 Parking brake does not hold

Parking brake cables improperly adjusted (Chapter 9).

SUSPENSION AND STEERING SYSTEMS

➡**Note: Before attempting to diagnose the suspension and steering systems, perform the following preliminary checks:**

a) Check the tire pressures and look for uneven wear.
b) Check the steering universal joints or coupling from the column to the steering gear for loose fasteners and wear.
c) Check the front and rear suspension and the steering gear assembly for loose and damaged parts.
d) Look for out-of-round or out-of-balance tires, bent rims and loose and/or rough wheel bearings.

49 Vehicle pulls to one side

1 Mismatched or uneven tires (Chapter 10).
2 Broken or sagging springs (Chapter 10).
3 Wheel alignment incorrect (Chapter 10).
4 Front brakes dragging (Chapter 9).

50 Abnormal or excessive tire wear

1 Front wheel alignment incorrect (Chapter 10).
2 Sagging or broken springs (Chapter 10).
3 Tire out-of-balance (Chapter 10).
4 Worn shock absorber (Chapter 10).
5 Overloaded vehicle.
6 Tires not rotated regularly.

51 Wheel makes a "thumping" noise

1 Blister or bump on tire (Chapter 1).
2 Improper shock absorber action (Chapter 10).

52 Shimmy, shake or vibration

1 Tire or wheel out-of-balance or out-of-round (Chapter 10).
2 Loose or worn wheel bearings (Chapter 10).
3 Worn tie-rod ends (Chapter 10).
4 Worn balljoints (Chapter 10).
5 Excessive wheel runout (Chapter 10).
6 Blister or bump on tire (Chapter 1).

53 Hard steering

1 Lack of lubrication at balljoints, tie-rod ends and steering gear assembly (Chapter 10).
2 Front wheel alignment incorrect (Chapter 10).
3 Low tire pressure (Chapter 1).

54 Steering wheel does not return to center position correctly

1 Lack of lubrication at balljoints and tie-rod ends (Chapters 1 and 10).
2 Binding in steering column (Chapter 10).
3 Defective rack-and-pinion assembly (Chapter 10).
4 Front wheel alignment problem (Chapter 10).

55 Abnormal noise at the front end

1 Lack of lubrication at balljoints and tie-rod ends (Chapter 1).
2 Loose upper strut mount (Chapter 10).
3 Worn tie-rod ends (Chapter 10).
4 Loose stabilizer bar (Chapter 10).
5 Loose wheel lug nuts (Chapter 1).
6 Loose suspension bolts (Chapter 10).

56 Wander or poor steering stability

1 Mismatched or uneven tires (Chapter 10).
2 Lack of lubrication at balljoints or tie-rod ends (Chapters 1 and 10).
3 Worn shock absorbers (Chapter 10).
4 Loose stabilizer bar (Chapter 10).
5 Broken or sagging springs (Chapter 10).
6 Front wheel alignment incorrect.
7 Worn steering gear clamp bushings (Chapter 10).

57 Erratic steering when braking

1 Wheel bearings worn (Chapter 10).
2 Broken or sagging springs (Chapter 10).
3 Leaking caliper (Chapter 9).
4 Warped rotors (Chapter 9).
5 Worn steering gear clamp bushings (Chapter 10).
6 Wheel alignment incorrect.

58 Excessive pitching and/or rolling around corners or during braking

1 Loose stabilizer bar (Chapter 10).
2 Worn shock absorbers or mounts (Chapter 10).
3 Broken or sagging springs (Chapter 10).
4 Overloaded vehicle.

59 Suspension bottoms

1 Overloaded vehicle.
2 Worn shock absorbers (Chapter 10).
3 Incorrect, broken or sagging springs (Chapter 10).

60 Cupped tires

1 Front wheel alignment incorrect (Chapter 10).
2 Worn shock absorbers (Chapter 10).
3 Wheel bearings worn (Chapter 10).
4 Excessive tire or wheel runout (Chapter 10).
5 Worn balljoints (Chapter 10).

61 Excessive tire wear on outside edge

1 Inflation pressures incorrect (Chapter 1).
2 Excessive speed in turns.
3 Wheel alignment incorrect (excessive toe-in or positive camber). Have professionally aligned.
4 Suspension arm bent or twisted (Chapter 10).

62 Excessive tire wear on inside edge

1 Inflation pressures incorrect (Chapter 1).
2 Wheel alignment incorrect (toe-out or excessive negative camber). Have professionally aligned.
3 Loose or damaged steering components (Chapter 10).

63 Tire tread worn in one place

1 Tires out-of-balance.
2 Damaged or buckled wheel. Inspect and replace if necessary.
3 Defective tire (Chapter 1).

64 Excessive play or looseness in steering system

1 Wheel bearings worn (Chapter 10).
2 Tie-rod end loose or worn (Chapter 10).
3 Steering gear loose (Chapter 10).

65 Rattling or clicking noise in steering gear

1 Steering gear mounting bolts loose (Chapter 10).
2 Steering gear defective (Chapter 10).

1

TUNE-UP AND ROUTINE MAINTENANCE

Section

Reference to other Chapters

CHECK ENGINE light on - See Chapter 6

1 Toyota Sienna Maintenance Schedule

The maintenance intervals in this manual are provided with the assumption that you, not the dealer, will be doing the work. These are the minimum maintenance intervals recommended by the factory for vehicles that are driven daily. If you wish to keep your vehicle in peak condition at all times, you may wish to perform some of these procedures even more often. Because frequent maintenance enhances the efficiency, performance and resale value of your vehicle, we encourage you to do so. If you drive in dusty areas, tow a trailer, idle or drive at low speeds for extended periods or drive for short distances (less than four miles) in below freezing temperatures, shorter intervals are also recommended.

When your vehicle is new, it should be serviced by a factory authorized dealer service department to protect the factory warranty. In many cases, the initial maintenance check is done at no cost to the owner.

EVERY 250 MILES OR WEEKLY, WHICHEVER COMES FIRST

Check the engine oil level (Section 4)
Check the engine coolant level (Section 4)
Check the windshield washer fluid level (Section 4)
Check the brake fluid level (Section 4)
Check the tires and tire pressures (Section 5)

EVERY 3000 MILES OR 3 MONTHS, WHICHEVER COMES FIRST

All items listed above plus:
Check the power steering fluid level (Section 6)
Check the automatic transaxle fluid level (Section 7)
Change the engine oil and oil filter (Section 8)
Check the torque of the driveaxle flange bolts (Chapter 8)

EVERY 6000 MILES OR 6 MONTHS, WHICHEVER COMES FIRST

Inspect and replace if necessary the windshield wiper blades (Section 9)
Check and service the battery (Section 10)
Check and adjust if necessary the engine drivebelts (Section 11)
Inspect and replace if necessary all underhood hoses (Section 12)
Check the cooling system (Section 13)
Rotate the tires (Section 14)

Typical engine compartment layout

1	Brake master cylinder reservoir	5	Engine oil filler cap	9	Windshield washer fluid reservoir
2	Air filter housing	6	Engine oil filter	10	Engine coolant reservoir
3	Battery	7	Engine oil dipstick	11	Power steering fluid reservoir
4	Automatic transaxle fluid dipstick	8	Radiator hose	12	Cooling system pressure cap

EVERY 15,000 MILES OR 12 MONTHS, WHICHEVER COMES FIRST

All items listed above plus:
    Inspect the brake system (Section 15)*
    Replace the air filter (Section 16)
    Inspect the fuel system (Section 17)
    Inspect the suspension and steering components (Section 18)*
    Check the driveaxle boots (Section 18)
    Replace the cabin air filter (2004 and later models) (Section 19)
    Inspect the exhaust system (Section 20)

EVERY 30,000 MILES OR 24 MONTHS, WHICHEVER COMES FIRST

All items listed above plus:
    Service the cooling system (drain, flush and refill) (Section 21)
    Inspect the evaporative emissions control system (Section 22)
    Check and tighten critical chassis and body fasteners (Section 23)

EVERY 60,000 MILES OR 48 MONTHS, WHICHEVER COMES FIRST

    Replace the fuel filter (Section 25)
    Replace the spark plugs (Section 26)
    Inspect and replace if necessary the spark plug wires (Section 27)

Inspect and if necessary adjust the valve clearances (Section 28)
Replace the fuel tank cap gasket (Section 29)
Check and replace if necessary the PCV valve (Section 30)

EVERY 90,000 MILES

Replace the timing belt (Chapter 2A) ***

* This item is affected by "severe" operating conditions as described below. If your vehicle is operated under "severe" conditions, perform all maintenance indicated with an asterisk (*) at 3000 mile/3 month intervals. Severe conditions are indicated if you mainly operate your vehicle under one or more of the following conditions:

Operating in dusty areas
Towing a trailer
Idling for extended periods and/or low speed operation
Operating when outside temperatures remain below freezing and
    when most trips are less than 4 miles

** If operated under one or more of the following conditions, change the automatic transaxle fluid and differential lubricant every 30,000 miles:

In heavy city traffic where the outside temperature regularly reaches
    90-degrees F (32-degrees C) or higher In hilly or mountainous
    terrain
Frequent trailer pulling

*** Replace the timing belt at 60,000 miles only if operated under severe conditions.

Typical front underside components

1	Engine oil drain plug	5	Automatic transaxle drain plug	8	Brake hose
2	Front brake caliper	6	Exhaust pipe	9	Differential drain plug
3	Outer driveaxle boot	7	Inner driveaxle boot		(2000 and earlier models)
4	Steering gear boot				

Typical rear underside components

1	Rear axle beam	3	Fuel tank	5	Parking brake cable
2	Shock absorber	4	Exhaust pipe	6	Coil spring

2 Introduction

This Chapter is designed to help the home mechanic maintain his vehicle for peak performance, economy, safety and long life.

Included is a master maintenance schedule, followed by sections dealing specifically with each item on the schedule. Visual checks, adjustments, component replacement and other helpful items are included. Refer to the accompanying illustrations of the engine compartment and the underside of the vehicle for the location of various components.

Servicing your vehicle in accordance with the mileage/time maintenance schedule and the following Sections will provide it with a planned maintenance program that should result in a long and reliable service life. This is a comprehensive plan, so maintaining some items but not others at the specified service intervals won't produce the same results.

As you service your vehicle, you will discover that many of the procedures can - and should - be grouped together because of the nature of the particular procedure you're performing or because of the close proximity of two otherwise unrelated components to one another.

For example, if the vehicle is raised for any reason, you should inspect the exhaust, suspension, steering and fuel systems while you're under the vehicle. When you're rotating the tires, it makes good sense

to check the brakes and wheel bearings since the wheels are already removed.

Finally, let's suppose you have to borrow or rent a torque wrench. Even if you only need to tighten the spark plugs, you might as well check the torque of as many critical fasteners as time allows.

The first step of this maintenance program is to prepare yourself before the actual work begins. Read through all sections pertinent to the procedures you're planning to do, then make a list of and gather together all the parts and tools you will need to do the job. If it looks as if you might run into problems during a particular segment of some procedure, seek advice from your local parts man or dealer service department.

OWNER'S MANUAL AND VECI LABEL INFORMATION

Your vehicle Owner's Manual was written for your year and model and contains very specific information on component locations, specifications, fuse ratings, part numbers, etc. The Owner's Manual is an important resource for the do-it-yourselfer to have; if one was not supplied with your vehicle, it can generally be ordered from a dealer parts department.

Among other important information, the Vehicle Emissions Control Information (VECI) label contains specifications and procedures for tune-up adjustments (if applicable) and, in some instances, spark plugs (see Chapter 6 for more information on the VECI label). The information on this label is the exact maintenance data recommended by the manufacturer. This data often varies by intended operating altitude, local emissions regulations, month of manufacture, etc.

This Chapter contains procedural details, safety information and more ambitious maintenance intervals than you might find in the manufacturer's literature. However, you may also find procedures or specifications in your Owner's Manual or VECI label that differ with what's printed here. In these cases, the Owner's Manual or VECI label can be considered correct, since it is specific to your particular vehicle.

3   Tune-up general information

The term tune-up is used in this manual to represent a combination of individual operations rather than one specific procedure.

If, from the time the vehicle is new, the routine maintenance schedule is followed closely and frequent checks are made of fluid levels and high wear items, as suggested throughout this manual, the engine will be kept in relatively good running condition and the need for additional work will be minimized.

More likely than not, however, there will be times when the engine is running poorly due to lack of regular maintenance. This is even more likely if a used vehicle, which has not received regular and frequent maintenance checks, is purchased. In such cases, an engine tune-up will be needed outside of the regular routine maintenance intervals.

The first step in any tune-up or engine diagnosis to help correct a poor running engine would be a cylinder compression check. A check of the engine compression (see Chapter 2C) will give valuable information regarding the overall performance of many internal components and should be used as a basis for tune-up and repair procedures. If, for instance, a compression check indicates serious internal engine wear, a conventional tune-up will not help the running condition of the engine and would be a waste of time and money. Also in Chapter 2, Part C is information on checking engine vacuum, which also gives information on the engine's state-of-tune and condition.

The following series of operations are those most often needed to bring a generally poor-running engine back into a proper state of tune.

MINOR TUNE-UP

Clean, inspect and test the battery (Section 10)
Check all engine related fluids (Section 4)
Check and adjust the drivebelts (Section 11)
Check all underhood hoses (Section 12)
Check the cooling system (Section 13)
Check the air filter (Section 16)
Inspect the spark plug wires (Section 27)

MAJOR TUNE-UP

All items listed under Minor tune-up, plus . . .
Check the charging system (Chapter 5)
Replace the air filter (Section 16)
Check the fuel system (Section 17)
Replace the spark plugs (Section 26)
Replace the spark plug wires (Section 27)

4   Fluid level checks (every 250 miles or weekly)

1   Fluids are an essential part of the lubrication, cooling, brake and other systems. Because these fluids gradually become depleted and/or contaminated during normal operation of the vehicle, they must be periodically replenished. See *Recommended lubricants and fluids* and *Capacities* at the end of this Chapter before adding fluid to any of the following components.

➡Note: The vehicle must be on level ground before fluid levels can be checked.

ENGINE OIL

▶ Refer to illustrations 4.2, 4.4 and 4.6

2   The engine oil level is checked with a dipstick located at the front side of the engine (see illustration). The dipstick extends through a metal tube down into the engine oil pan.

3   The oil level should be checked before the vehicle has been driven, or about 5 minutes after the engine has been shut off. If the oil is checked immediately after driving the vehicle, some of the oil will remain in the upper engine components, producing an inaccurate reading on the dipstick.

4.2 The engine oil dipstick is mounted on the front (radiator) side of the engine

4   Pull the dipstick from the tube and wipe all the oil from the end with a clean rag or paper towel. Insert the clean dipstick all the way back into its metal tube and pull it out again. Observe the oil at the end of the dipstick. At its highest point, the level should be between the L and F marks (see illustration). On later models, the oil dipstick has two dots on it, one for the Low position, one for the High position.

5   It takes one quart of oil to raise the level from the lower mark to the upper mark (full) on the dipstick. Do not allow the level to drop below the lower mark or oil starvation may cause engine damage. Conversely, overfilling the engine (adding oil above the upper mark) may cause oil-fouled spark plugs, oil leaks or oil seal failures.

6   Remove the threaded cap from the valve cover to add oil (see illustration). Use a funnel to prevent spills. After adding the oil, install the filler cap hand tight. Start the engine and look carefully for any small leaks around the oil filter or drain plug. Stop the engine and check the oil level again after it has had sufficient time to drain from the upper block and cylinder head galleys.

7   Checking the oil level is an important preventive maintenance step. A continually dropping oil level indicates oil leakage through damaged seals, from loose connections, or past worn rings or valve guides. If the oil looks milky in color or has water droplets in it, a cylinder head gasket may be blown. The engine should be checked immediately. The condition of the oil should also be checked. Each time you check the oil level, slide your thumb and index finger up the dipstick before wiping off the oil. If you see small dirt or metal particles clinging to the dipstick, the oil should be changed (see Section 8).

ENGINE COOLANT

♦ Refer to illustration 4.8

❋❋ WARNING:

Do not allow antifreeze to come in contact with your skin or painted surfaces of the vehicle. Flush contaminated areas immediately with plenty of water. Don't store new coolant or leave old coolant lying around where it's accessible to children or pets - they're attracted by its sweet smell. Ingestion of even a small amount of coolant can be fatal! Wipe up garage floor and drip pan spills immediately. Keep antifreeze containers covered and repair cooling system leaks as soon as they're noticed.

4.4 The oil level should be at or near the upper dot or mark (Full) on the dipstick - if it isn't, add enough oil to bring the level to or near the upper mark (it takes one quart to raise the level from the lower mark to the upper, do not overfill)

8   All models covered by this manual are equipped with a coolant recovery system. The coolant reservoir is located in the right front corner of the engine compartment and is connected by a hose to the water outlet (see illustration). If the coolant heats up during engine operation, coolant can escape through the pressurized filler cap and connecting hose into the reservoir. As the engine cools, the coolant is automatically drawn back into the cooling system to maintain the correct level.

9   The coolant level should be checked regularly. It must be between the Full and Low lines on the tank. The level will vary with the temperature of the engine. When the engine is cold, the coolant level should be at or slightly above the Low mark on the tank. Once the engine has warmed up, the level should be at or near the Full mark. If it isn't, allow the fluid in the tank to cool, then remove the cap from the reservoir and add coolant to bring the level up to the Full line. Use only ethylene/glycol type coolant and water in the mixture ratio recommended by your owner's manual. Do not use supplemental inhibitors or additives. If only a small amount of coolant is required to bring the system up to the proper level, water can be used. However, repeated additions of water will dilute the recommended antifreeze and water solution. In order to maintain the proper ratio of antifreeze and water, it is advisable to top up the coolant level with the correct mixture. Refer to your owner's manual for the recommended ratio.

10 If the coolant level drops within a short time after replenishment, there may be a leak in the system. Inspect the radiator, hoses, cooling system pressure cap, drain plugs, air bleeder plugs and water pump. If no leak is evident, have the radiator cap pressure tested.

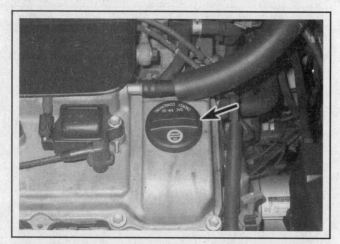

4.6 The threaded oil filler cap is located on the valve cover - to prevent dirt from contaminating the engine, always make sure the area around this opening is clean before removing the cap

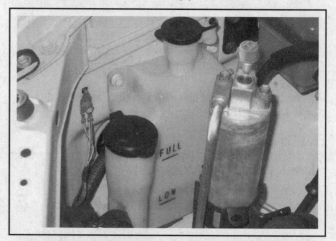

4.8 Make sure the coolant level is between the Full and Low lines - if it's below the Low line, add a sufficient quantity of the specified mixture of antifreeze and water

4.14 The windshield washer fluid reservoir is located at the right front corner of the engine compartment - fluid can be added after flipping up the cap

4.16a The access cap for the brake fluid reservoir is in the left corner of the cowl cover

4.16b The brake fluid should be kept between the MIN and MAX marks on the reservoir (shown with cowl cover removed - when looking in from the top of the cylinder, the level should be about 1 to 1.5 inches below the cap

✳✳ WARNING:

Never remove the cooling system pressure cap when the engine is running or has just been shut down, because the cooling system is hot. Escaping steam and scalding liquid could cause serious injury.

11 If it is necessary to open the cooling system pressure cap, wait until the system has cooled completely, then wrap a thick cloth around the cap and turn it 1/8-turn counterclockwise. If any steam escapes, wait until the system has cooled further, then remove the cap.

12 When checking the coolant level, always note its condition. It should be relatively clear. If it is brown or rust colored, the system should be drained, flushed and refilled. Even if the coolant appears to be normal, the corrosion inhibitors wear out with use, so it must be replaced at the specified intervals.

13 Do not allow antifreeze to come in contact with your skin or painted surfaces of the vehicle. Flush contacted areas immediately with plenty of water.

WINDSHIELD WASHER FLUID

▶ **Refer to illustration 4.14**

14 Fluid for the windshield washer system is stored in a plastic reservoir, which is located at the right front corner of the engine compartment (see illustration). In milder climates, plain water can be used to top up the reservoir, but the reservoir should be kept no more than two-thirds full to allow for expansion should the water freeze. In colder climates, the use of a specially designed windshield washer fluid, available at your dealer and any auto parts store, will help lower the freezing point of the fluid. Mix the solution with water in accordance with the manufacturer's directions on the container. Do not use regular antifreeze. It will damage the vehicle's paint.

BRAKE FLUID

▶ **Refer to illustrations 4.16a and 4.16b**

15 The brake master cylinder is mounted on the front of the power booster unit in the engine compartment. A remote fluid reservoir for the brake master cylinder is located on the firewall, under the cowl cover.

16 To check the fluid level of the brake master cylinder reservoir, simply look at the MAX and MIN marks on the reservoir (see illustrations).

17 If the level is low, wipe the top of the reservoir cover with a clean rag to prevent contamination of the brake system before lifting the cover.

18 Add only the specified brake fluid to the brake reservoir (refer to *Recommended lubricants and fluids* at the end of this Chapter or to your owner's manual). Mixing different types of brake fluid can damage the system. Fill the brake master cylinder reservoir only to the MAX line.

✳✳ WARNING:

Use caution when filling the reservoir - brake fluid can harm your eyes and damage painted surfaces. Do not use brake fluid that has been opened for more than one year or has been left open. Brake fluid absorbs moisture from the air. Excess moisture can cause a dangerous loss of braking.

19 While the reservoir cap is removed, inspect the master cylinder reservoir for contamination. If deposits, dirt particles or water droplets are present, the system should be drained and refilled (see Chapter 9).

20 After filling the reservoir to the proper level, make sure the lid is properly seated to prevent fluid leakage and/or system pressure loss.

21 The brake fluid in the master cylinder will drop slightly as the brake pads at each wheel wear down during normal operation. If the master cylinder requires repeated replenishing to keep it at the proper level, this is an indication of leakage in the brake system, which should be corrected immediately. Check all brake lines and connections, along with the wheel cylinders and booster (see Section 15 for more information).

22 If, upon checking the master cylinder fluid level, you discover the reservoir empty or nearly empty, the brake system should be filled, bled (see Chapter 9), and checked for leaks.

5   Tire and tire pressure checks (every 250 miles or weekly)

♦ **Refer to illustrations 5.2, 5.3, 5.4a, 5.4b and 5.8**

1   Periodic inspection of the tires may spare you from the inconvenience of being stranded with a flat tire. It can also provide you with vital information regarding possible problems in the steering and suspension systems before major damage occurs.

2   Normal tread wear can be monitored with a simple, inexpensive device known as a tread depth indicator (see illustration). When the tread depth reaches the specified minimum, replace the tire(s).

5.2 Use a tire tread depth gauge to monitor tire wear - they are available at auto parts stores and service stations and cost very little

3   Note any abnormal tread wear (see illustration). Tread pattern irregularities such as cupping, flat spots and more wear on one side than the other are indications of front end alignment and/or balance problems. If any of these conditions are noted, take the vehicle to a tire shop or service station to correct the problem.

4   Look closely for cuts, punctures and embedded nails or tacks. Sometimes a tire will hold its air pressure for a short time or leak down very slowly even after a nail has embedded itself into the tread. If a slow leak persists, check the valve stem core to make sure it is tight (see illustration). Examine the tread for an object that may have embedded itself into the tire or for a "plug" that may have begun to leak (radial tire punctures are repaired with a plug that is fitted in a puncture). If a puncture is suspected, it can be easily verified by spraying a solution of soapy water onto the puncture area (see illustration). The soapy solution will bubble if there is a leak. Unless the puncture is inordinately large, a tire shop or gas station can usually repair the punctured tire.

5   Carefully inspect the inner sidewall of each tire for evidence of brake fluid leakage. If you see any, inspect the brakes immediately.

6   Correct tire air pressure adds miles to the lifespan of the tires, improves mileage and enhances overall ride quality. Tire pressure cannot be accurately estimated by looking at a tire, particularly if it is a radial. A tire pressure gauge is therefore essential. Keep an accurate gauge in the glovebox. The pressure gauges fitted to the nozzles of air hoses at gas stations are often inaccurate.

7   Always check tire pressure when the tires are cold. "Cold," in this case, means the vehicle has not been driven over a mile in the

UNDERINFLATION

CUPPING

OVERINFLATION

Cupping may be caused by:
● Underinflation and/or mechanical irregularities such as out-of-balance condition of wheel and/or tire, and bent or damaged wheel.
● Loose or worn steering tie-rod or steering idler arm.
● Loose, damaged or worn front suspension parts.

INCORRECT TOE-IN
OR EXTREME CAMBER

FEATHERING DUE
TO MISALIGNMENT

5.3 This chart will help you determine the condition of the tires, the probable cause(s) of abnormal wear and the corrective action necessary

5.4a If a tire loses air on a steady basis, check the valve core first to make sure it's snug (a special inexpensive wrench is commonly available at auto parts stores)

5.4b If the valve core is tight, raise the corner of the vehicle with the low tire and spray a soapy water solution onto the tread as the tire is turned slowly - leaks will cause small bubbles to appear

5.8 To extend the life of the tires, check the air pressure at least once a week with an accurate gauge (don't forget the spare)

three hours preceding a tire pressure check. A pressure rise of four to eight pounds is not uncommon once the tires are warm.

8   Unscrew the valve cap protruding from the wheel or hubcap and push the gauge firmly onto the valve (see illustration). Note the reading on the gauge and compare this figure to the recommended tire pressure shown on the tire placard in the glovebox. Be sure to reinstall the valve cap to keep dirt and moisture out of the valve stem mechanism. Check all four tires and, if necessary, add enough air to bring them up to the recommended pressure levels.

9   Don't forget to keep the spare tire inflated to the specified pressure (consult your owner's manual). Note that the air pressure specified for a compact spare is significantly higher than the pressure of the regular tires.

6   Power steering fluid level check (every 3000 miles or 3 months)

▶ **Refer to illustration 6.4**

1   Unlike manual steering, the power steering system relies on fluid which may, over a period of time, require replenishing.

2   The fluid reservoir for the power steering pump is located on the right (passenger side) inner fender panel near the front of the engine.

3   For the check, the front wheels should be pointed straight ahead and the engine should be off.

4   The reservoir is translucent plastic and the fluid level can be checked visually (see illustration).

5   If additional fluid is required, pour the specified type directly into the reservoir, using a funnel to prevent spills.

6   If the reservoir requires frequent fluid additions, all power steering hoses, hose connections, the power steering pump and the rack and pinion assembly should be carefully checked for leaks.

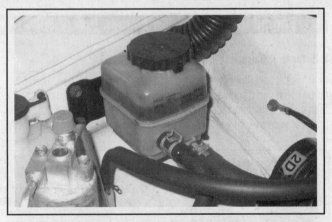

6.4 The power steering fluid reservoir is located on the right side of the engine compartment - the reservoir is translucent so the fluid level can be checked either hot or cold without removing the cap

7   Automatic transaxle fluid level check (every 3000 miles or 3 months)

▶ **Refer to illustrations 7.4a and 7.4b**

1   The level of the automatic transaxle fluid should be carefully maintained. Low fluid level can lead to slipping or loss of drive, while overfilling can cause foaming, loss of fluid and transaxle damage.

2   The transaxle fluid level should only be checked when the transaxle is hot (at its normal operating temperature). If the vehicle has just been driven over 10 miles (15 miles in a frigid climate), and the fluid temperature is 160 to 175-degrees F, the transaxle is hot.

✳✳ CAUTION:

If the vehicle has just been driven for a long time at high speed or in city traffic in hot weather, or if it has been pulling a trailer, an accurate fluid level reading cannot be obtained. Allow the fluid to cool down for about 30 minutes.

3   If the vehicle has not just been driven, park the vehicle on level ground, set the parking brake and start the engine. While the engine is idling, depress the brake pedal and move the selector lever through all the gear ranges, beginning and ending in Park.

4   With the engine still idling, remove the dipstick from its tube (see illustration). Check the level of the fluid on the dipstick (see illustration) and note its condition.

5   Wipe the fluid from the dipstick with a clean rag and reinsert it back into the filler tube until the cap seats.

7.4a The automatic transaxle dipstick is located at the left-front of the engine

6   Pull the dipstick out again and note the fluid level. If the transaxle is cold, the level should be in the COLD or COOL range on the dipstick. If it is hot, the fluid level should be in the HOT range. If the level is at the low side of either range, add the specified automatic transaxle fluid through the dipstick tube with a funnel.

7   Add just enough of the recommended fluid to fill the transaxle to the proper level. It takes about one pint to raise the level from the low mark to the high mark when the fluid is hot, so add the fluid a little at a time and keep checking the level until it is correct.

8   The condition of the fluid should also be checked along with the level. If the fluid at the end of the dipstick is black or a dark reddish brown color, or if it emits a burned smell, the fluid should be changed. If you are in doubt about the condition of the fluid, purchase some new fluid and compare the two for color and smell.

7.4b If the automatic transaxle fluid is cold, the level should be between the lower two notches; if it's at normal operating temperature, the level should be between the upper notches on the dipstick

8   Engine oil and oil filter change (every 3000 miles or 3 months)

▶ **Refer to illustrations 8.2, 8.7, 8.13 and 8.15**

1   Frequent oil changes are the best preventive maintenance the home mechanic can give the engine, because aging oil becomes diluted and contaminated, which leads to premature engine wear.

2   Make sure that you have all the necessary tools before you begin this procedure (see illustration). You should also have plenty of rags or newspapers handy for mopping up any spills.

3   Access to the underside of the vehicle is greatly improved if the vehicle can be lifted on a hoist, driven onto ramps or supported by jack stands.

8.2 These tools are required when changing the engine oil and filter

1   *Drain pan* - It should be fairly shallow in depth, but wide to prevent spills

2   *Rubber gloves* - When removing the drain plug and filter, you will get oil on your hands (the gloves will prevent burns)

3   *Breaker bar* - Sometimes the oil drain plug is tight, and a long breaker bar is needed to loosen it

4   *Socket* - To be used with the breaker bar or a ratchet (must be the correct size to fit the drain plug)

5   *Filter wrench* - This is a metal band-type wrench, which requires clearance around the filter to be effective

6   *Filter wrench* - This type fits on the bottom of the filter and can be turned with a ratchet or breaker bar (different-size wrenches are available for different types of filters)

8.7 Use the proper size box-end wrench or socket to remove the oil drain plug without rounding off the corners

8.13 It's a good idea to pack rags around the filter before removal to minimize the mess - since it is usually on very tight, you'll need a special wrench for removal - DO NOT use the wrench to tighten the new filter

8.15 Lubricate the oil filter gasket with clean engine oil before installing the filter on the engine

---

❋❋ WARNING:

Do not work under a vehicle which is supported only by a bumper, hydraulic or scissors-type jack.

---

4   If this is your first oil change, get under the vehicle and familiarize yourself with the location of the oil drain plug. The engine and exhaust components will be warm during the actual work, so try to anticipate any potential problems before the engine and accessories are hot.

5   Park the vehicle on a level spot. Start the engine and allow it to reach its normal operating temperature (the needle on the temperature gauge should be at least above the bottom mark). Warm oil and sludge will flow out more easily. Turn off the engine when it's warmed up. Remove the filler cap.

6   Raise the vehicle and support it securely on jackstands.

❋❋ WARNING:

To avoid personal injury, never get beneath a vehicle when it is supported only by a jack. The jack provided with your vehicle is designed solely for raising the vehicle to remove and replace the wheels. Always use jackstands to support the vehicle when it becomes necessary to place your body underneath the vehicle.

---

7   Being careful not to touch the hot exhaust components, place the drain pan under the drain plug in the bottom of the pan and remove the plug (see illustration). You may want to wear gloves while unscrewing the plug the final few turns if the engine is really hot.

8   Allow the old oil to drain into the pan. It may be necessary to move the pan farther under the engine as the oil flow slows to a trickle. Inspect the old oil for the presence of metal shavings and chips.

9   After all the oil has drained, wipe off the drain plug with a clean rag. Even minute metal particles clinging to the plug would immediately contaminate the new oil.

10   Clean the area around the drain plug opening, reinstall the plug (using a new sealing washer) and tighten it to the torque listed in this Chapter's Specifications.

11   Move the drain pan into position under the oil filter.

2006 AND EARLIER MODELS

12   Remove all tools, rags, etc. from under the vehicle, being careful not to spill the oil in the drain pan, then lower the vehicle.

13   Loosen the oil filter (see illustration) by turning it counterclockwise with an oil filter wrench. Once the filter is loose, use your hands to unscrew it from the block. Just as the filter is detached from the block, immediately tilt the open end up to prevent the oil inside the filter from spilling out.

❋❋ WARNING:

The engine exhaust manifold may still be hot, so be careful.

---

14   With a clean rag, wipe off the mounting surface on the block. If a residue of old oil is allowed to remain, it will smoke when the block is heated up. It will also prevent the new filter from seating properly. Also make sure that none of the old gasket remains stuck to the mounting surface. It can be removed with a scraper if necessary.

15   Compare the old filter with the new one to make sure they are the same type. Smear some engine oil on the rubber gasket of the new filter and screw it into place (see illustration). Because overtightening the filter will damage the gasket, do not use a filter wrench to tighten the filter. Tighten it by hand until the gasket contacts the seating surface. Then seat the filter by giving it an additional 3/4-turn.

2007 AND LATER MODELS

▸ Refer to illustrations 8.16a, 8.16b and 8.16c

16   Use a ratchet with an extension to remove the plug from the bottom of the oil filter housing, being careful to minimize the inevitable spillage (see illustrations). You can then use a blunt tool to push up the inner valve and allow the canister to drain.

➥Note: Dealers offer a special tool for this that includes a drain hose in order to make the job as clean as possible.

Unscrew the main oil filter housing. If it's too tight to be removed by hand, you can use an oil filter wrench.

17   Remove the filter element and the large O-ring from the housing.

➥Note: Don't use a metal tool to remove the O-ring, as this may scratch the soft housing.

18   Carefully clean all components and the engine block sealing area. Install a new O-ring and filter, then screw the assembly back onto the engine. Tighten it to the torque listed in this Chapter's Specifications. If you removed the drain plug, clean it thoroughly, install a new

8.16a Use a 3/8-inch extension to remove the oil filter housing drain plug - the entire filter housing can be removed instead, but it creates more spillage

8.16b The filter housing can be drained by inserting a blunt tool to lift the drain valve - make sure to have the drain pan centered under the filter

8.16c The main filter housing can usually be unscrewed by hand - if it's stuck you'll have to use an oil filter wrench, but be careful as the housing can be easily damaged

O-ring and tighten the plug to the torque listed in this Chapter's Specifications.

ALL MODELS

19 Add new oil to the engine through the oil filler cap in the valve cover. Use a funnel to prevent oil from spilling onto the top of the engine. Pour three quarts of fresh oil into the engine. Wait a few minutes to allow the oil to drain into the pan, then check the level on the oil dipstick (see Section 4 if necessary). If the oil level is at or near the F mark, install the filler cap hand tight, start the engine and allow the new oil to circulate.

20 Allow the engine to run for about a minute. While the engine is running, look under the vehicle and check for leaks at the oil pan drain plug and around the oil filter. If either is leaking, stop the engine and tighten the plug or filter slightly.

21 Wait a few minutes to allow the oil to trickle down into the pan, then recheck the level on the dipstick and, if necessary, add enough oil to bring the level to the F mark.

22 During the first few trips after an oil change, make it a point to check frequently for leaks and proper oil level.

23 The old oil drained from the engine cannot be reused in its present state and should be discarded. Oil reclamation centers, auto garages and gas stations will normally accept the oil, which can be refined and used again. After the oil has cooled, it can be drained into a suitable container (capped plastic jugs, topped bottles, milk cartons, etc.) for transport to one of these disposal sites.

SERVICE REMINDER LIGHT RESETTING (2004 AND LATER MODELS)

24 Turn the ignition key to the On position and depress the button to the right of the speedometer until the odometer is displayed.

25 Turn the ignition key to the Off position.

26 Depress the button again and hold it, then turn the ignition key to the On position. Hold the button in the depressed position for five seconds.

27 The odometer should indicate "000000" and the MAINT REQD light should turn off.

9 Windshield wiper blade inspection and replacement (every 6000 miles or 6 months)

♦ Refer to illustrations 9.5, 9.6, 9.7, 9.8, 9.9 and 9.10

1 The windshield wiper and blade assembly should be inspected periodically for damage, loose components and cracked or worn blade elements.

2 Road film can build up on the wiper blades and affect their efficiency, so they should be washed regularly with a mild detergent solution.

3 The action of the wiping mechanism can loosen bolts, nuts and fasteners, so they should be checked and tightened, as necessary, at the same time the wiper blades are checked.

4 If the wiper blade elements are cracked, worn or warped, or no longer clean adequately, they should be replaced with new ones.

5 Lift the arm assembly away from the glass for clearance (see illustration).

TYPE A

6 Working from the end of the wiper closest to the arm, pull the rubber blade element from the frame and discard it (see illustration).

7 To install a new rubber wiper element, insert the end with the small protrusions into the replacement hole and work the rubber along the slot in the blade frame see illustration).

TYPE B

8 Squeeze the end of the wiper element and pull it out of the frame (see illustration).

9 Insert the end of the new element without cutouts into the end of the frame (see illustration).

10 Work the rubber along the slot in the blade frame until the cutouts are locked into place by the wiper frame claw (see illustration).

9.5 Push the tab to release the wiper blade frame assembly from the wiper arm

9.6 Pull the type A wiper element tabs out of the frame

9.7 To install a new element, insert the end of the blade with the small protrusions into the frame

9.8 Squeeze the end of the type B wiper element and pull it straight out of the frame

9.9 Insert the end without the cutout into the frame

9.10 Slide the element into place until the cutouts seat into the locking claw

10 Battery check, maintenance and charging (every 6000 miles or 6 months)

▶ Refer to illustrations 10.1, 10.7a, 10.7b, 10.8a, 10.8b and 10.13

✳✳ WARNING:

Certain precautions must be followed when checking and servicing the battery. Hydrogen gas, which is highly flammable, is always present in the battery cells, so keep lighted tobacco and all other open flames and sparks away from the battery. The electrolyte inside the battery is actually dilute sulfuric acid, which will cause injury if splashed on your skin or in your eyes. It will also ruin clothes and painted surfaces. When removing the battery cables, always detach the negative cable first and hook it up last!

CHECK

1 A routine preventive maintenance program for the battery in your vehicle is the only way to ensure quick and reliable starts. But before performing any battery maintenance, make sure that you have the proper equipment necessary to work safely around the battery (see illustration).

10.1 Tools and materials required for battery maintenance

1 *Face shield/safety goggles* - When removing corrosion with a brush, the acidic particles can easily fly up into your eyes
2 *Baking soda* - A solution of baking soda and water can be used to neutralize corrosion
3 *Petroleum jelly* - A layer of this on the battery posts will help prevent corrosion
4 *Battery post/cable cleaner* - This wire-brush cleaning tool will remove all traces of corrosion from the battery posts and cable clamps
5 *Treated felt washers* - Placing one of these on each post, directly under the cable clamps, will help prevent corrosion
6 *Puller* - Sometimes the cable clamps are very difficult to pull off the posts, even after the nut/bolt has been completely loosened. This tool pulls the clamp straight up and off the post without damage
7 *Battery post/cable cleaner* - Here is another cleaning tool that is a slightly different version of Number 4 above, but it does the same thing
8 *Rubber gloves* - Another safety item to consider when servicing the battery; remember that's acid inside the battery!

10.7a Battery terminal corrosion usually appears as light, fluffy powder

10.7b Loosen the battery cable clamp bolt with a wrench - sometimes special battery pliers are required for this procedure if corrosion has deteriorated the hex nut - always remove the negative cable first and reconnect it last!

2   There are also several precautions that should be taken whenever battery maintenance is performed. Before servicing the battery, always turn the engine and all accessories off and disconnect the cable from the negative terminal of the battery.

3   The battery produces hydrogen gas, which is both flammable and explosive. Never create a spark, smoke or light a match around the battery. Always charge the battery in a ventilated area.

4   Electrolyte contains poisonous and corrosive sulfuric acid. Do not allow it to get in your eyes, on your skin or on your clothes. Never ingest it. Wear protective safety glasses when working near the battery. Keep children away from the battery.

5   Note the external condition of the battery. If the positive terminal and cable clamp on your vehicle's battery is equipped with a rubber protector, make sure that it's not torn or damaged. It should completely cover the terminal. Look for any corroded or loose connections, cracks in the case or cover or loose hold-down clamps. Also check the entire length of each cable for cracks and frayed conductors.

6   Some models with sealed batteries have a battery condition indicator on top of the battery. Compare the color showing in the window to the condition color chart on the battery. You may catch a low-charge battery condition before it strands you on the roadside. If the color indicates a low state of charge, charge the battery and examine the charging system (see Chapter 5 and this Section).

MAINTENANCE

7   If corrosion, which looks like white, fluffy deposits (see illustration) is evident, particularly around the terminals, the battery should be removed for cleaning. Loosen the cable clamp bolts with a wrench, being careful to remove the negative cable first, and slide them off the terminals (see illustration). Then disconnect the hold-down clamp bolt and nut, remove the clamp and lift the battery from the engine compartment.

8   Clean the cable clamps thoroughly with a battery brush or a terminal cleaner and a solution of warm water and baking soda. Wash the terminals and the top of the battery case with the same solution but make sure that the solution doesn't get into the battery. When cleaning the cables, terminals and battery top, wear safety goggles and rubber gloves to prevent any solution from coming in contact with your eyes or hands. Wear old clothes too - even diluted, sulfuric acid splashed onto clothes will burn holes in them. If the terminals have been extensively corroded, clean them up with a terminal cleaner (see illustrations). Thoroughly wash all cleaned areas with plain water.

9   Whenever the battery is removed for cleaning or charging, inspect the battery carrier before reinstalling the battery in the engine compartment. If the carrier is dirty or covered with corrosion, clean it in the same solution of warm water and baking soda. Inspect the metal brackets that support the carrier to make sure that they are not covered with corrosion. If they are, wash them off. If corrosion is extensive, sand the brackets down to bare metal and spray them with a zinc-based primer (available in spray cans at auto paint and body supply stores).

10   Reinstall the battery back into the engine compartment. Make sure that no parts or wires are laying on the carrier during installation of the battery. Information on removing and installing the battery can be found in Chapter 5. Information on jump-starting can be found at the front of this manual.

11   Install a pair of specially-treated felt washers around the terminals (available at auto parts stores), then coat the terminals and the cable clamps with petroleum jelly or grease to prevent further corrosion. Install the cable clamps and tighten the nuts, being careful to install the negative cable last.

12   Install the hold-down clamp and nuts. Tighten the nuts only enough to hold the battery firmly in place. Overtightening these nuts can crack the battery case.

13   Make sure that the battery tray is in good condition and the hold-down clamp bolts are tight (see illustration). If the battery is removed from the tray, make sure no parts remain in the bottom of the tray when the battery is reinstalled. When reinstalling the hold-down clamp nut and bolt, do not overtighten them.

CHARGING

✳✳ WARNING:

When batteries are being charged, hydrogen gas, which is very explosive and flammable, is produced. Do not smoke or allow open flames near a charging or a recently charged battery. Wear eye protection when near the battery during charging. Also, make sure the charger is unplugged before connecting or disconnecting the battery from the charger.

14   Slow-rate charging is the best way to restore a battery that's discharged to the point where it will not start the engine. It's also a good way to maintain the battery charge in a vehicle that's only driven a few miles between starts. Maintaining the battery charge is particularly important in the winter when the battery must work harder to start the engine and electrical accessories that drain the battery are in greater use.

15 It's best to use a one or two-amp battery charger (sometimes called a "trickle" charger). They are the safest and put the least strain on the battery. They are also the least expensive. For a faster charge, you can use a higher amperage charger, but don't use one rated more than 1/10th the amp/hour rating of the battery. Rapid boost charges that claim to restore the power of the battery in one to two hours are hardest on the battery and can damage batteries not in good condition. This type of charging should only be used in emergency situations.

16 The average time necessary to charge a battery should be listed in the instructions that come with the charger. As a general rule, a trickle charger will charge a battery in 12 to 16 hours.

10.8a When cleaning the cable clamps, all corrosion must be removed (the inside of the clamp is tapered to match the taper on the post, so don't remove too much material)

10.8b Regardless of the type of tool used on the battery posts, a clean, shiny surface should be the result

10.13 Make sure the battery hold-down nut and bolt are tight

11 Drivebelt check, adjustment and replacement (every 6000 miles or 6 months)

2006 AND EARLIER MODELS

Check

▶ **Refer to illustrations 11.3 and 11.5**

1 The alternator/air conditioning compressor and power steering pump drivebelts, also referred to as V-ribbed belts or simply "fan" belts, are located at the right end of the engine. The good condition and proper adjustment of the alternator belt is critical to the operation of the engine. Because of their composition and the high stresses to which they are subjected, drivebelts stretch and deteriorate as they get older. They must therefore be periodically inspected.

2 These vehicles are equipped with two belts. One belt transmits power from the crankshaft to the alternator and air conditioning compressor. The power steering pump is driven by its own belt.

3 With the engine off, open the hood and locate the drivebelts at the right end of the engine. With a flashlight, check each belt for any unde-sirable conditions. Both sides of the belt should be inspected, which means you will have to twist the belt to check the underside. Use your fingers to feel the belt where you can't see it. If the belt is worn, replace it (go to Step 8).

4 To check the tension of each belt in accordance with factory spec-ifications, install either a Nippondenso or Burroughs belt tension gauge on the belt. Measure the tension in accordance with the tool manufac-turer's instructions and compare your measurement to the specified drivebelt tension for either a used or new belt.

➡ **Note: A "used" belt is defined as any belt which has been operated more than five minutes on the engine; a "new" belt is one that has been used for less than five minutes.**

5 If you don't have either of the above tools, and cannot borrow one, the following rule of thumb method is recommended: Push firmly

11.3 Check a multi-ribbed belt for signs like these - if the belt looks worn, replace it

ACCEPTABLE

Cracks Running Across "V" Portions of Belt

1/2" Missing Two or More Adjacent Ribs 1/2" or longer

UNACCEPTABLE

Cracks Running Parallel to "V" Portions of Belt

RULER BELT DEFLECTION

STRAIGHT EDGE

MAKE SURE RULER IS PERPENDICULAR TO STRAIGHT EDGE

11.5 Measuring drivebelt deflection with a straightedge and ruler (2006 and earlier models)

on the belt with your thumb at a distance halfway between the pulleys and note how far the belt can be pushed (deflected). Measure this deflection with a ruler (see illustration). The belt should deflect 1/4-inch if the distance from pulley center to pulley center is between 7 and 11 inches; the belt should deflect 1/2-inch if the distance from pulley center to pulley center is between 12 and 16 inches.

Adjustment

▶ **Refer to illustration 11.6**

6   If the alternator/air conditioner compressor belt must be adjusted, loosen the alternator pivot bolt located on the front left corner of the block. Loosen the locking bolt and turn the adjusting bolt (see illustration). Measure the belt tension in accordance with one of the above methods. Repeat this step until the air conditioning compressor drivebelt is adjusted.

7   Adjust the power steering pump belt by loosening the adjustment bolt that secures the pump to the slotted bracket and pivot the pump (away from the engine to tighten the belt, toward it to loosen it). Repeat the procedure until the drivebelt tension is correct and tighten the bolt.

Replacement

8   To replace a belt, follow the above procedures for drivebelt adjustment but slip the belt off the crankshaft pulley and remove it. If you are replacing the power steering pump belt, you will have to remove the air conditioning compressor belt first because of the way they are arranged on the crankshaft pulley. Because of this and because belts tend to wear out more or less together, it is a good idea to replace both belts at the same time. Mark each belt and its appropriate pulley groove so the replacement belts can be installed in their proper positions.

9   Take the old belts to the parts store in order to make a direct comparison for length, width and design.

10   After replacing the drivebelt, make sure that it fits properly in the ribbed grooves in the pulleys. It is essential that the belt be properly centered.

11   Adjust the belt(s) in accordance with the procedure outlined above.

2007 AND LATER MODELS

Check

12   These vehicles are equipped with one belt that is automatically

11.6   After loosening the pivot bolt (A) and the adjustment pinch bolt, turn the adjustment bolt (B) clockwise to tighten the belt, or counterclockwise to loosen the belt (2006 and earlier models)

tensioned by a tensioner pulley. The checks of belt condition are the same as those for earlier models. Refer to Step 3 in this Section and check for any belt aging, wear or damage.

Replacement

13   Loosen the lug nuts of the right front wheel. Raise the vehicle and support it securely on jackstands. Remove the right front wheel.

14   Remove the inner fender splash shield for access to the tensioner pulley (see Chapter 11, Section 13).

15   Turn the center pivot bolt of the tensioner counterclockwise to loosen it, then pull the belt off.

➡**Note: Working room is very limited. It may be necessary to use a special tool, such as Toyota #09249-63010, or an equivalent.**

16   Install the replacement belt referring to the underhood routing diagram sticker.

➡**Note: New belts are difficult to place into position. It may be easiest to slip the belt over the tensioner pulley and the idler pulley last as you turn the tensioner pulley.**

17   Verify that the belt is correctly centered on each of the pulleys

---

12   Underhood hose check and replacement (every 6000 miles or 6 months)

❋ WARNING:

Replacement of air conditioning hoses must be left to a dealer service department or air conditioning shop that has the equipment to depressurize the system safely. Never remove air conditioning components or hoses until the system has been evacuated and the refrigerant recovered by a dealer service department or air conditioning shop.

GENERAL

1   High temperatures in the engine compartment can cause the deterioration of the rubber and plastic hoses used for engine, accessory and emission systems operation. Periodic inspection should be made for cracks, loose clamps, material hardening and leaks.

2   Information specific to the cooling system hoses can be found in Section 13.

3   Some, but not all, hoses are secured to the fittings with clamps.

Where clamps are used, check to be sure that they haven't lost their tension, allowing the hose to leak. If clamps aren't used, make sure the hose has not expanded and/or hardened where it slips over the fitting, allowing it to leak.

VACUUM HOSES

4   It's quite common for vacuum hoses, especially those in the emissions system, to be color-coded or identified by colored stripes molded into them. Various systems require hoses with different wall thickness, collapse resistance and temperature resistance. When replacing hoses, be sure the new ones are made of the same material.

5   Often the only effective way to check a hose is to remove it completely from the vehicle. If more than one hose is removed, be sure to label the hoses and fittings to ensure correct installation.

6   When checking vacuum hoses, be sure to include any plastic T-fittings in the check. Inspect the fittings for cracks and the hose where it fits over the fitting for distortion, which could cause leakage.

7   A small piece of vacuum hose (1/4-inch inside diameter) can be used as a stethoscope to detect vacuum leaks. Hold one end of the hose to your ear and probe around vacuum hoses and fittings, listening for the "hissing" sound characteristic of a vacuum leak.

❋❋ WARNING:

When probing with the vacuum hose stethoscope, be very careful not to come into contact with moving engine components such as the drivebelts, cooling fan, etc.

FUEL HOSE

❋❋ WARNING:

Gasoline is extremely flammable, so take extra precautions when you work on any part of the fuel system. Don't smoke or allow open flames or bare light bulbs near the work area, and don't work in a garage where a gas-type appliance (such as a water heater or a clothes dryer) is present. Since gasoline is carcinogenic, wear fuel resistant gloves when there's a possibility of being exposed to fuel, and, if you spill any fuel on your skin, rinse it off immediately with soap and water. Mop up any spills immediately and do not store fuel-soaked rags where they could ignite. The fuel system is under constant pressure, so, if any fuel lines are to be disconnected, the fuel pressure in the system must be relieved first. When you perform any kind of work on the fuel system, wear safety glasses and have a Class B type fire extinguisher on hand.

8   Check all rubber fuel lines for deterioration and chafing. Check especially for cracks in areas where the hose bends and just before fittings, such as where a hose attaches to the fuel filter.

9   High quality fuel line, marked specifically for use on fuel-injected engines, should be used for fuel line replacement. Never, under any circumstances, use unreinforced vacuum line, clear plastic tubing or water hose for fuel lines.

10   Spring-type clamps are commonly used on fuel lines. These clamps often lose their tension over a period of time, and can be "sprung" during removal. Replace all spring-type clamps with screw clamps whenever a hose is replaced.

METAL LINES

11   Sections of metal line are often used for fuel delivery between the fuel pump and the engine. Check carefully to be sure the line has not been bent or crimped and that cracks have not started in the line.

12   If a section of metal fuel line must be replaced, only seamless steel tubing should be used, since copper and aluminum tubing don't have the strength necessary to withstand normal engine vibration.

13   Check the metal brake lines where they enter the master cylinder and brake proportioning unit (if used) for cracks in the lines or loose fittings. Any sign of brake fluid leakage calls for an immediate thorough inspection of the brake system.

13 Cooling system check (every 6000 miles or 6 months)

▶ **Refer to illustration 13.4**

1   Many major engine failures can be attributed to a faulty cooling system. If the vehicle is equipped with an automatic transaxle, the cooling system also cools the transaxle fluid and thus plays an important role in prolonging transaxle life.

2   The cooling system should be checked with the engine cold. Do this before the vehicle is driven for the day or after the engine has been shut off for at least three hours.

❋❋ WARNING:

Never remove the cooling system pressure cap when the engine is running or has just been shut down, because the cooling system is hot. Escaping steam and scalding liquid could cause serious injury. Wait until the engine has cooled completely.

3   Remove the cooling system pressure cap by turning it counterclockwise 1/8-turn. If you hear a hissing sound (indicating there is still pressure in the system), wait until it stops. Now press down on the cap with the palm of your hand and continue turning until the cap can be removed. Thoroughly clean the cap, inside and out, with clean water. Also clean the filler neck on the water outlet. All traces of corrosion should be removed. The coolant inside the water outlet should be relatively transparent. If it's rust colored, the system should be drained and refilled (see Section 23). If the coolant level isn't up to the top, add additional antifreeze/coolant mixture (see Section 4).

4   Carefully check the large upper and lower radiator hoses along with the smaller diameter heater hoses that run from the engine to the firewall. Inspect each hose along its entire length, replacing any hose that is cracked, swollen or shows signs of deterioration. Cracks may

Check for a chafed area that could fail prematurely.

Overtightening the clamp on a hardened hose will damage the hose and cause a leak.

Check each hose for swelling and oil-soaked ends. Cracks and breaks can be located by squeezing the hose.

Check for a soft area indicating the hose has deteriorated inside.

13.4 Hoses, like drivebelts, have a habit of failing at the worst possible time - to prevent the inconvenience of a blown radiator or heater hose, inspect them carefully as shown here

become more apparent if the hose is squeezed (see illustration). Regardless of condition, it's a good idea to replace hoses with new ones every two years.

5   Make sure that all hose connections are tight. A leak in the cooling system will usually show up as white or rust colored deposits on the areas adjoining the leak. If wire-type clamps are used at the ends of the hoses, it may be a good idea to replace them with more secure screw-type clamps.

6   Use compressed air or a soft brush to remove bugs, leaves, etc. from the front of the radiator or air conditioning condenser. Be careful not to damage the delicate cooling fins or cut yourself on them.

7   Every other inspection, or at the first indication of cooling system problems, have the cap and system pressure tested. If you don't have a pressure tester, most gas stations and garages will do this for a minimal charge.

14 Tire rotation (every 6000 miles or 6 months)

♦ **Refer to illustration 14.2**

1   The tires should be rotated at the specified intervals and whenever uneven wear is noticed. Since the vehicle will be raised and the tires removed anyway, check the brakes (see Section 15) at this time.

2   Radial tires must be rotated in a specific pattern (see illustration).

3   Refer to the information in Jacking and towing at the front of this manual for the proper procedures to follow when raising the vehicle and changing a tire. If the brakes are to be checked, do not apply the parking brake as stated. Make sure the tires are blocked to prevent the vehicle from rolling.

4   Preferably, the entire vehicle should be raised at the same time. This can be done on a hoist or by jacking up each corner and then lowering the vehicle onto jackstands placed under the frame rails. Always use four jackstands and make sure the vehicle is firmly supported.

5   After rotation, check and adjust the tire pressures as necessary and be sure to check the wheel lug nut torque.

6   For further information on the wheels and tires, refer to Chapter 10.

14.2 The recommended tire rotation pattern for these models

15 Brake check (every 15,000 miles or 12 months)

☀ WARNING:

Brake system dust is hazardous to your health. DO NOT blow it out with compressed air and DO NOT inhale it. An approved filtering mask should be worn when working on the brakes. DO NOT use gasoline or solvents to remove the dust. Use brake system cleaner only!

➡Note: For detailed photographs of the brake system, refer to Chapter 9.

1   In addition to the specified intervals, the brakes should be inspected every time the wheels are removed or whenever a defect is suspected. Any of the following symptoms could indicate a potential brake system defect: The vehicle pulls to one side when the brake pedal is depressed; the brakes make squealing or dragging noises when applied; brake travel is excessive; the pedal pulsates; brake fluid leaks, usually onto the inside of the tire or wheel.

2   The disc brake pads have built-in wear indicators, which should make a high-pitched squealing or scraping noise when they are worn to the replacement point. When you hear this noise, replace the pads immediately or expensive damage to the discs can result.

3   Loosen the wheel nuts.

4   Raise the vehicle and place it securely on jack stands.

5   Remove the wheels (see *Jacking and towing* at the front of this book, or your owner's manual, if necessary).

DISC BRAKES

♦ **Refer to illustration 15.6**

6   There are two pads - an outer and an inner - in each caliper. The pads are visible through inspection holes in each caliper (see illustration).

7   Check the pad thickness by looking at each end of the caliper and through the inspection hole in the caliper body. If the lining material is less than the thickness listed in this Chapter's Specifications, replace the pads.

➡Note: Keep in mind that the lining material is riveted or bonded to a metal backing plate and the metal portion is not included in this measurement.

8   If it is difficult to determine the exact thickness of the remaining pad material by the above method, or if you are at all concerned about the condition of the pads, remove the caliper(s), then remove the pads for further inspection (refer to Chapter 9).

9   Once the pads are removed from the calipers, clean them with brake cleaner and remeasure them with a ruler or a vernier caliper.

10 Measure the disc thickness with a micrometer to make sure that it still has service life remaining. If any disc is thinner than the specified minimum thickness, replace it (refer to Chapter 9). Even if the disc has service life remaining, check its condition. Look for scoring, gouging and burned spots. If these conditions exist, remove the disc and have it resurfaced (see Chapter 9).

11 Before installing the wheels, check all brake lines and hoses for damage, wear, deformation, cracks, corrosion, leakage, bends and twists, particularly in the vicinity of the rubber hoses at the calipers. Check the clamps for tightness and the connections for leakage. Make sure that all hoses and lines are clear of sharp edges, moving parts and the exhaust system. If any of the above conditions are noted, repair, reroute or replace the lines and/or fittings as necessary (see Chapter 9).

12 When checking the brake lines and hoses, use a small mechanic's mirror to help you see both sides of the hose.

15.6 You'll find an inspection hole like this in each caliper through which you can view the inner and outer brake pad lining

15.13 A quick check of the remaining drum brake shoe lining material can be made by removing the rubber plug in the backing plate and looking through the inspection hole

15.15 If the lining is bonded to the brake shoe, measure the lining thickness from the outer surface to the metal shoe, as shown here; if the lining is riveted to the shoe, measure from the lining outer surface to the rivet head

REAR DRUM BRAKES

▶ Refer to illustrations 15.13, 15.15 and 15.17

13 To check the brake shoe lining thickness without removing the brake drums, remove the rubber plug from the backing plate and use a flashlight to inspect the linings (see illustration). For a more thorough brake inspection, follow the procedure below.

14 Refer to Chapter 9 and remove the rear brake drums.

❋❋ WARNING:

Brake dust produced by lining wear and deposited on brake components is hazardous to your health. DO NOT blow it out with compressed air and DO NOT inhale it!

15 Note the thickness of the lining material on the rear brake shoes (see illustration) and look for signs of contamination by brake fluid and grease. If the lining material is with-in 1/16-inch of the recessed rivets or metal shoes, replace the brake shoes with new ones. The shoes should also be replaced if they are cracked, glazed (shiny lining surfaces) or contaminated with brake fluid or grease. See Chapter 9 for the replacement procedure.

16 Check the shoe return and hold-down springs and the adjusting mechanism to make sure they're fitted correctly and in good condition. Deteriorated or distorted springs, if not replaced, could allow the linings to drag and wear prematurely.

15.17 Carefully peel back the wheel cylinder boot and check for leaking fluid indicating that the cylinder must be replaced

17 Check the wheel cylinders for leakage by carefully peeling back the rubber boots (see illustration). If brake fluid is noted behind the boots, the wheel cylinders must be replaced (see Chapter 9).

18 Check the drums for cracks, score marks, deep scratches and hard spots, which will appear as small discolored areas. If imperfections cannot be removed with emery cloth, the drums must be resurfaced by an automotive machine shop (see Chapter 9 for more detailed information).

19 Refer to Chapter 9 and install the brake drums.

20 Install the wheels and snug the wheel nuts finger tight.

21 Remove the jackstands and lower the vehicle.

22 Tighten the wheel nuts to the torque listed in this Chapter's Specifications.

BRAKE BOOSTER CHECK

23 Sit in the driver's seat and perform the following sequence of tests.

24 With the brake fully depressed, start the engine - the pedal should move down a little when the engine starts.

25 With the engine running, depress the brake pedal several times - the travel distance should not change.

26 Depress the brake, stop the engine and hold the pedal in for about 30 seconds - the pedal should neither sink nor rise.

27 Restart the engine, run it for about a minute and turn it off. Then firmly depress the brake several times - the pedal travel should decrease with each application.

28 If your brakes do not operate as described above when the preceding tests are performed, the brake booster is either in need of repair or has failed. Refer to Chapter 9 for the removal procedure.

PARKING BRAKE

29 Slowly push down on the parking brake pedal and count the number of clicks you hear until the pedal is down as far as it will go. The adjustment is correct if you hear the specified number of clicks. If you hear more or fewer clicks, it's time to adjust the parking brake (refer to Chapter 9).

30 An alternative method of checking the parking brake is to park the vehicle on a steep hill with the parking brake set and the transaxle in Neutral (be sure to stay in the vehicle for this check!) If the parking brake cannot prevent the vehicle from rolling, it is in need of adjustment (see Chapter 9).

16 Air filter replacement (every 15,000 miles or 12 months)

▶ **Refer to illustrations 16.1 and 16.3**

1   The air filter is inside a housing at the left (driver's) side of the engine compartment. To remove the cover on 2006 and earlier models, release the two spring clips (see illustration).

2   On 2007 and later models, first disconnect the three vacuum hoses from the air filter cover, then remove the other interfering vacuum hoses. Disconnect the wiring from the air intake tube, then loosen the tube's clamp. Remove the two air filter cover bolts and lift off the cover.

3   Lift the cover up and remove the air filter element (see illustration).

4   Inspect the outer surface of the filter element. If it is dirty, replace it. If it is only moderately dusty, it can be reused by blowing it clean from the back to the front surface with compressed air.

✳✳ **WARNING:**

Always wear eye protection when using compressed air!

Because it is a pleated paper type filter, it cannot be washed or oiled. If it cannot be cleaned satisfactorily with compressed air, discard and replace it.

✳✳ **CAUTION:**

Never drive the vehicle with the air cleaner removed. Excessive engine wear could result and backfiring could even cause a fire under the hood.

5   Installation is the reverse of removal.

16.1 Detach the two air-cleaner housing clips (2006 and earlier models)

16.3 Lift the cover up and remove the filter

17 Fuel system check (every 15,000 miles or 12 months)

▶ **Refer to illustration 17.5**

✳✳ **WARNING:**

Gasoline is extremely flammable, so take extra precautions when you work on any part of the fuel system. Don't smoke or allow open flames or bare light bulbs near the work area, and don't work in a garage where a gas-type appliance (such as a water heater or a clothes dryer) is present. Since gasoline is carcinogenic, wear fuel resistant gloves when there's a possibility of being exposed to fuel, and, if you spill any fuel on your skin, rinse it off immediately with soap and water. Mop up any spills immediately and do not store fuel-soaked rags where they could ignite. The fuel system is under constant pressure, so, if any fuel lines are to be disconnected, the fuel pressure in the system must be relieved first. When you perform any kind of work on the fuel system, wear safety glasses and have a Class B type fire extinguisher on hand.

1   If you smell fuel while driving or after the vehicle has been sitting in the sun, inspect the fuel system immediately.

2   Remove the fuel filler cap and inspect if for damage and corrosion. The gasket should have an unbroken sealing imprint. If the gasket is damaged or corroded, remove it and install a new one (Section 29).

3   Inspect the fuel feed line for cracks. Make sure the banjo bolt that secures the banjo fitting to the in-line fuel filter is tight. Also check that there are no fuel leaks around the fuel injectors and fuel rail (see Chapter 4).

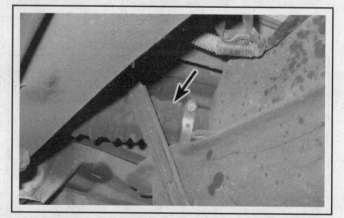

17.5 Check the fuel tank filler hose connection for leaks and damage

4   Since some components of the fuel system - the fuel tank and part of the fuel feed and return lines, for example - are underneath the vehicle, they can be inspected more easily with the vehicle raised on a hoist. If that's not possible, raise the vehicle and support it securely on jackstands.

5   With the vehicle raised and safely supported, inspect the fuel tank and filler neck for punctures, cracks and other damage. The connection between the filler neck and the tank is particularly critical. Sometimes a rubber filler neck will leak because of loose clamps or deteriorated rubber (see illustration). These are problems a home mechanic can usually rectify.

✳✳ WARNING:

Do not, under any circumstances, try to repair a fuel tank (except rubber components).

6   Carefully check all rubber hoses and metal lines leading away from the fuel tank. Check for loose connections, deteriorated hoses, crimped lines and other damage. Carefully inspect the lines from the tank to the engine. Repair or replace damaged sections as necessary (see Chapter 4).

18 Steering, suspension and driveaxle boot check (every 15,000 miles or 12 months)

▸ **Refer to illustrations 18.7 and 18.8**

➡**Note: For detailed illustrations of the steering and suspension components, refer to Chapter 10.**

1   With the vehicle on the ground and the front wheels pointed straight ahead, rock the steering wheel gently back and forth. If freeplay is excessive, a front wheel bearing, main shaft yoke, intermediate shaft yoke, lower arm balljoint or tie-rod end is worn or the steering gear is out of adjustment or broken. Steering wheel freeplay is the amount of travel (measured at the rim of the steering wheel) between the initial steering input and the point at which the front wheels begin to turn (indicated by slight resistance). Refer to Chapter 10 for the appropriate repair procedure.

2   Other symptoms, such as excessive vehicle body movement over rough roads, swaying (leaning) around corners and binding as the steering wheel is turned, may indicate faulty steering and/or suspension components.

3   Check the shock absorbers by pushing down and releasing the vehicle several times at each corner. If the vehicle does not come back to a level position within one or two bounces, the shocks/struts are worn and must be replaced. When bouncing the vehicle up and down, listen for squeaks and noises from the suspension components. Additional information on suspension components can be found in Chapter 10.

4   Raise the vehicle and support it securely on jackstands.

5   Check the tires for irregular wear patterns and proper inflation. See Section 5 in this Chapter for information regarding tire wear and Chapter 10 for the wheel bearing replacement procedures.

6   Inspect the universal joint between the steering shaft and the steering gear housing. Check the steering gear housing for lubricant leakage or oozing. Make sure that the dust seals and boots are not damaged and that the boot clamps are not loose. Check the steering linkage for looseness or damage. Check the tie-rod ends for excessive play. Look for loose bolts, broken or disconnected parts and deteriorated rubber bushings on all suspension and steering components. While an assistant turns the steering wheel from side to side, check the steering components for free movement, chafing and binding. If the steering components do not seem to be reacting with the movement of the steering wheel, try to determine where the slack is located.

7   Check the balljoints for wear by trying to move each control arm up and down with a prybar (see illustration) to ensure that its balljoint has no play. If any balljoint does have play, replace it (see Chapter 10).

8   Inspect the balljoint boots for damage and leaking grease (see illustration). Replace the balljoints with new ones if they are damaged (see Chapter 10).

DRIVEAXLE BOOT CHECK

▸ **Refer to illustration 18.10**

9   The driveaxle boots are very important because they prevent dirt, water and foreign material from entering and damaging the constant velocity (CV) joints. Oil and grease can cause the boot material to deteriorate prematurely, so it's a good idea to wash the boots with soap and water.

10   Inspect the boots for tears and cracks as well as loose clamps (see illustration). If there is any evidence of cracks or leaking lubricant, they must be replaced as described in Chapter 8.

18.7 To check the balljoints, attempt to move the lower arm up and down with a prybar to make sure there is no play in the balljoint (if there is, replace it)

18.8 Push on the balljoint boot to check for tears and grease leaks

18.10 Flex the driveaxle boots by hand to check for tears, cracks and leaking grease

19 Cabin air filter - replacement (every 15,000 miles or 12 months)

◆ **Refer to illustration 19.3**

➡**Note: This procedure applies to 2004 and later models only.**

1 2004 and later models are equipped with a cabin air filter in the blower housing. The filter traps dust and pollen before the air enters the passenger compartment.

2 For access to the cabin air filter, swing the glove box down.

3 Pull out the filter case and lift out the filter (see illustration).

4 Installation is the reverse of the removal procedure.

19.3 Release the tabs at each end of the filter cover, then slide the filter and cover out

20 Exhaust system check (every 15,000 miles or 12 months)

◆ **Refer to illustration 20.2**

1 With the engine cold (at least three hours after the vehicle has been driven), check the complete exhaust system from its starting point at the engine to the end of the tailpipe. This should be done on a hoist where unrestricted access is available.

2 Check the pipes and connections for evidence of leaks, severe corrosion or damage. Make sure that all brackets and hangers are in good condition and tight (see illustration).

3 At the same time, inspect the underside of the body for holes, corrosion, open seams, etc. which may allow exhaust gases to enter the passenger compartment. Seal all body openings with silicone or body putty.

4 Rattles and other noises can often be traced to the exhaust system, especially the mounts and hangers. Try to move the pipes, silencer and catalytic converter. If the components can come in contact with the body or suspension parts, secure the exhaust system with new mounts.

5 Check the running condition of the engine by inspecting inside the end of the tailpipe. The exhaust deposits here are an indication of

20.2 Check the exhaust system for rust, damage, or worn rubber hangers

engine state-of-tune. If the pipe is black and sooty or coated with white deposits, the engine is in need of a tune-up, including a thorough fuel system inspection.

21 Cooling system servicing (draining, flushing and refilling) (every 30,000 miles or 24 months)

✳✳ **WARNING:**

Do not allow engine coolant (antifreeze) to come in contact with your skin or painted surfaces of the vehicle. Rinse off spills immediately with plenty of water. Antifreeze is highly toxic if ingested. Never leave antifreeze lying around in an open container or in puddles on the floor; children and pets are attracted by its sweet smell and may drink it. Check with local authorities about disposing of used antifreeze. Many communities have collection centers that will see that antifreeze is disposed of safely.

➡**Note: Non-toxic antifreeze is available at most auto parts stores. Although the antifreeze is non-toxic when fresh, proper disposal is still required.**

1 Periodically, the cooling system should be drained, flushed and refilled to replenish the antifreeze mixture and prevent formation of rust and corrosion, which can impair the performance of the cooling system and cause engine damage. When the cooling system is serviced, all hoses and the cooling system pressure cap should be checked and replaced if necessary.

DRAINING

◆ **Refer to illustrations 21.4 and 21.5**

✳✳ **WARNING:**

Wait until the engine is completely cool before beginning this procedure.

2 Apply the parking brake and block the wheels. If the vehicle has just been driven, wait several hours to allow the engine to cool down before beginning this procedure.

3 Once the engine is completely cool, remove the cooling system pressure cap.

4 Move a large container under the radiator drain to catch the coolant, then open the drain fitting at the bottom of the radiator (a pair of pliers may be required to turn it) (see illustration).

5 After the coolant stops flowing out of the radiator, move the container under the engine block drain plug (see illustration). Loosen the

21.4 The drain fitting is located at the bottom of the radiator

21.5 The engine has a coolant drain like this located on both sides of the block (2006 and earlier models shown)

plug and allow the coolant in the block to drain.

6   While the coolant is draining, check the condition of the radiator hoses, heater hoses and clamps (refer to Section 13 if necessary).

7   Replace any damaged clamps or hoses (see Chapter 3).

FLUSHING

▶ Refer to illustration 21.10

8   Once the system is completely drained, remove the thermostat from the engine (see Chapter 3). Then reinstall the thermostat housing without the thermostat. This will allow the system to be flushed.

9   Tighten the engine block drain plugs and the radiator drain plug. Turn your heating system controls to Hot, so that the heater core will be flushed at the same time as the rest of the cooling system. Install the cooling system pressure cap.

10   Disconnect the upper radiator hose from the radiator. Place a garden hose in the upper radiator inlet, turn the water on and flush the system until the water runs clear out of the upper radiator hose (see illustration).

11   In severe cases of contamination or clogging of the radiator, remove the radiator (see Chapter 3) and have a radiator repair facility clean and repair it if necessary. Many deposits can be removed by the

chemical action of a cleaner available at auto parts stores. Follow the procedure outlined in the manufacturer's instructions.

➡ **Note: When the coolant is regularly drained and the system refilled with the correct antifreeze/water mixture, there should be no need to use chemical cleaners or descalers.**

12   After flushing, drain the radiator and   block once again to drain the water from the system.

REFILLING

▶ Refer to illustration 21.15

13   Tighten the radiator and block drain plugs. Reinstall the thermostat.

14   Place the heater temperature control in the maximum heat position.

15   Remove the cooling system pressure cap and slowly add new coolant (a 50/50 mixture of water and antifreeze) to the water outlet until it's full. Add coolant to the reservoir up to the lower mark. On 2007 and later models, loosen the air bleed valve at the top of the radiator. Close the valve when air-free coolant flows out of the valve.

16   Leave the pressure cap off and run the engine in a well-ventilated area until the thermostat opens (coolant will begin flowing through the radiator and the upper radiator hose will become hot).

17   Turn the engine off and let it cool. Add more coolant mixture to bring the level back up to the lip on the radiator filler neck.

18   Squeeze the upper radiator hose to expel air, then add more coolant mixture if necessary. Reinstall the pressure cap.

19   Start the engine, allow it to reach normal operating temperature and check for leaks.

21.10 With the thermostat removed, disconnect the upper radiator hose and flush the radiator and engine block with a garden hose

21.15 2007 and later models have this fitting to allow bleeding air from the cooling system

22 Evaporative emissions control system check (every 30,000 miles or 24 months)

◆ **Refer to illustrations 22.2**

1   The function of the evaporative emissions control system is to draw fuel vapors from the fuel tank and fuel system, store them in a charcoal canister and then burn them during normal engine operation. On 1998 to 2000 models, the canister is up front, under the air filter housing. On later models, it is at the rear of the vehicle, near the fuel tank. A cover may have to be removed for access on the later models.

2   The most common symptom of a fault in the evaporative emissions system is a strong fuel odor in or around the vehicle. If a fuel odor is detected, inspect the charcoal canister. Check the canister and all hoses for damage and deterioration (see illustration).

3   The evaporative emissions control system is explained in more detail in Chapter 6.

22.2 Check the charcoal canister for damage and the hose connections for cracks and damage (1998 through 2000 models shown) - on 2001 and later models, the EVAP canister is located at the rear of the vehicle, ahead of the fuel tank

23 Chassis and body fastener check (every 30,000 miles or 24 months)

◆ **Refer to illustrations 23.1a and 23.1b**

1   Tighten the following fasteners to the torque values listed in this Chapter's Specifications (see illustrations):

a) *Front seat mounting bolts.*
b) *Front suspension subframe-to-body mounting bolts and rear suspension axle beam pivot bolts/nuts.*

23.1a Periodically check the tightness of the bolts on the front suspension subframe (two front bolts are accessed after plastic splash shields are removed) . . .

23.1b . . . and rear suspension axle pivot bolts/nuts

24 Automatic transaxle/differential fluid change (every 60,000 miles or 48 months)

◆ **Refer to illustrations 24.7, 24.8a, 24.8b, 24.9, 24.12 and 24.14**

1   At the specified time intervals, the automatic transaxle and differential fluid should be drained and replaced.

➥**Note: Although the manufacturer doesn't specify it, it is a good idea to clean the transaxle fluid strainer periodically to remove accumulated dirt and metal particles.**

2   Before beginning work, purchase the specified transaxle fluid (see *Recommended lubricants and fluids* in this Chapter's Specifications).

3   Other tools necessary for this job include jackstands to support the vehicle in a raised position, a 10 mm hex bit or Allen wrench, a

drain pan capable of holding at least five quarts, newspapers and clean rags.

4   The fluid should be drained immediately after the vehicle has been driven. Hot fluid is more effective than cold fluid at removing built up sediment.

✳✳ **WARNING:**

Fluid temperature can exceed 350-degrees F in a hot transaxle. Wear protective gloves.

24.7 Use a 10-mm hex bit or Allen wrench to remove the automatic transaxle drain plug

24.8a After loosening the front bolts, remove the rear pan bolts and . . .

24.8b . . . allow the remaining fluid to drain out

24.9 Remove the strainer bolts and lower the strainer

5   After the vehicle has been driven to warm up the fluid, raise it and place it on jackstands for access to the transaxle and, on 2000 and earlier models, differential drain plugs.

6   Move the necessary equipment under the vehicle, being careful not to touch any of the hot exhaust components.

7   Place the drain pan under the drain plug in the transaxle pan and remove the drain plug (see illustration). Be sure the drain pan is in position, as fluid will come out with some force. Once the fluid is drained, reinstall the drain plug securely. If you aren't going to clean the strainer, proceed to Step 14.

8   To clean the strainer, remove the front transaxle pan bolts, then loosen the rear bolts and carefully pry the pan loose with a screwdriver and allow the remaining fluid to drain (see illustrations). Once the fluid has drained, remove the bolts and lower the pan.

9   Remove the strainer retaining bolts, disconnect the clip (some models) and lower the strainer from the transaxle (see illustration). Be careful when lowering the strainer as it contains residual fluid.

10   Wash the strainer thoroughly in clean solvent, then dry it.

11   Place the strainer in position, connect the clip (if equipped) and install the bolts. Tighten the bolts to the torque listed in this Chapter's Specifications.

12   Carefully clean the gasket surfaces of the fluid pan, removing all traces of old gasket material. Noting their location, remove the magnets, wash the pan in clean solvent, then dry it.

❋❋ **WARNING:**

Always wear eye protection when using compressed air! Be sure to clean and reinstall the magnets in the pan (see illustration).

24.12 Noting their locations, remove the magnets and wash them and the pan in solvent before installing them

13 Install a new gasket, place the fluid pan in position and install the bolts in their original positions. Tighten the bolts to the torque listed in this Chapter's Specifications.

14 Locate the differential drain plug (this won't be necessary on 2001 and later models as they don't have a separate differential housing). Place the drain pan underneath the plug, remove it with a hex bit or Allen wrench and drain the fluid (see illustration). When the differential fluid has drained, reinstall the plug (using a new sealing washer) and tighten it to the torque listed in this Chapter's Specifications.

15 Lower the vehicle.

16 With the engine off, add new fluid to the transaxle through the dipstick tube (see *Recommended lubricants and fluids* for the recommended fluid type and capacity). Use a funnel to prevent spills. It is best to add a little fluid at a time, continually checking the level with the dipstick (see Section 7). Allow the fluid time to drain into the pan.

17 Start the engine and move the gearshift selector into all positions from P through L, then shift into P and apply the parking brake.

18 With the engine idling, check the fluid level. Add fluid up to the two lower notches on the dipstick.

24.14 Automatic transaxle differential drain plug location

25 Fuel filter replacement (every 60,000 miles or 48 months)

▶ **Refer to illustration 25.4**

1 Refer to Chapter 4 and relieve the fuel system pressure.

➡**Note: 2001 and later models do not have a separate serviceable fuel filter. These models have a filter in the fuel tank, which is designed to last for 100,000 miles or more (see Chapter 4).**

2 Disconnect the negative battery cable.

3 If necessary for access, remove the air cleaner assembly (see Chapter 4) and evaporative canister (see Chapter 6).

4 Unscrew the banjo bolt from the top of the filter and disconnect the fitting from the filter (see illustration). Loosen the fitting at the bottom of the fuel filter with a flare nut wrench while holding the filter canister from turning with an open-end wrench.

5 Remove the bracket bolts from the inner fender panel and remove the filter and bracket assembly.

6 Note that the inlet and outlet pipes are clearly labeled on their respective ends of the filter and that the flanged end of the filter faces down. Make sure the new filter is installed so that it's facing the proper direction as noted above. When correctly installed, the filter should be fitted so that the outlet faces up and the inlet faces down.

7 Connect the inlet fitting to the bottom of the filter, then mount the bracket to the inner fender panel, tightening the bolts securely. Now tighten the inlet fitting securely.

8 Connect the outlet fitting to the top of the filter, using new sealing washers on either side of the fitting. Tighten the banjo bolt to the torque listed in this Chapter's Specifications.

9 The remainder of installation is the reverse of the removal procedure.

25.4 Disconnect the fuel line fitting at the top and bottom of the fuel filter (1998 through 2000 models only)

26 Spark plug check and replacement (every 60,000 miles or 48 months)

▶ **Refer to illustrations 26.1a, 26.1b, 26.4a, 26.4b, 26.7, 26.8, 26.10, 26.11, 26.12a and 26.12b**

1 Spark plug replacement requires a spark plug socket that fits onto a ratchet. This socket is lined with a rubber grommet to protect the porcelain insulator of the spark plug and to hold the plug while you insert it into the spark plug hole. You will also need a wire-type feeler gauge to check and adjust the spark plug gap and a torque wrench to tighten the new plugs to the specified torque (see illustration). On engines equipped with a V-bank cover, remove the three 5-mm cap nuts and detach the cover for access (see illustrations).

2 If you are replacing the plugs, purchase the new plugs, adjust them to the proper gap and then replace each plug one at a time.

➡**Note: The manufacturer specifies that only platinum- or iridium-tipped spark plugs be used on these models. When buying new spark plugs, it's essential that you obtain the correct plugs for your specific vehicle. This information can be found in the Specifications Section at the end of this Chapter.**

26.1a Tools required for changing spark plugs

1 **Spark plug socket** - *This will have special padding inside to protect the spark plug's porcelain insulator*
2 **Torque wrench** - *Although not mandatory, using this tool is the best way to ensure the plugs are tightened properly*
3 **Ratchet** - *Standard hand tool to fit the spark plug socket*
4 **Extension** - *Depending on model and accessories, you may need special extensions and universal joints to reach one or more of the plugs*
5 **Spark plug gap gauge** - *This gauge for checking the gap comes in a variety of styles. Make sure the gap for your engine is included*

3   Inspect each of the new plugs for defects. If there are any signs of cracks in the porcelain insulator of a plug, don't use it.
4   Check the electrode gaps of the new plugs.

➡**Note: Do not adjust the gap on the iridium spark plugs used on some later models because using a gapping tool on them could damage the iridium plating on the electrodes. These spark plugs are pre-gapped by the manufacturer.**

On other types of spark plugs, check the gap by inserting the wire

26.1b Remove the three 5-mm cap nuts on 2001 and later models - earlier models have two nuts and two clips

gauge of the proper thickness between the electrodes at the tip of the plug (see illustration). The gap between the electrodes should be identical to that listed in this Chapter's Specifications. If the gap is incorrect, use the notched adjuster on the feeler gauge body to bend the curved side electrode slightly (see illustration).
5   If the side electrode is not exactly over the center electrode, use the notched adjuster to align them.

❈❈ **CAUTION:**

If the gap of a new plug must be adjusted, bend only the base of the negative electrode - do not touch the tip.

6   Remove the upper intake manifold for access to the rear spark plugs (see Chapter 2B).
7   Remove the bolts and detach each ignition coil assembly from the spark plugs (front bank only on 1998 through 2000 models) (see illustration).
8   To prevent the possibility of mixing up spark plug wires, work on

26.4a Spark plug manufacturers recommend using a wire-type gauge when checking the gap - if the wire does not slide between the electrodes with a slight drag, adjustment is required

26.4b To change the gap, bend the side electrodes only, be very careful not to crack or chip the porcelain insulator surrounding the center electrode

26.7 Remove the retaining bolt (A), disconnect the electrical connector (B) and detach the individual coils to reach the front spark plugs - the spark plug wires (C) lead to the rear bank spark plugs on 1998 to 2000 models

26.8 When removing spark plug wires, pull only on the boot using a twisting/pulling motion - on individual coils, pull straight up

26.10 Because they are deeply recessed, the proper spark plug socket and an extension will be required when removing or installing the spark plugs

one spark plug at a time. Remove the wire and boot from one spark plug. Grasp the boot - not the cable - as shown, give it a half twisting motion and pull straight up (see illustration).

9   If compressed air is available, blow any dirt or foreign material away from the spark plug area before proceeding.

✳✳ WARNING:

Always wear eye protection when using compressed air!

10   Remove the spark plug (see illustration).

11   Whether you are replacing the plugs at this time or intend to re-use the old plugs, compare each old spark plug with those shown in the chart (see illustration) to determine the overall running condition of

the engine.

12   Apply a small amount of anti-seize compound to the spark plug threads, but do not get the compound on the spark plug electrodes (see illustration). It's often difficult to insert spark plugs into their holes without cross-threading them. To avoid this possibility, fit a short piece of rubber hose over the end of the spark plug (see illustration). The flexible hose acts as a universal joint to help align the plug with the spark plug hole. Should the plug begin to cross-thread, the hose will slip on the spark plug, preventing thread damage. Tighten the plug to the torque listed in this Chapter's Specifications.

13   Attach the plug wire to the new spark plug, again using a twisting motion on the boot until it is firmly seated on the end of the spark plug.

14   Follow the above procedure for the remaining spark plugs, replacing them one at a time to prevent mixing up the spark plug wires.

A normally worn spark plug should have light tan or gray deposits on the firing tip.

A carbon fouled plug, identified by soft, sooty, black deposits, may indicate an improperly tuned vehicle. Check the air cleaner, ignition components and engine control system.

An oil fouled spark plug indicates an engine with worn piston rings and/or bad valve seals allowing excessive oil to enter the chamber.

This spark plug has been left in the engine too long, as evidenced by the extreme gap- Plugs with such an extreme gap can cause misfiring and stumbling accompanied by a noticeable lack of power.

A physically damaged spark plug may be evidence of severe detonation in that cylinder. Watch that cylinder carefully between services, as a continued detonation will not only damage the plug, but could also damage the engine.

A bridged or almost bridged spark plug, identified by a build-up between the electrodes caused by excessive carbon or oil build-up on the plug.

26.11 Inspect the spark plug to determine engine running condition

26.12a A light coat of anti-seize compound applied to the threads of the spark plugs will keep the threads in the cylinder head from being damaged the next time the plugs are removed

26.12b A section of rubber hose will aid in getting the spark plug threads started

27 Spark plug wire - check and replacement (every 60,000 miles or 48 months)

1   The spark plug wires should be checked whenever new spark plugs are installed.

→Note: 2001 and later models have an individual coil for each spark plug, there are no secondary spark plug wires.

2   Begin this procedure by making a visual check of the spark plug wires while the engine is running. In a darkened garage (make sure there is ventilation) start the engine and observe each plug wire. Be careful not to come into contact with any moving engine parts. If there is a break in the wire, you will see arcing or a small spark at the damaged area. If arcing is noticed, obtain new wires.

3   The spark plug wires should be inspected one at a time to prevent mixing up the order, which is essential for proper engine operation. Each original plug wire should be numbered to help identify its location. If the number is illegible, a piece of tape can be marked with the correct number and wrapped around the plug wire.

→Note: There are three coilpacks, one mounted over each of the spark plugs on the front bank. From these coils, three spark plug wires are routed around the intake manifold to the rear bank spark plugs, which have a standard boot termination.

4   Disconnect the plug wire from the spark plug (refer to Section 26). A removal tool can be used for this purpose or you can grasp the rubber boot, twist the boot half a turn and pull the boot free. Do not pull on the wire itself.

5   Check inside the boot for corrosion, which will look like a white crusty powder.

6   Push the wire and boot back onto the end of the spark plug. It should fit tightly onto the end of the plug. If it doesn't, remove the wire and use pliers to carefully crimp the metal connector inside the wire boot until the fit is snug.

7   Using a clean rag, wipe the entire length of the wire to remove built-up dirt and grease. Once the wire is clean, check for burns, cracks and other damage. Do not bend the wire sharply, because the conductor might break.

8   Disconnect the wire from the coilpack. Use a small screwdriver to release the locking claw from the boot protector and pull only on the rubber boot. Check for corrosion and a tight fit. Replace the wire in the coilpack.

9   Inspect the remaining spark plug wires, making sure that each one is securely fastened at the coilpack and spark plug when the check is complete.

10 If new spark plug wires are required, purchase a set for your specific engine model. Remove and replace the wires one at a time to avoid mix-ups in the firing order.

11 For electrical checks of plug wires and coilpacks, refer to Chapter 5.

28 Valve clearance check and adjustment (every 60,000 miles or 48 months)

▶ Refer to illustrations 28.7a, 28.7b, 28.9a, 28.9b, 28.11a, 28.11b, 28.11c and 28.12

✳✳ WARNING:

Wait until the engine is completely cool before beginning this procedure.

→Note: The following procedure requires the use of a special lifter tool. It is impossible to perform this task without it.

→Note: 2007 and later 3.5L models have hydraulic valve systems that don't require checking or adjustment.

1   Disconnect the negative cable from the battery.

2   Remove the cowl covers (see Chapter 11).

3   Clamp off the coolant hoses leading to the tubes on the underside of the throttle body (it isn't necessary to drain the engine coolant). Remove the air cleaner assembly and air intake plenum (see Chapter 2C). On 1998 through 2000 models, disconnect the spark plug wires from the rear bank spark plugs and remove the ignition

28.7a When the no. 1 piston is at TDC on the compression stroke, the clearance of the indicated valves can be measured

28.7b Measure the clearance for each valve with a feeler gauge of the specified thickness - if the clearance is correct, you should feel a slight drag on the gauge as you pull it out

coil/spark plug wire assembly from the front bank. On 2001 and later models, remove all six coilpacks. Remove any other components that will interfere with valve cover removal.

4   Blow out the spark plug recesses with compressed air, if available, to remove any debris that might fall into the cylinders, then remove the spark plugs (see Section 27).

✳✳ WARNING:

Always wear eye protection when using compressed air!

5   Remove the valve cover(s) (see Chapter 2A or 2B).
6   Refer to Chapter 2A or 2B and position the number 1 piston at

TDC on the compression stroke.

7   Measure the clearance of the indicated valves with a feeler gauge of the specified thickness (see illustrations).

8   Record the clearance of each valve and note which ones are out of specification. This information will be used later to determine the required replacement shims.

9   Turn the crankshaft 2/3-turn (240-degrees) clockwise. Measure the valve clearance on the valves shown (see illustration). Rotate the crankshaft a further 2/3-turn and measure the clearance on the remaining valves (see illustration).

10 After measuring and recording the clearance of each valve, turn the crankshaft pulley until the camshaft lobe (above the first valve which you intend to adjust) is pointing upward, away from the shim.

28.9a After the engine has been rotated 240-degrees from TDC for the no. 1 piston, on the compression stroke, measure the clearance of the indicated valves

28.9b Rotate the crankshaft an additional 2/3 of a revolution (240-degrees) and measure the clearance of the remaining valves

28.11a Install the lifter tool as shown and squeeze the handles together to depress the lifter, then hold the lifter down with the smaller tool so the shim can be removed

28.11b Keep pressure on the lifter with the smaller tool and remove the shim with a small screwdriver . . .

11 Position the notch in the lifter toward the spark plug. Then depress the lifter with the special lifter tools (see illustrations). Place the special lifter tool in position as shown, with the longer jaw of the tool gripping the lower edge of the cast lifter boss and the upper, shorter jaw gripping the upper edge of the lifter itself. Depress the lifter by squeezing the handles of the lifter tool together, then hold the lifter down with the smaller tool and remove the larger one. Remove the adjusting shim with a small screwdriver or a pair of tweezers (see illustration). Note that the wire hook on the end of some lifter tool handles can be used to clamp both handles together to keep the lifter depressed while the shim is removed.

12 Measure the thickness of the shim with a micrometer (see illustration). To calculate the correct thickness of a replacement shim that will place the valve clearance within the specified value, use the following formula:

$N = T + (A - V)$

T = thickness of the old shim
A = valve clearance measured
N = thickness of the new shim
V = desired valve clearance (see this Chapter's Specifications)

13 Select a shim with a thickness as close as possible to the valve clearance calculated. Shims, which are available in 17 sizes in incre-

ments of 0.0020-inch (0.050 mm), range in size from 0.0984-inch (2.500 mm) to 0.1299-inch (3.300 mm).

➡**Note: Through careful analysis of the shim sizes needed to bring the out-of-specification valve clearance within specification, it is often possible to simply move a shim that has to come out anyway to another lifter requiring a shim of that particular size, thereby reducing the number of new shims that must be purchased.**

14 Place the special lifter tool in position as shown in illustration 28.11a, with the longer jaw of the tool gripping the lower edge of the cast lifter boss and the upper, shorter jaw gripping the upper edge of the lifter itself, press down the lifter by squeezing the handles of the lifter tool together and install the new adjusting shim (note that the wire hook on the end of one lifter tool handle can be used to clamp the handles together to keep the lifter depressed while the shim is inserted). Measure the clearance with a feeler gauge to make sure that your calculations are correct.

15 Repeat this procedure until all the valves that are out of clearance have been corrected.

16 Installation of the spark plugs, valve cover, spark plug wires and boots, accelerator cable bracket, etc. is the reverse of removal.

28.11c . . . a pair of tweezers or a magnet as shown here

28.12 Measure the shim thickness with a micrometer

29 Fuel tank cap gasket replacement (every 60,000 miles or 48 months)

♦ **Refer to illustration 29.2**

1 Obtain a new gasket.

2 Remove the tank cap and carefully pry the old gasket out of the recess (see illustration). Be very careful not to damage the sealing surface inside the cap.

3 Work the new gasket into the cap recess.

4 Install the cap, then remove it and make sure the gasket seals all the way around.

29.2 Use a small screwdriver to carefully pry out the old gasket - take care not to damage the cap

30 Positive Crankcase Ventilation (PCV) valve check and replacement (every 60,000 miles or 48 months)

♦ **Refer to illustration 30.4**

1 The PCV valve and hose is located in the valve cover for the rear cylinder bank, on the right (passenger's) side.

2 Disconnect the hose, remove the PCV valve from the cover, then reconnect the hose.

3 With the engine idling at normal operating temperature, place your finger over the valve opening. If there's no vacuum at the valve, check for a plugged hose or valve. Replace any plugged or deteriorated hoses.

4 Turn off the engine. Remove the PCV valve from the hose. Blow through the valve from the valve cover (cylinder head) end. If air will not pass through the valve in this direction, replace it with a new one (see illustration).

5 When purchasing a replacement PCV valve, make sure it's for your particular vehicle and engine size. Compare the old valve with the new one to make sure they're the same.

30.4 To check the PCV valve, first attach a clean section of hose to the cylinder head side of the valve and blow through it - air should pass through easily - then blow through the opposite side of the valve and verify that air doesn't pass through it

Specifications

Recommended lubricants and fluids

➡ **Note: Listed here are manufacturer recommendations at the time this manual was written. Manufacturers occasionally upgrade their fluid and lubricant specifications, so check with your auto parts store for current recommendations.**

Engine oil type	API grade "certified for gasoline engines"
Viscosity	See accompanying chart
Fuel	Unleaded fuel, 87 octane or higher
Coolant	
2004 and earlier models	50 to 70-percent ethylene glycol-based antifreeze and demineralized water

Recommended lubricants and fluids (continued)

2005 and later models

U.S.A. models — 50-percent Toyota Super Long Life Coolant or equivalent ethylene glycol-based non-silicate, non-amine, non-nitrate, non-borate coolant with long-life hybrid organic acid technology (H.O.A.T.) and demineralized water

Canada models — 55-percent Toyota Super Long Life Coolant or equivalent ethylene glycol-based non-silicate, non-amine, non-nitrate, non-borate coolant with long-life hybrid organic acid technology (H.O.A.T.) and demineralized water

Automatic transaxle (and front differential) fluid type
2003 and earlier models — DEXRON III automatic transmission fluid (or equivalent)
2004 and later models — Toyota Genuine automatic transmission fluid Type T-IV (or equivlent)
Brake fluid type — DOT 3 brake fluid
Power steering system fluid — DEXRON II or III automatic transmission fluid

Capacities*

Engine oil (including filter)
All except 3.5L engine — 5.0 qts
3.5L engine — 6.4 qts
Coolant
Without rear heater — Approximately 10.0 qts
With rear heater — Approximately 12.0 qts
Transaxle (drain and refill)
1998 through 2000 models — 3.7 qts, plus 0.8 qt for differential
2001 through 2003 models — Up to 5.0 qts
2004 and later models — Up to 3.7 quarts

*All capacities approximate. Add as necessary to bring to appropriate level.

SAE 10W-30

SAE 5W-30 (Preferred)

Engine oil viscosity chart

FOR GASOLINE ENGINES

LOOK FOR ONE OF THESE LABELS

Ignition system

Spark plug
Type
2000 and earlier models — NGK BKR6EKPB-11 or equivalent
2001 through 2006 3.3L models — NGK IFR6A-11 or equivalent
2007 and later 3.5L models — Denso FK20HR11 or equivalent
Gap — 0.043 inch
Spark plug wire resistance (2000 and earlier models) — Less than 25,000 ohms
Engine firing order — 1-2-3-4-5-6

Cylinder numbering and coil terminal location (2000 and earlier models shown - later models have one coil per spark plug)

Valve clearance (engine cold)

2006 and earlier 3.0L and 3.3L models
Intake — 0.006 to 0.010 inch
Exhaust — 0.010 to 0.014 inch
2007 and later 3.5L models — Hydraulic, self-adjusting

Cooling system

Thermostat rating	
Starts to open	176 to 183-degrees F
Fully open	203-degrees F

Accessory drivebelt tension (with Burroughs or Nippondenso tension gauge)

➡ Note: 2007 and later 3.5L models have self-tensioning drivebelts.

Alternator	
New belt	170 to 180 lbs
Used belt	95 to 135 lbs
Power steering pump	
New belt	150 to 185 lbs
Used belt	95 to 135 lbs

Brakes

Disc brake pad lining thickness (minimum)	1/8 inch
Drum brake shoe lining thickness (minimum)	1/16 inch
Brake pedal	
Freeplay	3/64 to 1/4 inch
Free height	6-9/32 to 6-43/64 inches
Brake light switch clearance	1/32 to 3/32 inch
Pedal reserve height	3-25/32 inches
Parking brake pedal adjustment	3 to 5 clicks at 66 lbs

Suspension and steering

Steering wheel freeplay limit	1-1/8 inches
Balljoint allowable movement	0 inch

Torque specifications   Ft-lbs (unless otherwise indicated)

➡ Note: Listed here are manufacturer recommendations at the time this manual was written. Manufacturers occasionally upgrade their fluid and lubricant specifications, so check with your auto parts store for current recommendations.

Automatic transaxle	
Pan bolts	70 in-lbs
Strainer bolts	96 in-lbs
Drain plug	36
Differential drain plug (2000 and earlier models)	40
Chassis and body	
Front seat mounting bolts	27
Front suspension subframe bolts	134
Rear suspension axle beam pivot bolt/nut	65
Fuel filter banjo bolt (2000 and earlier models)	21
Engine oil drain plug	33
Engine oil filter housing drain plug,	
2007 and later models	108 in-lbs
Engine oil filter housing, 2007 and later models	18
Spark plugs	156 in-lbs
Wheel lug nuts	77

Section

Reference to other Chapters

2A

3.0L AND 3.3L V6 ENGINES

1 General information

2003 and earlier models covered by this manual are equipped with the 1MZ-FE V6 engine. The design is a 3.0-liter, DOHC (dual overhead cam) with four valves per cylinder (24 in all), an aluminum engine block, distributorless ignition, and two-piece oil pan. 2004 and later models are equipped with the 3MZ-FE engine, which is essentially the same but with a larger displacement of 3.3 liters.

This Part of Chapter 2 is devoted to in-vehicle repair procedures for the V6 engine. All information concerning engine removal and installation and engine block and cylinder head overhaul can be found in Part C of this Chapter.

The following repair procedures are based on the assumption that the engine is installed in the vehicle. If the engine has been removed from the vehicle and mounted on a stand, many of the steps outlined in this Part of Chapter 2 will not apply.

The Specifications included in this Part of Chapter 2 apply only to the procedures contained in this Part. Part C of Chapter 2 contains the Specifications necessary for cylinder head and engine block rebuilding.

2 Repair operations possible with the engine in the vehicle

Many major repair operations can be accomplished without removing the engine from the vehicle.

Clean the engine compartment and the exterior of the engine with some type of degreaser before any work is done. It will make the job easier and help keep dirt out of the internal areas of the engine.

Depending on the components involved, it may be helpful to remove the hood to improve access to the engine as repairs are performed (refer to Chapter 11 if necessary). Cover the fenders to prevent damage to the paint. Special pads are available, but an old bedspread or blanket will also work.

If vacuum, exhaust, oil or coolant leaks develop, indicating a need for gasket or seal replacement, the repairs can generally be made with the engine in the vehicle. The intake and exhaust manifold gaskets, oil pan gasket, crankshaft oil seals and cylinder head gaskets are all accessible with the engine in place.

Exterior engine components, such as the intake and exhaust manifolds, the oil pan, the oil pump, the water pump, the starter motor, the alternator, and the fuel system components can be removed for repair with the engine in place.

Since the cylinder heads can be removed without pulling the engine, valve component servicing can also be accomplished with the engine in the vehicle. Replacement of the camshafts, timing belt and pulleys is also possible with the engine in the vehicle.

In extreme cases caused by a lack of necessary equipment, repair or replacement of piston rings, pistons, connecting rods and rod bearings is possible with the engine in the vehicle. However, this practice is not recommended because of the cleaning and preparation work that must be done to the components involved.

3 Top Dead Center (TDC) for number one piston - locating

♦ **Refer to illustrations 3.6 and 3.7**

1 Top Dead Center (TDC) is the highest point in the cylinder that each piston reaches as it travels up the cylinder bore. Each piston reaches TDC on the compression stroke and again on the exhaust stroke, but TDC generally refers to piston position on the compression stroke.

2 Positioning the piston(s) at TDC is an essential part of many procedures such as valve timing, camshaft and timing belt/pulley removal and distributor removal.

3 Before beginning this procedure, be sure to place the transaxle in Neutral and apply the parking brake or block the rear wheels. Also, disable the ignition system by disconnecting the primary electrical connectors at the ignition coil pack/modules (see Chapter 5). Remove the spark plugs (see Chapter 1).

4 In order to bring any piston to TDC, the crankshaft must be turned using one of the methods outlined below. When looking at the front of the engine, normal crankshaft rotation is clockwise.

a) *The preferred method is to turn the crankshaft with a socket and ratchet attached to the bolt threaded into the front of the crankshaft. Apply pressure on the bolt in a clockwise direction only. Never turn the bolt counterclockwise.*

b) *A remote starter switch, which may save some time, can also be used. Follow the instructions included with the switch. Once the piston is close to TDC, use a socket and ratchet as described in the previous paragraph.*

3.6 A compression gauge can be used in the number one plug hole to assist in finding TDC on 1MZ-FE engines

c) *If an assistant is available to turn the ignition switch to the Start position in short bursts, you can get the piston close to TDC without a remote starter switch. Make sure your assistant is out of the vehicle, away from the ignition switch, then use a socket and ratchet as described in Paragraph (a) to complete the procedure.*

3.7 Turn the crankshaft until the notch in the pulley aligns with the zero on the timing plate

5   The engine does not have a distributor, but rather three ignition coils, fired in sequence by signals from the computer. The three coils sit directly on top of cylinders 2, 4 and 6, with spark plug wires connecting these coils to the cylinders on the rear bank.

6   Remove the spark plug and install a compression pressure gauge in the number one spark plug hole (see Chapter 2C). It should be a gauge with a screw-in fitting and a hose at least six inches long (see illustration).

7   Rotate the crankshaft using one of the methods described above while observing the compression gauge. When TDC for the compression stroke of number one cylinder is reached, compression pressure will show on the gauge as the marks are beginning to line up on the crankshaft pulley (see illustration). If you go past the marks, release the gauge pressure and rotate the crankshaft around two more revolutions.

→Note: The most positive method for finding TDC on the V6 engine is to remove the upper timing belt cover and examine the crankshaft timing marks and camshaft sprocket timing marks (see Section 8).

4   Variable Valve Timing (VVT) system - description, check and component replacement

DESCRIPTION

→Note: A Variable Valve Timing (VVT) system is used on 2001 and later models. The following procedures apply to the oil control valve, oil filter or intake camshaft sprocket/actuator on either cylinder head.

1   The VVT system varies intake camshaft timing by directing oil pressure to advance or retard the intake camshaft sprocket/actuator assembly. Changing the intake camshaft timing during certain engine conditions increases engine torque and fuel economy and reduces emissions.

2   System components include the Powertrain Control Module (PCM), an Oil Control Valve (OCV) in each cylinder head, an oil filter for each OCV and an intake camshaft sprocket/actuator assembly.

3   The PCM uses inputs from the Vehicle Speed Sensor (VSS), the Throttle Position Sensor (TPS), the Mass Air Flow (MAF) sensor and the Engine Coolant Temperature (ECT) sensor to turn the oil control valve ON or OFF.

4   When the OCV is energized by the PCM, it directs a specified amount of oil pressure from the engine to advance or retard the intake camshaft sprocket/actuator assembly.

5   The intake camshaft sprocket/actuator assembly is equipped with an inner hub that is attached to the camshaft. The inner hub consists of a series of fixed vanes that use oil pressure as a wedge against the vanes to rotate the camshaft. The higher the oil pressure, the greater the amount of actuator rotation and, therefore, the amount of camshaft advance or retard. How does greater oil pressure advance or retard the cam? By directing the oil to the advance or retard side of the fixed vanes.

6   When oil is applied to the advance side of the vanes, the actuator can advance the camshaft up to 21 degrees in a clockwise direction. When oil is applied to the retard side of the vanes, the actuator will start to rotate the camshaft counterclockwise back to 0 degrees, which is the normal position of the actuator during engine operation under no load or at idle. The PCM can also send a signal to the oil control valve to stop oil flow to both (advance and retard) passages to hold camshaft advance in its current position.

7   Under light engine loads, the VVT system retards the camshaft timing to decrease valve overlap and stabilize engine output. Under medium engine loads, the VVT system advances the camshaft timing to increase valve overlap, thereby increasing fuel economy and decreasing exhaust emissions. Under heavy engine loads at low RPM, the VVT system advances the camshaft timing to help close the intake valve faster, which improves low to midrange torque. Under heavy engine loads at high RPM, the VVT system retards the camshaft timing to slow the closing of the intake valve to improve engine horsepower.

CHECK AND COMPONENT REPLACEMENT

→Note 1: A problem in the VVT oil control valve circuit will set a diagnostic trouble code and turn on the Check Engine light on the dash. Refer to Chapter 6 for accessing trouble codes.

→Note 2: Most problems in the VVT system originate from the oil control valve(s) and filter(s). Regular engine oil and filter changes are necessary for trouble-free operation of the OCVs.

→Note 3: Some checks and inspections of the VVT system require removal of the valve cover and the intake camshaft.

Oil control valve (OCV) filter

▶ Refer to illustrations 4.8a and 4.8b

8   A clogged OCV filter screen is often the cause of VVT system problems. Remove the OCV filter from the rear of the cylinder head (see illustration) and then inspect the filter for clogging. Clean the filter if necessary and reinstall it using a new O-ring. Make sure that the big end of the filter faces toward the head (see illustration). Be sure to tighten the filter plug to the torque listed in this Chapter's Specifications.

4.8a The oil control valve (OCV) filters are located at the rear of each cylinder head

Oil control valve (OCV)

♦ **Refer to illustrations 4.9, 4.10, 4.11a and 4.11b**

9 Disconnect the electrical connector from the oil control valve and measure the resistance between the terminals of the control valve (see illustration). There should be 6.9 to 7.9 ohms resistance. If the indicated resistance is out of range, go to the next Step and replace the OCV. If the resistance is within range, go to Step 11.

10 To replace the OCV, unplug the electrical connector, remove the hold-down bolt (see illustration) and pull the OCV out of the cylinder head. Use a new O-ring when installing the new OCV. Be sure to tighten the OCV hold-down bolt to the torque listed in this Chapter's Specifications.

4.8b If you suspect a problem with the VVT system, inspect the OCV filter for obstructions; when you install the filter, use a new O-ring and make sure that the big end of the filter faces toward the head

11 Remove the OCV from the cylinder head (see previous Step) and check the operation of the OCV plunger. Using a pair of fused jumper wires, ground terminal No. 2 of the OCV connector, and then apply battery voltage to terminal No. 1 (see illustration). When voltage is applied, the plunger should move out; when voltage is cut, the plunger should move back inward (see illustration). If the OCV doesn't operate as described, replace it (see Step 10). Always use a new O-ring when reinstalling the OCV.

Camshaft sprocket/actuator assembly

♦ **Refer to illustrations 4.13, 4.16, 4.18 and 4.20**

12 Remove the valve cover (see Section 5), the timing belt (see Section 8) and the intake camshaft (see Section 10).

➡**Note 1: DO NOT remove the exhaust camshaft or sprocket from the engine.**

➡**Note 2: Do not remove the VVT actuator unless the actuator or the camshaft is to be replaced.**

13 Mount the camshaft in a bench vise. Secure the camshaft in the vise by clamping up the hexagonal "nut" part of the cam (see illustration).

⁑ **CAUTION:**

Be careful not to damage the camshaft or any of the cam lobes or journals.

4.9 To measure the resistance of the OCV coil, unplug the electrical connector and hook up an ohmmeter across the two terminals; there should be 6.9 to 7.9 ohms resistance

4.10 To remove the OCV, unplug the electrical connector, remove the hold-down bolt and pull the OCV out of the cylinder head

4.11a Using a pair of fused jumper wires, ground terminal No. 2 of the OCV connector, and then apply battery voltage to terminal No. 1

4.11b When voltage is applied, the OCV plunger (A), which you can see through the slots in the housing, should move out; when voltage is cut, the plunger should move in

4.13 Secure the camshaft in a bench vise by clamping up the hexagonal "nut" part of the cam; be careful not to damage the camshaft or any of the cam lobes or journals

4.16 Apply 14 psi of air pressure to the advance side oil port and try to rotate the actuator assembly by hand; the actuator should rotate freely from the locked position, with no obvious binding, for about 30 degrees in the advance angle direction (arrow)

4.18 To replace the sprocket/actuator assembly, put the camshaft in a bench vise and then remove the 46 mm nut by turning it clockwise (the nut is reverse-threaded)

4.20 When installing the sprocket/actuator assembly, make sure that the lock pin (in the camshaft) and lock pin groove (inside the sprocket/actuator) are aligned

14 Verify that the sprocket/actuator will not rotate from the locked position. The locked position is a "neutral position" in which the actuator is placed during idle and no load conditions, and anytime that the VVT system is not activated by the PCM.

15 Using lacquer thinner or acetone, remove all traces of oil from the front cam journals and the VVT oil control orifices. Apply vinyl tape over all the oil control orifices except the advance side oil port.

16 Apply 14 psi of air pressure to the advance side oil port and try to rotate the actuator assembly by hand. The actuator should rotate freely, with no obvious binding, for about 30 degrees in the advance angle direction from the locked position (see illustration).

→Note: It is critical to have an air tight seal between the air gun nozzle and the advance oil port hole, because if air leaks out at the air nozzle, or at any of the other oil control orifices, the lock pin in the actuator won't be forced out of its locating hole. If leakage occurs, apply a little more air pressure to the advance side oil port to force the lock pin from the locating hole.

17 If the actuator does not rotate freely as described, replace the intake camshaft sprocket/actuator assembly.

18 To replace the sprocket/actuator assembly, put the camshaft in a bench vise (see Step 13), and then remove the 46 mm nut by turning it *clockwise* (the nut is reverse-threaded) (see illustration).

19 Remove the sprocket/actuator assembly. If it's hard to pull off the camshaft, tap it lightly with a plastic-tip hammer.

✳✳ CAUTION:

DO NOT try to disassemble the sprocket/actuator assembly - it's NOT rebuildable.

20 Lubricate the sprocket/actuator seating surface on the camshaft with clean engine oil. Before installing the sprocket/actuator assembly, make sure that the lock pin (in the camshaft) and lock pin groove (inside the sprocket/actuator) are aligned (see illustration). Install the sprocket/actuator assembly. Using a NEW sprocket/actuator assembly retaining nut, tighten the retaining nut to the torque listed in this Chapter's Specifications (don't forget, it's reverse-threaded).

21 Install the intake camshaft (see Section 10), the timing belt (see Section 8) and the valve cover (see Section 5).

5 Valve covers - removal and installation

REMOVAL

♦ **Refer to illustrations 5.2, 5.3, 5.4a, 5.4b and 5.5**

1 Disconnect the negative cable from the battery.

2 Remove the V-bank cover (see illustration). If you're removing the rear (firewall side) cover, remove the intake plenum assembly (see Section 6) and the cowl cover (see Chapter 11).

3 If you're working on the front (radiator side) or both covers, remove the coil connectors, coils and spark plugs from the front bank (see illustration).

4 Detach the engine wiring harness from the left side of the engine, the number 3 timing belt cover, the rear of the engine and right-hand side (see illustrations).

5 Remove the retaining bolts and sealing washers, then detach the cover(s) (see illustration). If the cover is stuck to the head, bump the

5.2 Using an Allen wrench, remove the two bolts and pull up the V-bank cover, which has two clips under the "finned" area (1998 to 2000 models) - later models have three nuts and one large wingnut

5.3 Disconnect the ignition coils from the harness and remove the coils

5.4a Remove two nuts and disconnect the left-hand engine harness . . .

end with a wood block and a hammer to jar it loose. If that doesn't work, try to slip a flexible putty knife between the head and cover to break the seal.

⁂ CAUTION:

Don't pry at the cover-to-head joint or damage to the sealing surfaces may occur, leading to oil leaks after the cover is reinstalled.

INSTALLATION

▶ **Refer to illustration 5.8**

6   The mating surfaces of the cylinder head and cover must be clean when the cover is installed. Use a gasket scraper to remove all traces of sealant and old gasket material, then clean the mating surfaces with lacquer thinner or acetone. If there's residue or oil on the mating surfaces when the cover is installed, oil leaks may develop.

7   Install new spark plug tube seals.

8   Apply RTV sealant to the gasket/seal joints at the front and rear camshaft-to-head mounts and install the valve cover with a new gasket (see illustration).

5.4b . . . disconnect the wire clips at the timing belt cover and the five bolts retaining the right-hand harness, then move the harness away from the rear valve cover

9   Tighten the nuts to the torque listed in this Chapter's Specifications in three or four equal steps.

10 Reinstall the remaining parts, run the engine and check for oil leaks.

5.5 Remove the bolts and sealing washers and remove the valve cover

5.8 Apply RTV sealant to the areas indicated and install the cover with a new gasket

6   Intake manifold - removal and installation

✳✳ WARNING:

Wait until the engine is completely cool before beginning this procedure.

REMOVAL

1   Relieve the fuel system pressure, then disconnect the negative cable from the battery.

Upper intake plenum

▶ **Refer to illustration 6.8**

2   Drain the coolant into a clean container (see Chapter 1).
3   Remove the V-bank cover (see illustration 5.2).
4   Remove the air cleaner assembly (see Chapter 4).
5   Disconnect the electrical connectors, vacuum and coolant bypass hoses from the throttle body, then disconnect the throttle linkage (see Chapter 4). The throttle body can remain attached to the intake plenum unless it is being removed for cleaning or gasket service.
6   On models with EGR, disconnect the EGR pipe at the intake plenum.
7   Unbolt the brace to the throttle body, and the engine lifting.

8   Remove the bolts and nuts holding the plenum to the lower intake manifold and lift the plenum off (see illustration).

Lower intake manifold

▶ **Refer to illustrations 6.10, 6.11 and 6.12**

9   Disconnect the electrical connectors from the fuel injectors.

➡**Note: The intake manifold can be removed with the injectors and fuel rails in place or removed, depending on the work to be done.**

10   Disconnect the air assist and heater hoses at the left end of the intake manifold (see illustration). Also detach the fuel line from the fuel rail (see Chapter 4).

✳✳ CAUTION:

Use no tools when disconnecting the quick-connect fuel line fittings; use only your hand.

11   Remove the eight mounting nuts/bolts, then detach the manifold from the engine (see illustration). If it's stuck, don't pry between the gasket mating surfaces or damage may result.
12   There is a water transfer hose (see illustration) that is exposed

6.8   Remove the bolts (A) and nuts (B), then remove the intake plenum

6.10   Detach the heater hoses (A) and the air assist hose (B)

6.11   Remove the bolts and nuts, then remove the lower intake manifold - numbers indicate tightening sequence for reassembly

6.12   This water transfer hose should be replaced whenever the intake manifold is off for other repairs

only when the intake manifold is removed. Because of the difficulty in getting at this hose for replacement, we recommend that it be replaced with a new hose if the intake manifold is removed for other work.

INSTALLATION

13 Use a scraper to remove all traces of old gasket material and sealant from the manifold and cylinder heads, then clean the mating surfaces with lacquer thinner or acetone.

7 Exhaust manifolds - removal and installation

▶ **Refer to illustrations 7.2 and 7.5**

✴✴ WARNING:

The engine must be completely cool before beginning this procedure.

1 Disconnect the negative cable from the battery.
2 Remove the exhaust manifold heat shield (see illustration), then spray penetrating oil on the exhaust manifold fasteners and allow it to soak in.
3 Remove the heated oxygen sensors from the front and rear manifolds.
4 Remove the EGR pipe from the rear exhaust manifold and cylinder head (see Chapter 6).
5 Remove the nuts retaining the exhaust pipes to the front and rear exhaust manifolds, and the exhaust manifold braces from the block (see illustration).
6 Disconnect the electrical connector from the oxygen sensor at each manifold.
7 Unbolt the exhaust manifolds from the cylinder heads and slip them off the mounting studs.

➡**Note: The rear exhaust manifold bolts are difficult to access. You'll need to access them from below with a long, flexible extension on your ratchet.**

8 Carefully inspect the manifolds and fasteners for cracks and damage.
9 Use a scraper to remove all traces of old gasket material and carbon deposits from the manifolds and cylinder head mating surfaces. If the gasket was leaking, check the manifolds for warpage on the cylinder head mounting surface by placing a straightedge over the surface and trying to insert a feeler gauge. If the clearance exceeds the limit listed in this Chapter's Specifications, have the manifold resurfaced at an automotive machine shop.
10 Position new gaskets over the cylinder head studs.
11 Install the manifolds and thread the mounting nuts into place.
12 Working from the center out, tighten the nuts to the torque listed

14 Install new gaskets, then position the manifold on the engine. Make sure the gaskets haven't shifted, then install the nuts/bolts.
15 Tighten the nuts/bolts, in three or four equal steps, to the torque listed in this Chapter's Specifications. Tighten the bolts in the sequence shown in illustration 6.11.
16 Install the remaining parts in the reverse order of removal. Use a new gasket between the intake manifold and the plenum.
17 Refill the cooling system. Run the engine and check for fuel, vacuum and coolant leaks.

7.2 Remove these bolts and detach the heat shield from the exhaust manifold

in this Chapter's Specifications in three or four equal steps.
13 Reinstall the remaining parts in the reverse order of removal. Use new gaskets when connecting the exhaust pipes.
14 Run the engine and check for exhaust leaks.

7.5 Remove the support bracket and the two nuts at the exhaust pipe/manifold joint

8 Timing belt and sprockets - removal, inspection and installation

REMOVAL

▶ **Refer to illustrations 8.9, 8.11a, 8.11b, 8.12, 8.13, 8.14, 8.17, 8.21 and 8.24**

✴✴ CAUTION:

The timing system is complex. Severe engine damage will occur if you make any mistakes. Do not attempt this procedure unless you are highly experienced with this type of repair. If you

are at all unsure of your abilities, consult an expert. Double-check all your work and be sure everything is correct before you attempt to start the engine.

1 Disconnect the negative cable from the battery.
2 Remove the coolant overflow tank and windshield washer tank (see Chapter 3).
3 Remove the cowl cover (see Chapter 11).
4 Remove the right front inner fender apron (see Chapter 11).

5 Remove the drivebelts from the alternator and power steering pump (see Chapter 1). Remove the alternator brace.

6 Loosen the lug nuts on the right front wheel, but don't remove them yet.

7 Raise the front of the vehicle and support it securely on jack-stands. Apply the parking brake and block the rear wheels. Remove the right front wheel.

8 Position the number one cylinder at TDC (see Section 3).

9 Support the engine with a jack from below and remove the engine movement control rod and its bracket on the engine (see illustration). Place a wood block on the jack head and do not place the jack directly under the oil pan drain plug.

10 Remove the spark plugs (see Chapter 1).

11 Remove the upper (no. 2) timing belt cover and gasket (see illustrations).

→Note: Unclip the wiring harness above the cover and push it back enough to remove the belt cover.

12 Check to see if there are installation marks on the timing belt - if you intend to re-use the belt and the marks have been obscured, make new ones (see illustration).

13 Make sure the camshaft pulley timing marks are properly aligned (see illustration).

8.9 Remove the two through-bolts (A) and the engine movement control rod (B)

14 Remove the timing belt tensioner (see illustration). Be sure to remove the rubber boot as well; it may stick in the tensioner recess.

8.11a Timing belt and related components

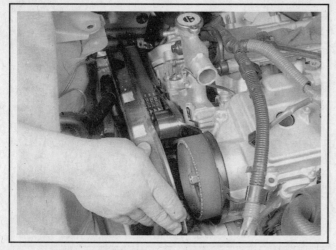

8.11b Remove the number 2 timing belt cover

> ✳✳ **CAUTION:**
>
> Loosen the bolts a little at a time, alternating from side-to-side until the tensioner pressure is off.

15 Relieve the tension between the rear (right-hand) and front (left-hand) camshaft sprockets by turning the rear sprocket slightly clockwise.

> ✳✳ **CAUTION:**
>
> Don't turn the sprocket any more than is necessary to provide enough slack to allow you to slip the belt off the sprockets.

16 Remove the timing belt from the camshaft sprockets.
17 The camshaft sprockets can be removed at this point, if they are worn or damaged. Use a two-pin spanner to hold the sprocket while you use a socket to loosen the sprocket bolt. If the spanner is not available, remove the valve cover(s) (see Section 5) and hold the camshaft with a wrench on the cast-in hex while loosening the sprocket bolt (see illustration). Remove the bolt and detach the sprocket.

8.14 Remove the two bolts and detach the timing belt tensioner

8.12 If you intend to re-use the belt and the original installation marks are obscured or missing, make new ones

8.13 Both camshaft sprocket timing marks should align with the marks on the rear cover

18 Remove the upper (no. 2) idler pulley (see illustration 8.11a).
19 Remove the crankshaft (drivebelt) pulley bolt. Wedge a large screwdriver into the flywheel/driveplate ring gear teeth or against a converter bolt to keep the engine from turning. Use a breaker bar and

8.17 If the camshaft sprockets are damaged, or the cams are to be removed, hold the hex portion of the camshaft with a wrench while removing the sprocket bolt

8.21 A puller should not be necessary to remove the crankshaft pulley - if it is stuck use two prybars behind it

socket to loosen the pulley bolt.

20 When the crankshaft pulley bolt is loosened, the TDC position of the crankshaft may be disturbed. Check and align again, if necessary.

➡ Note: The crankshaft timing belt sprocket has a TDC alignment mark that lines up with a mark on the oil pump housing, making it easy to check the TDC alignment even after the crankshaft pulley and lower timing belt cover are removed.

21 The crankshaft pulley should come off with strong hand pressure (see illustration). If not, use two prybars behind it to lever it off. Do not use a jaw-type puller.

22 Remove the lower (no. 1) timing belt cover and gasket (see illustration 8.11a).

23 Slip the timing belt guide off the crankshaft.

24 If you're re-using the belt, check for a mark on the belt adjacent to the drilled mark on the crankshaft sprocket (see illustration). If the original mark is gone, make a new one, then slip the belt off the sprocket.

25 Using an Allen wrench, remove the no. 1 idler pulley and plate washer (see illustration 8.11a).

26 If it's worn or damaged, or if you're replacing the crankshaft front

8.29 Check the timing belt for cracked or missing teeth - wear on one side of the belt indicates misalignment problems

8.24 There should be a mark on the belt next to the drilled mark on the sprocket

oil seal, the crankshaft sprocket can now be removed. If it won't come off by hand, a steering wheel type puller may be needed to remove the sprocket. Be careful not to damage the crankshaft sensor portion of the sprocket during the removal process. If necessary, remove the lower sprocket retainer (see illustration 8.38).

INSPECTION

◆ Refer to illustrations 8.29, 8.34 and 8.35

✳✳ CAUTION:

Do not bend, twist or turn the timing belt inside out. Do not allow it to come in contact with oil, coolant or fuel. Do not utilize timing belt tension to keep the camshaft or crankshaft from turning when installing the sprocket bolt(s). Do not turn the crankshaft or camshaft more than a few degrees (if necessary for tooth alignment) while the timing belt is removed.

27 Remove the idler pulleys and check the bearings for smooth operation and excessive play.

28 If the timing belt broke during engine operation, the belt may have been contaminated or overtightened.

29 If the belt teeth are cracked or missing (see illustration), the oil pump or camshaft(s) may have seized.

✳✳ CAUTION:

If the timing belt broke during engine operation, the valves may have come in contact with the pistons, causing damage. Check the valve clearance (see Chapter 1) - bent valves usually will have excessive clearance, indicating damage that will require cylinder head removal to repair.

30 If there is noticeable wear or cracks on the face of the belt, check to see if there are nicks or burrs on the idler pulleys.

31 If there is wear or damage on only one side of the belt, check the belt guide and the alignment of the sprockets.

32 Replace the timing belt with a new one if obvious wear or damage is noted or if it is the least bit questionable. Correct any problems that contributed to belt failure prior to belt installation.

➡ Note: Professionals recommend replacing the belt whenever it is removed, since belt failure can lead to expensive engine damage. The manufacturer recommends changing the belt at 60,000-mile intervals.

8.34 Check the tensioner for signs of leakage and test for leakdown by forcing it against an immovable object

8.35 Measure the tensioner pushrod protrusion and compare it to the Specifications (2003 and earlier models)

8.38 Align the marks on the crankshaft timing sprocket with the marks on the oil pump case (A), and install the sprocket retainer (B) and bolt

33 Check the belt tensioner for visible oil leakage. If there's only a faint trace of oil on the pushrod side, the tensioner seal is in satisfactory condition.

34 Hold the tensioner in both hands and push it forcefully against an immovable object (see illustration). If the pushrod moves, replace the tensioner.

35 If you're working on a 2003 or earlier model, measure the protrusion of the pushrod from the housing end (see illustration). Compare your measurement to this Chapter's Specifications. If the protrusion is not as specified, replace the tensioner.

➡Note: When the tensioner is stored off the engine, keep the pushrod UP.

36 Check that the idler pulleys turn smoothly.

INSTALLATION

▶ Refer to illustrations 8.38 and 8.53

✳✳ CAUTION:

Before starting the engine, carefully rotate the crankshaft by hand through at least two full revolutions (use a socket and breaker bar on the crankshaft pulley centerbolt). If you feel any resistance, STOP! There is something wrong - most likely, valves are contacting the pistons. You must find the problem before proceeding. Check your work and see if any updated repair information is available.

37 Remove all dirt, oil and grease from the timing belt area at the front of the engine.

38 Align the crankshaft timing sprocket keyway with the crankshaft key and install the sprocket with the flange side up against the engine (see illustration 8.11a). Be careful not to damage the crankshaft sensor portion of the crankshaft sprocket. Check the alignment of the TDC marks on the sprocket and the oil pump housing, and reinstall the retainer and bolt (see illustration).

39 Apply thread-locking compound to the first two or three threads on the lower (no. 1) idler pulley bolt, then position the idler pulley and washer and install the bolt. Tighten the bolt to the torque listed in this Chapter's Specifications.

40 Install the timing belt, starting at the crankshaft sprocket. If you're re-using the original belt, align the marks on the belt with the marks on the sprockets and covers. Install the belt over the lower (no. 1) idler and

water pump pulleys.

41 Slip the belt guide over the end of the crankshaft with the cupped side facing out.

42 Install the lower (no. 1) timing belt cover and gasket (see illustration 8.11a).

43 Slip the crankshaft (drivebelt) pulley onto the crankshaft, aligning the pulley keyway with the crankshaft key. Install the bolt and tighten it to the torque listed in this Chapter's Specifications. Prevent the crankshaft from turning by using the method described in Step 19.

44 Install the upper (no. 2) idler pulley. Tighten the bolt to the torque listed in this Chapter's Specifications. Make sure the pulley turns smoothly.

45 Install the front camshaft sprocket (if it was removed) on the camshaft with the flange side facing OUT. Align the pin hole in the sprocket with the pin in the end of the camshaft.

46 Install the sprocket retaining bolt and tighten it to the torque listed in this Chapter's Specifications. Use the method described in Step 17 to keep the camshaft from turning.

47 Recheck the timing marks to be sure the crankshaft hasn't turned (see illustration 8.38). If you're re-using the original belt, the installation mark should line up as it did in Step 12. If not, change the position of the timing belt on the crankshaft sprocket. The mark on the front (left-hand) camshaft sprocket should be at the top (12 o'clock position), aligned with the mark on the rear (no. 3) timing cover.

48 The rear (right-hand) camshaft knock pin hole should be at the top (12 o'clock position). If necessary, remove the valve cover and turn the camshaft slightly with a wrench to align the sprocket with the mark on the rear (no. 3) cover (see illustration 8.13).

49 Install the rear (right-hand) camshaft sprocket (if it was removed) on the camshaft with the flange side facing IN. Align the pin hole in the sprocket with the knock pin in the end of the camshaft.

50 Install the retaining bolt and tighten it to the torque listed in this Chapter's Specifications. Use the method described in Step 17 to keep the camshaft from turning. Be sure the timing mark is still aligned with the rear (no. 3) cover.

51 Turn the front (left-hand) camshaft sprocket clockwise slightly (about one tooth) with a pin spanner. If the special tool isn't available, grip the hex on the camshaft with a wrench and turn it (see illustration 8.17). If you're re-using the original belt, align the installation mark with the camshaft timing mark. Slip the belt onto the sprocket, then turn the camshaft counterclockwise, back to its original position. There should now be slight tension on the belt.

52 Slip the belt onto the rear sprocket. If you're re-using the original

belt, align the installation marks.

53 Using a press or vise, slowly compress the timing belt tensioner pushrod (see illustration). Insert a metal pin, drill bit or Allen wrench through the holes in the pushrod and housing. Release the pressure from the press or vise.

54 Install the timing belt tensioner and tighten the bolts to the torque listed in this Chapter's Specifications. Remove the retaining pin.

55 Using a socket and breaker bar on the crankshaft pulley bolt, turn the crankshaft slowly (clockwise) through two complete revolutions (720-degrees). Recheck the timing marks (see illustrations 3.7 and 8.13).

❋❋ CAUTION:

If the timing marks are not aligned exactly as shown, repeat the timing belt installation procedure. DO NOT start the engine until you're absolutely certain that the timing belt is installed correctly. Serious and costly engine damage could occur if the belt is installed wrong.

56 Reinstall the engine movement control rod's mounting bracket.
57 Install the upper (no. 2) timing belt cover and gasket.
58 Install the engine movement control rod and braces and tighten the bolts securely.
59 Reinstall the remaining parts in the reverse order of removal.

8.53 Restrain the tensioner pushrod by compressing the unit in a vise and inserting a pin approximately 0.050-inch (1.27 mm) in diameter - make sure the rubber boot is in place

9   Oil seals - replacement

CRANKSHAFT OIL SEAL

◆ **Refer to illustrations 9.3 and 9.5**

1   Remove the timing belt and crankshaft timing belt sprocket (see Section 8).
2   Note how far the seal is recessed in the bore, then cut away the seal lip with a razor knife.
3   Carefully pry the seal out of the engine with a screwdriver or seal removal tool (see illustration). If you use a screwdriver, wrap tape around the tip - don't scratch the housing bore or damage the crankshaft (if the crankshaft is damaged, the new seal will end up leaking).
4   Clean the bore in the engine and coat the outer edge of the new seal with engine oil or multi-purpose grease. Apply the same grease to the seal lip.
5   Using a seal driver or a socket with an outside diameter slightly smaller than the outside diameter of the seal, carefully drive the new seal into place with a hammer (see illustration). Make sure it's installed

squarely and driven in to the same depth as the original. Check the seal after installation to make sure the spring didn't pop out of place.
6   Reinstall the crankshaft timing sprocket and timing belt (see Section 8). Be careful not to scratch the crankshaft sensor portion of the sprocket.
7   With everything installed, run the engine and check for oil leaks at the front seal.

CAMSHAFT OIL SEALS

◆ **Refer to illustration 9.12**

8   Remove the timing belt and camshaft sprocket(s) (see Section 8).
9   Remove the bolts and detach the rear (no. 3) timing belt cover.
10 Note how far the seal is seated in the bore, then carefully pry it out with a screwdriver. Wrap the screwdriver tip with tape - don't scratch the bore or damage the camshaft (if the camshaft is damaged, the new seal will end up leaking).

9.3 Cut away the crankshaft seal lip, wrap a screwdriver tip with tape and pry out the seal

9.5 Lubricate the seal lip and drive the new crankshaft seal into place with a seal driver or a large socket and a hammer

11 Clean the bore and coat the outer edge of the new seal with engine oil or multi-purpose grease. Apply multi-purpose grease to the seal lip.

12 Using a seal driver or a socket with an outside diameter slightly smaller than the outside diameter of the seal, carefully drive the new seal into place with a hammer (see illustration). Make sure it's installed squarely and driven in to the same depth as the original.

13 Reinstall the rear timing belt cover and tighten the bolts.

14 Reinstall the camshaft sprocket(s) and timing belt (see Section 8).

15 With everything installed, run the engine and check for oil leaks at the camshaft seal.

9.12 Lubricate the seal lip and tap the new camshaft seal into place with a seal driver or a large socket and a hammer

10 Camshafts and lifters - removal, inspection and installation

➡Note: Before beginning this procedure, obtain two 6 x 1.0 mm bolts 16 to 20 mm long. They will be referred to as service bolts in the text.

REMOVAL

◆ Refer to illustrations 10.1, 10.3, 10.4, 10.10, 10.12, 10.13 and 10.14

1   Position the engine at TDC (see Section 3), then remove the valve covers (see Section 5), the timing belt and the camshaft sprocket (see Section 8). Measure the camshaft thrust clearance (endplay) with a dial indicator (see illustration). If the clearance is greater than the service limit, replace the camshaft and/or the cylinder head.

2   The following steps apply to the removal of each of the four camshafts. On each head, the exhaust camshaft subgear is secured first, the intake cam removed, then the exhaust camshaft is removed.

3   Make sure the cam timing marks on the drive and driven gears are in alignment (see illustration).

➡Note: On the right (rear) cylinder head, align the two dots on the intake camshaft gear. On the left (front) cylinder head, align

10.1 Mount a dial indicator as shown to measure camshaft endplay

the one dot on the intake camshaft gear with the one dot on the exhaust camshaft gear.

4   Secure the exhaust camshaft sub-gear to the driven gear with a service bolt installed in the threaded hole (see illustration).

10.3 Align the timing marks on the backside of the camshaft gears

10.4 Install a service bolt through the sub-gear into the main gear

10.10 Mark up a cardboard box to store the lifters/shims and camshaft bearing caps - use a separate box for each set to avoid mix-ups and mark the FRONT, INTAKE and EXHAUST orientation

10.12 With the hex portion of the camshaft held in a vise, use a two-pin spanner to remove the tension from the sub-gear and remove the service bolt, then release the sub-gear

10.13 Remove the snap-ring with a pair of snap-ring pliers

⁂ CAUTION:

Since the camshaft thrust clearance is minimal, the camshafts must be held level as they are being removed. If they aren't, the portion of the cylinder head next to the cam gears may crack or be damaged by the gear leverage. Before lifting a camshaft out of the head, make certain that the torsional spring force of the sub-gear has been eliminated by the service bolt.

5 Loosen the intake camshaft bearing cap bolts in 1/4-turn increments until they can be removed by hand. Follow the reverse of the recommended tightening sequence (see illustrations 10.39a and 10.39b).

6 Remove the bearing caps and gently lift out the intake camshaft. Be sure to keep it level.

7 Loosen the exhaust camshaft bearing cap bolts in 1/4-turn increments until they can be removed by hand. Follow the reverse of the recommended tightening sequence (see illustrations 10.34a and 10.34b).

8 Remove the exhaust camshaft bearing caps and oil seal and gently lift out the exhaust camshaft. Be sure to keep it level.

9 Repeat the steps for the other cylinder head.

10 Store the bearing caps in the correct order.

➥Note: If necessary, the valve lifters and shims can now be removed with a magnetic tool. Be sure to store them separately so they can be reinstalled in their original locations (see illustration).

11 To disassemble an exhaust camshaft gear, mount the cam in a vise with the jaws gripping the large hex on the shaft.

12 Install a second service bolt in the unthreaded hole in the camshaft sub-gear. Using a screwdriver positioned against the service bolt just installed, rotate the sub-gear clockwise and remove the first service bolt. The second bolt isn't needed if you have a two-pin spanner (see illustration).

13 Remove the sub-gear snap-ring (see illustration).

14 The wave washer, sub-gear and camshaft gear spring can now be removed from the camshaft (see illustration). Be sure to keep the parts from the rear cylinder head cams separate from the front cylinder head parts.

INSPECTION

◆ Refer to illustrations 10.15, 10.16, 10.17, 10.21, 10.22, 10.23a, 10.23b and 10.25

15 Measure the end gap (distance between the ends) of the camshaft gear spring (see illustration) and compare it to this Chapter's Specifications. If not as specified, replace the spring.

10.14 Remove the wave washer (1), the camshaft sub-gear (2) and the gear spring (3)

10.15 Measure the distance between the ends of the camshaft gear spring

10.16 Wipe the oil off the valve shims and mark the intakes I and the exhausts E - a magnetic tool works well for removing lifters

10.17 Wipe off the oil and inspect each lifter for wear and scuffing

10.21 Measure the lobe heights on each camshaft - if any lobe height is less than the specified allowable minimum, replace that camshaft

16 Carefully label, then remove the valve lifters and shims (see illustration).

17 Inspect each lifter for scuffing and score marks (see illustration).

18 Measure the outside diameter of each lifter and the corresponding lifter bore inside diameter. Subtract the lifter diameter from the lifter bore diameter to determine the oil clearance. Compare it to this Chapter's Specifications. If the oil clearance is excessive, a new head and/or new lifters will be required.

19 Store the lifters in a clean box, separated from each other, so they won't be damaged. Make sure the shims stay with the lifters (don't mix them up).

20 Visually examine the cam lobes and bearing journals for score marks, pitting, galling and evidence of overheating (blue, discolored areas). Look for flaking away of the hardened surface layer of each lobe.

21 Using a micrometer, measure the height of each camshaft lobe (see illustration). Compare your measurements with this Chapter's Specifications. If the height for any one lobe is less than the specified minimum, replace the camshaft.

22 Using a micrometer, measure the diameter of each journal at several points (see illustration). Compare your measurements with this Chapter's Specifications. If the diameter of any one journal is less than

specified, replace the camshaft.

23 Check the oil clearance for each camshaft journal as follows:

a) *Clean the bearing caps and the camshaft journals with lacquer thinner or acetone.*

b) *Carefully lay the camshaft(s) in place in the head. Don't install the lifters and don't use any lubrication.*

c) *Lay a strip of Plastigage on each journal (see illustration).*

d) *Install the bearing caps with the arrows pointing toward the front (timing belt end) of the engine.*

e) *Tighten the bolts to the specified torque in 1/4-turn increments.*

➡**Note: Don't turn the camshaft while the Plastigage is in place.**

f) *Remove the bolts and detach the caps.*

g) *Compare the width of the crushed Plastigage (at its widest point) to the scale on the Plastigage envelope (see illustration).*

h) *If the clearance is greater than specified, replace the camshaft and/or cylinder head.*

i) *Scrape off the Plastigage with your fingernail or the edge of a credit card - don't scratch or nick the journals or bearing caps.*

24 Temporarily install the camshafts without installing the lifters or exhaust camshaft sub-gear.

10.22 Measure each journal diameter with a micrometer (if any journal measures less than the specified limit, replace the camshaft)

10.23a Lay a strip of Plastigage on each camshaft journal

10.23b Compare the width of the crushed Plastigage to the scale on the envelope to determine the oil clearance

10.25 Position a dial indicator as shown here to measure gear backlash

10.31a On the right (rear) cylinder, set the exhaust camshaft into place with the two dots facing the intake camshaft . . .

10.31b . . . on the left (front) cylinder head, set the exhaust camshaft into place with the one dot facing the intake camshaft

10.32 Apply RTV sealant to the shaded areas on the bearing cap

25 Measure the gear backlash (the freeplay between the gear teeth) with a dial indicator (see illustration) and compare it to this Chapter's Specifications.

INSTALLATION

♦ Refer to illustrations 10.31a, 10.31b, 10.32, 10.33a, 10.33b, 10.34a, 10.34b, 10.37, 10.38a, 10.38b, 10.39a and 10.39b

26 Reassemble the exhaust camshaft gear(s) by installing the camshaft gear spring, sub-gear, wave washer and snap-ring.

27 Mount the camshaft in a padded vise.

28 Insert a service bolt into the unthreaded hole in the camshaft subgear. Using a screwdriver, align the holes of the camshaft driven gear and sub-gear by turning the camshaft sub-gear clockwise. Install a second service bolt in the threaded hole, tightening it to clamp the gears together. Remove the service bolt from the unthreaded hole. Repeat the procedure for the other exhaust camshaft.

29 Apply moly-base grease or engine assembly lube to the lifters, then install them in their original locations in the cylinder heads. Make sure the valve adjustment shims are in place in the lifters, and that all lifters are installed in their original bores.

30 Apply camshaft installation lubricant to the exhaust camshaft lobes, bearing journals and gear thrust faces.

31 Set the exhaust camshaft in place in the cylinder head with the timing mark on the subgear facing the center of the head (see illustrations).

32 Apply a thin coat of RTV sealant to the outer edges of the front bearing cap cylinder head mating surfaces (see illustration).

33 Install the bearing caps in numerical order with the arrows pointing toward the timing belt end of the engine (see illustrations).

10.33a Install the exhaust camshaft bearing caps with the arrows pointing toward the timing belt end of the engine; this is the rear (right) cylinder head . . .

10.33b . . . and this is the front (left) cylinder head

10.34a Exhaust camshaft bearing cap bolt tightening sequence - rear cylinder head

10.34b Exhaust camshaft bearing cap bolt tightening sequence - front cylinder head

10.37 Align the dots on the exhaust camshaft subgear with the dots on the intake gear (rear cylinder head shown, front head similar except align one dot with one dot)

10.38a Install the intake camshaft bearing caps with the arrows pointing toward the timing belt end of the engine; this is the rear (right) cylinder head . . .

34 Tighten the bearing cap bolts in 1/4-turn increments to the torque listed in this Chapter's Specifications. Follow the recommended sequence (see illustrations).

35 Refer to Section 9 and install a new camshaft oil seal.

36 Apply camshaft installation lubricant to the intake camshaft lobes, bearing journals and gear thrust faces.

37 Set the intake camshaft in place in the cylinder head, with the timing mark aligned with the exhaust camshaft timing mark (see illustration).

➡**Note: On the right (rear) cylinder head, align the two dots on the intake camshaft gear. On the left (front) cylinder head, align the one dot on the intake camshaft gear with the one dot on the exhaust camshaft gear.**

38 Install the bearing caps in numerical order with the arrows pointing toward the front (timing belt end) of the engine (see illustrations).

10.38b . . . and this is the front (left) cylinder head

10.39a Intake camshaft bearing cap bolt tightening sequence - rear cylinder head

10.39b Intake camshaft bearing cap bolt tightening sequence - front cylinder head

39 Tighten the bearing cap bolts in 1/4-turn increments to the torque listed in this Chapter's Specifications. Follow the recommended sequence (see illustrations).

40 Remove the service bolt from the exhaust camshaft subgear.

41 Reinstall the camshaft sprockets and the timing belt (see Section 8).

42 Reinstall the remaining components in the reverse order of removal.

43 Before reinstalling the valve covers, apply RTV sealant in the areas indicated (see illustration 5.8). Clean the rubber half-circle plugs for the back of the heads and reinstall with new RTV sealant.

44 The remainder of the installation is the reverse of the disassembly sequence.

45 Run the engine, then check for leaks and proper operation.

11 Cylinder heads - removal and installation

※※ WARNING:

Wait until the engine is completely cool before beginning this procedure.

REMOVAL

♦ Refer to illustrations 11.7, 11.8 and 11.11

1 Disconnect the negative cable from the battery.

2 Drain the cooling system, including the block (see Chapter 1).

3 Remove the air intake plenum and intake manifold (see Section 6).

4 Remove the exhaust manifold(s) (see Section 7).

5 Remove the alternator (see Chapter 5).

6 Remove the timing belt, camshaft sprockets and upper idler pulley (see Section 8).

➡Note: If the timing belt is not being replaced at the time the heads are removed, the timing belt and lower timing belt cover don't have to be completely removed. Follow the Steps in Section 8, marking the belt location at the lower cover at TDC, and removing the belt only from the camshaft sprockets and idler pulley.

7 Remove the bolts holding the number 3 timing belt cover (see illustration).

8 Disconnect the coolant sensor connectors and remove the water transfer casting (see illustration).

9 Remove the camshaft(s) from the head(s) you intend to remove (see Section 10).

10 Remove the bolts at the rear of the cylinder heads and move the

11.7 Release the three wiring harness clips, pull the harness back and remove the number 3 timing belt cover

engine wiring harnesses away from the heads.

11 Using an 8 mm hex bit or Allen wrench, remove the recessed head bolts (one in each head) (see illustration).

12 Using a 12-point socket, loosen the rest of the cylinder head bolts in 1/4-turn increments until they can be removed by hand. Follow the reverse order of the recommended tightening sequence (see illustration 11.23).

13 Lift the cylinder head off the engine block. If the head is stuck, place a wood block against it and strike the wood with a hammer.

11.8 Remove the bolts and the coolant transfer casting (A) - the transfer hose (B) should be replaced whenever the intake manifold is removed

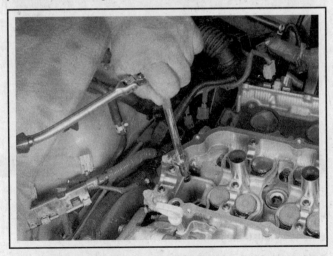

11.11 Remove the recessed bolt with an 8 mm hex bit socket

※※ CAUTION:

Don't pry between the head and block. The gasket surfaces may be damaged and leaks could result.

14 Repeat the procedure for the other head.

INSTALLATION

♦ **Refer to illustrations 11.20 and 11.23**

15 The mating surfaces of the cylinder heads and block must be perfectly clean when the heads are installed.

16 Use a gasket scraper to remove all traces of carbon and old gasket material, then clean the mating surfaces with lacquer thinner or acetone. If there's oil on the mating surfaces when the head is installed, the gasket may not seal correctly and leaks could develop. When working on the block, stuff the cylinders with clean shop rags to keep out debris. Use a vacuum cleaner to remove material that falls into the cylinders.

17 Check the block and head mating surfaces for nicks, deep scratches and other damage. If damage is slight, it can be removed with a file; if it's excessive, machining may be the only alternative.

18 Use a tap of the correct size to chase the threads in the cylinder head bolt holes, then clean the holes with compressed air - make sure that nothing remains in the holes.

※※ WARNING:

Wear eye protection when using compressed air!

19 Mount each bolt in a vise and run a die down the threads to remove corrosion and restore the threads. Dirt, corrosion, sealant and damaged threads will affect torque readings. Using a micrometer, measure the thickness of the head bolts at their "necked-down" thinnest section and compare the results to this Chapter's Specifications. If the bolt is thinner than specified, it has been stretched and should be replaced. It is advisable to replace all of the head bolts if any fail to meet minimum specs.

20 Position the new gaskets over the dowel pins in the block (see illustration).

21 Carefully set the head on the block without disturbing the gasket.

22 Before installing the head bolts, apply a small amount of clean engine oil to the threads.

23 Install the bolts in their original locations and tighten them finger tight. Following the recommended sequence, tighten the bolts to the torque listed in this Chapter's Specifications (see illustration). Don't tighten the recessed bolt at this time.

24 Mark the front of each bolt head with paint. You can also mark the socket you are using. Place the socket over the 12-point bolt so that you can observe the mark.

25 Following the same sequence, tighten each 12-point bolt an additional 1/4-turn (90-degrees) (see illustration 11.23).

26 Tighten the recessed bolt to the torque listed in this Chapter's Specifications.

27 Repeat the entire procedure to install the other cylinder head.

28 The remaining installation steps are the reverse of removal.

29 Refill the cooling system, change the oil and filter (see Chapter 1), run the engine and check for leaks.

11.20 Be sure the new head gaskets are positioned right side up (check all holes and coolant passages for correct alignment) and over the block dowels

11.23 Cylinder head bolt TIGHTENING sequence

12 Oil pan - removal and installation

REMOVAL

♦ **Refer to illustrations 12.7, 12.8, 12.9 and 12.11**

1 The oil pan is a two-part assembly, with an aluminum casting attached to the block and transaxle, and a lower stamped-steel pan section at the bottom.

2 Disconnect the negative cable from the battery.

3 Raise the vehicle and support it securely on jackstands.

4 Remove the engine splash shields.

5 Drain the engine oil and remove the oil filter.

6 Disconnect the front exhaust pipe from the catalytic converter, the two bolts and the support bracket, and the nuts holding the pipe to the front and rear exhaust manifolds (see Chapter 4 and Section 6).

12.7 Remove two bolts and the flywheel housing cover

12.8 Remove the two bolts securing the aluminum upper pan to the transaxle

12.9 Remove the steel section of the oil pan

7   Remove the flywheel housing cover (see illustration).

8   Remove the two bolts holding the aluminum oil pan section to the transaxle (see illustration).

9   Remove the 10 bolts and two nuts securing the steel oil pan section, and detach the steel pan (see illustration). If it's stuck, pry it loose very carefully with a small screwdriver or putty knife. Don't damage the mating surfaces of the pan or oil leaks could develop.

10   Remove the oil pump strainer/pickup (see illustration 13.4).

11   Remove the bolts securing the aluminum oil pan section to the block (see illustration).

➡**Note: Some bolts are within the area formerly covered by the steel pan.**

12   Remove the oil pan baffle plate, if necessary.

INSTALLATION

♦ **Refer to illustration 12.18**

13   Use a scraper to remove all traces of old sealant from the block and oil pan. Clean the mating surfaces with lacquer thinner or acetone.

14   Make sure the threaded bolt holes in the block are clean.

15   Check the flange of the steel pan section for distortion, particularly around the bolt holes. If necessary, place the pan on a wood block and use a hammer to flatten and restore the gasket surface.

16   If the baffle had been removed, reinstall it now.

17   Clean the mating surfaces of the engine block and aluminum pan

section, being careful not to gouge the soft metal, which could lead to leaks.

18   Apply RTV sealant to the aluminum pan section, following the grooves, which indicates where to apply the bead of sealant inside and outside the bolts (see illustration).

19   Install the aluminum pan section within five minutes and uniformly tighten the bolts to the torque listed in this Chapter's Specifications in several passes. Work from the center out towards the ends of the pan.

20   Inspect the oil pump pick-up/strainer assembly for cracks and a blocked strainer. If the pick-up was removed, clean it with solvent or thinner and install it now, using a new gasket (see Section 13). Tighten the fasteners to the torque listed in this Chapter's Specifications.

21   Apply a 3 to 4 mm wide bead of RTV sealant to the flange of the steel oil pan section.

➡**Note: The steel pan section must be installed within five minutes once the sealant has been applied.**

22   Carefully position the steel pan on the aluminum section and install the bolts. Working from the center out, tighten them to the torque listed in this Chapter's Specifications in three or four steps.

23   The remainder of installation is the reverse of removal. Be sure to add oil and install a new oil filter.

24   Run the engine and check for oil pressure and leaks.

12.11 Remove the bolts retaining the aluminum portion of the pan

12.18 Follow the grooves for an indication of where to position the bead of new RTV sealant on the aluminum pan section and install the pan

13 Oil pump - removal, inspection and installation

REMOVAL

♦ Refer to illustrations 13.4, 13.7, 13.8, 13.9, 13.11 and 13.12

1 Remove the oil pan (see Section 12).
2 Remove the timing belt (see Section 8) and lower timing belt idler pulley.
3 Remove the crankshaft sprocket (see Section 8).
4 Remove the oil pick-up tube (see illustration).
5 Remove the alternator (see Chapter 5).
6 Unbolt the air conditioning compressor and set it aside without disconnecting the refrigerant lines.
7 Remove the compressor bracket (see illustration).
8 Remove the power steering pump adjusting bar and pry the pump away from the oil pump body (see illustration).
9 Remove the lower timing belt idler pulley (see illustration).
10 Remove the bolts and detach the oil pump from the engine. You may have to pry carefully between the front main bearing cap and the pump body with a screwdriver.
11 Remove the O-ring. Remove the oil pressure relief valve snap-ring, retainer, spring and valve (see illustration).

✸✸ WARNING:

The spring is tightly compressed - be careful and wear eye protection.

12 Use a large Phillips screwdriver to remove the screws retaining the body cover to the rear of the oil pump (see illustration).
13 Lift the cover off and remove the pump rotors.
14 Use a scraper to remove all traces of sealant and old gasket material from the pump body and engine block, then clean the mating surfaces with lacquer thinner or acetone.

INSPECTION

♦ Refer to illustrations 13.17a, 13.17b and 13.17c

15 Clean all components with solvent, then inspect them for wear and damage.
16 Check the oil pressure relief valve sliding surface and valve spring. If either the spring or the valve is damaged, they must be replaced as a set.

13.4 The oil pick-up tube is held in place with three fasteners

13.7 Unbolt the air conditioning compressor bracket from the block

13.8 Remove the power steering pump adjuster bar and pry the pump away from the oil pump body

13.9 Using a 10 mm hex bit or Allen wrench, remove the lower timing belt idler pulley

13.11 Remove the oil pressure relief plug, spring and valve

13.12 Use a large Phillips screwdriver or bit to remove the screws retaining the pump cover

13.17a Measure the driven rotor-to-body clearance with a feeler gauge

13.17b Measure the rotor side clearance with a precision straightedge and feeler gauge

13.17c Measure the rotor tip clearance with a feeler gauge - note the rotor marks are facing out (when the pump body cover is installed, the marks will be against the cover)

17 Check the clearance of the following components with a feeler gauge and compare the measurements to this Chapter's Specifications (see illustrations):

a) Driven rotor-to-oil pump body clearance
b) Rotor side clearance
c) Rotor tip clearance

INSTALLATION

▶ **Refer to illustration 13.26**

18 Pry the old crankshaft seal out with a screwdriver.

19 Apply multi-purpose grease or engine oil to the outer edge of the new seal and carefully drive it into place with a seal driver and a hammer. Also apply multi-purpose grease to the seal lip.

20 Place the drive and driven rotors into the pump body with the marks facing out (see illustration 13.17c).

21 Pack the pump cavity with petroleum jelly and install the cover. Tighten the screws securely following a criss-cross pattern.

22 Lubricate the oil pressure relief valve with engine oil and install the valve components in the pump body.

23 Use acetone or lacquer thinner and a clean rag to remove all traces of oil from the gasket surfaces.

24 Apply a 2 to 3 mm wide bead of anaerobic sealant to the oil pump. Avoid using an excessive amount of sealant, especially around oil passages and bolt holes. Assembly must be completed within five minutes of sealant application, otherwise the material must be removed and reapplied.

25 Position a new O-ring on the block.

26 Engage the spline teeth on the oil pump drive rotor with the large

13.26 Be sure to align the drive rotor and the crankshaft as the oil pump is installed, and install a new O-ring on the block

teeth on the crankshaft and slide the pump into place (see illustration).

27 Install the oil pump mounting bolts in their original locations and tighten them to the torque listed in this Chapter's Specifications in a criss-cross pattern.

28 Using a new gasket, install the oil pick-up tube and tighten the fasteners to the torque listed in this Chapter's Specifications.

29 Reinstall the remaining parts in the reverse order of removal.

30 Add oil, start the engine and check for oil leaks.

31 Recheck the engine oil level.

14 Driveplate - removal and installation

▶ **Refer to illustration 14.4**

REMOVAL

1 Raise the vehicle and support it securely on jackstands, then refer to Chapter 7 and remove the transaxle and torque converter. If it's leaking, now would be a very good time to replace the front pump seal/O-ring.

2 Use a center punch or paint to make alignment marks on the driveplate and crankshaft to ensure correct alignment during reinstallation.

3 Remove the bolts that secure the driveplate to the crankshaft. If the crankshaft turns, wedge a screwdriver in the ring gear teeth to jam the driveplate.

4 Remove the driveplate from the crankshaft.

✳✳ CAUTION:

Wear gloves when removing the driveplate, since the ring gear teeth may be sharp.

There are spacers on both sides of the driveplate (see illustration). Keep them with the driveplate.

INSTALLATION

5　Check for cracked and broken ring gear teeth and any damage or warpage.

6　Clean and inspect the mating surfaces of the driveplate and the crankshaft. If the crankshaft rear seal is leaking, replace it before reinstalling the driveplate.

7　Position the driveplate against the crankshaft. Be sure to align the marks made during removal. Note that some engines have an alignment dowel or staggered bolt holes to ensure correct installation. Before installing the bolts, apply thread locking compound to the threads.

8　Wedge a screwdriver in the ring gear teeth to keep the driveplate from turning and tighten the bolts to the torque listed in this Chapter's Specifications. Follow a criss-cross pattern and work up to the final

14.4　When removing the driveplate, keep track of which position the two spacer plates are installed

torque in three or four steps.

9　The remainder of installation is the reverse of the removal procedure.

15　Rear main oil seal - replacement

▶ Refer to illustrations 15.2, 15.5, 15.6 and 15.7

1　The transaxle must be removed from the vehicle for this procedure (see Chapter 7).

2　The seal can be replaced without removing the oil pan or removing the seal retainer. However, this method is not recommended because the lip of the seal is quite stiff and it's possible to cock the seal in the retainer bore or damage it during installation. If you want to take the chance, pry out the old seal with a screwdriver (see illustration). Apply multi-purpose grease to the crankshaft seal journal and the lip of the new seal and carefully push the new seal into place. The lip is stiff, so carefully work it onto the seal journal of the crankshaft with a

smooth object like the end of an extension as you tap the seal into place. Don't rush it or you may damage the seal.

3　The following method is recommended but requires removal of the oil pan (see Section 12) and the seal retainer.

4　After the oil pan has been removed, remove the bolts, detach the seal retainer and remove all the old gasket material.

5　Position the seal and retainer assembly between two wood blocks on a workbench and drive the old seal out from the back side with a screwdriver (see illustration).

6　Drive the new seal into the retainer with a block of wood (see illustration) or a section of pipe slightly smaller in diameter than the outside diameter of the seal.

15.2　The quick way to replace the rear crankshaft oil seal is to simply pry the old one out with a screwdriver, lubricate the crankshaft journal and the lip of the new seal with multi-purpose grease and push the new seal into place - the seal lip is very stiff and can be easily damaged during installation if you're not careful

15.5　After removing the retainer assembly from the block, support it between two wood blocks and drive out the old seal with a screwdriver and hammer

15.6　Drive the new seal into the retainer with a block of wood or a section of pipe, if you have one large enough - make sure that you don't cock the seal in the retainer bore

7   Lubricate the crankshaft seal journal and the lip of the new seal with multi-purpose grease. Apply a 2 to 3 mm wide bead of anaerobic sealant to the retainer flange (see illustration) before attaching the retainer to the block.

8   Slowly and carefully push the seal onto the crankshaft. The seal lip is stiff, so work it onto the crankshaft with a smooth object such as the end of an extension as you push the retainer against the block.

9   Install and tighten the retainer bolts to the torque listed in this Chapter's Specifications. The bottom sealing flange of the retainer must not extend below the bottom sealing flange (oil pan rail) of the block.

10 The remaining steps are the reverse of removal.

15.7 Apply sealant to the oil seal retainer-to-block mating surface

16 Engine mounts - check and replacement

▶ **Refer to illustration 16.4**

1   Engine mounts seldom require attention, but broken or deteriorated mounts should be replaced immediately or the added strain placed on the driveline components may cause damage or wear.

CHECK

2   During the check, the engine must be raised slightly to remove the weight from the mounts.

3   Raise the vehicle and support it securely on jackstands, then position a jack under the engine oil pan. Place a large block of wood between the jack head and the oil pan, then carefully raise the engine just enough to take the weight off the mounts. Do not position the wood block under the drain plug.

✳✳ WARNING:

DO NOT place any part of your body under the engine when it's supported only by a jack!

4   Check the mounts (see illustration) to see if the rubber is cracked, hardened or separated from the metal plates. Sometimes the rubber will split right down the center.

5   Check for relative movement between the mount plates and the engine or frame (use a large screwdriver or pry bar to attempt to move the mounts). If movement is noted, lower the engine and tighten the mount fasteners.

6   Rubber preservative should be applied to the mounts to slow deterioration.

REPLACEMENT

7   Disconnect the negative battery cable from the battery, then raise the vehicle and support it securely on jackstands (if not already done). Support the engine as described in Step 3.

8   To remove the right engine mount (movement control rod), remove the two stays, one mounted on either side of the bracket on the engine.

9   Remove the mount-to-bracket nuts and detach the mount.

10 The rear mount bracket is a casting that cradles the insulator, which is retained by a through-bolt to the chassis bracket. To remove the rear engine mount, remove the throughbolt, then the insulator bolts.

11 To remove the front engine mount, remove the nut holding the

16.4 Typical engine mounting components

insulator to the engine bracket, then the three bolts holding the insulator to the chassis.

12 In addition to the front engine mount, there is also a shock-absorbing mount, mounted between the engine and chassis, to the left of the conventional front engine mount. Remove the throughbolt where the mount is connected to the suspension subframe, then remove the nut and bushing at the top of the shock absorber and remove the shock from the engine bracket.

13 Installation is the reverse of removal. Use thread locking compound on the mount bolts/nuts and be sure to tighten them securely.

14 See Chapter 7 for transaxle mount replacement.

Specifications

General

Engine designation

    2003 and earlier models   1MZ-FE

    2004 and later models   3MZ-FE

Cylinder numbers (timing belt end-to-transaxle end)

    Right (firewall) side   1-3-5

    Left (radiator) side   2-4-6

    Firing order   1-2-3-4-5-6

Displacement

    2003 and earlier models   183 cubic inches (3.0 liters)

    2004 and later models   202 cubic inches (3.3 liters)

Cylinder numbering and coil terminal location (2000 and earlier shown - later models have one coil per spark plug)

Cylinder head

Warpage limits

    Cylinder head   0.0039 inch

    Intake manifold   0.0031 inch

    Exhaust manifolds   0.0196 inch

Cylinder head bolt diameter (thinnest section)   0.3445 (min)

Camshaft and related components

Valve clearance (engine cold)

    1998 to 2000

        Intake   0.005 to 0.009 inch

        Exhaust   0.011 to 0.015 inch

    2001 and later

        Intake   0.006 to 0.009 inch

        Exhaust   0.010 to 0.014 inch

Bearing journal diameter

    1998 to 2000   1.0610 to 1.0616 inches

    2001 and later   1.0614 to 1.0620 inches

Bearing oil clearance

    Standard

        Intake   0.0014 to 0.0028 inch

        Exhaust   0.0010 to 0.0024 inch

    Service limit

        Intake   0.0039 inch

        Exhaust   0.0035 inch

Lobe height

    1998 to 2000

        Intake

             Standard   1.6579 to 1.6618 inches

            Service Limit   1.6520 inches

        Exhaust

             Standard   1.6520 to 1.6559 inches

            Service limit   1.6461 inches

    2001 through 2003

        Intake

             Standard   1.6902 to 1.6942 inches

            Service Limit   1.6842 inches

Exhaust	
Standard	1.6838 to 1.6876 inches
Service limit	1.6776 inches
2004 and later	
Intake	
Standard	1.6981 to 1.7020 inches
Service limit	1.6921 inches
Exhaust	
Standard	1.6933 to 1.6972 inches
Service limit	1.6874 inches
Thrust clearance (endplay)	
Standard	0.0016 to 0.0035 inch
Service limit	0.0047 inch
Runout limit (total indicator reading)	0.0024 inch
Camshaft gear backlash	
Standard	0.0008 to 0.0079 inch
Service limit	0.0188 inch
Camshaft gear spring end gap	0.712 to 0.740 inch
Timing belt tensioner protrusion	
(2003 and earlier models)	0.394 to 0.425 inch
Lifters	
Outside diameter	1.2191 to 1.2195 inch
Bore diameter	1.2205 to 1.2211 inch
Lifter-to-bore (oil) clearance	
Standard	0.0009 to 0.0020 inch
Service limit	0.0028 inch

Oil pump

Driven rotor-to-pump body clearance	
2000 and earlier	
Standard	0.0039 to 0.0069 inch
Service limit	0.0118 inch
2001 through 2003	
Standard	0.0098 to 0.0128 inch
Service limit	0.0157 inch
2004 and later	
Standard	0.0050 to 0.0064 inch
Service limit	0.0118 inch
Rotor tip clearance	
Standard	0.0043 to 0.0094 inch
Service limit	0.0138 inch
Rotor side clearance	
Standard	0.0012 to 0.0035 inch
Service limit	0.0059 inch

Torque specifications   Ft-lbs (unless otherwise indicated)

➡ Note: One foot-pound (ft-lb) of torque is equivalent to 12 inch-pounds (in-lbs) of torque. Torque values below approximately 15 ft-lbs are expressed in inch-pounds, since most foot-pound torque wrenches are not accurate at these smaller values.

Air conditioning compressor bracket mounting bolts	19
Intake manifold bolts/nuts	132 in-lbs
Throttle body brace bolts	168 in-lbs
Engine lift hanger bolts	29

Torque specifications (continued)   Ft-lbs (unless otherwise indicated)

➡Note: One foot-pound (ft-lb) of torque is equivalent to 12 inch-pounds (in-lbs) of torque. Torque values below approximately 15 ft-lbs are expressed in inch-pounds, since most foot-pound torque wrenches are not accurate at these smaller values.

Exhaust manifold nuts	36
Crankshaft pulley bolt	
2003 and earlier	159
2004 and later	162
Timing belt cover bolts (no. 3)	74 in-lbs
Idler pulley bolts	
No. 1	25
No. 2	32
Timing belt tensioner bolts	20
Camshaft pulley bolts	94
Camshaft bearing cap bolts	144 in-lbs
Cylinder head bolts (12-point)	
Step 1	40
Step 2	Tighten an additional 90-degrees (1/4-turn)
Cylinder head bolt (recessed)	
2003 and earlier	156 in-lbs
2004 and later	168 in-lbs
Oil pan bolts	
2003 and earlier models	
Aluminum section	
10 mm bolt head	69 in-lbs
12 mm bolt head	168 in-lbs
14 mm bolt head (to transaxle)	27
Steel section	69 in-lbs
2004 and later models	
Aluminum section	
10 mm bolt head	71 in-lbs
12 mm bolt head	168 in-lbs
14 mm bolt head	27
Steel section	71 in-lbs
Oil pump mounting bolts	
10 mm bolt head	69 in-lbs
12 mm bolt head	168 in-lbs
14 mm bolt head (2004 and later)	32
Oil pick-up tube mounting bolts	69 in-lbs
Driveplate bolts*	61
Rear crankshaft oil seal retainer mounting bolts	69 in-lbs
Valve cover nuts/bolts	69 in-lbs
Variable Valve Timing (VVT) system (2001 and later models)	
Oil control valve filter plug	33
Oil control valve hold-down bolt	66 in-lbs
Camshaft sprocket/actuator assembly	
retaining nut**	110
Engine mounts	
Engine movement control rod mounting bolts	47
Front engine mount insulator-to-chassis bolts	
Green	48
Silver	32
Front (shock absorber) mount bolts	35
Rear engine mount insulator nuts	48

Apply thread locking compound to the threads prior to installation
**Reverse-threaded.*

2B

3.5L V6 ENGINE

Section

Reference to other Chapters

1 General information

This Part of Chapter 2 is devoted to in-vehicle repair procedures for the 3.5L (2GR-FE) engine. Information concerning engine removal and installation and engine overhaul can be found in Part C of this Chapter.

The following repair procedures are based on the assumption that the engine is installed in the vehicle. If the engine has been removed from the vehicle and mounted on a stand, many of the steps outlined in this Part of Chapter 2 will not apply.

The Specifications included in this Part of Chapter 2 apply only to the procedures contained in this Part. Additional specifications can be found in Chapter 2 Part C

2 Repair operations possible with the engine in the vehicle

1 Some major repair operations can be accomplished without removing the engine from the vehicle. Clean the engine compartment and the exterior of the engine with some type of degreaser before any work is done. It will make the job easier and help keep dirt out of the internal areas of the engine.

2 Depending on the components involved, it may be helpful to remove the hood to improve access to the engine as repairs are performed (refer to Chapter 11 if necessary). Cover the fenders to prevent damage to the paint. Special pads are available, but an old bedspread or blanket will also work.

3 The cowl assembly is removable and must be taken out for access to any components in the upper rear of the engine compartment. Refer to Section 4.

4 If vacuum, exhaust, oil or coolant leaks develop, indicating a need for gasket or seal replacement, the repairs can sometimes be made with the engine in the vehicle.

5 Although some major components can be removed with the engine in place, it is usually easier to first lower the engine/transaxle assembly out of the vehicle. Because of this, most procedures in this Section do not have details for in-the-vehicle service.

3 Top Dead Center (TDC) for number one piston - locating

▸ Refer to illustration 3.6

➡Note: With the engine in the vehicle, it is easier to find TDC on the number 4 cylinder. The crankshaft can then be rotated 360 degrees in order to put number 1 cylinder on TDC.

1 Top Dead Center (TDC) is the highest point in the cylinder that each piston reaches as it travels up the cylinder bore. Each piston reaches TDC on the compression stroke and again on the exhaust stroke, but TDC generally refers to piston position on the compression stroke.

2 Positioning the piston(s) at TDC is an essential part of certain procedures such as valve adjustment and timing chain/camshaft removal and installation.

3 Before beginning this procedure, remove the Number One spark plug (see Chapter 1, if necessary). Also, be sure to place the transmission in Neutral and apply the parking brake or block the rear wheels. If method b) or c) in Step 4 will be used to rotate the engine, also disable the ignition system by disconnecting the electrical connector from each ignition coil and disable the fuel pump (see Chapter 4, Section 2).

4 In order to bring any piston to TDC, the crankshaft must be turned using one of the methods outlined below. When looking at the front of the engine, normal crankshaft rotation is clockwise.

  a) *The preferred method is to turn the crankshaft with a socket and ratchet attached to the bolt threaded into the front of the crankshaft. Turn the crankshaft in a clockwise direction only.*

  b) *A remote starter switch, which may save some time, can also be used. Follow the instructions included with the switch. Once the piston is close to TDC, use a socket and ratchet as described in the previous paragraph.*

  c) *If an assistant is available to turn the ignition switch to the Start position in short bursts, you can get the piston close to TDC without a remote starter switch. Make sure your assistant is out of the vehicle, away from the ignition switch, then use a socket and ratchet as described in Paragraph (a) to complete the procedure.*

5 Install a compression pressure gauge in the number one spark plug hole (see Chapter 2C). It should be a gauge with a screw-in fitting and a hose at least six inches long.

6 Rotate the crankshaft using one of the methods described above while observing the compression gauge. When TDC for the compression stroke of number one cylinder is reached, compression pressure will show on the gauge as the marks on the crankshaft pulley are beginning to line up (see illustration). If you go past the marks, release the gauge pressure and rotate the crankshaft around two more revolutions.

7 After the number one piston has been positioned at TDC on the compression stroke, TDC for the next cylinder in the firing order can be located by turning the crankshaft another 120-degrees (refer to the firing order in this Chapter's Specifications). If you found TDC for number 4 cylinder, rotate the crankshaft 360 degrees to put number 1 cylinder at TDC.

3.6 Turn the crankshaft until the notch in the pulley aligns with the zero on the timing plate

4 Valve covers - removal and installation

▶ Refer to illustrations 4.2, 4.4, 4.5, 4.9, 4.10 and 4.11

➡Note: Steps 7 through 15 of this procedure assume that the engine has been lowered from the vehicle. If you attempt it with the engine in place, there are other Steps that must be performed that vary by model.

1   If the engine is in the vehicle, remove both windshield wiper arms and pull off the louvered plastic cowl (see Chapter 11).

2   Refer to Chapter 12 and remove the wiper motor and linkage (see illustration).

3   Remove the cowl brace bracket.

4   Remove the nut and remove the fuel pump resistor (see illustration). Unclip the interfering wiring from the cowl.

5   Remove the 7 bolts, then lift out the cowl assembly (see illustration).

6   Pull up on the front of the engine top cover to detach it from the two front retainers. Keep pulling it to detach the back retainer.

7   Disconnect the hose from the PCV valve.

8   Refer to Chapter 5 and remove the ignition coils. Disconnect the wiring from the sensors and actuators and secure the wiring harnesses out of the way.

9   Disconnect the oil line from the end of each valve cover (see illustration). Carefully set aside the oil control valve filter when you remove the upper banjo bolt from the valve cover. The sealing washers should be replaced with new ones if they're worn.

10 Remove the valve cover bolts and remove the valve cover (see illustration). There are 11 perimeter bolts and 1 center bolt.

11 Check the 3 small round interior gaskets as well as the large perimeter gasket (see illustration). They should be replaced with new ones if they show signs of deterioration.

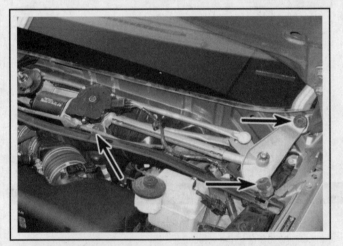

4.2 Wiper mounting bolts; the wiper and cowl must be removed to get access to the rear of the engine

4.4 Remove the fuel pump resistor and set it aside to remove the cowl

4.5 The front cowl (arrow) is secured with 7 screws

4.9 Take care with the oil filter (A) and the sealing washers (B) when disconnecting the oil line from the valve cover

12 Installation is the reverse of removal. Thoroughly clean all sealing surfaces prior to putting the new gaskets in place.

13 Apply dabs of RTV sealant to the joints where the timing chain cover meets the cylinder heads.

14 Evenly tighten the valve cover nuts and bolts to the torque listed in this Chapter's Specifications.

4.10 The valve cover is retained with 11 perimeter bolts (A) and a central bolt (B)

15 Start the engine and check for oil leaks around the edges of the valve cover.

4.11 Make sure that the gasket is fully seated into the valve cover groove, and that the spark plug tube seals are seated as well; arrows indicate areas where silicone sealer was applied on the joint between the timing cover and the cylinder head - clean old sealer from the gasket before reusing it

5   Intake manifold - removal and installation

⁕⁕ WARNING:

Wait until the engine is completely cool before beginning this procedure.

➡**Note: These procedure assume that the engine has been lowered from the vehicle. If you attempt it with the engine in place, there are other Steps that must be performed that vary by model.**

UPPER INTAKE MANIFOLD

◗ **Refer to illustrations 5.7 and 5.8**

➡**Note: Toyota refers to the upper intake manifold as the intake air surge tank. If you're buying a gasket for the upper intake manifold at a dealer parts department, use the Toyota terminology.**

1   Disconnect the cable from the negative terminal of the battery (see Chapter 5, Section 1).

⁕⁕ WARNING:

If you plan on removing the lower intake manifold, relieve the fuel system pressure before disconnecting the battery (see Chapter 4, Section 2).

2   Refer to Section 4 of this Chapter and perform Steps 1 through 6 if the engine is still in the vehicle.

3   Refer to Chapter 4 and disconnect all hoses and the wiring from the throttle body. The coolant hoses can be pinched off to avoid draining the cooling system. Label the hoses to avoid confusion later.

4   Disconnect the air intake tube from the throttle body.

5   Remove the throttle body bracket and the upper intake manifold brace.

6   Disconnect all wiring and hoses from the manifold.

7   Remove the two intake manifold mounting nuts and four mount-

5.7 Upper intake manifold fasteners

5.8 Check the condition of the upper intake manifold gasket, replacing it if necessary

5.14 To detach the lower intake manifold, remove these ten mounting bolts (fuel rail removed for clarity)

ing bolts and remove the upper intake manifold (see illustration).

8   Check the condition of the upper intake manifold gasket (see illustration). If it isn't cracked, hardened or flattened, it can be reused.

9   Installation is the reverse of removal. Be sure to tighten the upper intake manifold mounting bolts and nuts to the torque listed in this Chapter's Specifications.

LOWER INTAKE MANIFOLD

▶ **Refer to illustration 5.14**

➡**Note: Toyota refers to the lower intake manifold as the intake manifold. If you're buying a gasket for the lower intake manifold at a dealer parts department, use the Toyota terminology.**

10   Remove the upper intake manifold (see Steps 1 through 9).

11   If you're removing the lower intake manifold to replace it, remove

the fuel rail now (see Chapter 4).

12   If you're just removing the lower intake manifold to replace the gaskets, it's not necessary to remove the fuel rail, but you'll have to disconnect the fuel supply and return line connections by pinching the tabs of the fitting and pulling the lines apart (see Chapter 4).

13   Remove the interfering brace.

14   Remove the 10 lower intake manifold bolts and remove the lower intake manifold (see illustration).

15   Remove and discard the old lower intake manifold gaskets. Clean off all traces of old gasket material from the mating surfaces of the manifold and cylinder heads, then wipe the surfaces with brake system cleaner.

16   Installation is the reverse of removal. Be sure to use new gaskets and tighten the lower intake manifold bolts a little at a time, in a criss-cross pattern working from the center bolts outward, to the torque listed in this Chapter's Specifications.

6   Exhaust manifolds - removal and installation

☀☀ WARNING:

The engine must be completely cool before beginning this procedure.

➡**Note: This procedure assumes that the engine has been lowered from the vehicle. If you attempt it with the engine in place, there are other Steps that must be performed that vary by model.**

➡**Note: The following procedure applies to either exhaust manifold.**

1   Disconnect the electrical connectors from the left upstream oxygen sensor.

2   Remove the bolts that secure the exhaust manifold support bracket and remove it.

3   Disconnect any interfering wire clamps.

4   Remove the heat shield from the front exhaust manifold.

5   Evenly loosen the six nuts that secure each exhaust manifold and remove the exhaust manifold.

6   Remove and discard the old exhaust manifold gasket.

7   Installation is the reverse of removal. Be sure to use a new gasket and install it with the oval-shaped protruding tip facing in the correct direction. For the left (driver's side) manifold, the tip must face to the rear; on the right manifold it must face to the front.

8   Tighten the exhaust manifold nuts a little at a time, working from the center nuts outward, to the torque listed in this Chapter's Specifications.

7 Timing chains and sprockets - removal, inspection and installation

REMOVAL

▶ Refer to illustrations 7.3a, 7.3b, 7.3c, 7.6, 7.8a, 7.8b, 7.8c, 7.8d and 7.9

❊❊ WARNING:

Wait until the engine is completely cool before beginning this procedure.

❊❊ CAUTION:

The timing system is complex, and severe engine damage will occur if you make any mistakes. Do not attempt this procedure unless you are highly experienced with this type of repair. If you are at all unsure of your abilities, be sure to consult an expert. Double-check all your work and be sure everything is correct before you attempt to start the engine.

➡Note: There is an access plate for the timing chain tensioner in the right side of the timing chain cover.

➡Note: The manufacturer recommends that the oil pans be removed for this procedure. We have found this to be unnecessary.

➡Note: This procedure assumes that the engine has been lowered from the vehicle. If you attempt it with the engine in place, it's much more difficult and there are other steps that must be performed that vary by model.

1   Unbolt the drivebelt and the drivebelt tensioner (see "Drivebelt check and replacement" in Chapter 1).

2   Remove the idler pulley bolts and remove the two idler pulleys.

3   Set the engine to TDC (see Section 3). Remove the crankshaft pulley (see illustrations).

4   Remove the four timing cover bolts from the front of the upper oil pan.

5   Remove the water inlet (see Chapter 3). Remove the O-ring and gasket from the water inlet and discard them.

6   Remove the timing chain cover mounting fasteners and remove the timing chain cover. There are only a few spots where you can safely pry the cover off without damaging it (see illustration). Do NOT pry the timing chain cover loose at any other spot or you will damage the sealing surface of the cover.

7   After removing the timing chain cover, carefully pry out the old crankshaft seal with a screwdriver (see Section 8). Make sure that you don't scratch the seal bore. If you want to inspect or replace any oil pump parts, refer to Section 12.

➡Note: Keep track of the locations of all of the bolts. They are of different lengths and can't be interchanged.

8   Verify that the piston in the No. 1 cylinder is near TDC on its compression stroke. If not, install the crankshaft pulley bolt, then rotate the crankshaft until the dot on the crankshaft position trigger wheel (the toothed wheel behind the lower crankshaft sprocket) is at the 11 o'clock position and is aligned with the rib on the engine block (see illustration). You can also temporarily install the front cover and the crankshaft pulley and set the pulley at the 0 degree mark. Verify that the timing marks on the camshaft timing sprockets are aligned with their corresponding marks on top of the front camshaft bearing caps (see illustrations). If the marks are not aligned, rotate the crankshaft another 360-degrees and recheck the marks.

❊❊ CAUTION:

The upper timing marks on this engine do NOT align perfectly when the timing chains are correctly installed. Because of this, the only positive way to proceed is to carefully mark the positions of each timing chain on each camshaft sprocket as well as the crankshaft sprocket. Use a marker or paint that can't be rubbed off easily. It helps to use different colors to avoid confusion later.

7.3a Hold the crankshaft pulley with a pin spanner while removing the bolt

7.3b A chain wrench can also be used to hold the pulley, but only if special precautions are taken; note the sockets used as spacers to raise the chain over the timing scale, and the piece of old drivebelt used to pad the pulley

7.3c If the crankshaft pulley can't be removed by hand, use a puller that bolts to the hub of the pulley - not a jaw-type puller. Also, be sure to use the correct adapter between the nose of the crankshaft and the puller screw, so as not to damage the threads in the crankshaft

7.6 The timing chain cover can be pried loose at the lower corners and at the upper corners; prying anywhere else may damage the cover

7.8a Align the dot on the trigger wheel with the rib on the block - this should set the engine at TDC

7.8b The exhaust camshaft sprocket of the left (front) cylinder head with the engine at TDC - the timing marks (arrows) DO NOT exactly align at TDC

9   Turn the stopper plate on the No. 1 tensioner clockwise and push in the tensioner plunger (see illustration). To lock the plunger in this position, turn the stopper plate counterclockwise and insert a drill or punch (0.138-inch diameter) through the holes in the stopper plate and the tensioner body. Remove the tensioner mounting bolts and remove the No. 1 tensioner.

10 Remove the chain tensioner slipper.

11 Using a 10 mm hex wrench, unscrew the idler sprocket shaft and remove the idler shaft, sprocket and collar. Note which side of the sprocket faces out.

12 Remove the chain vibration dampers.

13 Note the positions of the timing marks on each camshaft sprocket and the crankshaft sprocket. Make sketches or take pictures if you have a camera. Remove the No. 1 timing chain.

7.8c The intake camshaft sprocket of the left (front) cylinder head with the engine at TDC - the timing marks (arrows) DO NOT exactly align at TDC

✳✳ CAUTION:

While the No. 1 timing chain is removed, DO NOT ROTATE THE CRANKSHAFT!

7.8d Alignment marks for the right (rear) camshaft sprockets - the timing marks DO NOT exactly align at TDC

7.9 To lock the tensioner in the retracted position, rotate the stopper plate clockwise and push the plunger in, then rotate the stopper plate counterclockwise and insert a pin through the hole in the stopper plate and the tensioner body

92078-2A-8.36 HAYNES

7.20 Measure timing chain stretch by measuring the distance between the closest points of 15 pins at three or more places around the length of the chain

14 Remove the crankshaft timing chain sprocket.

15 Compress chain tensioner No. 2 and insert a drill or punch (0.039-inch diameter) into the hole.

➡**Note: Timing chain No. 2 and the No. 2 chain tensioner are on the right (rear) cylinder head. Timing chain No. 3 and the No. 3 tensioner are on the left (front) cylinder head.**

16 Hold the hex on the exhaust camshaft with a wrench and unscrew the two bolts that secure the camshaft timing sprockets to the camshafts. Remove the sprockets and chain as an assembly. Keep the components in a resealable plastic bag to ensure that none of these components is mixed with the other timing chain set.

❋❋ **CAUTION:**

Don't attempt to disassemble the adjustable intake sprocket assembly. If disassembled, it will have to be replaced.

17 Remove the chain tensioner No. 2 mounting bolt and remove chain tensioner No. 2. Store the tensioner in the plastic bag with the other No. 2 timing chain components.

18 To remove the No. 3 timing chain and tensioner, repeat these Steps. Again, store the components in a resealable plastic bag.

❋❋ **CAUTION:**

While the timing chains are removed, DO NOT ROTATE THE CRANKSHAFT!

INSPECTION

◆ **Refer to illustrations 7.20 and 7.21**

19 Inspect all parts of the timing chain assembly for wear and damage. Inspect the three timing chains for loose pins, cracks, and worn rollers and side plates. Inspect the sprockets for hook-shaped, chipped and/or broken teeth.

20 Inspect timing chain No. 1 for stretching. To measure timing chain stretch, measure the distance between 15 pins at three or more places around the length of the chain (see illustration). Measure between the inside of the rollers. Compare your measurements with the distance listed in this Chapter's Specifications.

21 Measure the diameter of each timing chain sprocket and idler

7.21 Wrap the chain around each of the timing chain sprockets and measure the diameter of the sprockets across the chain rollers. If the measurement is less than the minimum sprocket diameter, replace the chain and the timing sprockets

sprocket with the appropriate timing chain installed on the sprocket (see illustration). The sprocket diameter, with the chain in place, should not exceed the dimensions listed in this Chapter's Specifications.

22 Measure the idler sprocket oil clearance as follows. First, measure the diameter of the idler sprocket collar with a micrometer and record your measurement. Then measure the inside diameter of the idler sprocket and record that measurement as well. Subtract the idler sprocket collar diameter from the inside diameter of the idler sprocket and compare the result with the clearance listed in this Chapter's Specifications. If the clearance is excessive, replace the idler sprocket and/or collar, as necessary.

23 Some scoring and wear of the timing chain tensioners and vibration dampers is normal, but excessive wear will increase chain noise, accelerate chain and sprocket wear and could damage the engine if a chain jumps timing. Inspect chain tensioners No. 2 and 3, the timing chain tensioner slipper and the timing chain vibration dampers for excessive wear. If the measured chain wear for any of these components exceeds the depth listed in this Chapter's Specifications, replace the component.

24 Check the chain tensioners for correct operation. On the No. 1 tensioner, raise the ratchet pawl and verify that the plunger moves smoothly in and out of the tensioner, then release the ratchet pawl and verify that it prevents the plunger from sliding back into the tensioner. Also verify that the plungers on the No. 2 and No. 3 tensioners move in and out smoothly.

INSTALLATION

◆ **Refer to illustrations 7.26, 7.28, 7.33a, 7.33b and 7.40**

❋❋ **CAUTION:**

Before starting the engine, carefully rotate the crankshaft by hand through at least two full revolutions (use a socket and breaker bar on the crankshaft pulley center bolt). If you feel any resistance, STOP! There is something wrong - most likely, valves are contacting the pistons. You must find the problem before proceeding. Check your work and see if any updated repair information is available.

7.26 The small No. 2 timing chain maintains the alignment of the intake and exhaust camshaft sprockets of the right (rear) cylinder head; set the yellow links on the single line and single dot of the camshaft sprockets

7.28 Set the yellow links of the No. 3 timing chain of the left (front) cylinder head on the double lines and double dots of the camshaft sprockets

7.33a The orange links of the No. 1 (main) timing chain must align with the correct marks on each intake sprocket - the rear single line on the right (rear) head and the large arrowhead on the left (front) head

25 Push in the tensioner plunger on chain tensioner No. 2 and insert a drill or punch (0.039 inch diameter) into the hole of the tensioner to lock the plunger in the retracted position. Install the tensioners and tighten the mounting bolts to the torque listed in this Chapter's Specifications.

26 Install the No. 2 (right bank inner) timing chain on the camshaft sprockets. Make sure that the yellow mark links on the chain are aligned with the single timing dots or lines on the camshaft sprockets (see illustration).

27 Align the yellow links on the No. 2 timing chain with the timing marks on the bearing caps and install timing chain No. 2 and the camshaft sprockets as an assembly. Install the two bolts that secure the timing sprockets to the camshafts. Immobilize the hex on the exhaust camshaft with an adjustable wrench and tighten these two bolts to the torque listed in this Chapter's Specifications. Remove the drill or punch that was used to lock the tensioner plunger in its retracted position and verify that the plunger tensions the chain.

28 Install the other inner timing chain by repeating Steps 25 through 27. Align the yellow links with the double line or dot marks on the sprockets (see illustration). Also align its yellow links with the marks on the bearing caps.

29 Install the chain guides and tighten the bolts to the torque listed in this Chapter's Specifications.

30 Install the crankshaft timing sprocket on the crankshaft. Be sure to align the timing sprocket keyway with the keys on the crankshaft.

31 Apply a light coat of engine oil to the bearing surface of the idler sprocket collar. Install the idler sprocket collar, sprocket and shaft. Make sure that the teeth on the idler sprocket are facing forward. Tighten the idler sprocket shaft to the torque listed in this Chapter's Specifications.

32 Verify that the timing marks on the camshaft timing sprockets are aligned with their corresponding marks on top of the front camshaft bearing caps.

33 Install the long timing chain (No. 1) on the camshaft timing sprockets and on the idler sprocket. Turn the camshaft sprockets to remove the slack in the upper part of the chain, then install the chain over the crankshaft sprocket. Make sure that the yellow link is aligned with the timing dot on the crankshaft timing sprocket (it's near the 3 o'clock position) and that the orange links are aligned with the timing marks on the intake camshaft sprockets (see illustrations). There is a dot on the crankshaft position trigger wheel (the toothed wheel behind the lower crankshaft sprocket) that must be at the 11 o'clock position and aligned with the rib on the engine block (see illustration 7.8a).

34 Turn the stopper plate on the No. 1 tensioner clockwise and push in the tensioner plunger. To lock the plunger in this position, turn the stopper plate counterclockwise and insert a drill or punch (0.138-inch diameter) through the holes in the stopper plate and the tensioner.

7.33b The lower yellow link of the No. 1 timing chain aligns with the dots on the crankshaft at about the two o'clock position

Install the tensioner and tighten the tensioner mounting bolts to the torque listed in this Chapter's Specifications. Remove the drill or punch that you inserted into chain tensioner No. 1 and verify that it tensions timing chain No. 1.

✸✸ CAUTION:

Carefully rotate the crankshaft by hand through at least two full revolutions (use a socket and breaker bar on the crankshaft pulley center bolt). If you feel any resistance, STOP! There is something wrong - most likely, valves are contacting the pistons. You must find the problem before proceeding. Check your work to make sure all timing marks line-up properly, and see if any updated repair information is available.

35 Remove all old RTV sealant from the gasket mating surfaces of the timing chain cover and from the front of the cylinder heads and

7.40 Timing cover bolt tightening sequence

engine block.
36 Install a new crankshaft oil seal in the timing chain cover (see Section 8).
37 Install a new O-ring on the left cylinder head.
38 Apply gray RTV sealant on the timing chain cover in all areas where the cover seals to the engine block and oil pan. These beads should be about 1/8 to 3/16-inch (3 to 4.5 mm) wide.

✸✸ CAUTION:

Once you have installed the sealant on the engine and timing chain cover you have three minutes to install the cover. If you take longer than that, the sealant might not set up properly, so you'll have to remove the sealant and re-apply it.

Be sure to get sealant into the corners where the oil pan meets the engine block and avoid getting any on the O-rings.
39 Rotate the flats on the oil drive rotor to align it with the square part of the crankshaft timing sprocket and slide the timing chain cover into place.
40 Install all of the cover bolts, tightening them as you go.

✸✸ CAUTION:

Do not put long bolts in short holes or vice versa.

Tighten all of the bolts in the proper sequence to the torque listed in this Chapter's Specifications (see illustration).
41 Install and tighten the four oil pan bolts that go into the timing chain cover.
42 The remainder of installation is the reverse of the removal procedure.
43 Refill the engine with oil and coolant (see Chapter 1).
44 Reconnect the cable to the negative battery terminal.
45 Start the engine and check for leaks.

8   Crankshaft front oil seal - replacement

8.2 Pry the seal out of the timing chain cover, being careful not to scratch the crankshaft

▶ **Refer to illustrations 8.2 and 8.4**

➡ **Note: This procedure assumes that the engine has been lowered from the vehicle. If you attempt it with the engine in place, there are other Steps that must be performed that vary by model.**

1 Remove the crankshaft pulley (see Section 7).
2 Carefully pry the seal out of the timing chain cover with a screwdriver or seal removal tool (see illustration). If you use a screwdriver, wrap tape around the tip - don't scratch the housing bore or damage the crankshaft (if the crankshaft is damaged, the new seal will end up leaking).
3 Clean the bore in the timing chain cover and coat the lip and the outer edge of the new seal with engine oil or multi-purpose grease.
4 Using a seal driver or a socket with an outside diameter slightly smaller than the outside diameter of the seal, carefully drive the new

seal into place with a hammer (see illustration). Make sure it's installed squarely and driven in flush with the surface of the timing chain cover. Check the seal after installation to make sure the spring didn't pop out of place.

5   Reinstall the crankshaft pulley, tightening the bolt to the torque listed in this Chapter's Specifications.

6   Run the engine and check for oil leaks at the front seal.

8.4 Lubricate the seal lip and drive the new crankshaft seal into place with a large socket or piece of pipe and a hammer

9   Camshafts, rocker arms and valve adjusters - removal, inspection and installation

REMOVAL

➡Note: The following procedure is not for beginners. Please read the entire procedure carefully before deciding whether this is a job that you want to tackle at home.

➡Note: This procedure assumes that the engine has been lowered from the vehicle. If you attempt it with the engine in place, there are other Steps that must be performed that vary by model.

1   Disconnect the cable from the negative terminal of the battery (see Chapter 5, Section 1).

2   Drain the engine oil and coolant (see Chapter 1).

3   Remove the timing chains and sprockets (see Section 7).

4   To remove the camshafts from the right (passenger's side) cylinder head, rotate the camshafts counterclockwise so that the nose of the intake cam lobe for the No. 1 cylinder is facing toward 6 o'clock, and the nose of the exhaust cam lobe is facing 3 o'clock (the knock pins at the front of the camshaft should be at 12 o'clock for the exhaust cam and 1:30 for the intake cam). Use an open-end wrench on the integral hex cast into each camshaft to rotate the cams.

5   Gradually loosen and then remove the 8 bearing cap bolts in the reverse of the tightening sequence (see illustrations 9.19a and 9.19b).

6   Gradually loosen and remove the remaining 12 housing bolts in the reverse of the tightening sequence (see illustrations 9.18a and 9.18b).

7   Remove all 5 bearing caps and remove the intake and exhaust camshafts. Be sure to keep all of the components in the correct order. One way to do this is to put them in a box and label the cap numbers with a utility marker pen.

8   Carefully pry the camshaft housing from the top of the cylinder head.

✳✳ CAUTION:

Use a screwdriver wrapped with tape to avoid scratching the parts.

9   Remove all of the rocker arms and lash adjusters and put them in the same box with the cam bearing caps. Every component should be marked or labeled so that it can be returned to its original location.

10 If you're removing the camshafts from the other cylinder head, repeat Steps 5 through 9. Make sure that the front camshaft lobes are set on the intake cam at 9 o'clock and the exhaust cam at 1 o'clock (the knock pins at the front of the camshaft should be at 12 o'clock for both cams).

✳✳ CAUTION:

While the timing chains and camshafts are removed, DO NOT ROTATE THE CRANKSHAFT!

INSPECTION

▸ **Refer to illustrations 9.12, 9.13 and 9.14**

11 Inspect each rocker and lash adjuster arm for wear.

12 Visually examine the cam lobes and bearing journals for score marks, pitting, galling and evidence of overheating (blue, discolored areas). Look for flaking away of the hardened surface layer of each lobe. Using a micrometer, measure the height of each camshaft lobe (see illustration). Compare your measurements with this Chapter's Specifications. If the height for any one lobe is less than the specified minimum,

9.12 Measure the lobe heights on each camshaft - if any lobe height is less than the specified allowable minimum, replace that camshaft

9.13 Measure each journal diameter with a micrometer - if any journal measures less than the specified limit, replace the camshaft

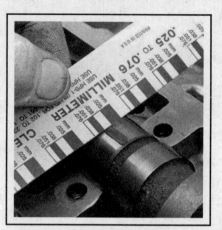

9.14 Compare the width of the crushed Plastigage to the scale on the envelope to determine the oil clearance

replace the camshaft.

13 Using a micrometer, measure the diameter of each journal at several points (see illustration). Compare your measurements with this Chapter's Specifications. If the diameter of any one journal is less than specified, replace the camshaft.

14 Check the oil clearance for each camshaft journal as follows:

a) *Clean the bearing caps and the camshaft journals with brake system cleaner.*

b) *Carefully lay the camshaft(s) in place in the cylinder head. Don't install the lifters and don't use any lubrication.*

c) *Lay a strip of Plastigage on each journal.*

d) *Install the bearing caps with the arrows pointing toward the front (timing chain end) of the engine.*

e) *Tighten the bolts to the torque listed in this Chapter's Specifications in 1/4-turn increments.*

➡**Note: Don't turn the camshaft while the Plastigage is in place.**

f) *Remove the bolts and detach the caps.*

g) *Compare the width of the crushed Plastigage (at its widest point) to the scale on the Plastigage envelope (see illustration).*

h) *If the clearance is greater than specified, replace the camshaft and/or cylinder head.*

i) *Scrape off the Plastigage with your fingernail or the edge of a credit card - don't scratch or nick the journals or bearing caps.*

INSTALLATION

▶ **Refer to illustrations 9.16a, 9.16b, 9.18a, 9.18b, 9.19a and 9.19b**

15 Lightly lubricate the lash adjuster bores and the adjusters themselves with clean engine oil, then install them in the same bores from which they were removed. Install the rocker arms in their original positions, oiling all wear points as you do so.

16 Right side: Lightly lubricate the camshaft journals with clean engine oil. Install the camshafts on the right camshaft housing so that the knock pin of the exhaust camshaft is at 12 o'clock and the intake camshaft's knock pin is rotated 45 degrees to 1:30. Apply a light coat of engine oil to the upper bearing caps, then install them in their correct locations. Tighten the bolts snug at this time in the correct sequence (see illustrations).

9.16a Snug the camshaft cap bolts of the right (rear) cylinder head in this sequence

9.16b Snug the camshaft cap bolts of the left (front) cylinder head in this sequence

9.18a Camshaft housing bolt tightening sequence - right (rear) cylinder head

9.18b Camshaft housing bolt tightening sequence - left (front) cylinder head

17 Thoroughly clean the sealing surfaces of the bottom of the camshaft bearing support and the top of the cylinder head. Apply a continuous 1/8-inch to 3/16-inch bead of RTV silicone sealer to the surface of the top of the cylinder head that mates with the camshaft bearing housing.

18 Set the camshaft housing assembly into place. Install the 12 mounting bolts and tighten them in the correct sequence to the torque listed in this Chapter's Specifications (see illustrations).

19 Loosen the 8 bearing cap bolts you previously tightened, then tighten them in the correct sequence to the torque listed in this Chapter's Specifications (see illustrations).

20 Left side: Lightly lubricate the camshaft journals with clean engine oil. Install the camshafts on the left cylinder head so that the knock pin of each camshaft is in the 12 o'clock position. Proceed as with the right cylinder head.

➡Note: There are 13 bolts in the camshaft housing instead of 12.

21 The remainder of installation is the reverse of removal. Install the timing chains, the timing chain cover and all of the components attached to the timing cover (see Section 7).

✳✳ CAUTION:

Carefully rotate the crankshaft by hand through at least two full revolutions (use a socket and breaker bar on the crankshaft pulley center bolt). If you feel any resistance, STOP! There is something wrong - most likely valves are contacting the pistons. You must find the problem before proceeding. Check your work to make sure all timing marks line-up properly and see if any updated repair information is available.

22 Refill the engine with oil and coolant (see Chapter 1), reconnect the cable to the negative battery terminal, start the engine and check for leaks.

➡Note: It may take a few minutes for lifter clatter to disappear.

9.19a Final camshaft cap bolt tightening sequence for the right (rear) cylinder head

9.19b Final camshaft cap bolt tightening sequence for the left (front) cylinder head

10 Cylinder heads - removal and installation

✳✳ WARNING:

The engine must be completely cool before starting this procedure.

➡ Note: This procedure applies to either cylinder head.

➡ Note: This procedure assumes that the engine has been lowered from the vehicle. If you attempt it with the engine in place, there are other Steps that must be performed that vary by model.

REMOVAL

1 Remove the camshafts and the camshaft housings (see Section 9).
2 Remove the exhaust manifolds (see Section 6).
3 If you're removing the left cylinder head, gradually loosen and remove the two front bolts.
4 Remove the cylinder head bolts gradually and evenly, in the order

10.14a Cylinder head bolt tightening sequence - left cylinder head

10.14b Cylinder head bolt tightening sequence - right cylinder head

opposite that of the tightening sequence then remove the cylinder head from the engine block.
5 Remove and discard the old cylinder head gasket.

INSTALLATION

▸ Refer to illustrations 10.14a, 10.14b and 10.16

6 The mating surfaces of the cylinder heads and the block must be perfectly clean as the heads are installed.
7 Use a gasket scraper to remove all traces of carbon and old gasket material, then clean the mating surfaces with brake system cleaner. If there's oil on the mating surfaces when the head is installed, the gasket may not seal correctly and leaks could develop.
8 When working on the block, stuff the cylinders with clean shop rags to keep out debris. Use a vacuum cleaner to remove material that falls into the cylinders.
9 Check the block and head mating surfaces for nicks, deep scratches and other damage. If damage is slight, it can be removed with a file; if it's excessive, machining may be the only alternative.
10 Use a tap of the correct size to chase the threads in the cylinder head bolt holes, then clean them with compressed air - make sure that nothing remains in the holes.

✳✳ WARNING:

Wear eye protection when using compressed air!

11 Mount each bolt in a vise and run a die down the threads to remove corrosion and restore the threads. Dirt, corrosion and damaged threads affect torque readings.
12 Measure the outside diameter of each cylinder head bolt 4 inches below the head, comparing your measurements to the minimum allowable diameter listed in this Chapter's Specifications. Replace any bolt with a diameter less than the allowable minimum.
13 Position the cylinder head gasket on the engine block so that the lot number stamp is on the center upper edge of the gasket facing up. Carefully place the cylinder head on the head gasket.

10.16 After you've tightened the other bolts of the left cylinder head, tighten these two in this order

14 Apply a light coat of oil to the cylinder head bolts, then install and tighten them (don't forget the washers!), gradually and evenly, in the proper sequence (see illustrations), to the initial torque listed in this Chapter's Specifications.

15 After tightening all eight bolts to the initial torque, put a paint mark on the front edge of each bolt (the edge facing toward the front of the engine), then retighten each bolt, in the same sequence, another 90-degrees. Repeat this one more time so that the bolts have turned 180-degrees from the initial torque. Make sure to use the proper sequence.

16 If you're installing the left cylinder head, install the two front head bolts and tighten them in the correct sequence to the torque listed in this Chapter's Specifications (see illustration).

17 If you removed both cylinder heads, install the other cylinder head now.

18 Install the intake and exhaust camshaft assemblies (see Section 9).

19 Install the camshaft timing oil control valve, the oil control valve filter and the VVT-i sensor (see "Variable Valve Timing-intelligent (VVT-i) - description and component replacement" in Chapter 6).

20 Install the timing chains, the timing chain cover and all components attached to the cover (see Section 7).

21 The remainder of installation is the reverse of the removal procedure.

22 Refill the engine with oil and coolant (see Chapter 1).

23 Reconnect the cable to the negative battery terminal, start the engine and check for leaks.

11 Oil pan - removal and installation

➡ **Note: This procedure assumes that the engine has been lowered from the vehicle. If you attempt it with the engine in place, there are other Steps that must be performed that vary by model.**

REMOVAL

1 Disconnect the cable from the negative terminal of the battery (see Chapter 5, Section 1). Drain the engine oil (see Chapter 1).

2 Remove the bolts and nuts that secure oil pan No. 2 (the smaller stamped steel pan) to the larger cast aluminum oil pan.

3 Oil pan No. 2 will probably be stuck to the oil pan with RTV sealant. Try tapping it loose with a rubber-tipped mallet. If you're unable to knock it loose, carefully cut the sealant with a putty knife and a hammer. Make sure that you don't damage the mating surfaces of the two pans.

4 Remove the two oil pump pickup tube/strainer mounting nuts and the brace bolt. Remove the pickup/strainer assembly.

5 Remove the 16 bolts and 2 nuts that secure the oil pan to the engine block.

6 Carefully pry the oil pan loose from the engine block.

❊❊ CAUTION:

Only pry in the small cutout areas along the side of the pan.

7 Remove the two O-rings from the bottom of the engine block. The sheet metal baffle plate can be removed at this time if necessary.

INSTALLATION

8 Install the baffle plate if you removed it. Tighten the fasteners to the torque listed in this Chapter's Specifications.

9 Use a scraper to remove all traces of old sealant from the block and oil pan. Clean the mating surfaces with brake system cleaner.

10 Make sure the threaded holes in the block are clean. Install new O-rings to the block, holding them in place with clean grease if required.

11 Check the flange of the steel oil pan for distortion around the bolt holes. If necessary, place it on a wood block and use a hammer to flatten and restore the gasket surface.

12 Inspect the strainer for cracks or blockage. Clean it with solvent and install it using a new gasket. Tighten the fasteners to the torque listed in this Chapter's Specifications.

13 Apply a 1/8 inch bead of RTV sealant to the upper oil pan flange.

14 Position the pan onto the block and install the fasteners. Working from the center out, tighten the fasteners to the torque listed in this Chapter's Specifications in several steps.

15 After you have installed the aluminum portion of the oil pan, apply a bead of RTV sealant to the flange of the No. 2 oil pan, carefully position it on the upper oil pan and install the bolts. Working from the center out, tighten them to the torque listed in this Chapter's Specifications in several steps.

16 The remainder of installation is the reverse of removal. Add oil and install a new filter (see Chapter 1). When you're done, run the engine and check for leaks.

12 Oil pump - removal, inspection and installation

REMOVAL

1 Remove the timing chain cover (see Section 7). The oil pump is on the inside of the cover.

2 Remove the relief valve plug using a 27 mm socket. Slide out the spring and the relief valve.

3 Remove the oil pump cover bolts and remove the oil pump cover. Remove the oil pump drive rotor and driven rotor.

INSPECTION

▶ **Refer to illustrations 12.6a, 12.6b and 12.6c**

4 Clean all components with solvent, then inspect them for wear and damage. Check that the oiled relief valve falls easily through its bore without sticking.

5 Check the oil pressure relief valve sliding surface and valve spring. If either the spring or the valve is damaged, they must be

replaced as a set.

6   Check the clearance of the following components with a feeler gauge and compare the measurements to this Chapter's Specifications (see illustrations):

   a)   *Driven rotor-to-oil pump body*
   b)   *Rotor side clearance*
   c)   *Rotor tip clearance*

7   Replace any worn parts or replace the entire oil pump assembly.

INSTALLATION

8   Pry the old crankshaft seal out of the timing chain cover with a screwdriver.

9   Apply multi-purpose grease or engine oil to the outer edge of the new crank seal and carefully drive it into place with a deep socket and a hammer. Apply multi-purpose grease or engine oil to the seal lip.

10   Apply a coat of petroleum jelly to the pump drive and driven rotors, then place the two rotors into position in the timing chain cover. Make sure that the pump marks (dimples) are facing out, toward the pump cover and away from the timing chain cover.

11   Pack the pump cavity with petroleum jelly (this will help to prime the pump) and install the cover. Tighten the cover bolts to the torque listed in this Chapter's Specifications.

12   Lubricate the oil pressure relief valve with clean engine oil and

12.6a Measure the driven rotor-to-body clearance with a feeler gauge

insert the valve, then the spring, into the pump cover. Screw in the plug and tighten it to the torque listed in this Chapter's Specifications.

13   Install the timing chain cover (see Section 7).

14   The remainder of installation is the reverse of removal. Add oil and install a new filter (see Chapter 1). When you're done, run the engine and check for leaks.

12.6b Measure the rotor side clearance with a precision straightedge and feeler gauge

12.6c Measure the rotor tip clearance with a feeler gauge - note the rotor marks are facing out (when the pump body cover is installed, the marks will be against the cover)

13   Driveplate - removal and installation

REMOVAL

1   Refer to Chapter 2C and remove the engine/transaxle assembly from the vehicle, then refer to Chapter 7 and remove the transaxle from the engine.

2   Make alignment marks on the driveplate and crankshaft to ensure correct alignment during reinstallation.

3   Remove the bolts securing the driveplate to the crankshaft. If the crankshaft turns, wedge a screwdriver in the ring gear teeth to hold the driveplate.

4   Remove the driveplate from the crankshaft. Be sure to support it while removing the last bolt. Automatic transmission equipped vehicles have spacers on both sides of the driveplate. Keep them with the driveplate.

INSTALLATION

5   Clean the driveplate to remove grease and oil. Inspect the surface for cracks. Check for cracked or broken ring gear teeth.

6   Clean and inspect the mating surfaces of the driveplate and the crankshaft. If the crankshaft rear seal is leaking, replace it before reinstalling the driveplate (see Section 14).

7   Position the driveplate against the crankshaft. Be sure to align the marks made during removal. Note that some engines have an alignment dowel or staggered bolt holes to ensure correct installation. Before installing the bolts, apply thread-locking compound to the threads.

8   Wedge a screwdriver in the ring gear teeth to keep it from turning and tighten the bolts to the torque listed in this Chapter's Specifications. Follow a criss-cross pattern and work up to the final torque in three or four steps.

9   The remainder of installation is the reverse of the removal procedure.

14   Rear main oil seal - replacement

▶ **Refer to illustration 14.4**

➡**Note: This procedure assumes that the engine has been removed from the vehicle.**

1   Remove the transmission (see Chapter 7). Refer to Section 13 and remove the driveplate.

2   The seal can be replaced without removing the oil pan or seal retainer. The easiest method involves using a seal-removal tool. If this tool isn't available, you can use a sharp knife to cut the lip off the old seal while carefully avoiding scratching the crankshaft. With the lip gone, use a screwdriver wrapped with tape to pry the seal out.

3   Lubricate the crankshaft seal journal and the lip of the new seal with multi-purpose grease.

4   Evenly drive the new seal into the retainer with a wood block or a section of pipe slightly smaller in diameter than the outside diameter of the seal (see illustration). The new seal should be approximately flush with the surface of the retainer.

5   The remainder of installation is the reverse of removal.

14.4 Drive the new seal into the retainer with a wood block or a section of pipe - make sure that you don't cock the seal in the retainer bore

15   Engine mounts - check and replacement

1   Engine mounts seldom require attention, but broken or deteriorated mounts should be replaced immediately or the added strain placed on the driveline components may cause damage or wear.

CHECK

2   During the check, the engine must be raised slightly to remove the weight from the mounts.

3   Raise the vehicle and support it securely on jackstands, then position a jack under the engine oil pan. Place a large wood block between the jack head and the oil pan, then carefully raise the engine just enough to take the weight off the mounts. Do not position the wood block under the drain plug.

✳✳ WARNING:

DO NOT place any part of your body under the engine when it's supported only by a jack!

4   Check the mounts to see if the rubber is cracked, hardened or separated from the metal plates. Sometimes the rubber will split down the center.

5   Check for relative movement between the mount plates and the engine or frame (use a large screwdriver or prybar to attempt to move the mounts).

6   If movement is noted, lower the engine and tighten the mount fasteners.

REPLACEMENT

7   Disconnect the cable from the negative terminal of the battery (see Chapter 5, Section 1), then raise the vehicle and support it securely on jackstands (if not already done). Support the engine as described in Step 3.

8   To remove an engine mount, remove the fasteners, raise the engine and detach the mount. The engine can be raised with an engine hoist, or with a floor jack and wood block placed under the oil pan.

➡**Note: Even if only one mount is being replaced, remove the mount-to-engine bracket nut from the other mount (this will allow the engine to be raised far enough for mount removal).**

9   Installation is the reverse of removal. Use non-hardening thread locking compound on the mount bolts/nuts and be sure to tighten them securely.

10   See Chapter 7 for transmission mount replacement.

Specifications

General

Engine designation	2GR-FE
Displacement	3.5 liters
Cylinder numbers (timing chain end-to-transmission end)	
Right (passenger) side	1-3-5
Left (driver) side	2-4-6
Firing order	1-2-3-4-5-6

92076-2B- HAYNES

Cylinder locations

Warpage limits

Cylinder head	0.0039 inch
Intake manifold	
Intake plenum side	0.031 inch
Cylinder head side	0.008 inch
Exhaust manifolds	0.028 inch

Camshaft and related components

Valve clearance	Hydraulic, non-adjustable
Bearing oil clearance	
Standard	
No. 1 journal	0.0016 to 0.0031 inch
Others	0.00098 to 0.0024 inch
Service limit	
No. 1 journal	0.0039 inch
Others	0.0035 inch
Lobe height	
Intake	
Standard	1.7447 to 1.7487 inches
Service limit	1.7388 inches
Exhaust	
Standard	1.7551 to 1.7591 inches
Service limit	1.7492 inches
Thrust clearance (endplay)	
Standard	0.031 to 0.051 inch
Service limit	0.06 inch
Runout limit (total indicator reading)	0.0016 inch

Cylinder head bolt diameter

Standard (measure at 4 inches below head)	0.4272 to 0.4331 inch
Minimum	0.421 inch

Timing chain

Timing chain (No. 1) stretch limit (between 15 pins)	5.390 inches
Timing chain (No. 2) stretch limit	5.417 inches
Timing chain sprocket wear limit	
(with No.1 chain installed)	2.417 inches
Idler sprocket wear limits	
With No. 1 chain installed	2.417 inches
Idler sprocket collar diameter	0.9050 to 0.9055 inch
Idler sprocket inside diameter	0.9063 to 0.9067 inch
Oil clearance	
Standard	0.0008 to 0.0017 inch
Maximum	0.0037 inch
Chain tensioner No. 2 wear limit	0.039 inch
Chain tensioner slipper wear limit	0.039 inch
Vibration damper No. 1 and No. 2 wear limit	0.039 inch

Oil pump

Driven rotor-to-pump body clearance	
Standard	0.0098 to 0.0128 inch
Service limit	0.0128 inch
Rotor tip clearance	
Standard	0.0024 to 0.0063 inch
Service limit	0.0063 inch
Rotor side clearance	
Standard	0.0012 to 0.0035 inch
Service limit	0.0035 inch

Torque specifications   Ft-lbs (unless otherwise indicated)

➡ **Note: One foot-pound (ft-lb) of torque is equivalent to 12 inch-pounds (in-lbs) of torque. Torque values below approximately 15 ft-lbs are expressed in inch-pounds, since most foot-pound torque wrenches are not accurate at these smaller values**

Intake manifold assembly	
Upper intake manifold bolts	156 in-lbs
Upper intake manifold nuts	144 in-lbs
Lower intake manifold bolts	15
Valve cover fasteners	
Small bolts	84 in-lbs
Large bolts	15
Exhaust manifold nuts	15
Crankshaft pulley bolt	184
Timing chain cover bolts/nuts - in sequence (see illustration 7.40)	
Bolt in center of upper vee	32
All others	15
Drivebelt idler pulley bolts	
Idler pulley No. 1 bolt (lower left of engine)	40
Idler pulley No. 2 bolt	29
Drivebelt tensioner mounting bolts	See Chapter 1
Camshaft housing bolts - in sequence	
(see illustration 9.18a or 9.18b)	21
Camshaft timing sprocket bolt	74
Camshaft bearing cap bolts - in sequence	
(see illustration 9.19a or 9.19b)	84 in-lbs

Torque specifications (continued) | **Ft-lbs (unless otherwise indicated)**

➡**Note: One foot-pound (ft-lb) of torque is equivalent to 12 inch-pounds (in-lbs) of torque. Torque values below approximately 15 ft-lbs are expressed in inch-pounds, since most foot-pound torque wrenches are not accurate at these smaller values**

Cylinder head bolts, in sequence (see illustrations 10.14a, 10.14b and 10.16)	
Step 1	27
Step 2	Tighten an additional 90-degrees
Step 3	Tighten an additional 90-degrees
Left cylinder head (two front 14 mm-head bolts)	22
Oil pan bolts/nuts	
Oil pan No. 1 (to engine block and front cover)	
2 small bolts	84 in-lbs
Other bolts	15
Oil pan No. 2 (to oil pan No. 1) nuts and bolts	84 in-lbs
Oil pan assembly-to-transmission	27
Oil pick-up tube nuts	84 in-lbs
Oil pump assembly	
Oil pump cover bolts	81 in-lbs
Oil pump relief valve plug	37
Driveplate-to-crankshaft bolts	61
Engine rear oil seal retainer	84 in-lbs
Timing chain tensioner bolts	
Chain tensioner No. 1	84 in-lbs
Chain tensioner No. 2	15
Chain tensioner No. 3	15
Timing chain guide bolts	17
Timing chain idler sprocket shaft	44

Section

Reference to other Chapters

2C

GENERAL
ENGINE
OVERHAUL
PROCEDURES

1 General information - engine overhaul

Included in this portion of Chapter 2 are the general overhaul procedures for the cylinder head and internal engine components.

The information ranges from advice concerning preparation for an overhaul and the purchase of replacement parts to detailed, step-by-step procedures covering removal and installation of internal engine components and the inspection of parts.

The following Sections have been written based on the assumption that the engine has been removed from the vehicle. For information concerning in-vehicle engine repair, as well as removal and installation of the external components necessary for the overhaul, see Chapter 2A or 2B.

The Specifications included in this Part are only those necessary for the inspection and overhaul procedures which follow. Refer to Chapter 2, Part A or B for additional Specifications.

It's not always easy to determine when, or if, an engine should be completely overhauled, as a number of factors must be considered.

High mileage is not necessarily an indication that an overhaul is needed, while low mileage doesn't preclude the need for an overhaul. Frequency of servicing is probably the most important consideration. An engine that's had regular and frequent oil and filter changes, as well as other required maintenance, will most likely give many thousands of miles of reliable service. Conversely, a neglected engine may require an overhaul very early in its life.

Excessive oil consumption is an indication that piston rings, valve seals and/or valve guides are in need of attention. Make sure that oil leaks aren't responsible before deciding that the rings and/or guides are bad. Perform an oil pressure check and a cylinder compression check to determine the extent of the work required (see Sections 2 and 3). Also check the vacuum readings under various conditions (see Section 4).

Loss of power, rough running, knocking or metallic engine noises, excessive valve train noise and high fuel consumption rates may also point to the need for an overhaul, especially if they're all present at the same time. If a complete tune-up doesn't remedy the situation, major mechanical work is the only solution.

An engine overhaul involves restoring the internal parts to the specifications of a new engine. During an overhaul, the piston rings are replaced and the cylinder walls are reconditioned (re-bored and/or honed). If a re-bore is done by an automotive machine shop, new oversize pistons will also be installed. The main bearings, connecting rod bearings and camshaft bearings are generally replaced with new ones and, if necessary, the crankshaft may be reground to restore the journals. Generally, the valves are serviced as well, since they're usually in less-than-perfect condition at this point. While the engine is being overhauled, other components, such as the starter and alternator, can be rebuilt as well. The end result should be a like-new engine that will give many trouble free miles.

➡Note: Critical cooling system components such as the hoses, drivebelts, thermostat and water pump should be replaced with new parts when an engine is overhauled. The radiator should be checked carefully to ensure that it isn't clogged or leaking (see Chapter 3). If you purchase a rebuilt engine or short block, some rebuilders will not warranty their engines unless the radiator has been professionally flushed. Also, be sure to check the oil pump carefully as described in Chapter 2A or 2B.

Before beginning the engine overhaul, read through the entire procedure to familiarize yourself with the scope and requirements of the job. Overhauling an engine isn't difficult, but it is time-consuming. Plan on the vehicle being tied up for a minimum of two weeks, especially if parts must be taken to an automotive machine shop for repair or reconditioning. Check on availability of parts and make sure that any necessary special tools and equipment are obtained in advance. Most work can be done with typical hand tools, although a number of precision measuring tools are required for inspecting parts to determine if they must be replaced. Often an automotive machine shop will handle the inspection of parts and offer advice concerning reconditioning and replacement.

➡Note: Always wait until the engine has been completely disassembled and all components, especially the engine block, have been inspected before deciding what service and repair operations must be performed by an automotive machine shop. Since the block's condition will be the major factor to consider when determining whether to overhaul the original engine or buy a rebuilt one, never purchase parts or have machine work done on other components until the block has been thoroughly inspected. As a general rule, time is the primary cost of an overhaul, so it doesn't pay to install worn or substandard parts.

As a final note, to ensure maximum life and minimum trouble from a rebuilt engine, everything must be assembled with care in a spotlessly-clean environment.

2 Oil pressure check

♦ **Refer to illustration 2.2**

1 Low engine oil pressure can be a sign of an engine in need of rebuilding. A "low oil pressure" indicator (often called an "idiot light") is not a test of the oiling system. Such indicators only come on when the oil pressure is dangerously low. Even a factory oil pressure gauge in the instrument panel is only a relative indication, although much better for driver information than a warning light. A better test is with a mechanical (not electrical) oil pressure gauge.

2 Locate the oil pressure sending unit. On 2006 and earlier models, it's at the front of the engine (see illustration), while on 2007 and later models, it's next to the oil filter.

3 Remove the oil pressure sending unit and install a fitting that will allow you to directly connect your hand-held, mechanical oil pressure gauge. Use Teflon tape or sealant on the threads of the adapter and the fitting on the end of your gauge's hose.

4 Connect an accurate tachometer to the engine, according to the tachometer manufacturer's instructions.

5 Check the oil pressure with the engine running (normal operating temperature) at the specified engine speed, and compare it to this Chapter's Specifications. If it's extremely low, the bearings and/or oil pump are probably worn out.

2.2 The oil pressure sending unit is located at the front of the engine, above the crankshaft position sensor

3   Cylinder compression check

▶ **Refer to illustration 3.6**

1   A compression check will tell you what mechanical condition the upper end of your engine (pistons, rings, valves, head gaskets) is in. Specifically, it can tell you if the compression is down due to leakage caused by worn piston rings, defective valves and seats or a blown head gasket.

➡ **Note: The engine must be at normal operating temperature and the battery must be fully charged for this check.**

2   Begin by cleaning the area around the spark plugs before you remove them (compressed air should be used, if available). The idea is to prevent dirt from getting into the cylinders as the compression check is being done.

3   Remove all of the spark plugs from the engine (see Chapter 1).

4   Block the throttle wide open.

3.6   A compression gauge with a threaded fitting for the spark plug hole is preferred over the type that requires hand pressure to maintain the seal - be sure to open the throttle valve as far as possible during the compression check! - start with the number 1 plug hole

5   Disable the ignition system by disconnecting the primary (low voltage) electrical connectors from the coil packs (see Chapter 5). The fuel pump circuit should also be disabled (see Chapter 4).

6   Install the compression gauge in the spark plug hole (see illustration).

7   Crank the engine over at least seven compression strokes and watch the gauge. The compression should build up quickly in a healthy engine. Low compression on the first stroke, followed by gradually increasing pressure on successive strokes, indicates worn piston rings. A low compression reading on the first stroke, which doesn't build up during successive strokes, indicates leaking valves or a blown head gasket (a cracked head could also be the cause). Deposits on the undersides of the valve heads can also cause low compression. Record the highest gauge reading obtained.

8   Repeat the procedure for the remaining cylinders and compare the results to this Chapter's Specifications.

9   Add some engine oil (about three squirts from a plunger-type oil can) to each cylinder, through the spark plug hole, and repeat the test.

10 If the compression increases after the oil is added, the piston rings are definitely worn. If the compression doesn't increase significantly, the leakage is occurring at the valves or head gasket. Leakage past the valves may be caused by burned valve seats and/or faces or warped, cracked or bent valves.

11 If two adjacent cylinders have equally low compression, there's a strong possibility that the head gasket between them is blown. The appearance of coolant in the combustion chambers or the crankcase would verify this condition.

12 If one cylinder is slightly lower than the others, and the engine has a slightly rough idle, a worn lobe on the camshaft could be the cause.

13 If the compression is unusually high, the combustion chambers are probably coated with carbon deposits. If that's the case, the cylinder head(s) should be removed and decarbonized.

14 If compression is way down or varies greatly between cylinders, it would be a good idea to have a leak-down test performed by an automotive repair shop. This test will pinpoint exactly where the leakage is occurring and how severe it is.

4   Vacuum gauge diagnostic checks

▶ **Refer to illustrations 4.4 and 4.6**

1   A vacuum gauge provides valuable information about what is going on in the engine at a low-cost. You can check for worn rings or cylinder walls, leaking head or intake manifold gaskets, incorrect carburetor adjustments, restricted exhaust, stuck or burned valves, weak valve springs, improper ignition or valve timing and ignition problems.

2   Unfortunately, vacuum gauge readings are easy to misinterpret, so they should be used in conjunction with other tests to confirm the diagnosis.

3   Both the absolute readings and the rate of needle movement are important for accurate interpretation. Most gauges measure vacuum in inches of mercury (in-Hg). The following references to vacuum assume the diagnosis is being performed at sea level. As elevation increases (or atmospheric pressure decreases), the reading will decrease. For every 1,000 foot increase in elevation above approximately 2000 feet, the gauge readings will decrease about one inch of mercury.

4   Connect the vacuum gauge directly to intake manifold vacuum, not to ported (throttle body) vacuum (see illustration). Be sure no hoses are left disconnected during the test or false readings will result.

5   Before you begin the test, allow the engine to warm up completely. Block the wheels and set the parking brake. With the transmission in Park, start the engine and allow it to run at normal idle speed.

✳✳ WARNING:

Keep your hands and the vacuum gauge clear of the fans.

6   Read the vacuum gauge; an average, healthy engine should normally produce about 17 to 22 in-Hg with a fairly steady needle (see illustration). Refer to the following vacuum gauge readings and what they indicate about the engine's condition:

7   A low steady reading usually indicates a leaking gasket between

the intake manifold and cylinder head(s) or throttle body, a leaky vacuum hose, late ignition timing or incorrect camshaft timing. Check ignition timing with a timing light and eliminate all other possible causes, utilizing the tests provided in this Chapter before you remove the timing chain cover to check the timing marks.

8 If the reading is three to eight inches below normal and it fluctuates at that low reading, suspect an intake manifold gasket leak at an intake port or a faulty fuel injector.

9 If the needle has regular drops of about two-to-four inches at a steady rate, the valves are probably leaking. Perform a compression check or leak-down test to confirm this.

10 An irregular drop or down-flick of the needle can be caused by a sticking valve or an ignition misfire. Perform a compression check or leak-down test and read the spark plugs.

11 A rapid vibration of about four in-Hg vibration at idle combined with exhaust smoke indicates worn valve guides. Perform a leak-down test to confirm this. If the rapid vibration occurs with an increase in engine speed, check for a leaking intake manifold gasket or head gasket, weak valve springs, burned valves or ignition misfire.

12 A slight fluctuation, say one inch up and down, may mean ignition problems. Check all the usual tune-up items and, if necessary, run the engine on an ignition analyzer.

13 If there is a large fluctuation, perform a compression or leak-down test to look for a weak or dead cylinder or a blown head gasket.

14 If the needle moves slowly through a wide range, check for a clogged PCV system, incorrect idle fuel mixture, carburetor/throttle body or intake manifold gasket leaks.

15 Check for a slow return after revving the engine by quickly snap-

4.4 A simple vacuum gauge can be very handy in diagnosing engine condition and performance - connect to a source of manifold vacuum

ping the throttle open until the engine reaches about 2,500 rpm and let it shut. Normally the reading should drop to near zero, rise above normal idle reading (about 5 in-Hg over) and then return to the previous idle reading. If the vacuum returns slowly and doesn't peak when the throttle is snapped shut, the rings may be worn. If there is a long delay, look for a restricted exhaust system (often the muffler or catalytic converter). An easy way to check this is to temporarily disconnect the exhaust ahead of the suspected part and redo the test.

0279H Low, steady reading

0282H Low, fluctuating needle

0280H Regular drops

0281H Irregular drops

0278H Rapid vibration

0284H Large fluctuation

0283H Slow fluctuation

4.6 Typical vacuum gauge readings

5   Engine removal - methods and precautions

If you've decided that an engine must be removed for overhaul or major repair work, several preliminary steps should be taken.

Locating a suitable place to work is extremely important. Adequate work space, along with storage space for the vehicle, will be needed. If a shop or garage isn't available, at the very least a flat, level, clean work surface made of concrete or asphalt is required.

Cleaning the engine compartment and engine before beginning the removal procedure will help keep tools clean and organized.

An engine hoist or A-frame will also be necessary. Make sure the equipment is rated in excess of the combined weight of the engine and transaxle. Safety is of primary importance, considering the potential hazards involved in lifting the engine out of the vehicle.

If the engine is being removed by a novice, an assistant should be available. Advice and aid from someone more experienced would also be helpful. There are many instances when one person cannot simultaneously perform all of the operations required when lifting the engine out of the vehicle.

Plan the operation ahead of time. Arrange for or obtain all of the tools and equipment you'll need prior to beginning the job. Some of the equipment necessary to perform engine removal and installation safely and with relative ease are (in addition to an engine hoist) a heavy duty floor jack, complete sets of wrenches and sockets as described in the front of this manual, wooden blocks and plenty of rags and cleaning solvent for mopping up spilled oil, coolant and gasoline. If the hoist must be rented, make sure that you arrange for it in advance and perform all of the operations possible without it beforehand. This will save you money and time.

Plan for the vehicle to be out of use for quite a while. A machine shop will be required to perform some of the work that the do-it-yourselfer can't accomplish without special equipment. These shops often have a busy schedule, so it would be a good idea to consult them before removing the engine in order to accurately estimate the amount of time required to rebuild or repair components that may need work.

Always be extremely careful when removing and installing the engine. Serious injury can result from careless actions. Plan ahead, take your time and a job of this nature, although major, can be accomplished successfully.

6   Engine - removal and installation

→Note: Read through the entire Section before beginning this procedure. The manufacturer recommends removing the engine and transaxle from below as a unit, then separating the engine from the transaxle on the shop floor. This is a difficult procedure for the home mechanic, as the vehicle has to be safely lifted and supported at a high enough position to allow removal of the engine/transaxle/suspension subframe as a unit from below. You also need enough room to set the drivetrain on a sturdy dolly to slide it out, and back in under the vehicle when reassembling. It is nearly essential that this procedure be performed with a vehicle lift.

REMOVAL

✳✳ WARNING 1:

The models covered by this manual are equipped with Supplemental Restraint Systems (SRS), more commonly known as airbags. Always disable the airbag system before working in the vicinity of the impact sensors, steering column or instrument panel to avoid the possibility of accidental deployment of the airbag, which could cause personal injury (see Chapter 12).

✳✳ WARNING 2:

Gasoline is extremely flammable, so take extra precautions when you work on any part of the fuel system. Don't smoke or allow open flames or bare light bulbs near the work area, and don't work in a garage where a gas-type appliance (such as a water heater or a clothes dryer) is present. Since gasoline is carcinogenic, wear latex gloves when there's a possibility of being exposed to fuel, and, if you spill any fuel on your skin, rinse it off immediately with soap and water. Mop up any spills immediately and do not store fuel-soaked rags where they could ignite. The fuel system is under constant pressure, so, if any fuel lines are to be disconnected, the fuel pressure in the system must be relieved first (see Chapter 4 for more information). When you perform any kind of work on the fuel system, wear safety glasses and have a Class B type fire extinguisher on hand.

2006 and earlier models

▸ Refer to illustrations 6.7 and 6.16

1   Relieve the fuel system pressure (see Chapter 4).
2   Disconnect the negative cable from the battery.
3   Remove the battery and battery tray.
4   Place protective covers on the fenders and remove the hood and cowl cover (see Chapter 11).
5   Remove the air cleaner assembly (see Chapter 4). Remove the inner fender splash shields.
6   Raise the vehicle and support it securely on jackstands. Drain the cooling system and engine oil and remove the drivebelts (see Chapter 1).
7   Clearly label, then disconnect all vacuum lines, coolant and emissions hoses, wiring harness connectors, ground straps and fuel lines. Masking tape and/or a touch up paint applicator work well for marking items (see illustration). Take instant photos or sketch the locations of components and brackets.
8   Remove the windshield washer tank and coolant reservoir tank.

6.7 Label both ends of each wire and hose before disconnecting it

6.16 Unbolt the A/C compressor and use wire or rope to tie it out of the way

6.41 Remove the bolts and nuts securing the subframe braces

9   Remove the cooling fan(s), shroud(s) and radiator (see Chapter 3).

10 Disconnect the heater hoses.

11 Release the residual fuel pressure in the tank by removing the gas cap, then undo the fuel lines connecting the engine to the chassis (see Chapter 4). Plug or cap all open fittings.

12 Disconnect the throttle linkage, transmission Throttle Valve (TV) linkage and speed control cable, if equipped, from the engine (see Chapter 4).

13 Disconnect the engine harness plugs and clips from the front and left side of the engine.

14 Disconnect the wire harness clips at the transaxle end of the engine and pull back the wiring on all sides to clear the engine.

15 Unbolt the power steering pump. If clearance allows, tie the pump aside without disconnecting the hoses. If necessary, remove the pump (see Chapter 10).

16 Unbolt the air conditioning compressor and set it aside (see illustration). Do not disconnect the refrigerant hoses.

17 Detach the exhaust pipes from the manifolds (see Chapter 4).

18 Disconnect the front stabilizer bar links from the struts, and disconnect the steering shaft coupler (see Chapter 10).

19 Attach a lifting sling to the engine, only at the factory engine-lifting brackets. Position a hoist and connect the sling to it. Take up the slack until there is slight tension on the hoist. Remove the engine movement control rod at the right end of the engine (see Chapter 2, Part A).

20 Remove both driveaxles (see Chapter 8). Remove the brake calipers and support them with wire to avoid stretching the brake hoses (see Chapter 9). Refer to Chapter 10 and disconnect the front struts from the top of the steering knuckle.

21 Disconnect the ABS sensors and wiring from the front suspension and wire them out of the way.

2007 and later models

22 Have the air conditioning system discharged and evacuated at an approved service facility.

23 Relieve the fuel system pressure (see Chapter 4).

24 Remove the battery (see Chapter 5).

25 Raise the vehicle and support it securely on jackstands. Remove the front wheels and the engine lower splash shield.

26 Remove both inner fender splash shields.

27 Drain the oil, coolant and transmission fluid (see Chapter 1).

28 Remove the upper intake manifold (see Chapter 2B). This involves removing the wiper assembly and both portions of the cowl.

29 Remove both air intake scoops from the top of the radiator support.

30 Remove the air filter lid and the filter, then remove the air filter housing and its support bracket.

31 Remove the air intake resonator. Remove the right engine mounting brace and the upper engine mount.

32 Disconnect all necessary coolant, oil and vacuum hoses. Label them to prevent confusion later.

33 Disconnect the fuel supply hose (see Chapter 4).

34 Disconnect the shift cable from the transaxle (see Chapter 7).

35 Label and then disconnect all wiring harnesses.

36 Remove the front exhaust pipe assembly for clearance.

37 Disconnect the stabilizer bar end links, then remove the axle hub nuts. Disconnect the front wheel speed sensors, disconnect the tie rod ends, then detach the lower control arms and pull them free of the axles (see Chapter 10).

38 Disconnect the steering shaft (see Chapter 10). Disconnect the power steering hoses from the pump.

39 Attach a lifting sling to the engine but only at the factory lifting brackets. Connect the sling to a hoist. Take up the slack in the sling until there's tension in it.

All models

▶ Refer to illustration 6.41

40 There should now be nothing to prevent the lowering of the suspension subframe with the engine and transaxle still attached to the subframe by the engine mounts.

41 Without placing any part of your body under the front suspension subframe, remove the bolts from the four braces that secure the subframe to the body (see illustration).

42 Slowly lower the engine/transaxle/subframe until they are secure on the dolly, then disconnect the lifting sling from the hoist.

43 Pull the dolly out from under the vehicle and reattach the hoist to the engine with the lifting sling.

44 Lift the hoist until the tension is taken from the engine mounts,

then disconnect all engine mounts from the engine (see Chapter 2A).

45 Refer to Chapter 7 to separate the engine from the transaxle, then remove the engine from the subframe, leaving the transaxle in place.

INSTALLATION

46 Check the engine/transaxle mounts. If they're worn or damaged, replace them.

47 With the engine hoist, carefully guide the engine into place to align with the transaxle, following the procedure outlined in Chapter 7.

✳✳ CAUTION:

Do not use the bolts to force the engine and transaxle into alignment. It may crack or damage major components.

48 Install the engine-to-transaxle bolts and tighten them securely.

49 Reconnect the engine mounts to the engine, then release the hoist and push the dolly under the vehicle.

50 Move the engine hoist over the engine, lower the lifting sling through the engine compartment and reattach the sling to the engine.

51 Have an assistant raise and position the engine/transaxle/subframe carefully until you can align the subframe and its braces.

52 Install the subframe brace bolts/nuts and torque them to this Chapter's Specifications.

53 Reinstall the remaining components and fasteners in the reverse order of removal.

54 Add coolant, oil, power steering and transmission fluids as needed (see Chapter 1).

55 Run the engine and check for proper operation and leaks. Shut off the engine and recheck the fluid levels.

7 Engine rebuilding alternatives

The do-it-yourselfer is faced with a number of options when performing an engine overhaul. The decision to replace the engine block, piston/connecting rod assemblies and crankshaft depends on a number of factors, with the number one consideration being the condition of the block. Other considerations are cost, access to machine shop facilities, parts availability, time required to complete the project and the extent of prior mechanical experience on the part of the do-it-yourselfer.

Some of the rebuilding alternatives include:

Individual parts - If the inspection procedures reveal that the engine block and most engine components are in reusable condition, purchasing individual parts may be the most economical alternative. The block, crankshaft and piston/connecting rod assemblies should all be inspected carefully. Even if the block shows little wear, the cylinder bores should be surface honed.

Short block - A short block consists of an engine block with a crankshaft and piston/connecting rod assemblies already installed. All new bearings are incorporated and all clearances will be correct. The existing camshaft, valve train components, cylinder head(s) and external parts can be bolted to the short block with little or no machine shop work necessary.

Long block - A long block consists of a short block plus an oil pump, oil pan, cylinder head(s), valve cover(s), camshaft and valve train components, timing sprockets and chain or gears and timing cover. All components are installed with new bearings, seals and gaskets incorporated throughout. The installation of manifolds and external parts is all that's necessary.

Used engine assembly - While overhaul provides the best assurance of a like-new engine, used engines available from wrecking yards and importers are often a very simple and economical solution. Many used engines come with warranties, but always give any engine a thorough diagnostic check-out before purchase. If possible, have the seller run the engine, ether in the vehicle or on a test stand so you can be sure it runs smoothly with no knocking or other noises. Check compression, vacuum and also for signs of oil leakage.

Give careful thought to which alternative is best for you and discuss the situation with local automotive machine shops, auto parts dealers and experienced rebuilders before ordering or purchasing replacement parts.

8 Engine overhaul - disassembly sequence

▶ **Refer to illustration 8.5**

1 It's much easier to disassemble and work on the engine if it's mounted on a portable engine stand. A stand can often be rented quite cheaply from an equipment rental yard. Before the engine is mounted on a stand, the flywheel/driveplate and rear oil seal retainer should be removed from the engine.

2 If a stand isn't available, it's possible to disassemble the engine with it blocked up on the floor. Be extra careful not to tip or drop the engine when working without a stand.

3 If you're going to obtain a rebuilt engine, all external components must come off first, to be transferred to the replacement engine, just as they will if you're doing a complete engine overhaul yourself. These include:

Alternator and brackets
Emissions control components
Coil packs, spark plug wires and spark plugs
Thermostat and housing cover
Water pump
EFI components
Intake/exhaust manifolds
Oil filter
Engine mounts
Clutch and flywheel/driveplate
Engine rear plate

➡**Note: When removing the external components from the engine, pay close attention to details that may be helpful or important during installation. Note the installed position of gaskets, seals, spacers, pins, brackets, washers, bolts and other small items.**

4 If you're obtaining a short block, which consists of the engine block, crankshaft, pistons and connecting rods all assembled, then the cylinder head(s), oil pan and oil pump will have to be removed as well. See *Engine rebuilding alternatives* for additional information regarding the different possibilities to be considered.

8.5 V6 engine lower end components - exploded view (2006 and earlier models)

5   If you're planning a complete overhaul, the engine must be disassembled and the internal components removed in the following order (see illustration).

Intake and exhaust manifolds
Valve cover(s)
Timing belt covers
Timing belt and sprockets
Cylinder head(s)
Oil pan
Oil pump
Piston/connecting rod assemblies
Crankshaft rear oil seal retainer
Crankshaft and main bearings

6   Before beginning the disassembly and overhaul procedures, make sure the following items are available. Also, refer to Section 20 for a list of tools and materials needed for engine reassembly.

Common hand tools
Small cardboard boxes or plastic bags for storing parts
Gasket scraper
Ridge reamer
Vibration damper puller
Micrometers
Telescoping gauges
Dial indicator set
Valve spring compressor
Cylinder surfacing hone
Piston ring groove cleaning tool
Electric drill motor
Tap and die set
Wire brushes
Oil gallery brushes
Cleaning solvent

9 Cylinder head - disassembly

◆ Refer to illustrations 9.2, 9.3 and 9.4

➡Note: New and rebuilt cylinder heads are commonly available for most engines at dealerships and auto parts stores. Due to the fact that some specialized tools are necessary for the disassembly and inspection procedures, and replacement parts may not be readily available, it may be more practical and economical for the home mechanic to purchase replacement head(s) rather than taking the time to disassemble, inspect and recondition the original(s).

1   Cylinder head disassembly involves removal of the intake and exhaust valves and related components. It's assumed that the lifters or rocker arms and camshaft(s) have already been removed (see Part A or B of this Chapter as needed).

2   Before the valves are removed, arrange to label and store them, along with their related components, so they can be kept separate and reinstalled in the same valve guides they are removed from (see illustration).

3   Compress the springs on the first valve with a spring compressor and remove the keepers (see illustration). Carefully release the valve spring compressor and remove the retainer, the spring and the spring seat (if used).

⚹⚹ CAUTION:

Be very careful not to nick or otherwise damage the lifter bores when compressing the valve springs.

➡Note: If your spring compressor does not have an end such as the one shown with cutouts on the side, an adapter is available to use with a standard spring compressor.

4   Pull the valve out of the head, then remove the oil seal from the guide. If the valve binds in the guide (won't pull through), push it back into the head and deburr the area around the keeper groove with a fine file or whetstone (see illustration).

5   Repeat the procedure for the remaining valves. Remember to keep all the parts for each valve together so they can be reinstalled in the same locations.

6   Once the valves and related components have been removed and stored in an organized manner, the head should be thoroughly cleaned and inspected. If a complete engine overhaul is being done, finish the engine disassembly procedures before beginning the cylinder head cleaning and inspection process.

9.2 A small plastic bag, with an appropriate label, can be used to store the valve train components so they can be kept together and reinstalled in the correct guide

9.3 Compress the spring until the keepers can be removed with a small magnetic screwdriver or needle-nose pliers

9.4 If the valve won't pull through the guide, deburr the edge of the stem end and the area around the top of the keeper groove with a file or whetstone

10 Cylinder head - cleaning and inspection

◆ Refer to illustrations 10.12, 10.14, 10.15, 10.16, 10.17 and 10.18

1   Thorough cleaning of the cylinder head(s) and related valve train components, followed by a detailed inspection, will enable you to decide how much valve service work must be done during the engine overhaul.

➡Note: If the engine was severely overheated, the cylinder head is probably warped (see Step 12).

CLEANING

2   Scrape all traces of old gasket material and sealing compound off

the head gasket, intake manifold and exhaust manifold sealing surfaces. Be very careful not to gouge the cylinder head. Special gasket removal solvents that soften gaskets and make removal much easier are available at auto parts stores.

3   Remove all built up scale from the coolant passages.

4   Run a stiff wire brush through the various holes to remove deposits that may have formed in them. If there are heavy rust deposits in the water passages, the bare head should be professionally cleaned at a machine shop.

5   Run an appropriate size tap into each of the threaded holes to remove corrosion and thread sealant that may be present. If compressed air is available, use it to clear the holes of debris produced by this operation.

10.12 Check the cylinder head gasket surfaces for warpage by trying to slip a feeler gauge under the precision straightedge (see the Specifications for the maximum warpage allowed and use a feeler gauge of that thickness)

✻✻ WARNING:

Wear eye protection when using compressed air!

6   Clean the exhaust and intake manifold stud threads with a wire brush.

7   Clean the cylinder head with solvent and dry it thoroughly. Compressed air will speed the drying process and ensure that all holes and recessed areas are clean.

➡Note: Decarbonizing chemicals are available and may prove very useful when cleaning cylinder heads and valve train components. They are very caustic and should be used with caution. Be sure to follow the instructions on the container.

8   Clean the lifters with solvent and dry them thoroughly (don't mix them up during the cleaning process). Compressed air will speed the drying process and can be used to clean out the oil passages.

9   Clean all the valve springs, spring seats, keepers and retainers with solvent and dry them thoroughly. Work on the components from one valve at a time to avoid mixing up the parts.

10   Scrape off any heavy deposits that may have formed on the valves, then use a motorized wire brush to remove deposits from the valve heads and stems. Again, make sure the valves don't get mixed up.

INSPECTION

➡Note: Be sure to perform all of the following inspection procedures before concluding that machine shop work is required. Make a list of the items that need attention. The inspection procedures for the lifters and the camshafts can be found in Part A or B of this Chapter.

Cylinder head

11   Inspect the head very carefully for cracks, evidence of coolant leakage and other damage. If cracks are found, check with an automotive machine shop concerning repair. If repair isn't possible, a new cylinder head should be obtained.

12   Using a straightedge and feeler gauge, check the head gasket mating surface for warpage (see illustration). If the warpage exceeds the limit found in this Chapter's Specifications, it can be resurfaced at an automotive machine shop.

➡Note: If the heads are resurfaced, the intake manifold flanges may also require machining.

10.14 A dial indicator can be used to measure valve stem-to-guide clearance - move the valve stem back and forth as shown

10.15 Check for valve wear at the points shown here

13   Examine the valve seats in each of the combustion chambers. If they're pitted, cracked or burned, the head will require valve service that's beyond the scope of the home mechanic.

14   Check the valve stem-to-guide clearance with a dial indicator (see illustration). Also, check the valve stem deflection with a dial indicator attached securely to the head. The valve must be in the guide and approximately 1/16-inch off the seat. The total valve stem movement indicated by the gauge needle must be noted, then divided by two to obtain the actual clearance value. If it exceeds the stem-to-guide clearance limit found in this Chapter's Specifications, the valve guides should be replaced. After this is done, if there's still some doubt regarding the condition of the valve guides they should be checked by an automotive machine shop (the cost should be minimal).

Valves

15   Carefully inspect each valve face for uneven wear, deformation, cracks, pits and burned areas (see illustration). Check the valve stem for scuffing and galling and the neck for cracks. Rotate the valve and check for any obvious indication that it's bent. Look for pits and excessive wear on the end of the stem. The presence of any of these conditions indicates the need for valve service by an automotive machine shop.

16   Measure the margin width on each valve (see illustration). Any valve with a margin narrower than that listed in this Chapter's Specifications will have to be replaced with a new one.

Valve components

17   Check each valve spring for wear (on the ends) and pits. Measure the free length and compare it to this Chapter's Specifications (see

10.16 The margin width on each valve must be as specified (if no margin exists, the valve cannot be re-used)

10.17 Measure the free length of each valve spring with a dial or vernier caliper

10.18 Check each valve spring for squareness

illustration). Any springs that are shorter than specified have sagged and should not be re-used. The tension of all springs should be pressure checked with a special fixture before deciding that they're suitable for use in a rebuilt engine (take the springs to an automotive machine shop for this check).

18 Stand each spring on a flat surface and check it for squareness (see illustration). If any of the springs are distorted or sagged, replace all of them with new parts.

19 Check the spring retainers and keepers for obvious wear and cracks. Any questionable parts should be replaced with new ones, as extensive damage will occur if they fail during engine operation.

20 Any damaged or excessively worn parts must be replaced with new ones.

21 If the inspection process indicates that the valve components are in generally poor condition and worn beyond the limits specified, which is usually the case in an engine that's being overhauled, reassemble the valves in the cylinder head and refer to Section 11 for valve servicing recommendations.

11 Valves - servicing

1 Because of the complex nature of the job and the special tools and equipment needed, servicing of the valves, the valve seats and the valve guides, commonly known as a valve job, should be done by a professional.

2 The home mechanic can remove and disassemble the head(s), do the initial cleaning and inspection, then reassemble and take them to a dealer service department or an automotive machine shop for the actual service work. Doing the inspection will enable you to see what condition the head(s) and valvetrain components are in and will ensure that you know what work and new parts are required when dealing with an automotive machine shop.

3 The dealer service department, or automotive machine shop, will remove the valves and springs, recondition or replace the valves and valve seats, recondition the valve guides, check and replace the valve springs, spring retainers and keepers (as necessary), replace the valve seals with new ones, reassemble the valve components and make sure the installed spring height is correct. The cylinder head gasket surface will also be resurfaced if it's warped.

4 After the valve job has been performed by a professional, the head(s) will be in like new condition. When the heads are returned, be sure to clean them again before installation on the engine to remove any metal particles and abrasive grit that may still be present from the valve service or head resurfacing operations. Use compressed air, if available, to blow out all the oil holes and passages.

12 Cylinder head - reassembly

▶ **Refer to illustrations 12.3 and 12.6**

1 Regardless of whether or not the head was sent to an automotive machine shop for valve servicing, make sure it's clean before beginning reassembly.

2 If the head was sent out for valve servicing, the valves and related components will already be in place. Begin the reassembly procedure with Step 8.

3 Install new seals on each of the valve guides.

➡**Note: Intake and exhaust valves require different seals - DO NOT mix them up!**

Gently tap each intake valve seal into place until it's seated on the guide (see illustration).

12.3 Gently tap the valve seals (arrow) into place with a deep socket and hammer - the intake seals are light brown and the exhaust seals are gray

❋❋ CAUTION:

Don't hammer on the valve seals once they're seated or you may damage them. Don't twist or cock the seals during installation or they won't seat properly on the valve stems.

4 Beginning at one end of the head, lubricate and install the first valve. Apply moly-base grease or clean engine oil to the valve stem.

5 Drop the spring seat or shim(s) over the valve guide and set the valve spring and retainer in place.

6 Compress the springs with a valve spring compressor and carefully install the keepers in the upper groove, then slowly release the compressor and make sure the keepers seat properly. Apply a small dab of grease to each keeper to hold it in place if necessary (see illustration).

7 Repeat the procedure for the remaining valves. Be sure to return the components to their original locations - don't mix them up!

8 Check the valve spring installed height with a dial or vernier caliper.

12.6 The small valve stem keepers are easier to position when coated with grease

13 Pistons/connecting rods - removal

♦ Refer to illustrations 13.2, 13.4 and 13.5

➥Note: Prior to removing the piston/connecting rod assemblies, remove the cylinder head(s), the oil pan and the oil pump pick-up tube by referring to the appropriate Sections in Chapter 2A or 2B.

1 Clean the top of the block and the upper cylinder walls with a cloth and lacquer thinner.

2 Use your fingernail to feel if a ridge has formed at the upper limit of ring travel (about 1/4-inch down from the top of each cylinder). If carbon deposits or cylinder wear have produced ridges, they must be completely removed with a special tool (see illustration). Follow the manufacturer's instructions provided with the tool. Failure to remove the ridges before attempting to remove the piston/connecting rod assemblies may result in piston damage.

3 After the cylinder ridges have been removed, turn the engine upside-down so the crankshaft is facing up.

4 Before the connecting rods are removed, check the endplay with feeler gauges. Slide them between the first connecting rod and the

crankshaft throw until the play is removed (see illustration). The endplay is equal to the thickness of the feeler gauge(s). If the endplay exceeds the specified service limit, new connecting rods will be required. If new rods (or a new crankshaft) are installed, the endplay may fall under the service limit (if it does, the rods will have to be machined to restore it - consult an automotive machine shop for advice if necessary). Repeat the procedure for the remaining connecting rods.

5 Check the connecting rods and caps for identification marks. If they aren't plainly marked, use a small center punch to make the appropriate number of indentations on each rod and cap (1, 2, 3, etc., depending on the engine type and cylinder they're associated with) (see illustration).

6 Loosen each of the connecting rod cap nuts 1/2-turn at a time until they can be removed by hand. Remove the number one connecting rod cap and bearing insert. Don't drop the bearing insert out of the cap.

7 The rods on V6 engines use rod bolts instead of nuts. To protect the crankshaft surface when removing or installing the pistons/rods, take two lengths of threaded rod that fit the connecting rod (or bolts

13.2 A ridge reamer is required to remove the ridge from the top of each cylinder - do this before removing the pistons!

13.4 Check the connecting rod side clearance (endplay) with a feeler gauge as shown here

13.5 The connecting rods and caps should be marked to indicate which cylinder they're installed in - if they aren't, mark them with a center punch to avoid confusion during reassembly - do not confuse the markings shown here as rod numbers; these are bearing size identifications

with the heads cut off), and slip a length of rubber tubing over them. Insert these "padded" bolts into the rod when removing or installing the piston/connecting rod assemblies, to avoid scratching the crankshaft journals or cylinder walls.

8   Push the connecting rod/piston assembly out through the top of the engine. Use a wooden hammer handle to push on the upper bearing surface in the connecting rod. If resistance is felt, double-check to make sure that all of the ridge was removed from the cylinder.

9   Repeat the procedure for the remaining cylinders.

→**Note: Turn the crankshaft as needed to put the rod to be removed close to parallel with the cylinder bore - don't try to drive it out while at a large angle to the bore.**

10   After removal, reassemble the connecting rod caps and bearing inserts in their respective connecting rods and install the cap nuts finger tight. Leaving the old bearing inserts in place until reassembly will help prevent the connecting rod bearing surfaces from being accidentally nicked or gouged.

11   Don't separate the pistons from the connecting rods (see Section 17 for additional information).

14 Crankshaft - removal

♦ **Refer to illustrations 14.1, 14.3 and 14.4**

→**Note: The crankshaft can be removed only after the engine has been removed from the vehicle. It's assumed that the flywheel or driveplate, vibration damper, timing belt, oil pan, oil pick-up tube, oil pump and piston/connecting rod assemblies have already been removed. The rear main oil seal and retainer must be removed from the block before proceeding with crankshaft removal.**

1   Before the crankshaft is removed, check the endplay. Mount a dial indicator with the stem in line with the crankshaft and touching the nose of the crank or one of the crank throws (see illustration).

2   Push the crankshaft all the way to the rear and zero the dial indicator. Next, pry the crankshaft to the front as far as possible and check the reading on the dial indicator. The distance that it moves is the endplay. If it's greater than specified, check the crankshaft thrust surfaces for wear. If no wear is evident, new thrust washers should correct the endplay.

3   If a dial indicator isn't available, feeler gauges can be used. Gently pry or push the crankshaft all the way to the front of the engine. Slip feeler gauges between the crankshaft and the front face of the thrust main bearing to determine the clearance (see illustration). The thrust bearing is on the number two journal.

4   The engine has main cap bolts along the sides of the block (see illustration). Check the main bearing caps to see if they're marked to indicate their locations. If they aren't, mark them with number stamping dies or a center punch. Remove those first (with their sealing washers) in the reverse order of the tightening sequence (see illustration 24.12c). Then remove the rest of the main cap bolts in the reverse order of the tightening sequence (see illustration 24.12a). Note if any stud bolts are used and make sure they're returned to their original locations when the crankshaft is reinstalled.

5   Gently tap the caps with a soft-face hammer, then separate them from the engine block. If necessary, use the bolts as levers to remove the caps. Try not to drop the bearing inserts if they come out with the caps.

6   Carefully lift the crankshaft out of the engine. It may be a good idea to have an assistant available, since the crankshaft is quite heavy. With the bearing inserts in place in the engine block and main bearing caps or cap assembly, return the caps to their respective locations on the engine block and tighten the bolts finger tight.

14.1 Checking crankshaft endplay with a dial indicator

14.3 Checking crankshaft endplay with a feeler gauge

14.4 The engine has side bolts into the main caps (rear bolt on this side not seen here) - the engine mount must be removed to access the bolt in the center of this photo

15 Engine block - cleaning and inspection

CLEANING

▶ **Refer to illustrations 15.1 and 15.8**

1 To allow complete cleaning of the block, the core plugs must be removed. These engines do not have conventional core plugs in the aluminum block, but rather bolted-on plates with RTV sealant (see illustration).

2 Using a gasket scraper, remove all traces of gasket material from the engine block. Be very careful not to nick or gouge the gasket sealing surfaces.

3 Remove the main bearing caps or cap assembly and separate the bearing inserts from the caps and the engine block. Tag the bearings, indicating which cylinder they were removed from and whether they were in the cap or the block, then set them aside.

4 Remove all of the threaded oil gallery plugs from the block. The plugs are usually very tight - they may have to be drilled out and the holes re-tapped. Use new plugs when the engine is reassembled.

5 If the engine is extremely dirty, it should be taken to an automotive machine shop for cleaning.

6 After the block is returned, clean all oil holes and oil galleries one more time. Brushes specifically designed for this purpose are available at most auto parts stores. Flush the passages with warm water until the water runs clear, dry the block thoroughly and wipe all machined surfaces with a light, rust preventive oil. If you have access to compressed air, use it to speed the drying process and to blow out all the oil holes and galleries.

✳✳ WARNING:

Wear eye protection when using compressed air!

7 If the block isn't extremely dirty or sludged up, you can do an adequate cleaning job with hot soapy water and a stiff brush. Take plenty of time and do a thorough job. Regardless of the cleaning

15.1 The equivalent of a core plug is this bolted-on plate, sealed with sealant

method used, be sure to clean all oil holes and galleries very thoroughly, dry the block completely and coat all machined surfaces with light oil.

8 The threaded holes in the block must be clean to ensure accurate torque readings during reassembly. Run the proper size tap into each of the holes to remove rust, corrosion, thread sealant or sludge and restore damaged threads (see illustration). If possible, use compressed air to clear the holes of debris produced by this operation. Now is a good time to clean the threads on the head bolts and the main bearing cap bolts as well.

9 Reinstall the main bearing caps and tighten the bolts finger tight.

10 Apply a 1/8 to 3/16-inch bead of RTV sealant to the water seal plate, then install the plate to the block and tighten the nuts to the torque listed in this Chapter's Specifications.

11 Apply non-hardening sealant (such as Permatex no. 2 or Teflon

15.8 All bolt holes in the block - particularly the main bearing cap and head bolt holes - should be cleaned and restored with a tap (be sure to remove debris from the holes after this is done)

15.16a Measure the diameter of each cylinder at a right angle to the engine centerline (A), and parallel to engine centerline (B) - out-of-round is the difference between A and B, taper is the difference between A and B at the top of the cylinder and A and B at the bottom of the cylinder

15.16b The ability to "feel" when the telescoping gauge is at the correct point will be developed over time, so work slowly and repeat the check until you're satisfied that the bore measurement is accurate

15.16c The gauge is then measured with a micrometer to determine the bore size

15.20 Check the block deck on both banks for distortion with a precision straightedge and feeler gauges - check straight along and diagonally

pipe sealant) to the new oil gallery plugs and thread them into the holes in the block. Make sure they're tightened securely.

12 If the engine isn't going to be reassembled right away, cover it with a large plastic trash bag to keep it clean.

INSPECTION

▶ **Refer to illustrations 15.16a, 15.16b, 15.16c and 15.20**

13 Before the block is inspected, it should be cleaned as described earlier in this Section.

14 Visually check the block for cracks, rust and corrosion. Look for stripped threads in the threaded holes. It's also a good idea to have the block checked for hidden cracks by an automotive machine shop that has the special equipment to do this type of work, especially if the vehicle had a history of overheating or using coolant. If defects are found, have the block repaired, if possible, or replaced.

15 Check the cylinder bores for scuffing and scoring.

16 Measure the diameter of each cylinder at the top (just under the

ridge area), center and bottom of the cylinder bore, parallel to the crankshaft axis (see illustrations).

17 Next, measure each cylinder's diameter at the same three locations across the crankshaft axis. Compare the results to this Chapter's Specifications.

18 Repeat the procedure for the remaining pistons and cylinders.

19 If the cylinder walls are badly scuffed or scored, or if they're out-of-round or tapered beyond the limits given in this Chapter's Specifications, have the engine block rebored and honed at an automotive machine shop. If a rebore is done, oversize pistons and rings will be required.

20 Using a precision straightedge and feeler gauge, check the block deck (the surface that mates with the cylinder heads) for distortion (see illustration). If it's distorted beyond the specified limit, it can be resurfaced by an automotive machine shop.

21 If the cylinders are in reasonably good condition and not worn to the outside of the limits, and if the piston-to-cylinder clearances can be maintained properly, then they don't have to be rebored. Honing is all that's necessary (refer to Section 16).

16 Cylinder honing

▶ **Refer to illustrations 16.3a and 16.3b**

1 Prior to engine reassembly, the cylinder bores must be honed so the new piston rings will seat correctly and provide the best possible combustion chamber seal.

➡**Note: If you don't have the tools or don't want to tackle the honing operation, most automotive machine shops will do it for a reasonable fee.**

2 Before honing the cylinders, install the main bearing caps or cap assembly (without bearing inserts) and tighten the bolts to the specified torque.

3 Two types of cylinder hones are commonly available - the flex hone or "bottle brush" type and the more traditional surfacing hone with spring-loaded stones. Both will do the job, but for the less experienced mechanic the "bottle brush" hone will probably be easier to use. You'll also need some kerosene or honing oil, rags and an electric drill motor. The drill motor should be operated at a steady, slow speed. Use a large 1/2-inch drill or a 3/8-inch variable-speed drill. Proceed as follows:

16.3a A "bottle brush" hone is the easiest type of hone to use

a) Mount the hone in the drill motor, compress the stones and slip it into the first cylinder (see illustration).

✳✳ WARNING:

Be sure to wear safety goggles or a face shield!

b) Lubricate the cylinder with plenty of honing oil, turn on the drill and move the hone up-and-down in the cylinder at a pace that will produce a fine crosshatch pattern on the cylinder walls. Ideally, the crosshatch lines should intersect at approximately a 60-degree angle (see illustration). Be sure to use plenty of lubricant and don't take off any more material than is absolutely necessary to produce the desired finish.

➡**Note: Piston ring manufacturers may specify a smaller crosshatch angle than the traditional 60-degrees - read and follow any instructions included with the new rings.**

c) Don't withdraw the hone from the cylinder while it's running. Instead, shut off the drill and continue moving the hone up-and-down in the cylinder until it comes to a complete stop, then compress the stones and withdraw the hone. If you're using a "bottle brush" type hone, stop the drill motor, then turn the chuck in the normal direction of rotation while withdrawing the hone from the cylinder.

d) Wipe the oil out of the cylinder and repeat the procedure for the remaining cylinders.

4   After the honing job is complete, chamfer the top edges of the cylinder bores with a small file so the rings won't catch when the pistons are installed. Be very careful not to nick the cylinder walls with the end of the file.

5   The entire engine block must be washed again very thoroughly with warm, soapy water to remove all traces of the abrasive grit pro-

16.3b The cylinder hone should leave a smooth, crosshatch pattern with the lines intersecting at approximately a 60-degree angle

duced during the honing operation.

➡**Note: The bores can be considered clean when a lint-free white cloth - dampened with clean engine oil - used to wipe them out doesn't pick up any more honing residue, which will show up as gray areas on the cloth. Be sure to run a brush through all oil holes and galleries and flush them with running water.**

6   After rinsing, dry the block and apply a coat of light rust preventive oil to all machined surfaces. Wrap the block in a plastic trash bag to keep it clean and set it aside until reassembly.

17 Pistons/connecting rods - inspection

▶ **Refer to illustrations 17.4a, 17.4b, 17.10 and 17.11**

1   Before the inspection process can be carried out, the piston/connecting rod assemblies must be cleaned and the original piston rings removed from the pistons.

➡**Note: Always use new piston rings when the engine is reassembled.**

2   Using a piston ring installation tool, carefully remove the rings

from the pistons. Be careful not to nick or gouge the pistons in the process.

3   Scrape all traces of carbon from the top of the piston. A handheld wire brush or a piece of fine emery cloth can be used once the majority of the deposits have been scraped away. Do not, under any circumstances, use a wire brush mounted in a drill motor to remove deposits from the pistons. The piston material is soft and may be eroded away by the wire brush.

17.4a The piston ring grooves can be cleaned with a special tool, as shown here . . .

17.4b . . . or a section of a broken ring

17.10 Check the ring groove clearance with a feeler gauge at several points around the groove

4   Use a piston ring groove-cleaning tool to remove carbon deposits from the ring grooves. If a tool isn't available, a piece broken off the old ring will do the job. Be very careful to remove only the carbon deposits - don't remove any metal and do not nick or scratch the sides of the ring grooves (see illustrations).

5   Once the deposits have been removed, clean the piston/rod assemblies with solvent and dry them with compressed air (if available). Make sure the oil return holes in the back sides of the ring grooves and the oil hole in the lower end of each rod are clear.

6   If the pistons and cylinder walls aren't damaged or worn excessively, and if the engine block is not rebored, new pistons won't be necessary. Normal piston wear appears as even vertical wear on the piston thrust surfaces and slight looseness of the top ring in its groove. New piston rings, however, should always be used when an engine is rebuilt.

7   Carefully inspect each piston for cracks around the skirt, at the pin bosses and at the ring lands.

8   Look for scoring and scuffing on the thrust faces of the skirt, holes in the piston crown and burned areas at the edge of the crown. If the skirt is scored or scuffed, the engine may have been suffering from overheating and/or abnormal combustion, which caused excessively high operating temperatures. The cooling and lubrication systems should be checked thoroughly. A hole in the piston crown is an indication that abnormal combustion (preignition) was occurring. Burned areas at the edge of the piston crown are usually evidence of spark knock (detonation). If any of the above problems exist, the causes must be corrected or the damage will occur again. The causes may include intake air leaks, incorrect air/fuel mixture, incorrect ignition timing and EGR system malfunctions.

9   Corrosion of the piston, in the form of small pits, indicates that coolant is leaking into the combustion chamber and/or the crankcase. Again, the cause must be corrected or the problem may persist in the rebuilt engine.

10 Measure the piston ring groove clearance by laying a new piston ring in each ring groove and slipping a feeler gauge in beside it (see illustration). Check the clearance at three or four locations around each groove. Be sure to use the correct ring for each groove - they are different. If the clearance is greater than that listed in this Chapter's Specifications, new pistons will have to be used.

11 Check the piston-to-bore clearance by measuring the bore (see Section 15) and the piston diameter. Make sure the pistons and bores

17.11 Measure the piston diameter at a 90-degree angle to the piston pin, at the specified distance from the top (2003 and earlier) or bottom (2004 and later) of the piston.

are correctly matched. Measure the piston across the skirt, at a 90-degree angle to the piston pin at the specified distance from the top or bottom of the piston (see illustration). Subtract the piston diameter from the bore diameter to obtain the clearance. If it's greater than specified, the block will have to be rebored and new pistons and rings installed.

12 Check the piston-to-rod clearance by twisting the piston and rod in opposite directions. Any noticeable play indicates excessive wear, which must be corrected.

13 If the pistons must be removed from the connecting rods for any reason, the rods should be taken to an automotive machine shop, to be checked for bend and twist, since automotive machine shops have special equipment for this purpose.

14 Check the connecting rods for cracks and other damage. Temporarily remove the rod caps, lift out the old bearing inserts, wipe the rod and cap bearing surfaces clean and inspect them for nicks, gouges and scratches. After checking the rods, replace the old bearings, slip the caps into place and tighten the nuts finger tight.

→Note: If the engine is being rebuilt because of a connecting rod knock, be sure to install new rods.

18 Crankshaft - inspection

▶ Refer to illustration 18.5

1   Clean the crankshaft with solvent and dry it with compressed air (if available). Be sure to clean the oil holes with a stiff brush and flush them with solvent.

2   Check the main and connecting rod bearing journals for uneven wear, scoring, pits and cracks.

3   Remove all burrs from the crankshaft oil holes with a stone, file or scraper.

4   Check the rest of the crankshaft for cracks and other damage. It should be magnafluxed to reveal hidden cracks - an automotive machine shop will handle the procedure.

5   Using a micrometer, measure the diameter of the main and connecting rod journals and compare the results to this Chapter's Specifications (see illustration). By measuring the diameter at a number of points around each journal's circumference, you'll be able to determine whether or not the journal is out-of-round. Take the measurement at

18.5 Measure the diameter of each crankshaft journal at several points to detect taper and out-of-round conditions

each end of the journal, near the crank throws, to determine if the journal is tapered. Crankshaft runout should be checked also, but large V-blocks and a dial indicator are needed to do it correctly. If you don't have the equipment, have a machine shop check the runout.

6   If the crankshaft journals are damaged, tapered, out-of-round or worn beyond the limits given in the Specifications, have the crankshaft reground by an automotive machine shop. Be sure to use the correct size bearing inserts if the crankshaft is reconditioned.

7   Check the oil seal journals at each end of the crankshaft for wear and damage. If the seal has worn a groove in the journal, or if it's nicked or scratched, the new seal may leak when the engine is reassembled. In some cases, an automotive machine shop may be able to repair the journal by pressing on a thin sleeve. If repair isn't feasible, a new or different crankshaft should be installed.

8   Refer to Section 19 and examine the main and rod bearing inserts.

19 Main and connecting rod bearings - inspection and selection

INSPECTION

▶ **Refer to illustration 19.1**

1   Even though the main and connecting rod bearings should be replaced with new ones during the engine overhaul, the old bearings should be retained for close examination, as they may reveal valuable information about the condition of the engine (see illustration).

2   Bearing failure occurs because of lack of lubrication, the presence of dirt or other foreign particles, overloading the engine and corrosion. Regardless of the cause of bearing failure, it must be corrected before the engine is reassembled to prevent it from happening again.

3   When examining the bearings, remove them from the engine block, the main bearing caps, the connecting rods and the rod caps and lay them out on a clean surface in the same general position as their location in the engine. This will enable you to match any bearing problems with the corresponding crankshaft journal.

4   Dirt and other foreign particles get into the engine in a variety of ways. It may be left in the engine during assembly, or it may pass through filters or the PCV system. It may get into the oil, and from there into the bearings. Metal chips from machining operations and normal engine wear are often present. Abrasives are sometimes left in engine components after reconditioning, especially when parts are not thoroughly cleaned using the proper cleaning methods. Whatever the source, these foreign objects often end up embedded in the soft bearing material and are easily recognized. Large particles will not embed in the bearing and will score or gouge the bearing and journal. The best prevention for this cause of bearing failure is to clean all parts thoroughly and keep everything spotlessly clean during engine assembly. Frequent and regular engine oil and filter changes are also recommended.

5   Lack of lubrication (or lubrication breakdown) has a number of interrelated causes. Excessive heat (which thins the oil), overloading (which squeezes the oil from the bearing face) and oil leakage or throw off (from excessive bearing clearances, worn oil pump or high engine speeds) all contribute to lubrication breakdown. Blocked oil passages, which usually are the result of misaligned oil holes in a bearing shell, will also oil starve a bearing and destroy it. When lack of lubrication is the cause of bearing failure, the bearing material is wiped or extruded from the steel backing of the bearing. Temperatures may increase to the point where the steel backing turns blue from overheating.

6   Driving habits can have a definite effect on bearing life. Low speed operation in too high a gear (lugging the engine) puts very high loads on bearings, which tends to squeeze out the oil film. These loads cause the bearings to flex, which produces fine cracks in the bearing face (fatigue failure). Eventually the bearing material will loosen in pieces and tear away from the steel backing. Short trip driving leads to

corrosion of bearings because insufficient engine heat is produced to drive off the condensed water and corrosive gases. These products collect in the engine oil, forming acid and sludge. As the oil is carried to the engine bearings, the acid attacks and corrodes the bearing material.

7   Incorrect bearing installation during engine assembly will lead to bearing failure as well. Tight-fitting bearings leave insufficient bearing oil clearance and will result in oil starvation. Dirt or foreign particles trapped behind a bearing insert result in high spots on the bearing which lead to failure.

SELECTION

▶ **Refer to illustrations 19.10 and 19.11**

8   If the original bearings are worn or damaged, or if the oil clearances are incorrect (see Sections 22 or 24), the following procedures should be used to select the correct new bearings for engine reassembly. However, if the crankshaft has been reground, new undersize bearings must be installed - the following procedure should not be used if undersize bearings are required! The automotive machine shop that reconditions the crankshaft will provide or help you select the correct size bearings. Regardless of how the bearing sizes are determined, use the oil clearance, measured with Plastigage, as a guide to ensure the bearings are the right size.

19.1 When inspecting the main and connecting rod bearings, look for these problems

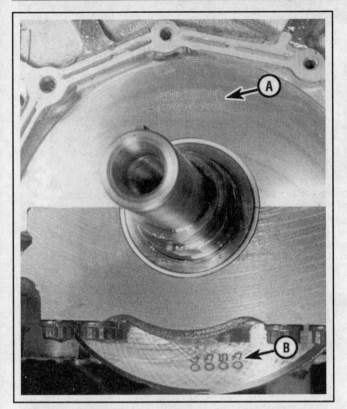

19.10 Grade numbers are located on the front of the block above the crankshaft (A); and crankshaft journal grades are on the side of the first counterweight (B)

Main bearings

9   If you need to use a STANDARD size main bearing, install one that has the same number as the original bearing (see illustration 19.10 for the bearing number locations). There are five sizes of main bearings.

10   The block numbers are on the front of the block, just above the first main bearing, and the crankshaft numbers are on the first counter-

Number 1 and 4 Bearings (2003 and earlier) or 1 and 2 (2004 through 2006)

	Total number				" ": Number mark
Cylinder block (A) + Crankshaft (B)	0 – 5	6 – 11	12 – 17	18 – 23	24 – 28
Use bearing	"3"	"4"	"5"	"6"	"7"

EXAMPLE: Cylinder block "06" (A)
 + Crankshaft "08" (B)
 = Total number 14 (Use bearing "5")

Number 2 and 3 Bearings (2003 and earlier) or 3 and 4 (2004 through 2006)

	Total number				" ": Number mark
Cylinder block (A) + Crankshaft (B)	0 – 5	6 – 11	12 – 17	18 – 23	24 – 28
Use bearing	"1"	"2"	"3"	"4"	"5"

EXAMPLE: Cylinder block "06" (A)
 + Crankshaft "08" (B)
 = Total number 14 (Use bearing "3")

19.11 Select the proper bearings based on this chart - add the crank and block numbers and select the bearing size listed underneath

weight (see illustration).

11   Use the accompanying chart to determine the correct bearings for each journal on the engine (see illustration).

Connecting rod bearings

12   If you need to use a STANDARD size rod bearing, install one that has the same number as the number stamped into the connecting rod cap (see illustration 13.5).

All bearings

13   Remember, the oil clearance is the final judge when selecting new bearing sizes. If you have any questions or are unsure which bearings to use, get help from an auto parts store or a dealer parts or service department.

20 Engine overhaul - reassembly sequence

1   Before beginning engine reassembly, make sure you have all the necessary new parts, gaskets and seals as well as the following items on hand:

Common hand tools
A 1/2-inch drive torque wrench
Piston ring installation tool
Piston ring compressor
Short lengths of rubber or plastic hose to fit over connecting
    rod bolts
Plastigage
Feeler gauges
A fine-tooth file
New engine oil
Engine assembly lube or moly-base grease
Gasket sealer
Thread locking compound

2   In order to save time and avoid problems, engine reassembly must be done in the following general order:

Piston rings
Crankshaft and main bearings
Piston/connecting rod assemblies
Rear main oil seal/retainer
Oil pump
Oil pan
Cylinder heads
Camshafts and lifters
Timing belt or chains and sprockets
Timing belt covers
Valve covers
Intake and exhaust manifolds
Flywheel/driveplate

ENGINE BEARING ANALYSIS

Debris

Babbitt bearing embedded with debris from machinings

Microscopic detail of debris

Microscopic detail of gouges

Overplated copper alloy bearing gouged by cast iron debris

Aluminum bearing embedded with glass beads

Microscopic detail of glass beads

Damaged lining caused by dirt left on the bearing back

Misassembly

Result of a lower half assembled as an upper - blocking the oil flow

Excessive oil clearance is indicated by a short contact arc

Polished and oil-stained backs are a result of a poor fit in the housing bore

Result of a wrong, reversed, or shifted cap

Overloading

Damage from excessive idling which resulted in an oil film unable to support the load imposed

Damaged upper connecting rod bearings caused by engine lugging; the lower main bearings (not shown) were similarly affected

The damage shown in these upper and lower connecting rod bearings was caused by engine operation at a higher-than-rated speed under load

Misalignment

A poorly finished crankshaft caused the equally spaced scoring shown

A tapered housing bore caused the damage along one edge of this pair

A warped crankshaft caused this pattern of severe wear in the center, diminishing toward the ends

A bent connecting rod led to the damage in the "V" pattern

Lubrication

Corrosion

Microscopic detail of corrosion

Corrosion is an acid attack on the bearing lining generally caused by inadequate maintenance, extremely hot or cold operation, or inferior oils or fuels

Result of dry start: The bearings on the left, farthest from the oil pump, show more damage

Microscopic detail of cavitation

Example of cavitation - a surface erosion caused by pressure changes in the oil film

Result of a low oil supply or oil starvation

Severe wear as a result of inadequate oil clearance

Damage from excessive thrust or insufficient axial clearance

Bearing affected by oil dilution caused by excessive blow-by or a rich mixture

21 Piston rings - installation

♦ **Refer to illustrations 21.3, 21.4, 21.9a, 21.9b and 21.12**

1   Before installing the new piston rings, the ring end gaps must be checked. It's assumed that the piston ring groove clearance has been checked and verified correct (see Section 17).

2   Lay out the piston/connecting rod assemblies and the new ring sets so the ring sets will be matched with the same piston and cylinder during the end gap measurement and engine assembly.

3   Insert the top (number one) ring into the first cylinder and square it up with the cylinder walls by pushing it in with the top of the piston (see illustration). The ring should be near the bottom of the cylinder, at the lower limit of ring travel.

4   To measure the end gap, slip feeler gauges between the ends of the ring until a gauge equal to the gap width is found (see illustration). The feeler gauge should slide between the ring ends with a slight amount of drag. Compare the measurement to that found in this Chapter's Specifications. If the gap is larger or smaller than specified, double-check to make sure you have the correct rings before proceeding.

5   If the gap is too small, replace the rings - DO NOT file the ends to increase the clearance.

6   Excess end gap isn't critical unless it's greater than 0.040-inch.

Again, double-check to make sure you have the correct rings for your engine.

7   Repeat the procedure for each ring that will be installed in the first cylinder and for each ring in the remaining cylinders. Remember to keep rings, pistons and cylinders matched up.

8   Once the ring end gaps have been checked/corrected, the rings can be installed on the pistons.

9   The oil control ring (lowest one on the piston) is usually installed first. It's composed of three separate components. Slip the spacer/expander into the groove (see illustration). If an anti-rotation tang is used, make sure it's inserted into the drilled hole in the ring groove. Refer to illustration 24.5 for the orientation of the expander gap to the piston. Next, install the lower side rail. Don't use a piston ring installation tool on the oil ring side rails, as they may be damaged. Instead, place one end of the side rail into the groove between the spacer/expander and the ring land, hold it firmly in place and slide a finger around the piston while pushing the rail into the groove (see illustration). Next, install the upper side rail in the same manner.

10   After the three oil ring components have been installed, check to make sure that both the upper and lower side rails can be turned smoothly in the ring groove.

21.3 When checking piston ring end gap, the ring must be square in the cylinder bore (this is done by pushing the ring down with the top of a piston as shown)

21.4 With the ring square in the cylinder, measure the end gap with a feeler gauge

21.9a Install the spacer/expander in the oil control ring groove

21.9b DO NOT use a piston ring installation tool when installing the oil ring side rails

21.12 Install the compression rings with a ring expander - the mark must face up (top rings are marked 1R, G1 or T, second rings are marked 2R, G2 or T2) - 2006 and earlier models

11 The number two (middle) ring is installed next. It's usually stamped with a mark, which must face up, toward the top of the piston.

➡ **Note: Always follow the instructions printed on the ring package or box - different manufacturers may require different approaches. Do not mix up the top and middle rings, as they have different cross-sections.**

12 Use a piston ring installation tool and make sure the ring's identification mark is facing the top of the piston, then slip the ring into the middle groove on the piston (see illustration). Don't expand the ring any more than necessary to slide it over the piston.

13 Install the number one (top) ring in the same manner. Make sure the mark is facing up. Be careful not to confuse the number one and number two rings.

14 Repeat the procedure for the remaining pistons and rings.

22 Crankshaft - installation and main bearing oil clearance check

▶ **Refer to illustrations 22.10, 22.12a, 22.12b, 22.12c, 22.14 and 22.20**

1 Crankshaft installation is the first major step in engine reassembly. It's assumed at this point that the engine block and crankshaft have been cleaned, inspected and repaired or reconditioned.

2 Position the engine with the bottom facing up.

3 Remove the main bearing cap bolts and lift out the caps or cap assembly. Lay the caps out in the proper order.

4 If they're still in place, remove the old bearing inserts from the block and the main bearing caps. Wipe the main bearing surfaces of the block and caps with a clean, lint free cloth. They must be kept spotlessly clean!

MAIN BEARING OIL CLEARANCE CHECK

5 Clean the back sides of the new main bearing inserts and lay the bearing half with the oil groove in each main bearing saddle in the block. Lay the other bearing half from each bearing set in the corresponding main bearing cap. Make sure the tab on each bearing insert fits into the recess in the block or cap. Also, the oil holes in the block must line up with the oil holes in the bearing insert.

❊❊ **CAUTION:**

Do not hammer the bearings into place and don't nick or gouge the bearing faces. No lubrication should be used at this time.

6 The thrust bearings (washers) must be installed in the number two cap and saddle. Install the thrust bearings with the oil grooves facing out.

7 Clean the faces of the bearings in the block and the crankshaft main bearing journals with a clean, lint free cloth. Check or clean the oil holes in the crankshaft, as any dirt here can go only one way - straight through the new bearings.

8 Once you're certain the crankshaft is clean, carefully lay it in position in the main bearings.

9 Before the crankshaft can be permanently installed, the main bearing oil clearance must be checked.

10 Trim several pieces of the appropriate size Plastigage (they must be slightly shorter than the width of the main bearings) and place one piece on each crankshaft main bearing journal, parallel with the journal axis (see illustration).

11 Clean the faces of the bearings in the caps and install the caps in their respective positions (don't mix them up) with the arrows pointing toward the front of the engine. Don't disturb the Plastigage. Apply a light coat of oil to the bolt threads and the under-sides of the bolt heads, then install them.

12 Following the recommended sequence (see illustration), tighten the main bearing cap bolts, in three steps, to the torque listed in this Chapter's Specifications. Don't rotate the crankshaft at any time during this operation!

➡ **Note: After reaching the specified torque on all of the bolts, tighten each bolt in sequence an additional 90-degrees (except the six-point bolts) (see illustration).**

22.10 Lay the Plastigage strips on the main bearing journals, parallel to the crankshaft centerline

22.12a Main bearing cap bolt tightening sequence

22.12b After reaching the specified torque, mark the front side of each bolt with paint as shown here, plus a paint mark on the socket, then turn the bolts an additional 1/4-turn - the paint marks should now be 90-degrees from their original position

The side bolts are torqued after the main cap bolts (see illustration).

13 Remove the bolts and carefully lift off the main bearing caps or cap assembly. Keep them in order. Don't disturb the Plastigage or rotate the crankshaft. If any of the main bearing caps are difficult to remove, tap them gently from side-to-side with a soft-face hammer to loosen them.

14 Compare the width of the crushed Plastigage on each journal to the scale printed on the Plastigage envelope to obtain the main bearing oil clearance (see illustration). Check the Specifications to make sure it's correct.

15 If the clearance is not as specified, the bearing inserts may be the wrong size (which means different ones will be required - see Section 19). Before deciding that different inserts are needed, make sure that no dirt or oil was between the bearing inserts and the caps or block when the clearance was measured. If the Plastigage is noticeably wider at one end than the other, the journal may be tapered (see Section 18).

16 Carefully scrape all traces of the Plastigage material off the main bearing journals and/or the bearing faces. Don't nick or scratch the bearing faces.

FINAL CRANKSHAFT INSTALLATION

17 Carefully lift the crankshaft out of the engine. Clean the bearing faces in the block, then apply a thin, uniform layer of clean moly-base grease or engine assembly lube to each of the bearing surfaces. Coat the thrust washers as well.

18 Lubricate the crankshaft surfaces that contact the oil seals with multi-purpose grease or clean engine oil.

19 Make sure the crankshaft journals are clean, then lay the crankshaft back in place in the block. Clean the faces of the bearings in the caps or cap assembly, then apply lubricant to them. Install the caps in their respective positions with the arrows pointing toward the front of the engine.

➡Note: Be sure to install the thrust washers on the number 2 main journal.

The upper (block side) thrust washers can be rotated into position around the crank with the crank in the block, with the thrust washer grooves facing OUT. The tanged lower thrust washers should be placed on the caps with their grooves OUT and the tangs fitting into the cap slots.

20 Apply a light coat of oil to the bolt threads and the under sides of the bolt heads, then install them. Tighten all main bearing cap bolts to the torque listed in this Chapter's Specifications, following the recommended sequence.

➡Note: Install the inner (closest to the crankshaft) bolts first, tap the caps down lightly with a plastic-faced hammer, then install the outer bolts and begin the torque sequence. The side bolts are not installed and tightened until all of the inner bolts have been tightened to the proper torque (see illustrations 22.12a, 22.12b and 22.12c). Be sure to use new sealing washers on the hex-head (side) bolts (see illustration).

21 Rotate the crankshaft a number of times by hand to check for any obvious binding.

22 Check the crankshaft endplay with a feeler gauge or a dial indicator as described in Section 14. The endplay should be correct if the crankshaft thrust faces aren't worn or damaged and new thrust washers have been installed.

23 Install a new rear main oil seal, then bolt the retainer to the block (see Section 23).

22.12c Main bearing cap side bolt tightening sequence - tighten the side bolts after tightening the cap bolts

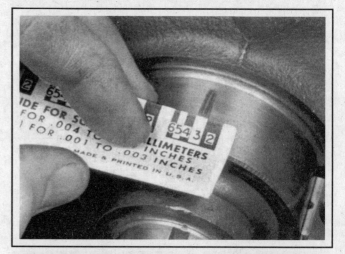

22.14 Compare the width of the crushed Plastigage to the scale on the envelope to determine the main bearing oil clearance (always take the measurement at the widest point of the Plastigage) - be sure to use the correct scale; standard and metric scales are included

22.20 Hex-headed bolts secure the sides of the main caps - when final-assembling this engine use new sealing washers on these bolts

23 Rear main oil seal installation

▶ **Refer to illustrations 23.3 and 23.5**

1   The crankshaft must be installed first and the main bearing caps or cap assembly bolted in place, then the new seal should be installed in the retainer and the retainer bolted to the block.

2   Check the seal contact surface on the crankshaft very carefully for scratches and nicks that could damage the new seal lip and cause oil leaks. If the crankshaft is damaged, the only alternative is a new or different crankshaft.

3   The old seal can be removed from the retainer by driving it out from the back side with a hammer and punch (see illustration). Be sure to note how far it's recessed into the bore before removing it; the new seal will have to be recessed an equal amount. Be very careful not to scratch or otherwise damage the bore in the retainer or oil leaks could develop.

4   Make sure the retainer is clean, then apply a thin coat of engine oil to the outer edge of the new seal. The seal must be pressed squarely into the bore, so hammering it into place isn't recommended. If you don't have access to a press, sandwich the housing and seal between two smooth pieces of wood and press the seal into place with the jaws of a large vise. The pieces of wood must be thick enough to distribute the force evenly around the entire circumference of the seal. Work slowly and make sure the seal enters the bore squarely.

5   As a last resort, the seal can be tapped into the retainer with a hammer. Use a block of wood to distribute the force evenly and make sure the seal is driven in squarely (see illustration).

6   The seal lips must be lubricated with clean engine oil or multi-purpose grease before the seal/retainer is slipped over the crankshaft and bolted to the block. No gasket is required, instead apply a 3/32-inch wide bead of anaerobic sealant to the retainer-to-block surface.

7   Tighten the bolts a little at a time to the torque listed in Chapter 2A or 2B Specifications.

23.3 After removing the retainer from the block, support it on a couple of wood blocks and drive out the old seal with a punch and hammer

23.5 Drive the new seal into the retainer with a wood block or a section of pipe, if you have one large enough - make sure you don't cock the seal in the retainer bore

24 Pistons/connecting rods - installation and rod bearing oil clearance check

▶ **Refer to illustrations 24.3, 24.5, 24.9, 24.11, 24.13, 24.15 and 24.17**

1   Before installing the piston/connecting rod assemblies, the cylinder walls must be perfectly clean, the top edge of each cylinder must be chamfered, and the crankshaft must be in place.

2   Remove the cap from the end of the number one connecting rod (refer to the marks made during removal). Remove the original bearing inserts and wipe the bearing surfaces of the connecting rod and cap with a clean, lint-free cloth. They must be kept spotlessly clean.

CONNECTING ROD BEARING OIL CLEARANCE CHECK

3   Clean the back side of the new upper bearing insert, then lay it in place in the connecting rod. Make sure the tab on the bearing fits into the recess in the rod so the oil holes line up (see illustration). Don't hammer the bearing insert into place and be very careful not to nick or gouge the bearing face. Don't lubricate the bearing at this time.

4   Clean the back side of the other bearing insert and install it in

24.3 On all rods, align the bearing tang with the notch in the rod

the rod cap. Again, make sure the tab on the bearing fits into the recess in the cap, and don't apply any lubricant. It's critically important that the mating surfaces of the bearing and connecting rod are perfectly clean and oil free when they're assembled.

GLOSSARY

B

Backlash - The amount of play between two parts. Usually refers to how much one gear can be moved back and forth without moving the gear with which it's meshed.

Bearing Caps - The caps held in place by nuts or bolts which, in turn, hold the bearing surface. This space is for lubricating oil to enter.

Bearing clearance - The amount of space left between shaft and bearing surface. This space is for lubricating oil to enter.

Bearing crush - The additional height which is purposely manufactured into each bearing half to ensure complete contact of the bearing back with the housing bore when the engine is assembled.

Bearing knock - The noise created by movement of a part in a loose or worn bearing.

Blueprinting - Dismantling an engine and reassembling it to EXACT specifications.

Bore - An engine cylinder, or any cylindrical hole; also used to describe the process of enlarging or accurately refinishing a hole with a cutting tool, as to bore an engine cylinder. The bore size is the diameter of the hole.

Boring - Renewing the cylinders by cutting them out to a specified size. A boring bar is used to make the cut.

Bottom end - A term which refers collectively to the engine block, crankshaft, main bearings and the big ends of the connecting rods.

Break-in - The period of operation between installation of new or rebuilt parts and time in which parts are worn to the correct fit. Driving at reduced and varying speed for a specified mileage to permit parts to wear to the correct fit.

Bushing - A one-piece sleeve placed in a bore to serve as a bearing surface for shaft, piston pin, etc. Usually replaceable.

C

Camshaft - The shaft in the engine, on which a series of lobes are located for operating the valve mechanisms. The camshaft is driven by gears or sprockets and a timing chain. Usually referred to simply as the cam.

Carbon - Hard, or soft, black deposits found in combustion chamber, on plugs, under rings, on and under valve heads.

Cast iron - An alloy of iron and more than two percent carbon, used for engine blocks and heads because it's relatively inexpensive and easy to mold into complex shapes.

Chamfer - To bevel across (or a bevel on) the sharp edge of an object.

Chase - To repair damaged threads with a tap or die.

Combustion chamber - The space between the piston and the cylinder head, with the piston at top dead center, in which air-fuel mixture is burned.

Compression ratio - The relationship between cylinder volume (clearance volume) when the piston is at top dead center and cylinder volume when the piston is at bottom dead center.

Connecting rod - The rod that connects the crank on the crankshaft with the piston. Sometimes called a con rod.

Connecting rod cap - The part of the connecting rod assembly that attaches the rod to the crankpin.

Core plug - Soft metal plug used to plug the casting holes for the coolant passages in the block.

Crankcase - The lower part of the engine in which the crankshaft rotates; includes the lower section of the cylinder block and the oil pan.

Crank kit - A reground or reconditioned crankshaft and new main and connecting rod bearings.

Crankpin - The part of a crankshaft to which a connecting rod is attached.

Crankshaft - The main rotating member, or shaft, running the length of the crankcase, with offset throws to which the connecting rods are attached; changes the reciprocating motion of the pistons into rotating motion.

Cylinder sleeve - A replaceable sleeve, or liner, pressed into the cylinder block to form the cylinder bore.

D

Deburring - Removing the burrs (rough edges or areas) from a bearing.

Deglazer - A tool, rotated by an electric motor, used to remove glaze from cylinder walls so a new set of rings will seat.

E

Endplay - The amount of lengthwise movement between two parts. As applied to a crankshaft, the distance that the crankshaft can move forward and back in the cylinder block.

F

Face - A machinist's term that refers to removing metal from the end of a shaft or the face of a larger part, such as a flywheel.

Fatigue - A breakdown of material through a large number of loading and unloading cycles. The first signs are cracks followed shortly by breaks.

Feeler gauge - A thin strip of hardened steel, ground to an exact thickness, used to check clearances between parts.

Free height - The unloaded length or height of a spring.

Freeplay - The looseness in a linkage, or an assembly of parts, between the initial application of force and actual movement. Usually perceived as slop or slight delay.

Freeze plug - See Core plug.

G

Gallery - A large passage in the block that forms a reservoir for engine oil pressure.

Glaze - The very smooth, glassy finish that develops on cylinder walls while an engine is in service.

H

Heli-Coil - A rethreading device used when threads are worn or damaged. The device is installed in a retapped hole to reduce the thread size to the original size.

I

Installed height - The spring's measured length or height, as installed on the cylinder head. Installed height is measured from the spring seat to the underside of the spring retainer.

J

Journal - The surface of a rotating shaft which turns in a bearing.

K

Keeper - The split lock that holds the valve spring retainer in position on the valve stem.

Key - A small piece of metal inserted into matching grooves machined into two parts fitted together - such as a gear pressed onto a shaft - which prevents slippage between the two parts.

Knock - The heavy metallic engine sound, produced in the combustion chamber as a result of abnormal combustion - usually detonation. Knock is usually caused by a loose or worn bearing. Also referred to as detonation, pinging and spark knock. Connecting rod or main bearing knocks are created by too much oil clearance or insufficient lubrication.

L

Lands - The portions of metal between the piston ring grooves.

Lapping the valves - Grinding a valve face and its seat together with lapping compound.

Lash - The amount of free motion in a gear train, between gears, or in a mechanical assembly, that occurs before movement can begin. Usually refers to the lash in a valve train.

Lifter - The part that rides against the cam to transfer motion to the rest of the valve train.

M

Machining - The process of using a machine to remove metal from a metal part.

Main bearings - The plain, or babbitt, bearings that support the crankshaft.

Main bearing caps - The cast iron caps, bolted to the bottom of the block, that support the main bearings.

O

O.D. - Outside diameter.

Oil gallery - A pipe or drilled passageway in the engine used to carry engine oil from one area to another.

Oil ring - The lower ring, or rings, of a piston; designed to prevent excessive amounts of oil from working up the cylinder walls and into the combustion chamber. Also called an oil-control ring.

Oil seal - A seal which keeps oil from leaking out of a compartment. Usually refers to a dynamic seal around a rotating shaft or other moving part.

O-ring - A type of sealing ring made of a special rubberlike material; in use, the O-ring is compressed into a groove to provide the sealing action.

Overhaul - To completely disassemble a unit, clean and inspect all parts, reassemble it with the original or new parts and make all adjustments necessary for proper operation.

P

Pilot bearing - A small bearing installed in the center of the flywheel (or the rear end of the crankshaft) to support the front end of the input shaft of the transmission.

Pip mark - A little dot or indentation which indicates the top side of a compression ring.

Piston - The cylindrical part, attached to the connecting rod, that moves up and down in the cylinder as the crankshaft rotates. When the fuel charge is fired, the piston transfers the force of the explosion to the connecting rod, then to the crankshaft.

Piston pin (or wrist pin) - The cylindrical and usually hollow steel pin that passes through the piston. The piston pin fastens the piston to the upper end of the connecting rod.

Piston ring - The split ring fitted to the groove in a piston. The ring contacts the sides of the ring groove and also rubs against the cylinder wall, thus sealing space between piston and wall. There are two types of rings: Compression rings seal the compression pressure in the combustion chamber; oil rings scrape excessive oil off the cylinder wall.

Piston ring groove - The slots or grooves cut in piston heads to hold piston rings in position.

Piston skirt - The portion of the piston below the rings and the piston pin hole.

Plastigage - A thin strip of plastic thread, available in different sizes, used for measuring clearances. For example, a strip of plastigage is laid across a bearing journal and mashed as parts are assembled. Then parts are disassembled and the width of the strip is measured to determine clearance between journal and bearing. Commonly used to measure crankshaft main-bearing and connecting rod bearing clearances.

Press-fit - A tight fit between two parts that requires pressure to force the parts together. Also referred to as drive, or force, fit.

Prussian blue - A blue pigment; in solution, useful in determining the area of contact between two surfaces. Prussian blue is commonly used to determine the width and location of the contact area between the valve face and the valve seat.

R

Race (bearing) - The inner or outer ring that provides a contact surface for balls or rollers in bearing.

Ream - To size, enlarge or smooth a hole by using a round cutting tool with fluted edges.

Ring job - The process of reconditioning the cylinders and installing new rings.

Runout - Wobble. The amount a shaft rotates out-of-true.

S

Saddle - The upper main bearing seat.

Scored - Scratched or grooved, as a cylinder wall may be scored by abrasive particles moved up and down by the piston rings.

Scuffing - A type of wear in which there's a transfer of material between parts moving against each other; shows up as pits or grooves in the mating surfaces.

Seat - The surface upon which another part rests or seats. For example, the valve seat is the matched surface upon which the valve face rests. Also used to refer to wearing into a good fit; for example, piston rings seat after a few miles of driving.

Short block - An engine block complete with crankshaft and piston and, usually, camshaft assemblies.

Static balance - The balance of an object while it's stationary.

Step - The wear on the lower portion of a ring land caused by excessive side and back-clearance. The height of the step indicates the ring's extra side clearance and the length of the step projecting from the back wall of the groove represents the ring's back clearance.

Stroke - The distance the piston moves when traveling from top dead center to bottom dead center, or from bottom dead center to top dead center.

Stud - A metal rod with threads on both ends.

T

Tang - A lip on the end of a plain bearing used to align the bearing during assembly.

Tap - To cut threads in a hole. Also refers to the fluted tool used to cut threads.

Taper - A gradual reduction in the width of a shaft or hole; in an engine cylinder, taper usually takes the form of uneven wear, more pronounced at the top than at the bottom.

Throws - The offset portions of the crankshaft to which the connecting rods are affixed.

Thrust bearing - The main bearing that has thrust faces to prevent excessive endplay, or forward and backward movement of the crankshaft.

Thrust washer - A bronze or hardened steel washer placed between two moving parts. The washer prevents longitudinal movement and provides a bearing surface for thrust surfaces of parts.

Tolerance - The amount of variation permitted from an exact size of measurement. Actual amount from smallest acceptable dimension to largest acceptable dimension.

U

Umbrella - An oil deflector placed near the valve tip to throw oil from the valve stem area.

Undercut - A machined groove below the normal surface.

Undersize bearings - Smaller diameter bearings used with re-ground crankshaft journals.

V

Valve grinding - Refacing a valve in a valve-refacing machine.

Valve train - The valve-operating mechanism of an engine; includes all components from the camshaft to the valve.

Vibration damper - A cylindrical weight attached to the front of the crankshaft to minimize torsional vibration (the twist-untwist actions of the crankshaft caused by the cylinder firing impulses). Also called a harmonic balancer.

W

Water jacket - The spaces around the cylinders, between the inner and outer shells of the cylinder block or head, through which coolant circulates.

Web - A supporting structure across a cavity.

Woodruff key - A key with a radiused backside (viewed from the side).

24.5 Stagger the ring end gaps around the piston as shown, before installing the pistons

24.9 Check to be sure both the mark on the piston and the mark on the connecting rod are aligned as shown

5   Position the piston ring gaps at staggered intervals around the piston (see illustration).

6   Use cut-off bolts covered with rubber tubing inserted in place of rod bolts to protect the crankshaft when installing pistons/rods.

7   Lubricate the piston and rings with clean engine oil and attach a piston ring compressor to the piston. Leave the skirt protruding about 1/4-inch to guide the piston into the cylinder. The rings must be compressed until they're flush with the piston.

8   Rotate the crankshaft until the number one connecting rod journal is at BDC (bottom dead center) and apply a coat of engine oil to the cylinder wall.

9   With the dimple on top of the piston (see illustration) facing the front of the engine, gently insert the piston/connecting rod assembly into the number one cylinder bore and rest the bottom edge of the ring compressor on the engine block.

10 Tap the top edge of the ring compressor to make sure it's contacting the block around its entire circumference.

11 Gently tap on the top of the piston with the end of a wooden hammer handle (see illustration) while guiding the end of the connecting rod into place on the crankshaft journal. The piston rings may try to pop out of the ring compressor just before entering the cylinder bore, so keep some downward pressure on the ring compressor. Work slowly, and if any resistance is felt as the piston enters the cylinder, stop immediately. Find out what's hanging up and fix it before proceeding.

24.11 The piston can be driven (gently) into the cylinder bore with the end of a wooden or plastic hammer handle

✳✳ CAUTION:

Do not, for any reason, force the piston into the cylinder - you might break a ring and/or the piston.

12 Once the piston/connecting rod assembly is installed, the connecting rod bearing oil clearance must be checked before the rod cap is permanently bolted in place.

13 Cut a piece of the appropriate-size Plastigage slightly shorter than the width of the connecting rod bearing and lay it in place on the number one connecting rod journal, parallel with the journal axis (see illustration).

14 Clean the connecting rod cap bearing face, remove the protective hoses from the connecting rod bolts and install the rod cap. Make sure the mating mark on the cap is on the same side as the mark on the connecting rod. Check the cap to make sure the front mark is facing the timing belt end of the engine.

15 Apply a light coat of oil to the under sides of the nuts, then install and tighten them to the torque listed in this Chapter's Specifications, working up to it in three steps. Use a thin-wall socket to avoid erroneous torque readings that can result if the socket is wedged between the rod cap and nut. If the socket tends to wedge itself between the nut and the cap, lift up on it slightly until it no longer contacts the cap. Do not rotate the crankshaft at any time during this operation.

➡Note: After reaching the specified torque, tighten each nut an additional 90-degrees (1/4-turn) (see illustration).

16 Remove the nuts and detach the rod cap, being very careful not to disturb the Plastigage.

17 Compare the width of the crushed Plastigage to the scale printed on the Plastigage envelope to obtain the oil clearance (see illustration). Compare it to this Chapter's Specifications to make sure the clearance is correct.

18 If the clearance is not as specified, the bearing inserts may be the wrong size (which means different ones will be required). Before deciding that different inserts are needed, make sure that no dirt or oil was between the bearing inserts and the connecting rod or cap when the clearance was measured. Also, recheck the journal diameter. If the Plastigage was wider at one end than the other, the journal may be tapered (refer to Section 19).

24.13 Lay the Plastigage strips on each rod bearing journal, parallel to the crankshaft centerline

FINAL CONNECTING ROD INSTALLATION

19 Carefully scrape all traces of the Plastigage material off the rod journal and/or bearing face. Be very careful not to scratch the bearing, use your fingernail or the edge of a credit card to remove the Plastigage.

20 Make sure the bearing faces are perfectly clean, then apply a uniform layer of clean moly-base grease or engine assembly lube to both of them. You'll have to push the piston higher into the cylinder to expose the face of the bearing insert in the connecting rod, be sure to slip the protective hoses over the rod bolts first.

21 Slide the connecting rod back into place on the journal, remove the protective hoses from the rod cap bolts, install the rod cap and tighten the nuts to the torque listed in this Chapter's Specifications. Again, work up to the torque in three steps.

22 Repeat the entire procedure for the remaining pistons/connecting rods.

23 The important points to remember are:

a) Keep the back sides of the bearing inserts and the insides of the connecting rods and caps perfectly clean when assembling them.
b) Make sure you have the correct piston/rod assembly for each cylinder.
c) The dimple on the piston must face the front of the engine.
d) Lubricate the cylinder walls with clean oil.
e) Lubricate the bearing faces when installing the rod caps after the oil clearance has been checked.

24 After all the piston/connecting rod assemblies have been properly installed, rotate the crankshaft a number of times by hand to check for

24.15 Install the connecting rod caps with the front mark facing the timing belt end of the engine, and torque to Specifications - for the 90-degree second step, use an angle gauge as shown, or use paint reference marks on the rod nuts/bolts and the socket

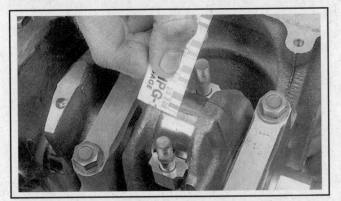

24.17 Measure the width of the crushed Plastigage to determine the rod bearing oil clearance (be sure to use the correct scale - standard and metric scales are included)

any obvious binding.

25 As a final step, the connecting rod endplay must be checked. Refer to Section 13 for this procedure.

26 Compare the measured endplay to this Chapter's Specifications to make sure it's correct. If it was correct before disassembly and the original crankshaft and rods were reinstalled, it should still be right. If new rods or a new crankshaft were installed, the endplay may be inadequate. If so, the rods will have to be removed and taken to an automotive machine shop for resizing.

25 Initial start-up and break-in after overhaul

⁕ WARNING:

Have a fire extinguisher handy when starting the engine for the first time.

1 Once the engine has been installed in the vehicle, double-check the engine oil and coolant levels.

2 With the spark plugs out of the engine and the ignition system and fuel pump disabled (see Section 3), crank the engine until oil pressure registers on the gauge or the light goes out.

3 Install the spark plugs, hook up the plug wires and restore the ignition system and fuel pump functions (see Section 3).

4 Start the engine. It may take a few moments for the fuel system to build up pressure, but the engine should start without a great deal of effort.

5 After the engine starts, it should be allowed to warm up to normal operating temperature. While the engine is warming up, make a thorough check for fuel, oil and coolant leaks.

6 Shut the engine off and recheck the engine oil and coolant levels.

7 Drive the vehicle to an area with minimum traffic, accelerate from 30 to 50 mph, then allow the vehicle to slow to 30 mph with the throttle closed. Repeat the procedure 10 or 12 times. This will load the piston rings and cause them to seat properly against the cylinder walls.

Check again for oil and coolant leaks.

8   Drive the vehicle gently for the first 500 miles (no sustained high speeds) and keep a constant check on the oil level. It is not unusual for an engine to use oil during the break-in period.

9   At approximately 500 to 600 miles, change the oil and filter.

10 For the next few hundred miles, drive the vehicle normally. Do not pamper it or abuse it.

11 After 2000 miles, change the oil and filter again and consider the engine broken in.

Specifications

General

Engine designation	
2003 and earlier models	1MZ-FE
2004 and later models	3MZ-FE
Displacement	
2003 and earlier models	183 cubic inches (3.0 liters)
2004 and later models	202 cubic inches (3.3 liters)
Cylinder compression pressure	
Standard	218 psi
Minimum	145 psi
Oil pressure (engine hot)	
At 3000 rpm	43 to 78 psi
At idle	4.3 psi minimum

Cylinder head

Warpage limits	
Block surface	0.004 inch
Manifold surfaces	0.003 inch

Valves and related components

Valve margin width	
Standard	0.039 inch
Minimum	0.020 inch
Valve stem diameter	
Intake	0.2154 to 0.2159 inch
Exhaust	0.2152 to 0.2157 inch
Valve stem-to-guide clearance	
Intake	
Standard	0.001 to 0.0024 inch
Service limit	0.0031 inch
Exhaust	
Standard	0.0012 to 0.0026 inch
Service limit	0.0039 inch
Valve spring	
Out-of-square limit	0.079 inch
Free length	1.7913 inches
Installed height	1.331 inches
Valve lifter, 2006 and earlier models	
Diameter	1.2191 to 1.2195 inches
Lifter bore diameter	
2003 and earlier	1.2205 to 1.2211 inches
2004 through 2006	1.2208 to 1.2215

Lifter-to-bore clearance
    2003 and earlier
        Standard   0.0009 to 0.0020 inch
        Service limit   0.0028 inch
    2004 through 2006
        Standard   0.0013 to 0.0023 inch
        Service limit   0.0028 inch

Crankshaft and connecting rods

Connecting rod journal
    Diameter   2.0863 to 2.0866 inches
    Taper and out-of-round limits   0.0008 inch
    Bearing oil clearance
        Standard   0.0015 to 0.0025 inch
        Service limit   0.003 inch
Connecting rod side clearance (endplay)
    2006 and earlier models
        Standard   0.0059 to 0.0118 inch
        Service limit   0.0138 inch
    2007 and later models
        Standard   0.006 to 0.015 inch
        Service limit   0.020 inch
Main bearing journal
    Diameter   2.4011 to 2.4016 inches
    Taper and out-of-round limits   0.0008 inch
    Bearing oil clearance
        2006 and earlier models
            Standard
               Numbers 1 and 4   0.0006 to 0.0014 inch
               Numbers 2 and 3   0.0010 to 0.0019 inch
           Service limit
               Numbers 1 and 4   0.0020 inch
               Numbers 2 and 3   0.0024 inch
        2007 and later models
            Standard   0.0010 to 0.0019 inch
           Service limit   0.0020 inch
Crankshaft endplay
    Standard   0.0016 to 0.0095 inch
    Service limit   0.0118 inch
    Thrust washer thickness
        2006 and earlier models   0.0760 to 0.0780 inch
        2007 and later models   0.096 to 0.098 inch

Engine block

Deck warpage limit
    2003 and earlier   0.0028 inch
    2004 and later   0.0020 inch
Cylinder bore diameter
    2003 and earlier
        Standard   3.4449 to 3.4453 inches
        Service limit   3.4457 inches

Engine block (continued)

Cylinder bore diameter (continued)
  2004 through 2006
    Standard   3.6220 to 3.6225 inches
    Service limit   3.6252 inches
  2007 and later
    Standard   3.701 inches
    Service limit   3.709 inches

Pistons and rings

2003 and earlier
  Piston diameter (standard)
    Aisin-made (measured 0.9 inch from
      top of piston)   3.4412 to 3.4416 inches
    Mahle-made (measured 1.6 inch from
      top of piston)   3.4430 to 3.4436 inches
  Piston-to-bore clearance
    Standard
      Aisin-made   0.0033 to 0.0042 inch
      Mahle-made   0.0013 to 0.0023 inch
    Service limit
      Aisin-made   0.0051 inch
      Mahle-made   0.0031 inch
  Piston ring end gap
    No. 1 (top) compression ring
      Standard   0.0098 to 0.0138 inch
      Service limit   0.0374 inch
    No. 2 (middle) compression ring
      Standard   0.0138 to 0.0177 inch
      Service limit   0.0413 inch
    Oil ring
      Standard   0.0059 to 0.0157 inch
      Service limit   0.0394 inch
  Piston ring groove clearance
    No. 1 (top) compression ring   0.0008 to 0.0028 inch
    No. 2 (middle) compression ring   0.0008 to 0.0024 inch
2004 through 2006
  Piston diameter (standard, measured 4.412 inch
    from bottom of piston)   3.6202 to 3.6207 inches
  Piston-to-bore clearance   0.0013 to 0.0023 inch
    Service limit   0.0051 inch
  Piston ring end gap
    No. 1 (top) compression ring
      Standard   0.0118 to 0.0157 inch
      Service limit   0.0374 inch
    No. 2 (middle) compression ring
      Standard   0.0197 to 0.0236 inch
      Service limit   0.0413 inch
    Oil ring
      Standard   0.0059 to 0.0157 inch
      Service limit   0.0394 inch

Piston ring groove clearance
    No. 1 (top) compression ring   0.0012 to 0.0031 inch
    No. 2 (middle) compression ring   0.0008 to 0.0024 inch
    Oil ring   0.0012 to 0.0043 inch

2007 and later
    Piston diameter, measured at 8.9 mm from the bottom of the piston
        Standard   3.699 to 3.700 inches
        Minimum   3.694 inches
    Piston-to-bore clearance
        Standard   0.0008 to 0.0020 inch
        Maximum   0.0024 inch
    Piston ring end gap
        Top compression ring
            Standard   0.0098 to 0.0138 inch
            Maximum   0.0197 inch
        Second compression ring
            Standard   0.0197 to 0.0236 inch
            Maximum   0.0335 inch
        Oil ring
            Standard   0.0039 to 0.0157 inch
            Maximum   0.0236 inch
    Piston ring groove clearance
        Top compression ring   0.0008 to 0.0028 inch
        Second compressing ring   0.0008 to 0.0024 inch
        Oil ring   0.0028 to 0.0059 inch

Torque specifications*   Ft-lbs (unless otherwise indicated)

➡ **Note:** One foot-pound (ft-lb) of torque is equivalent to 12 inch-pounds (in-lbs) of torque. Torque values below approximately 15 ft-lbs are expressed in inch-pounds, since most foot-pound torque wrenches are not accurate at these smaller values.

Main bearing cap assembly bolts
    12-point bolts
        Step 1   45
        Step 2   Tighten an additional 90-degrees (1/4-turn)
    6-point bolts (side bolts)   38
Connecting rod cap nuts
    Step 1   18
    Step 2   Tighten an additional 90-degrees (1/4-turn)
Suspension subframe brace fasteners
    2003 and earlier
        Large bolts   134
        Smaller bolts   24
        Nuts   27
    2004 and later
        Large bolts   63
        Smaller bolts   24
        Nuts   24
Water seal plate nuts   120 in-lbs

* Refer to Chapter 2 Part A or B for additional torque specifications

NOTES

Section

Reference to other Chapters

3

COOLING, HEATING AND AIR CONDITIONING SYSTEMS

1   General information

ENGINE COOLING SYSTEM

♦ **Refer to illustrations 1.1 and 1.2**

All vehicles covered by this manual employ a pressurized engine cooling system with thermostatically controlled coolant circulation (see illustration). An impeller type water pump mounted on the front of the block pumps coolant through the engine. The coolant flows around each cylinder and toward the rear of the engine. Cast-in coolant passages direct coolant around the intake and exhaust ports, near the spark plug areas and in proximity to the exhaust valve guides.

A wax pellet-type thermostat is located in the thermostat housing near the front of the engine (see illustration). During warm up, the closed thermostat prevents coolant from circulating through the radiator. When the engine reaches normal operating temperature, the thermostat opens and allows hot coolant to travel through the radiator, where it is cooled before returning to the engine.

The cooling system is sealed by a pressure-type radiator cap. This raises the boiling point of the coolant, and the higher boiling point of the coolant increases the cooling efficiency of the radiator. If the system pressure exceeds the cap pressure relief value, the excess pressure in the system forces the spring-loaded valve inside the cap off its seat and allows the coolant to escape through the overflow tube into a coolant reservoir. When the system cools, the excess coolant is automatically drawn from the reservoir back into the radiator.

The coolant reservoir does double duty as both the point at which fresh coolant is added to the cooling system to maintain the proper fluid level and as a holding tank for overheated coolant.

This type of cooling system is known as a closed design because coolant that escapes past the pressure cap is saved and reused.

HEATING SYSTEM

The heating system consists of a blower fan and heater core located within the heater box, the inlet and outlet hoses connecting the heater core to the engine cooling system and the heater/air conditioning control head on the dashboard. Hot engine coolant is circulated through the heater core. When the heater mode is activated, a flap door opens to expose the heater box to the passenger compartment. A fan switch on the control head activates the blower motor, which forces air through the core, heating the air.

AIR CONDITIONING SYSTEM

♦ **Refer to illustrations 1.7a and 1.7b**

The air conditioning system consists of a condenser mounted in front of the radiator, an evaporator mounted adjacent to the heater core under the dashboard, a compressor mounted on the engine, a filter-drier (accumulator) which contains a high pressure relief valve and the

1.1 Typical cooling system component locations

1	Radiator	3	Cooling fans	5	Thermostat	7	Coolant pressure cap
2	Condenser	4	Water pump	6	Coolant recovery tank		

plumbing connecting all of the above (see illustrations). In addition, most models have rear-mounted components to heat/cool the rear of the vehicle.

A blower fan forces the warmer air of the passenger compartment through the evaporator core (sort of a radiator-in-reverse), transferring the heat from the air to the refrigerant. The liquid refrigerant boils off into low pressure vapor, taking the heat with it when it leaves the evaporator. The compressor keeps refrigerant circulating through the system, pumping the warmed coolant through the condenser where it is cooled and then circulated back to the evaporator.

Some models are equipped with an optional Automatic Air Conditioning system. With this system, you select the desired interior temperature with a knob on the controls, similar to setting the temperature on a home heating/cooling thermostat, and the system automatically adds the right blend of cool or warm air to maintain this temperature. The system has sensors that detect both the interior and outside temperature.

1.2 A typical thermostat

1 Flange
2 Piston
3 Jiggle valve
4 Main coil spring
5 Secondary coil spring
6 Frame
7 Valve
8 Valve seat

1.7a Major components of the front heating and air conditioning system

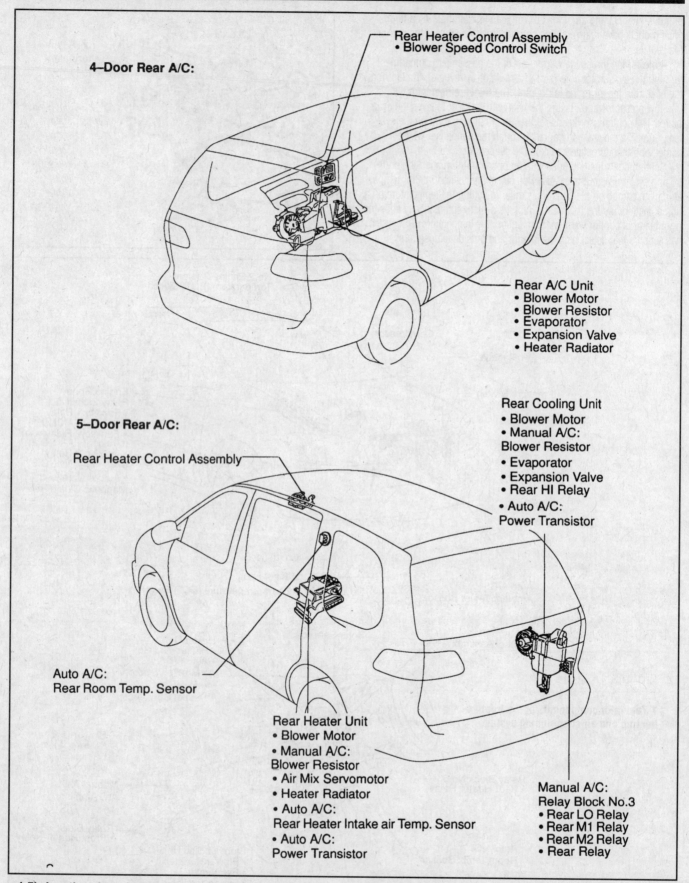

4–Door Rear A/C:

Rear Heater Control Assembly
• Blower Speed Control Switch

Rear A/C Unit
• Blower Motor
• Blower Resistor
• Evaporator
• Expansion Valve
• Heater Radiator

Rear Cooling Unit
• Blower Motor
• Manual A/C:
Blower Resistor
• Evaporator
• Expansion Valve
• Rear HI Relay
• Auto A/C:
Power Transistor

5–Door Rear A/C:

Rear Heater Control Assembly

Auto A/C:
Rear Room Temp. Sensor

Rear Heater Unit
• Blower Motor
• Manual A/C:
Blower Resistor
• Air Mix Servomotor
• Heater Radiator
• Auto A/C:
Rear Heater Intake air Temp. Sensor
• Auto A/C:
Power Transistor

Manual A/C:
Relay Block No.3
• Rear LO Relay
• Rear M1 Relay
• Rear M2 Relay
• Rear Relay

1.7b Location of rear heating and air-conditioning components - four-door models were available from 1998 to 2000, later models are five-door only

2 Antifreeze - general information

♦ **Refer to illustration 2.4**

❋❋ WARNING:

Do not allow antifreeze to come in contact with your skin or painted surfaces of the vehicle. Rinse off spills immediately with plenty of water. Antifreeze is highly toxic if ingested. Never leave antifreeze lying around in an open container or in puddles on the floor; children and pets are attracted by it's sweet smell and may drink it. Check with local authorities about disposing of used antifreeze. Many communities have collection centers that will see that antifreeze is disposed of safely. Never dump used antifreeze on the ground or into drains.

➡Note: Non-toxic coolant is available at local auto parts stores. Although the coolant is non-toxic when fresh, proper disposal of used coolant is still required.

The cooling system should be filled with a water/ethylene-glycol based antifreeze solution, which will prevent freezing down to at least -20 degrees F, or lower if local climate requires it. It also provides protection against corrosion and increases the coolant boiling point.

The cooling system should be drained, flushed and refilled at least every other year (see Chapter 1). The use of antifreeze solutions for periods of longer than two years is likely to cause damage and encourage the formation of rust and scale in the system. If your tap water is "hard", i.e. contains a lot of dissolved minerals, use distilled water with the antifreeze.

Before adding antifreeze to the system, check all hose connections, because antifreeze tends to search out and leak through very minute

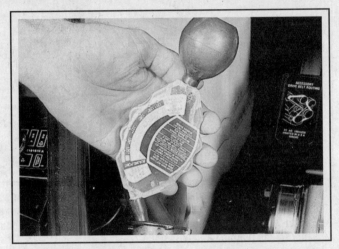

2.4 An inexpensive hydrometer can be used to test the condition of your coolant

openings. Engines do not normally consume coolant. Therefore, if the level goes down find the cause and correct it.

The exact mixture of antifreeze-to-water that you should use depends on the relative weather conditions. The mixture should contain at least 50 percent antifreeze, but should never contain more than 70 percent antifreeze. Consult the mixture ratio chart on the antifreeze container before adding coolant. Hydrometers are available at most auto parts stores to test the ratio of antifreeze to water (see illustration). Use antifreeze that meets the vehicle manufacturer's specifications.

3 Thermostat - check and replacement

❋❋ WARNING:

Do not attempt to remove the radiator cap, coolant or thermostat until the engine has cooled completely.

GENERAL CHECK

1 Before assuming the thermostat is responsible for a cooling system problem, check the coolant level (see Chapter 1), drivebelt tension (see Chapter 1) and temperature gauge (or light) operation.

2 If the engine takes a long time to warm up (as indicated by the temperature gauge or heater operation), the thermostat is probably stuck open. Replace the thermostat with a new one.

3 If the engine runs hot, use your hand to check the temperature of the lower radiator hose. If the hose is not hot, but the engine is, the thermostat is probably stuck in the closed position, preventing the coolant inside the engine from escaping to the radiator. Replace the thermostat.

❋❋ CAUTION:

Do not drive the vehicle without a thermostat. The computer

may stay in open loop and emissions and fuel economy will suffer.

4 If the lower radiator hose is hot, it means that the coolant is flowing and the thermostat is open. Consult the *Troubleshooting* Section at the front of this manual for further diagnosis.

THERMOSTAT TEST

♦ **Refer to illustration 3.7**

5 A more thorough test of the thermostat can only be made when it is removed from the vehicle (see below). If the thermostat remains in the open position at room temperature, it is faulty and must be replaced.

6 To test it fully, suspend the (closed) thermostat on a length of string or wire in a container of cold water, with a thermometer (cooking type that reads beyond 212-degrees F). A clear Pyrex cooking container is easiest to use.

7 Heat the water on a stove while observing the temperature and the thermostat. Neither should contact the sides of the container (see illustration).

3.7 A thermostat can be accurately checked by heating it in a container of water with a thermometer and observing the opening and fully-open temperature

3.12 Unbolt the water inlet pipe from the cylinder head and pull it out of the thermostat housing

3.13a The thermostat housing is at the back of the intake manifold, above the transaxle - you'll have to remove wiring and hoses to get at it

8   Note the temperature when the thermostat begins to open and when it is fully open. Compare the temperatures to the Specifications in this Chapter. The number stamped into the thermostat is generally the fully-open temperature. Some manufacturers provide Specifications for the beginning-to-open temperature, the fully-open temperature, and sometimes the amount the valve should open.

9   If the thermostat doesn't open and close as specified, or sticks in any position, replace it.

REPLACEMENT

2006 and earlier models

▶ **Refer to illustrations 3.12, 3.13a and 3.13b**

10 Disconnect the negative cable from the battery.

11 Drain the coolant from the radiator (see Chapter 1). Disconnect the radiator hose from the water inlet pipe.

12 Unbolt the water inlet pipe and remove the pipe and O-ring (see illustration).

13 Remove the fasteners and electrical connectors from the thermo-stat housing and detach the housing from the engine (see illustrations). Be prepared for some coolant to spill as the gasket seal is broken.

➡**Note: Access is easier with the air cleaner cover and hose removed.**

2007 and later models

14 Pull up the front of the engine cover to disengage the clips. Keep lifting it farther until the rear clip detaches. Set the cover aside.

15 Loosen the lug nuts on the right front wheel. Raise the vehicle and support it securely on jackstands. Remove the plastic lower engine splash shield.

16 Drain the coolant from the radiator (see Chapter 1).

17 Remove the right inner fender splash shield (see Chapter 11).

18 Remove the drivebelt (see Chapter 1).

19 Disconnect the upper radiator hose from the engine.

20 Remove the interfering drivebelt idler pulley, the bolt and the inner and outer washers.

➡**Note: The larger washer goes under the bolt head, the smaller under the pulley.**

21 Remove the water inlet/thermostat housing.

3.13b The thermostat housing is held on by three nuts

3.23 The thermostat gasket fits around the edge of the thermostat like a grooved sealing ring

All models

▶ **Refer to illustration 3.23**

22 Remove the thermostat, noting the direction in which it was installed in the housing, and thoroughly clean the sealing surfaces.

23 Install a new gasket onto the thermostat (see illustration). Make sure it is evenly fitted all the way around.

24 Install the thermostat and housing, positioning the jiggle pin at the highest point.

25 Tighten the housing fasteners to the torque listed in this Chapter's Specifications and reinstall the remaining components in the reverse order of removal. Use a new O-ring on the water inlet pipe and lubricate the O-ring with soapy water.

26 Refill the cooling system and bleed the air from the system (see Chapter 1). Run the engine and check for leaks and proper operation.

4　Engine cooling fans and circuit - check and replacement

✳✳ WARNING:

To avoid possible injury, keep clear of the fan blades, as they may start turning at any time!

CHECK

▶ **Refer to illustration 4.1**

1　To test an inoperative fan motor (one that doesn't come on when the engine gets hot or when the air conditioner is on), first check the fuses and/or fusible links (see Chapter 12). Then disconnect the electrical connector at the motor and use fused jumper wires to connect the fan directly to the battery (see illustration). If the fan still does not work, replace the fan motor.

✳✳ WARNING:

Do not allow the test clips to contact each other or any metallic part of the vehicle.

2　If the motor tested OK, the problem could lie in the relay(s), temperature switch, or the wiring. See Chapter 12 for relay checking procedures.

REPLACEMENT

2006 and earlier models

▶ **Refer to illustrations 4.6, 4.7 and 4.8**

✳✳ WARNING:

Wait until the engine is completely cool before beginning this procedure.

3　Disconnect the negative battery cable. If you're removing the condenser (right side) fan, drain the cooling system (see Chapter 1) and disconnect the upper radiator hose from the radiator.

4　Disconnect the wiring connector at the fan motor.

➡ **Note: All models have two fans. Both fans should operate all the time at low speed. When the air conditioning is On, both fans should operate at a higher speed.**

4.1 Disconnect the fan wiring connector and connect jumper wires directly to the positive and negative terminals of the battery

5　On models with cruise control, disconnect the cruise control actuator wire from the fan shroud for easier removal of fan number 1.

6　Unbolt the fan/shroud from the radiator and lift it from the vehicle (see illustration). On models with air conditioning, the number 2 fan may have to be removed first to allow room for removal of the number 1 fan.

4.6 Unbolt the fan and shroud and remove the assembly from the radiator - the upper bolts at each fan are indicated; there are more at the bottom of the shroud

7 Hold the fan blades and remove the fan retaining clip (see illustration).

8 Unbolt the fan motor from the shroud (see illustration).

9 Installation is the reverse of removal. When installing the blade to fan motor use a new clip, and orient the clip's open side to clear the projecting bump on the blade. If a new fan switch is installed, lubricate the O-ring with soapy water before installation.

10 If the cooling system was drained, refill it with the proper type of coolant (see Chapter 1).

2007 and later models

11 Remove the fan assembly with the radiator (see Section 5).

4.7 Remove the nut, then remove the fan from the motor

4.8 Remove the screws and separate the motor from the shroud

5 Radiator and coolant reservoir - removal and installation

※ WARNING:

Do not start this procedure until the engine is completely cool. Do not allow antifreeze to come in contact with your skin or painted surfaces of the vehicle. Rinse off spills immediately with plenty of water. Antifreeze is highly toxic if ingested. Never leave antifreeze lying around in an open container or in puddles on the floor; children and pets are attracted by it's sweet smell and may drink it. Check with local authorities about disposing of used antifreeze. Many communities have collection centers that will see that antifreeze is disposed of safely. Never dump used antifreeze on the ground or into drains.

➡Note: Non-toxic coolant is available at local auto parts stores. Although the coolant is non-toxic when fresh, proper disposal of used coolant is still required.

RADIATOR REMOVAL

2006 and earlier models

▶ Refer to illustrations 5.6 and 5.7

1 Disconnect the negative battery cable.

2 Drain the coolant into a container (see Chapter 1).

3 Remove both the upper and lower radiator hoses.

4 Disconnect the reservoir hose from the radiator filler neck.

5 The radiator can be removed with the cooling fans still attached.

6 Disconnect the transaxle cooler lines from the radiator (see illustration). Place a drip pan to catch the fluid and cap the fittings.

7 Remove the bolts that attach the radiator to its support (see illustration).

5.6 Remove the automatic transaxle cooler lines

5.7 Remove the hold-down clamps from each end of the radiator

8   Lift out the radiator. Be aware of dripping fluids and the sharp fins.

9   With the radiator removed, it can be inspected for leaks, damage and internal blockage. If in need of repairs, have a professional radiator shop or dealer service department perform the work, as special techniques are required.

10   Bugs and dirt can be cleaned from the radiator with compressed air and a soft brush. Don't bend the cooling fins as this is done.

❋ WARNING:

Wear eye protection.

2007 and later models

11   Pull up the front of the engine cover to disengage the clips. Keep lifting it farther until the rear clip detaches. Set the cover aside.

12   Loosen the lug nuts on the right front wheel. Raise the vehicle and support it securely on jackstands. Remove the plastic lower engine splash shield.

13   Drain the coolant from the radiator (see Chapter 1).

14   Remove both air inlets.

15   Remove the battery (see Chapter 5).

16   Remove the front bumper assembly (see Chapter 11). Also remove the front bumper energy absorber foam.

17   Disconnect all hoses from the radiator.

18   Detach the four clips, then remove the cover from the front of the hood latch. Remove the hood latch (see Chapter 11).

19   Disconnect the wiring from the air temperature sensor and the horns, then remove the vertical hood latch support bar.

20   Disconnect the fan wiring.

21   Remove the four bolts, then lift out the horizontal upper radiator support bar with the horns attached.

22   Disconnect the transmission fluid and oil hoses from the radiator. Detach the tube assembly from the top of the radiator.

23   Remove the right headlight assembly (see Chapter 12).

24   Unclip and remove the side air deflector from the right front side of the radiator.

25   Remove the right headlight support bracket.

26   Remove the pressure tube assembly from the lower right front of the radiator.

27   Remove the two round radiator support cushions from the top of the upper radiator support. Remove the six bolts, then remove the upper radiator support.

28   Remove the two bolts at the bottom of the radiator and separate the radiator and the condenser.

29   Carefully lift the radiator and fan assembly up and out of the vehicle. The fan assembly is attached with two bolts at the bottom and can be separated now. The lower radiator support and the inlet assembly can be removed if the radiator is being replaced.

RADIATOR INSTALLATION

30   Installation is the reverse of the removal procedure. Be sure the rubber mounts are in place.

31   After installation, fill the cooling system with the proper mixture of antifreeze and water. Refer to Chapter 1 if necessary.

32   Start the engine and check for leaks. Allow the engine to reach normal operating temperature, indicated by the upper radiator hose becoming hot. Recheck the coolant level and add more if required.

33   Check and add transaxle fluid as needed.

COOLANT RESERVOIR - REMOVAL AND INSTALLATION

▶ **Refer to illustration 5.34**

34   On most models, remove two bolts and the coolant reservoir simply pulls up and out of the bracket on the fenderwell (see illustration).

35   Pour the coolant into a container. Wash out and inspect the reservoir for cracks and chafing. Replace it if damaged.

36   Installation is the reverse of removal.

5.34 Typical coolant reservoir removal - remove the upper bolts

---

6   Water pump - check

1   A failure in the water pump can cause serious engine damage due to overheating.

2   With the engine running and warmed to normal operating temperature, squeeze the upper radiator hose. If the water pump is working properly, a pressure surge should be felt as the hose is released.

❋ WARNING:

Keep hands away from fan blades!

3   Water pumps are equipped with weep or vent holes. If a failure occurs in the pump seal, coolant will leak from this hole. In most cases it will be necessary to use a flashlight to find the hole on the water pump by looking through the space behind the pulley just below the water pump shaft. A slight gray discoloration around the weep hole is normal, while dark brown stains indicate a problem.

4   If the water pump shaft bearings fail there may be a howling sound at the front of the engine while it is running. Bearing wear can be felt if the water pump pulley is rocked up and down. Do not mistake drivebelt slippage, which causes a squealing sound, for water pump failure. Spray automotive drivebelt dressing on the belts to eliminate the belt as a possible cause of the noise.

7   Water pump - replacement

✳✳ WARNING:

Do not start this procedure until the engine is completely cool. Do not allow antifreeze to come in contact with your skin or painted surfaces of the vehicle. Rinse off spills immediately with plenty of water. Antifreeze is highly toxic if ingested. Never leave antifreeze lying around in an open container or in puddles on the floor; children and pets are attracted by it's sweet smell and may drink it. Check with local authorities about disposing of used antifreeze. Many communities have collection centers that will see that antifreeze is disposed of safely. Never dump used antifreeze on the ground or into drains.

➡Note: Non-toxic coolant is available at local auto parts stores. Although the coolant is non-toxic when fresh, proper disposal of used coolant is still required.

2006 AND EARLIER MODELS

◆ **Refer to illustrations 7.3, 7.4 and 7.6**

1   Disconnect the negative battery cable and drain the cooling system.

2   Remove the timing belt and camshaft sprockets (see Chapter 2A).

3   Remove the bolt retaining the water inlet pipe to the alternator adjuster and remove the water inlet pipe and thermostat (see Section 3). Remove the number 3 timing belt cover (see illustration).

4   Remove the water pump retaining bolts/nuts and separate the pump from the engine.

➡Note: There are two long studs (some engines may have bolts) that hold the engine mounting bracket and the water pump. The studs have a small hex-head that is used to remove the stud (see illustration). If it is stuck, remove the stud with locking pliers and replace the stud with a new bolt of the same

length. At least one of these long studs may have to be removed to allow the water pump to be removed.

5   Thoroughly clean all sealing surfaces, removing all traces of old gaskets, sealer and O-rings. Remove any traces of oil with acetone or lacquer thinner and a clean rag.

6   These models use a metal and rubber gasket (see illustration).

7   Reinstall the pump and the remaining parts in the reverse order of removal. Tighten the water pump bolts in several steps to the torque listed in this Chapter's Specifications.

8   Refill the cooling system (see Chapter 1) and run the engine, checking for leaks and proper operation.

2007 AND LATER MODELS

9   Remove the engine/transaxle assembly (see Chapter 2C).

10 Remove the alternator (see Chapter 5).

11 Remove the air conditioning compressor (see Section 16).

12 Remove the six bolts and the upper front engine mount bracket.

13 Remove both the front and rear drivebelt idler pulley assemblies. Keep them in order and note that the larger of the washers goes under the head of the pulley bolt. The smaller goes between the pulley and the engine block.

14 Remove the six bolts and the drivebelt tensioner.

15 Hold the water pump pulley with a special pin-spanner wrench. If you don't have one, you can use a chain wrench or a strap wrench instead. Remove the pulley.

16 Remove the thermostat housing (see Section 3).

17 Remove the water pump. There are 16 bolts securing it - make sure they are all accounted for. Remove the gasket.

18 Installation is the reverse of removal. Tighten the bolts to the torque listed in this Chapter's Specifications.

19 Refill the cooling system (see Chapter 1) and run the engine, checking for leaks and proper operation.

7.3 Release the three wiring harness clips, pull the harness back and remove the number three belt cover (2006 and earlier models)

7.4 The water pump has two long studs - at least one must be removed with a small wrench to allow water pump removal (2006 and earlier models)

7.6 A new metal/rubber gasket is used when installing the water pump (2006 and earlier models)

8   Coolant temperature sending unit - check and replacement

❄❄ WARNING:

Do not start this procedure until the engine is completely cool. Do not allow antifreeze to come in contact with your skin or painted surfaces of the vehicle. Rinse off spills immediately with plenty of water. Antifreeze is highly toxic if ingested. Never leave antifreeze lying around in an open container or in puddles on the floor; children and pets are attracted by it's sweet smell and may drink it. Check with local authorities about disposing of used antifreeze. Many communities have collection center s which will see that antifreeze is disposed of safely. Never dump used antifreeze on the ground or into drains.

➡Note: Non-toxic coolant is available at local auto parts stores. Although the coolant is non-toxic when fresh, proper disposal of used coolant is still required.

➡Note: This procedure applies only to 2006 and earlier models. 2007 and later models use the engine coolant temperature sensor to operate the temperature gauge. Refer to Chapter 6 for information about this sensor.

CHECK

8.3 Remove the V-bank cover to locate the coolant temperature gauge sending unit - don't confuse it with the coolant temperature sensor (for the computer), which is next to it but has two wires attached to it - 2006 and earlier models

◆ **Refer to illustration 8.3**

1   If the coolant temperature gauge is inoperative, check the fuses first (see Chapter 12).

2   If the temperature gauge indicates excessive temperature after running awhile, see the Troubleshooting Section in the front of the manual.

3   If the temperature gauge indicates Hot as soon as the engine is started cold, disconnect the wire at the coolant temperature sender (see illustration). If the gauge reading drops, replace the sending unit. If the reading remains high, the wire to the gauge may be shorted to ground or the gauge is faulty.

4   If the coolant temperature gauge fails to show any indication after the engine has been warmed up, (approx. 10 minutes) and the fuses checked out OK, shut off the engine. Disconnect the single-wire con-

nector at the sending unit and, using a jumper wire, connect the wire to a clean ground on the engine. Briefly turn on the ignition without starting the engine. If the gauge now indicates Hot, replace the sending unit.

5   If the gauge fails to respond, the circuit may be open or the gauge may be faulty - see Chapter 12 for additional information.

REPLACEMENT

6   Drain the coolant (see Chapter 1).

7   Disconnect the wiring connector from the sending unit.

8   Using a deep socket or a wrench, remove the sending unit.

9   Install the new unit and tighten it securely. Do not use thread sealer as it may electrically insulate the sending unit.

10 Reconnect the wiring connector, refill the cooling system and check for coolant leakage and proper gauge function.

9   Blower motor circuit - check

◆ **Refer to illustrations 9.4, 9.8, 9.9a, 9.9b, 9.9c and 9.10**

➡Note 1: This procedure does not apply to models with Automatic Air Conditioning. For models with Automatic Air Conditioning, refer to Section 13, Steps 24 to 28.

➡Note 2: Most models have rear heating/air conditioning units. Rear units have their own controls and blower motor.

1   If the blower motor doesn't operate, first check all connections in the circuit for looseness and corrosion. Make sure the battery is fully charged. Check the Heater fuse in the fuse panel below the driver's side of the dashboard. Also check the blower relay in the underhood fuse/relay box. Remove the relay and test it according to the procedure in Chapter 12.

2   Locate the blower motor relay in the underhood fuse/relay box. Remove the relay and test it for proper operation (see Chapter 12). If the relay fails the tests, replace it.

3   With the transmission in Park and the parking brake securely set, turn the ignition switch to the ON position. It isn't necessary to start the vehicle.

4   The blower motor is located under the glove compartment area of the dash, near the firewall (see illustration). The rear blower motor is behind a quarter panel trim (see illustration 1.7b).

5   Switch the heater controls to FLOOR and the blower speed to 4. Listen at the ducts to hear if the blower is operating. If it is, then switch the blower speed to 1 and listen again. Try all the speeds.

6   If the blower didn't operate, and you have checked the fuses and

9.4 Blower motor location (typical)

A   Blower motor   *B   Blower motor connector*

relay, test the blower. Locate the electrical connector at the blower motor (see illustration 9.4). Backprobe the Blue/red wire terminal; there should be at least 10 volts with the mode switch in any position other than Off and the ignition switch On. If not, there is a problem in the circuit from the fuse panel to the heater/air conditioning control panel, or from the control panel to the blower.

7   If there is voltage at the feed wire, but the blower does not operate, backprobe the Black/White wire and connect it to a known good chassis ground with a jumper wire. If it still doesn't operate, replace the blower motor. If the blower now operates there is a problem in the circuit from the blower to the blower speed switch to the resistor to ground. The most likely problem is a bad ground connection. Check the connection between the blower resistor and ground and the blower switch and ground (White/Black wires).

8   If the blower operates, but not at all speeds, check the blower

9.8 Location of the blower motor resistor

resistor. It's located on the blower housing under the center of the dash (see illustration). There are resistor elements mounted on the resistor board to provide blower speeds Lo, M1 and M2 (HI or 4 bypasses the resistor).

9   With the resistor removed from the vehicle, visually check the resistor for damage, indicated by the material melting out between the contacts. Check the resistor block with an ohmmeter between the terminals, as shown (see illustrations). If the resistance values are not as specified, replace the resistor.

10   If the blower operates, but not at all speeds and you have already checked the blower resistor, refer to Section 12 and remove the heater/air conditioning control panel. Disconnect the electrical connector from the back of the blower speed switch and test the terminals for continuity (see illustration). If the continuity is not as described, replace the blower speed switch.

Test between terminals	Resistance (approximate)
2 and 4	0.38 ohms
1 and 4	0.66 ohms
1 and 3	1.56 ohms

Test between terminals	Resistance (approximate)
2 and 6	0.38 ohms
3 and 6	0.97 ohms
1 and 3	1.69 ohms

Test between terminals	Resistance (approximate)
2 and 4	0.22 ohms
2 and 3	0.86 ohms
1 and 3	1.68 ohms

9.9a Continuity diagram for the front blower motor resistor (2006 and earlier models)

9.9b Continuity diagram for the rear blower motor resistor (2006 and earlier four-door models)

9.9c Continuity diagram for the rear blower motor resistor (2006 and earlier five-door models)

Terminal / Switch position	1	3	4	5	8	6	7
OFF	o						
LO	o	o					
M1	o	o	o			o	o
M2	o	o	o		o		
HI	o	o	o	o			

9.10 Continuity test for the blower speed switch (2006 and earlier models)

10 Blower motor - removal and installation

✳✳ WARNING:

The models covered by this manual are equipped with Supplemental Restraint systems (SRS), more commonly known as airbags. Always disconnect the negative battery cable, then the positive battery cable and wait two minutes before working in the vicinity of the impact sensors, steering column or instrument panel to avoid the possibility of accidental deployment of the airbag, which could cause personal injury (see Chapter 12). The yellow wiring harnesses and connectors routed through the console and instrument panel are for this system. Do not use electrical test equipment on any of the airbag system wiring or tamper with them in any way.

1   Disconnect the negative cable from the battery.

FRONT BLOWER MOTOR

▸ **Refer to illustrations 10.4, 10.5a, 10.5b and 10.6**

2   The blower unit is located in the passenger compartment above the right front foot-well.

3   Remove the right lower dash panel (see Chapter 11).

4   Remove the three bolts and pull the ECM out of the way (see illustration).

5   To remove the blower, remove the blower unit retaining screws and lower the unit from the housing (see illustrations).

6   If the motor is being replaced, transfer the fan to the new motor prior to installation (see illustration).

7   Installation is the reverse of removal. Check for proper operation.

REAR BLOWER MOTOR

▸ **Refer to illustrations 10.9, 10.10a and 10.10b**

8   Depending on whether you have a four-door or five-door model, remove the rear seats and either the left or right rear quarter panel trim (see illustration 1.7b). Five-door models have two rear blowers, one for the heating (located in the middle of the vehicle) and another for the air-conditioning, mounted in the right rear quarter.

9   On four-door models, disconnect the electrical connector, then remove the three blower motor mounting screws and the blower motor (see illustration).

10.4 Remove the ECM mounting bolts and move the ECM aside for blower motor removal (shown with connectors removed for clarity only, do not disconnect the ECM connectors)

10.5a Remove the two screws and the front blower motor cover

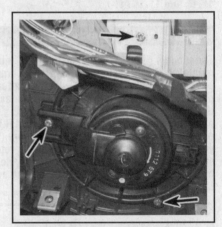

10.5b Front blower motor mounting screws

10.6 Use pliers to release and remove the clip, then lift the blower fan off the motor shaft

10.9 Rear blower motor mounting screws (four-door heater blowers and five-door cooling blowers)

10.10a To remove the mid-blower (heating) on 5-door models, remove the mounting screws and disconnect the electrical connector

10 On five-door models, once the rear heat unit has been removed, remove the air-mix motor, then remove all the screws of the unit cover (see illustrations). Flip the cover over and remove the blower fan (see illustration 10.6), then flip the cover back over and remove the three blower motor mounting screws.

10.10b To remove the rear cooling blower, remove the screws and lift the top from the cooling unit

11 Heater and air conditioning control assembly - removal and installation, cable adjustment and electrical checks

▶ Refer to illustrations 11.4, 11.5a, 11.5b, 11.5c, 11.9, 11.12, 11.13 and 11.15

❋❋ WARNING:

The models covered by this manual are equipped with Supplemental Restraint systems (SRS), more commonly known as airbags. Always disconnect the negative battery cable, then the positive battery cable and wait two minutes before working in the vicinity of the impact sensors, steering column or instrument panel to avoid the possibility of accidental deployment of the airbag, which could cause personal injury (see Chapter 12). The yellow wiring harnesses and connectors routed through the console and instrument panel are for this system. Do not use electrical test equipment on any of the airbag system wiring or tamper with them in any way.

REMOVAL AND INSTALLATION

1 Disconnect the negative cable from the battery.
2 On 2006 and earlier models, remove the kick panels, lower dash sound insulators, glove compartment, instrument cluster bezel and center instrument trim panel (see Chapter 11). Pull off the control knobs (if equipped).
3 On 2007 and later models, remove the center instrument cluster finish panels (see Chapter 11). Remove the shift knob (see Chapter 7).
4 Remove the radio (see Chapter 12).
5 Remove the heater control mounting screws. On 2006 and earlier models, pull the unit out a little, then push the temperature control shaft through and leave it in position as the control panel is pulled forward (see illustrations). Detach the connectors and remove the unit.
6 Installation is the reverse of the removal procedure.
7 Run the engine and check for proper functioning of the heater (and air conditioning, if equipped).

CABLE ADJUSTMENT (EXCEPT AUTOMATIC AIR CONDITIONING) (2006 AND EARLIER MODELS)

8 To adjust the air inlet control cable set the control lever to RECIRC, install the cable and clamp it in place.
9 To adjust the air mix control cable, set the air mix to COOL, install the cable and lock the clamp while applying slight pressure (away from the firewall) on the outer cable (see illustration).

11.4 Remove these screws to release the control assembly

11.5a Disconnect the electrical connectors from the control assembly

11.5b Disconnect the one cable at the top of the control assembly

11.9 The air mix control cable (arrow) should be attached when the control is in the COOL position

11.5c Disconnect the three cables from the bottom of the control assembly

11.12 With battery power applied to terminal 6 and ground to terminal 4, the AC switch light should come on when the switch is pressed - without the switch pressed in, the light should come on when the mode is turned to DEF

10 To adjust the mode control cable, set the mode to DEF, install the cable and lock the clamp while applying slight pressure (away from the firewall) on the outer cable.

11 To adjust the water control cable, set the water valve lever to COOL, install the cable and lock the clamp while applying slight pressure (away from the firewall) on the outer cable.

ELECTRICAL CHECKS (EXCEPT AUTOMATIC AIR CONDITIONING) (2006 AND EARLIER MODELS)

12 Check the air-conditioning switch operation by applying power

and ground to the terminals (see illustration). When the switch is pushed in (ON), the AC indicator light should come on. If it doesn't, replace the switch.

13 Using a self-powered continuity tester, test the terminals on the back of the control unit, starting with the mode control switch (see illustration).

14 Test the blower speed control switch for continuity (see Section 9). Any tests that do not meet specifications indicate the control unit should be replaced.

15 To replace any control panel components, remove the control knobs, then the screws on the back (see illustration).

11.13 Test the terminals at the back of the mode switch for continuity

Switch position	Continuity between
AC switch OFF	None
AC switch ON	6 and 5
Defrost OFF	None
Defrost ON	6 and 5
Switch illumination	3 and 1

11.15 To replace any of the air-conditioning control panel switches, remove the knobs at each switch, then remove the mounting screws from the back

12 Heater core - removal and installation

✳✳ WARNING 1:

The models covered by this manual are equipped with Supplemental Restraint systems (SRS), more commonly known as airbags. Always disconnect the negative battery cable, then the positive battery cable and wait two minutes before working in the vicinity of the impact sensors, steering column or instrument panel to avoid the possibility of accidental deployment of the airbag, which could cause personal injury (see Chapter 12).

✳✳ WARNING 2:

Wait until the engine is completely cool before beginning this procedure.

✳✳ WARNING 3:

Do not allow antifreeze to come in contact with your skin or painted surfaces of the vehicle. Rinse off spills immediately with plenty of water. Antifreeze is highly toxic if ingested. Never leave antifreeze lying around in an open container or in puddles on the floor; children and pets are attracted by it's sweet smell and may drink it. Check with local authorities about disposing of used antifreeze. Many communities have collection center s which will see that antifreeze is disposed of safely. Never dump used antifreeze on the ground or into drains.

➡Note: Non-toxic coolant is available at local auto parts stores. Although the coolant is non-toxic when fresh, proper disposal of used coolant is still required.

1 Disconnect the negative cable from the battery.
2 Drain the cooling system (see Chapter 1).

FRONT HEATER CORE

◆ Refer to illustrations 12.5, 12.6, 12.7 and 12.9

➡Note: Most 2007 and later models require the entire heater/

12.5 Remove the screws and the defroster ducting

12.6 Loosen the screws on the clamps where each pipe meets the heater core

12.7 Gently pull the heater pipes from the heater core - make sure the O-rings come out with the pipes

12.9 Pull the heater core up and out of the heating unit

12. 17 Exploded view of rear heating/ air conditioning unit (four-door models)

Rear Heater Duct

Rear A/C Unit

Heater Control Assembly

Water Hose

O-Ring

Suction Tube

Air Outlet Grill

LH Quarter Trim Panel

Liquid Tube

12.18 Remove the heater core from the heating/air conditioning unit (four-door models)

air conditioning unit to first be removed from the vehicle. While this is possible, it involves the removal of the instrument panel braces, other components and disassembly of the unit itself. This is beyond the scope of this manual.

3   Have the air conditioning system discharged and the refrigerant recovered, since the AC cooling unit must be removed before the heater core unit (see Section 18).

4   Refer to Chapter 11 and remove the instrument panel.

➡Note: This is a difficult procedure for the home mechanic, involving the tagging and disconnection/connection of many electrical connectors, and the removal of many plastic and metal fasteners, some of which are difficult to locate and release. This is a procedure recommended for a professional shop.

5   Remove the defroster ducting, located above the heating unit (see illustration).

6   Loosen the screws at the juncture of the heater pipes and the heater core (see illustration).

7   Separate the metal heater pipes from the heater core (see illustration).

8   Place old towels under the heater case to prevent any coolant drips from getting on the carpet.

9   The heater core can be pulled straight up out of the heating unit (see illustration). Make sure the foam sealing strips are intact.

10   Installation is the reverse order of removal. Use new O-rings to seal the heater core pipes.

11   Refill the cooling system, reconnect the battery and run the engine. Check for leaks and proper system operation.

REAR HEATER CORE

Four-door models

▶ **Refer to illustrations 12.17 and 12.18**

12   Have the air conditioning system discharged and the refrigerant recovered.

13   Place a drain pan under the vehicle and disconnect the coolant lines to the rear heater/air conditioning unit, under the floor. Also disconnect the AC line connections under the floor.

14   On these models, the rear heating and air conditioning are in one unit on the left side (see illustration 1.7b).

15   Refer to Chapter 12 and remove the rear seats, scuff plates for rear door and left side rear quarter panel trim panel.

16   Move the wiring harness out of the way and remove two screws and the heating duct.

17   Remove the two bolts and the rear heating/air conditioning unit (see illustration).

18   Remove the screws and clamps and the rear heater core (see illustration).

19   Installation is the reverse order of removal. Use new O-rings to seal the heater core pipes.

20   Refill the cooling system, reconnect the battery and run the engine. Check for leaks and proper system operation.

2003 and earlier five-door models

▶ **Refer to illustrations 12.23 and 12.25**

21   Place a drain pan under the vehicle and disconnect the coolant lines to the rear heater unit, under the floor near the center of the vehicle.

22   Refer to Chapter 11 and remove the front seats, the door sill scuff plates, kickpanels and the floor console.

23   Remove the three screws and the rear covers over the heating unit (see illustration).

12.23 Remove the covers from the rear heating unit (five-door models)

12.25 Basic components of the rear heating unit (five-door models)

24 After removing three bolts, the rear heating unit can be removed from the vehicle.

❄❄ CAUTION:

Keep old towels or rags on the carpeting to protect from coolant spills during heating unit removal.

25 Remove the heating unit cover, then remove the screws and clamps securing the heater core to the case (see illustration).

26 Installation is the reverse order of removal. Use new O-rings to seal the heater core pipes.

27 Refill the cooling system, reconnect the battery and run the engine. Check for leaks and proper system operation.2004 and later five-door models

2004 and later five-door models

28 Remove the right slide and rear door scuff plates (see illustration 18.16a), lower seat belt anchor, cargo net hooks and floor courtesy light. Using a trim panel tool, pry the rear quarter panel from the body, then remove it from the vehicle.

29 Release the heater hose spring clamps with a pair of pliers and slide the clamps an inch or two either way from their original positions. Disconnect the coolant hoses and remove them from the case.

30 Remove the bolts from the refrigerant lines and separate the lines from the A/C unit.

31 Remove the heater hoses from the coolant pipes.

32 Remove the clips and separate the air ducts from the vehicle.

33 Remove the mounting bolts and remove the A/C unit case from the rear of the vehicle.

34 Remove the blower motor (see Section 10).

35 Remove the power transistor and the thermistor.

36 Remove the three blower motor mounting screws and remove the blower motor from the case.

37 Remove the three fan shroud screws, then remove the shroud from the case.

38 Remove the water valve mounting bolts and separate the water valve from the A/C unit case.

39 Reassembly and installation is the reverse of disassembly and removal.

40 Refill the cooling system, reconnect the battery and run the engine. Check for leaks and proper operation. Have the air conditioning system recharged by the shop that discharged it.

13 Air conditioning and heating system - check and maintenance

AIR CONDITIONING SYSTEM

❄❄ WARNING:

The air conditioning system is under high pressure. Do not loosen any hose fittings or remove any components until the system has been discharged. Air conditioning refrigerant should be properly discharged into an EPA-approved recovery/recycling unit by a dealer service department or an automotive air conditioning repair facility. Always wear eye protection when disconnecting air conditioning system fittings.

1   The following maintenance checks should be performed on a regular basis to ensure that the air conditioner continues to operate at peak efficiency (see illustrations 1.7a and 1.7b).

  a) *Inspect the condition of the compressor drivebelt. If it is worn or deteriorated, replace it (see Chapter 1).*
  b) *Check the drivebelt tension and, if necessary, adjust it (see Chapter 1).*
  c) *Inspect the system hoses. Look for cracks, bubbles, hardening and deterioration. Inspect the hoses and all fittings for oil bubbles or seepage. If there is any evidence of wear, damage or leakage, replace the hose(s).*
  d) *Inspect the condenser fins for leaves, bugs and any other foreign material that may have embedded itself in the fins. Use a "fin comb" or compressed air to remove debris from the condenser.*
  e) *Make sure the system has the correct refrigerant charge.*

2   It's a good idea to operate the system for about ten minutes at least once a month. This is particularly important during the winter months because long term non-use can cause hardening, and subsequent failure, of the seals.

3   Because of the complexity of the air conditioning system and the special equipment necessary to service it, in-depth troubleshooting and repairs are beyond the scope of this manual. However, simple component replacement procedures are provided in this Chapter.

4   The most common cause of poor cooling is simply a low system refrigerant charge. If a noticeable drop in system cooling ability occurs, one of the following quick checks will help you determine whether the refrigerant level is low.

Check

▶ **Refer to illustration 13.8**

5   Warm the engine up to normal operating temperature.

6   Place the air conditioning temperature selector at the coldest setting and put the blower at the highest setting. Open the doors (to make sure the air conditioning system doesn't cycle off as soon as it cools the passenger compartment).

7   After the system reaches operating temperature, feel the two pipes connected to the evaporator at the firewall.

8   The pipe (thinner tubing) leading from the condenser outlet to the evaporator should be cold, and the evaporator outlet line (the thicker tubing that leads back to the compressor) should be slightly colder (3 to 10 degrees F). If the evaporator outlet is considerably warmer than the inlet, the system needs a charge. Insert a thermometer in the center

13.8 Place an accurate thermometer in the center dash vent, turn the air conditioning on and check the output temperature

13.10 A basic charging kit for R-134a systems is available at most auto parts stores - it must say R-134a (not R-12) and so must the can of refrigerant

air distribution duct (see illustration) while operating the air conditioning system - the temperature of the output air should be 35 to 40 degrees F below the ambient air temperature (down to approximately 40 degrees F). If the ambient (outside) air temperature is very high, say 110-degrees F, the duct air temperature may be as high as 60 degrees F, but generally the air conditioning is 35 to 40 degrees F cooler than the ambient air. If the air isn't as cold as it used to be, the system probably needs a charge.

9 Further inspection or testing of the system is beyond the scope of the home mechanic and should be left to a professional.

Adding refrigerant

▶ Refer to illustrations 13.10, 13.13 and 13.14

➡Note: All models covered by this manual use refrigerant R-134a. When recharging or replacing air conditioning components, use only refrigerant, refrigerant oil and seals compatible with this system. The seals and compressor oil used with older, conventional R-12 refrigerant are not compatible with the components in this system.

10 Buy an automotive charging kit at an auto parts store. A charging kit includes a can of R-134a refrigerant, a tap valve and a short section of hose that can be attached between the tap valve and the system low side service valve (see illustration). Because one can of refrigerant may not be sufficient to bring the system charge up to the proper level, it's a good idea to buy a couple of additional cans. Try to find at least one can that contains red refrigerant dye. If the system is leaking, the red dye will leak out with the refrigerant and help you pinpoint the location of the leak.

11 Connect the charging kit by following the manufacturer's instructions.

12 Back off the valve handle on the charging kit and screw the kit onto the refrigerant can, making sure first that the O-ring or rubber seal inside the threaded portion of the kit is in place.

13.13 Add R-134a only to the low side port - the procedure is easier if you wrap the can with a warm, wet towel to prevent icing

✳✳ WARNING:

Wear protective eye wear when dealing with pressurized refrigerant cans.

13 Remove the dust cap from the low-side charging port and attach the quick-connect fitting on the kit hose (see illustration).

✳✳ WARNING:

DO NOT hook the charging kit hose to the system high side! The fittings on the charging kit are designed to fit only on the low side of the system.

13.14 Pull the pressure switch connector off and temporarily bypass it with a jumper wire or paper clip between terminals 1 and 4 - put the connector back on as soon as you are through charging the system

13.23 This drain hose (at the firewall) from the heater/air conditioning unit should be kept clear to allow drainage of condensation

14 Warm the engine to normal operating temperature and turn on the air conditioning. Keep the charging kit hose away from the fan and other moving parts. In some cases, if the refrigerant charge is low enough, the air-conditioning system pressure switch may prevent the compressor from operating. For purposes of charging the system only, pull the pressure switch connector off and connect both pins on the connector with a paper clip or jumper wire (see illustration).

15 Turn the valve handle on the kit until the stem pierces the can, then back the handle out to release the refrigerant. You should be able to hear the rush of gas. Add refrigerant to the low side of the system until both the outlet and the evaporator inlet pipe feel about the same temperature. Allow stabilization time between each addition.

❄❄ WARNING:

Never add more than two cans of refrigerant to the system. The can may tend to frost up, slowing the procedure. Wet a shop towel with hot water and wrap it around the bottom of the can to keep it from frosting.

16 Put your thermometer back in the center register and check that the output air is getting colder.

17 When the can is empty, turn the valve handle to the closed position and release the connection from the low-side port. Replace the dust cap.

18 Remove the charging kit from the can and store the kit for future use with the piercing valve in the UP position, to prevent inadvertently piercing the can on the next use.

HEATING SYSTEMS

▶ **Refer to illustration 13.23**

19 If the air coming out of the heater vents isn't hot, the problem could stem from any of the following causes:

a) *The thermostat is stuck open, preventing the engine coolant from warming up enough to carry heat to the heater core. Replace the*

thermostat (see Section 3).

b) *A heater hose is blocked, preventing the flow of coolant through the heater core. Feel both heater hoses at the firewall. They should be hot. If one of them is cold, there is an obstruction in one of the hoses or in the heater core, or the heater control valve is shut. Detach the hoses and back flush the heater core with a water hose. If the heater core is clear but circulation is impeded, remove the two hoses and flush them out with a garden hose.*

c) *If flushing fails to remove the blockage from the heater core, the core must be replaced* (see Section 12).

20 If the blower motor speed does not correspond to the setting selected on the blower switch, the problem could be a bad fuse, circuit, blower relay, speed switch or blower resistor (see Section 9).

21 If there isn't any air coming out of the vents:

a) *Turn the ignition ON and activate the fan control. Place your ear at the heating/air conditioning register (vent) and listen. Most motors are audible. Can you hear the motor running?*

b) *If you can't (and have already verified that the blower switch and the blower motor resistor are good), the blower motor itself is probably bad* (see Section 10).

22 If the carpet under the heater core is damp, or if antifreeze vapor or steam is coming through the vents, the heater core is leaking. Remove it (see Section 12) and install a new unit (most radiator shops will not repair a leaking heater core).

23 Inspect the drain hose from the heater/evaporator assembly at the right-center of the firewall, make sure it is not clogged (see illustration). If there is a humid mist coming from the system ducts, this hose may be plugged with leaves or road debris.

AUTOMATIC AIR CONDITIONING

▶ **Refer to illustrations 13.24 and 13.25**

24 Some models may have an optional Automatic Air Conditioning system to control the temperature inside the vehicle. You set the desired temperature on the control panel and the climate control module (com-

13.24 Controls for Automatic Air Conditioning system (2006 and earlier models):

1 AC button
2 Air flow mode selector
3 Blower fan speed selector
4 Windshield airflow button
5 Temperature selector
6 Air intake selector
7 Auto button
8 Off button

puter) blends the right amount of cooled or heated air to maintain this cabin temperature (see illustration). The speed of the blower motor in this system is electronically controlled by the microprocessor through a linear controller that replaces the conventional blower motor resistor.

25 Most repairs or diagnostics of the system are beyond the scope of the home mechanic, but there is an on-board diagnostics function in the computer that will display trouble codes relating to the climate-control system. The codes (see illustration) can indicate what area, if any, is malfunctioning.

26 To begin the self-test function (vehicle interior at normal temperature), push the RECIRC/FR and AUTO buttons at the same time, while turning the ignition key to On. If all is normal with the system, the four indicator lights will cone on for one second then go off in sequence.

27 After the indicators display, the computer performs a search for Diagnostic Trouble Codes (DTC's). Any codes will appear on the control head where the temperature setting is usually displayed.

28 After the trouble code check, the system will operate all of the system's actuators at one-second intervals. The test mode can be exited any time by pressing the OFF button, but the computer will keep the codes in memory. If you want to clear the climate control DTC's, pull the fuse marked "DOME" from the underhood fuse/relay box and keep it disconnected for at least 10 seconds.

Trouble Code	Circuit
11	Room temp sensor, front
12	Ambient temp sensor circuit
13	Evap temp sensor, front
14	Engine coolant temp sensor
19	Room temp sensor, rear
21	Solar sensor circuit
22	Compressor drive
23	Pressure sensor
26	Intake air temp sensor, rear
31	Air mix damper position, front
32	Air inlet damper position
37	Air mix damper position, rear
41	Air mix damper servomotor, front
42	Air inlet damper servomotor, front
47	Air inlet damper servomotor, rear

13.25 Trouble codes for Automatic Air Conditioning system

14 Air conditioning compressor clutch circuit - check

♦ **Refer to illustration 14.5**

1 Proper operation of the compressor clutch is essential to the function of the air conditioning system. If your system doesn't seem to get cold, first check the clutch operation.

2 With the engine warmed up, set the air conditioning temperature selector on the coldest setting and the fan on high. Open the doors (to make sure the air conditioning system doesn't cycle off as soon as it cools the passenger compartment down).

3 Have an assistant push the AC button while you observe the front of the compressor. The clutch will make an audible click and the center of the clutch should rotate. If it doesn't, shut the engine off and disconnect the air conditioning system pressure switch. Insert a paper clip as a jumper and try the air conditioning again as in Steps 1 and 2 (see illustration 13.14). If it works now, the system pressure is too high or too low. Have your system tested by a dealer service department or air conditioning shop.

4 If the clutch still didn't operate, check the appropriate fuses. Inspect the fuse marked "heater" in the interior fuse panel under the driver's side of the dash.

5 While at the underhood relay/fuse box, pull the "MG CLT" (compressor clutch) relay and test it (see Chapter 12). With the relay out and the ignition Off, check for battery power at the number 1 socket for the compressor clutch relay (see illustration). There should be battery power. Also check the large heater relay (see Section 9).

6 With the engine running and the air conditioning on, connect sockets 3 and 5 for the compressor clutch relay with a jumper wire and

14.5 The clutch relay should exhibit no continuity between 3 and 5 unless it is powered, and there should be 62-91 ohms resistance between 1 and 2

listen for the clutch to click as you make the connection.

7 If the clutch still doesn't operate, turn off the engine, disconnect the clutch connector at the compressor and attach a jumper wire long enough to allow use of an ohmmeter to check for continuity between the number 3 terminal of the clutch relay socket and the socket in the compressor clutch connector. If there is no continuity, check for a open in the circuit between the relay box and the compressor clutch connector. If it has continuity, check for an open in the circuit from the PCM to the relay box.

15 Air conditioning receiver/drier - removal and installation

♦ **Refer to illustration 15.3**

❄ WARNING:

The air conditioning system is under high pressure. Do not loosen any hose fittings or remove any components until the system has been discharged. Air conditioning refrigerant should be properly discharged into an EPA-approved recovery/recycling unit by a dealer service department or an automotive air conditioning repair facility. Always wear eye protection when disconnecting air conditioning system fittings.

➡ **Note:** This component is only on 2006 and earlier models. On later models, it is an integral part of the condenser.

1 Have the refrigerant discharged by an air conditioning technician.

2 Disconnect the negative battery cable.

3 Disconnect the refrigerant lines (see illustration) from the receiver/drier and cap the open fittings to prevent entry of moisture.

4 Loosen the clamp bolt and slip the receiver/drier out of the bracket.

5 Installation is the reverse of removal.

6 Have the system evacuated, charged and leak tested by the shop that discharged it. If the receiver was replaced, have them add about 20

15.3 After the system has been discharged, unbolt the two refrigerant lines from the receiver/drier and cap them

cc (0.71 oz.) refrigeration oil to the compressor. Use only compressor oil compatible with R-134a refrigerant.

16 Air conditioning compressor - removal and installation

◆ Refer to illustration 16.4

❋❋ WARNING:

The air conditioning system is under high pressure. Do not loosen any hose fittings or remove any components until the system has been discharged. Air conditioning refrigerant should be properly discharged into an EPA-approved recovery/recycling unit by a dealer service department or an automotive air conditioning repair facility. Always wear eye protection when disconnecting air conditioning system fittings.

1   Have the refrigerant discharged and recovered by an automotive air conditioning technician.
2   Disconnect the negative cable from the battery.
3   Remove the drivebelt from the compressor (see Chapter 1). Remove the alternator (see Chapter 5).
4   On 2007 and later models, remove the radiator assembly (see Section 5). Detach the wiring connector and the refrigerant lines (see illustration).
5   Unbolt the compressor and lift it from the vehicle.
6   If a new or rebuilt compressor is being installed, follow the directions that come with it regarding the proper level of oil prior to installation.
7   Installation is the reverse of removal. Replace any O-rings with

16.4 Compressor details (shown with alternator removed)

A   Electrical connector
B   Mounting bolts (three shown here)

new ones specifically made for the purpose and lubricate them with refrigerant oil.
8   Have the system evacuated, recharged and leak tested by the shop that discharged it.

17 Air conditioning condenser - removal and installation

❋❋ WARNING:

The air conditioning system is under high pressure. Do not loosen any hose fittings or remove any components until the system has been discharged. Air conditioning refrigerant should be properly discharged into an EPA-approved recovery/recycling unit by a dealer service department or an automotive air conditioning repair facility. Always wear eye protection when disconnecting air conditioning system fittings.

1   Have the refrigerant discharged by an air conditioning technician.

2006 AND EARLIER MODELS

◆ Refer to illustrations 17.4a, 17.4b and 17.5

2   Remove the radiator upper mounts as described in Section 5.
3   Refer to Chapter 11 and remove the grille.
4   Disconnect the inlet and outlet fittings (see illustrations). Cap the open fittings immediately to keep moisture and dirt out of the system.
5   Remove the mounting nuts (see illustration). Push the radiator back toward the engine, then push the condenser rearward until it's free of the radiator support and can be pulled up and out if the vehicle.

17.4a Disconnect the liquid line using two wrenches (shown with fan removed for clarity)

17.4b Remove the bolt holding the refrigerant line to the right side of the condenser - on some models, the line is clamped to the side of the condenser as well

2007 AND LATER MODELS

6   Remove the front bumper assembly (see Chapter 11).

7   Disconnect the refrigerant lines and discard the O-rings. They must be replaced with new ones.

8   Remove both air inlet scoops.

9   Remove the hood latch and its vertical support (see Chapter 11).

10 Disconnect the cooling fan wiring.

11 Remove the four bolts and lift off the upper radiator support with the horns attached.

12 Disconnect the oil cooler tube assembly from the top of the radiator assembly.

13 Remove the six bolts and the upper radiator support.

14 Remove the two screws from the bottom of the condenser, then lift the condenser carefully out of the vehicle.

ALL MODELS

15 Install the condenser, brackets and bolts, making sure the rubber cushions fit on the mounting points properly.

17.5 Remove the mounting nuts on each side, near the top of the condenser

16 Reconnect the refrigerant lines, using new O-rings where needed. If a new condenser is installed, add 1.4 to 1.7 ounces of refrigerant oil.

17 Reinstall the remaining parts in the reverse order of removal. Have the system evacuated, charged and leak tested by the shop that discharged it.

18 Air conditioning evaporator and expansion valve - removal and installation

❊❊ WARNING 1:

The models covered by this manual are equipped with Supplemental Restraint systems (SRS), more commonly known as airbags. Always disconnect the negative battery cable, then the positive battery cable and wait two minutes before working in the vicinity of the impact sensors, steering column or instrument panel to avoid the possibility of accidental deployment of the airbag, which could cause personal injury (see Chapter 12). The yellow wiring harnesses and connectors routed through the console and instrument panel are for this system. Do not use electrical test equipment on any of the airbag system wiring or tamper with them in any way.

❊❊ WARNING 2:

The air conditioning system is under high pressure. Do not loosen any hose fittings or remove any components until after the system has been discharged. Air conditioning refrigerant should be properly discharged into an EPA-approved recovery/re-cycling unit at a dealer service department or an automotive air conditioning repair facility. Always wear eye protection when disconnecting air conditioning system fittings.

❊❊ CAUTION:

When replacing entire components, additional refrigerant oil should be added equal to the amount that is removed with the component being replaced. Be sure to read the can before adding any oil to the system, to make sure it is compatible with the R-134a system.

➠Note: This is a difficult procedure for the home mechanic, and involves removal of the dashboard. There are a number of hard-to-reach fasteners and many electrical connectors.

FRONT EVAPORATOR

▶ Refer to illustrations 18.3 and 18.6

➠Note: Most 2007 and later models require the entire heater/air conditioning unit to first be removed from the vehicle. While this is possible, it involves the removal of the instrument panel braces, other components and disassembly of the unit itself. This is beyond the scope of this manual.

1   Have the air conditioning system discharged and recovered by an air conditioning technician.

2   Disconnect the cable from the negative battery cable.

3   Disconnect the receiver line and suction line from the evaporator (see illustration). Plug both lines to prevent contaminants and moisture from entering the air conditioning system.

4   Remove the glove compartment and the right side lower dash panel (see Chapter 11).

5   Disconnect the electrical connectors from the evaporator housing.

6   From under the dash, remove the two rivets, 3 bolts and one nut securing the cooling unit to the firewall (see illustration).

7   Remove the screws, separate the housing and remove the evaporator core.

8   Remove the thermostat sensor from the evaporator. If the expansion valve is to be removed, use backup wrenches when disconnecting it.

9   Installation is the reverse of removal. Install new O-rings and coat them with R-134a refrigerant oil.

10 Have the system evacuated, charged and leak tested by an air conditioning technician. If a new evaporator was installed, add 1.4 ounces of new refrigerant oil.

18.3 Remove the two bolts to disconnect the refrigerant lines at the firewall

18.6 Remove the nut, bolts, and rivets to remove the cooling unit from the firewall (2006 and earlier models)

REAR EVAPORATOR

Four-door models

 Refer to illustration 18.12

11 Refer to Section 12 and remove the rear heating/air conditioning unit.

12 Remove the screws and separate the two halves of the unit case, then remove the evaporator (see illustration).

13 Installation is the reverse of removal. Install new O-rings and coat them with R-134a refrigerant oil.

14 Have the system evacuated, charged and leak tested by an air conditioning technician. If a new evaporator was installed, add 1.4 ounces of new refrigerant oil.

Five-door models

▶ **Refer to illustration 18.16a, 18.16b, 18.16c, 18.16d and 18.16e**

15 On these models, the rear cooling unit is located at the right rear of the vehicle, separate from the rear heating unit (see illustration 1.7b). Have the air conditioning system discharged and the

18.12 Remove the fourteen screws and one clamp, then separate the halves of the cooling case and remove the evaporator

refrigerant recovered.

16 Remove the rear seats, rear door scuff plate, upper quarter panel trim and the rear quarter trim panel (see illustrations).

18.16a To access the rear cooling unit on five-door models, first pry up the trim panel below the rear door

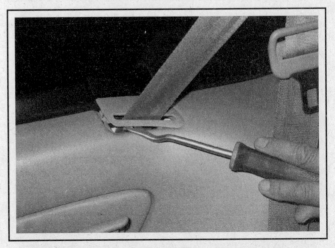

18.16b Pry up the seat belt trim plate on the right-rear quarter panel trim

17 From beneath the vehicle, disconnect the refrigerant lines.

18 Remove the three mounting bolts and pull the rear cooling unit from the vehicle.

19 Remove the screws and separate the two halves of the cooling unit housing.

20 Remove the evaporator from the case.

21 Installation is the reverse of removal. Install new O-rings and coat them with R-134a refrigerant oil.

22 Have the system evacuated, charged and leak tested by an air conditioning technician. If a new evaporator was installed, add 1.4 ounces of new refrigerant oil.

18.16c Using a trim tool, pry out the speaker grille from the quarter panel trim, and the grille from the rear corner panel

18.16d Remove the mounting screws from the quarter panel trim and the rear quarter panel

18.16e Pull the two panels out far enough to disconnect any electrical connectors - the panel can be pulled away far enough to access the unit if the seat belt is pulled all the way out and held with a clip

Specifications

General

Radiator cap pressure rating	12.1 to 16.4 psi
Thermostat rating	
Opens	176 to 183-degrees F
Fully open	203-degrees F
Thermostat housing nuts	69 in-lbs
Water pump-to-block bolts	69 in-lbs

Torque specifications   Ft-lbs (unless otherwise indicated)

➡**Note: One foot-pound (ft-lb) of torque is equivalent to 12 inch-pounds (in-lbs) of torque. Torque values below approximately 15 ft-lbs are expressed in inch-pounds, since most foot-pound torque wrenches are not accurate at these smaller values.**

Thermostat housing nuts	69 in-lbs
Water pump-to-block bolts	69 in-lbs

NOTES

4

FUEL AND EXHAUST SYSTEMS

1 General information

▶ **Refer to illustration 1.1**

The fuel system consists of a fuel tank, an electric fuel pump (located in the fuel tank), a fuel pressure regulator located next to the fuel pump, an EFI main relay, a fuel pump relay (circuit opening relay), the fuel rail and fuel injectors, an air cleaner assembly and a throttle body unit. All models are equipped with a Sequential Electronic Fuel Injection system (see illustration).

SEQUENTIAL ELECTRONIC FUEL INJECTION SYSTEM

Sequential Electronic Fuel Injection uses timed impulses to inject the fuel directly into the intake port of each cylinder according to its firing order. The injectors are controlled by the Powertrain Control Module (PCM). The PCM monitors various engine parameters and delivers the exact amount of fuel required into the intake ports. The throttle body serves only to control the amount of air passing into the system. Because each cylinder is equipped with its own injector, much better control of the fuel/air mixture ratio is possible.

FUEL PUMP AND LINES

Fuel is circulated from the fuel tank to the fuel injection system through a metal line running along the underside of the vehicle. An electric fuel pump and fuel level sending unit are located inside the fuel tank along with a fuel pressure regulator. A vapor return system routes all vapors back to the fuel tank through a separate return line.

The fuel pump relay is equipped with a primary and secondary voltage circuit. The primary circuit is controlled by the PCM and the secondary circuit is linked directly to the EFI main relay from the ignition switch. With the ignition switch ON (engine not running), the PCM will ground the relay for two seconds. During cranking, the PCM grounds the fuel pump relay as long as the camshaft position sensor sends its position signal (see Chapter 6). If there are no reference pulses, the fuel pump will shut off after two seconds.

EXHAUST SYSTEM

The exhaust system consists of two exhaust manifolds, exhaust pipes, catalytic converters, a muffler and a tail pipe. On some models, two catalytic converters are used, in which case the front catalytic converter is an integral component of the exhaust manifold. On 2001 and later models, there are three converters. A warm-up catalyst is part of the front exhaust manifold, another is part of the pipe from the rear bank, and the main three-way catalytic converter is part of the exhaust system after the front and rear pipes join together.

The catalytic converters are an emission control device added to the exhaust system to reduce pollutants. Refer to Chapter 6 for more information regarding the catalytic converters.

1.1 Fuel injection components (2006 and earlier models)

1   *Fuel injector*
2   *Air intake plenum*
3   *Fuel rail*
4   *Throttle body*
5   *Idle Air Control (IAC) valve (below throttle body)*

2 Fuel pressure relief

▶ **Refer to illustrations 2.1a and 2.1b**

❋❋ **WARNING:**

Gasoline is extremely flammable, so take extra precautions when you work on any part of the fuel system. Don't smoke or allow open flames or bare light bulbs near the work area, and don't work in a garage where a gas-type appliance (such as a water heater or a clothes dryer) is present. Since gasoline is carcinogenic, wear fuel-resistant gloves when there's a possibility of being exposed to fuel, and, if you spill any fuel on your skin, rinse it off immediately with soap and water. Mop up any spills immediately and do not store fuel-soaked rags where
they could ignite. The fuel system is under constant pressure, so, if any fuel lines are to be disconnected, the fuel pressure in the system must be relieved first. When you perform any kind of work on the fuel system, wear safety glasses and have a Class B type fire extinguisher on hand.

1   In the engine compartment fuse/relay box, remove the circuit opening relay (see illustrations).

2   Start the engine and allow it to run until it stops. Disconnect the cable from the negative terminal of the battery before working on the fuel system.

3   Be sure to place a shop rag around any fitting that's being loos-

2.1a To relieve the fuel system pressure, remove the circuit opening relay from the underhood fuse/relay box, then start the engine and let it run until it stalls. This fuse/relay box is typical of a 2003 and earlier model . . .

2.1b . . . and this is a 2004 through 2006 underhood fuse/relay box

ened to catch the residual fuel as it bleeds off. Dispose of the fuel soaked rag in an approved safety container.

4   The fuel system pressure is now relieved. When you're finished working on the fuel system, install the circuit opening relay and connect the negative cable to the battery.

---

3 Fuel pump/fuel pressure - check

※ WARNING:

Gasoline is extremely flammable, so take extra precautions when you work on any part of the fuel system. See the Warning in Section 2.

GENERAL CHECKS

1   Check that there is adequate fuel in the fuel tank.

2   Verify the fuel pump actually runs. Have an assistant turn the ignition switch to ON - you should hear a brief whirring noise (for approximately two seconds) as the pump comes on and pressurizes the system.

➡ **Note: The fuel pump is easily heard through the gas tank filler neck.**

If there is no response from the fuel pump (makes no sound) proceed to Step 8 and check the fuel pump electrical circuit. If the fuel pump runs, but a fuel system problem is suspected, continue with the fuel pump pressure check.

3.3 This aftermarket fuel pressure testing kit contains all the necessary fittings and adapters, along with the fuel pressure gauge, to test most automotive fuel systems

FUEL PUMP PRESSURE CHECK

▶ **Refer to illustrations 3.3**

➡ **Note: In order to perform the fuel pressure test, you will need to obtain a fuel pressure gauge capable of measuring high fuel pressure and the proper adapter set for the specific fuel injection system.**

3   Relieve the fuel system pressure (see Section 2). Disconnect the fuel filter outlet line and connect an adapter and fuel pressure gauge to the fuel filter and fuel line (see illustrations).

➡ **Note: On 1998 through 2000 models, the pressure gauge can be adapted to the fuel filter in the engine compartment. On later models, you'll have to adapt to the fuel rail connection. Each type will require a different adapter for the fuel pressure gauge assembly.**

4   Reinstall the circuit opening relay and connect the cable to the negative terminal of the battery. Turn all the accessories Off and switch the ignition key On. The fuel pump should run for about two seconds; note the reading on the gauge. After the pump stops running, the pressure should hold steady. After five minutes it should not drop below the minimum listed in this Chapter's Specifications.

5   Start the engine and let it idle at normal operating temperature. The pressure should remain the same. If all the pressure readings are within the limits listed in this Chapter's Specifications, the system is operating properly.

6   If the fuel pressure is not within specifications, check the following:

   a) *If the pressure is higher than specified, replace the fuel pressure regulator (see Section 6).*

   b) *If the pressure is lower than specified, check the fuel filter and fuel lines from the fuel rail to the fuel tank for restrictions or damage. Check the fuel injectors for leaks. If the pressure is still low, most likely the fuel pressure regulator and/or the fuel pump is defective. In this situation, it is recommended that both the fuel pressure regulator and fuel pump are replaced to prevent any future fuel pressure problems.*

7   After the testing is done, relieve the fuel pressure (see Section 2) and remove the fuel pressure gauge.

3.8 The EFI fuse and EFI relay are located in the engine compartment fuse/relay box - early model

3.9 On 2003 and earlier models, the fuel pump relay (circuit opening relay) is located in the engine compartment fuse/relay sub-box

FUEL PUMP ELECTRICAL CIRCUIT CHECK

▶ **Refer to illustrations 3.8 and 3.9**

8   If the pump does not turn on (makes no sound) with the ignition switch in the ON position, check the IGN fuse and the EFI fuse located in the engine compartment fuse center. If either fuse is blown, replace the fuse and see if the pump works (see illustration). If the pump now works, check for a short in the circuit between the fuel pump relay (circuit opening relay) and the fuel pump.

9   If the pump still does not work, remove the EFI main relay and check for battery voltage at the relay connector. One of the terminals should have battery voltage available at all times and another terminal should have battery voltage available with the ignition key On. If battery voltage does not exist, check the circuit from the fuse/relay box to the battery or ignition switch. If battery voltage exists at the relay socket, check the relays.

➡**Note: These models are equipped with an EFI main relay (see illustration 3.8) and a fuel pump relay (circuit opening relay), all located in the engine compartment fuse/relay**

box(es) (see illustration).

10   If the relays are good and the fuel pump does not operate, check for power to the fuel pump at the fuel pump electrical connector. Also check for continuity to chassis ground at the connector. If voltage is present at the fuel pump connector, the ground circuit is good and the fuel pump does not operate when connected, replace the fuel pump.

Relay check

▶ **Refer to illustrations 3.12 and 3.13**

➡**Note: The following checks apply to both the EFI main relay and fuel pump relay (circuit opening relay).**

11   Remove the relay from the engine compartment fuse/relay box or interior fuse/relay box.

12   Using an ohmmeter, check for continuity between terminals 1 and 2 (see illustration). If there's no continuity, replace the relay. Check that there is NO continuity between terminals 3 and 5.

13   Connect battery voltage to terminals 1 and 2 and verify that there's continuity between terminals 3 and 5 (see illustration). If there isn't, replace the relay.

3.12 EFI main relay continuity check

3.13 Apply battery voltage to terminals 1 and 2 and check for continuity between terminals 3 and 5

⁕⁕ WARNING:

Gasoline is extremely flammable, so take extra precautions when you work on any part of the fuel system. See the Warning in Section 2.

1   Always relieve the fuel pressure before servicing fuel lines or fittings (see Section 2).

2   The fuel line extends from the fuel tank to the engine compartment. The line is secured to the underbody with clip and screw assemblies. This line must be occasionally inspected for leaks, kinks and dents.

3   If evidence of dirt is found in the system or fuel filter during disassembly, the line should be disconnected and blown out. Check the fuel strainer on the fuel gauge sending unit (see Section 5) for damage and deterioration.

STEEL TUBING

4   If replacement of a fuel line or emission line is called for, use welded steel tubing meeting the manufacturer's specifications or its equivalent.

5   Don't use copper or aluminum tubing to replace steel tubing. These materials cannot withstand normal vehicle vibration.

6   Because fuel lines used on fuel-injected vehicles are under high pressure, they require special consideration.

4.12a When attaching a section of rubber hose to a metal fuel line, be sure to overlap the hose as shown, and secure it to the line with a new hose clamp of the proper type

7   Some fuel lines have threaded fittings with O-rings. Any time the fittings are loosened to service or replace components:

  a) *Always hold the stationary fitting with an open-end wrench while loosening or tightening the fitting nut.*
  b) *Check all O-rings for cuts, cracks and deterioration. Replace any that appear hardened, worn or damaged.*
  c) *If the lines are replaced, always use original equipment parts, or parts that meet the original equipment standards specified in this Section.*

FLEXIBLE HOSE

⁕⁕ WARNING:

Use only original equipment replacement hoses or their equivalent, marked specifically for fuel-injection use. Others may fail from the high pressures of this system.

8   Don't route fuel hose within four inches of any part of the exhaust system or within ten inches of the catalytic converter. Metal lines and rubber hoses must never be allowed to chafe against the frame. A minimum of 1/4-inch clearance must be maintained around a line or hose to prevent contact with the frame.

9   Some models may be equipped with nylon fuel line and quick-connect fittings at the fuel filter and/or fuel pump. The quick-connect fittings cannot be serviced separately. Do not attempt to service these types of fuel lines in the event the retainer tabs or the line becomes damaged. Replace the entire fuel line as an assembly.

REPLACEMENT

♦ **Refer to illustrations 4.12a, 4.12b, 4.12c and 4.12d**

10   In the event of any fuel line damage (metal or flexible lines) it is necessary to replace the damaged lines with factory replacement parts. Others may fail from the high pressures of this system.

11   Relieve the fuel pressure.

12   Remove all fasteners attaching the lines to the vehicle body. On fuel lines so equipped, detach the clamp(s) that attach the fuel hoses to the metal lines, then pull the hose off the fitting (see illustration).

4.12c On models with quick-connect fittings on the fuel filter (and on the fuel pump on all models), remove the fuel hose clamp (cover) . . .

4.12d . . . then pull the tab down to unlock the fuel line fitting

4.12b On quick-connect fuel line fittings, pinch the tabs, push and then pull the fitting off the fuel line. Be sure to replace the retainer on the fuel line once it has been disconnected

Twisting the hoses back and forth will allow them to separate more easily. If equipped with quick-connect fittings, hold the connector with one hand and depress the retaining tabs with the other hand, then separate the connector from the pipe (see illustrations). On connections that use banjo fittings, always use new sealing washers on either side of the fitting.

13 Installation is the reverse of removal. Be sure to use new O-rings at the threaded fittings (if equipped). On quick-connect fittings, align the retainer locking pawls with the connector grooves. Push the connector onto the pipe until both retaining pawls lock with a clicking sound.

5 Fuel pump - removal and installation

※※ **WARNING:**

Gasoline is extremely flammable, so take extra precautions when you work on any part of the fuel system. See the Warning in Section 2.

REMOVAL

♦ **Refer to illustrations 5.4a, 5.4b, 5.4c, 5.6, 5.8, 5.9a, 5.9b, 5.9c, 5.9d, 5.9e, 5.9f and 5.9g**

1 Relieve the fuel system pressure (see Section 2) and remove the fuel tank cap.

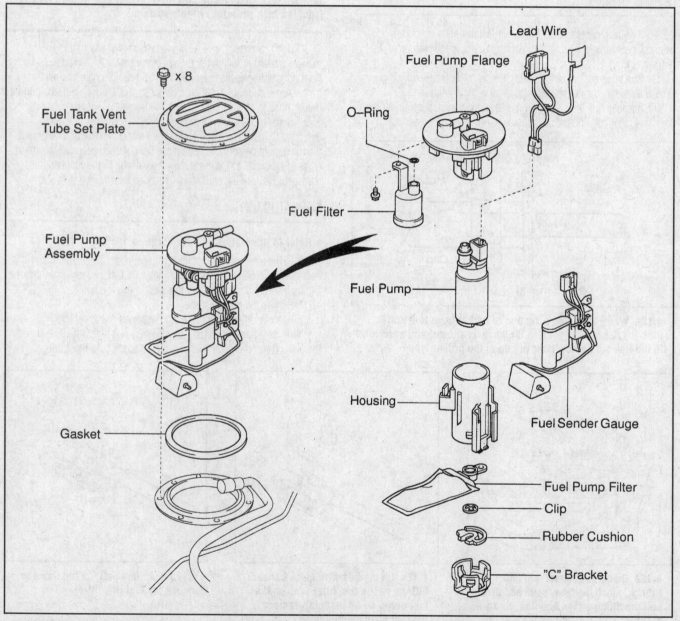

5.4a Exploded view of the fuel pump assembly - 1998 to 2000 models

Fuel Pump & Sender Gauge Connector

Vapor Pressure Sensor

Joint Clip

Tube Joint Clip

Fuel Suction Plate & Sender Gauge

Fuel Tube

O-Ring

Cap

X8

Fuel Tank Vent Tube Set Plate

Fuel Filter

Fuel Pump Assembly

Fuel Pump

No.2 Fuel Filter Cushion

Gasket

No.1 Fuel Suction Support

O-Ring

Fuel Pressure Regulator

Fuel Pump Filter

Clip

Rubber Cushion

No.2 Fuel Suction Support

5.4b Exploded view of the fuel pump assembly - 2001through 2003 models

Vapor Pressure Sensor

Tube Joint Clip

Fuel Suction Plate Sub-assy

Fuel pump Harness

O-ring

Fuel Pump Spacer

Fuel Pump

O-ring

Clip

O-ring

Fuel Pressure Regulator Assy

Fuel Tube Joint No. 1

O-ring

Fuel Filter Assy

O-ring

Clip

5.4c Exploded view of the fuel pump assembly - 2004 and later models

Fuel Suction Support No. 1

Fuel Sender Gage Assy

2   Disconnect the cable from the negative terminal of the battery.

3   Drain as much fuel from the fuel tank as possible into a proper gasoline container.

4   Refer to Section 8 and lower the fuel tank with a transmission-type jack until you can access the fuel pump connectors. There are slight differences between the fuel pump assembly for the 1998 to 2000 models, and the later models (see illustrations).

5   Disconnect the electrical connector. Disconnect the fuel line. If equipped with quick-connect fittings, see Section 4.

6   Remove the fuel pump/sending unit retaining screws (see illustration).

7   Carefully withdraw the fuel pump/fuel level sending unit assembly from the fuel tank.

5.6 Remove the fuel pump assembly cover mounting screws, lay the cover aside and pull the fuel pump assembly out with its gasket

5.8 Disconnect the fuel pump connector at the pump

5.9a Disconnect the electrical connectors, then push to release the fuel sender (1998 to 2000 models)

5.9b The fuel filter on 1998 to 2000 models is retained by a screw (A); to remove the fuel pressure regulator, remove screw (B) also . . .

5.9c . . . then pull the pressure regulator straight out

5.9d To remove the 1998 to 2000 model fuel pump, use screwdrivers to release the tabs in sequence, then disconnect the pump electrical connectors

5.9e Pry the snap-retainers on the bracket in sequence to release the housing from the upper section of the 1998 to 2000 model fuel pump assembly

8 Disconnect the electrical connector from the fuel pump (see illustration).

9 Remove the fuel pump from the assembly (see illustrations). On 2001 and later model pumps, pull the fuel filter/pump assembly off the plate after the plastic support has been removed. Disconnect the electrical connectors and remove the pump.

10 Inspect the fuel strainer for contamination. If it is dirty, replace it.

5.9f On 2001 and later model fuel pumps, pry at the bottom of the assembly to release the fuel pickup support

5.9g Remove the clip at the bottom of the assembly and the fuel strainer, then pry up to release the support (2001 and later)

INSTALLATION

11 Reassemble the fuel pump/sending unit in the reverse order of disassembly.

12 Install the fuel pump/sending unit assembly in the fuel tank. Connect the fuel line and electrical connector. If equipped with a quick-connect fitting, see Section 4.

13 The remainder of installation is the reverse of removal.

6   Fuel pressure regulator - removal and installation

▶ **Refer to illustration 6.3**

❊❊ **WARNING:**

Gasoline is extremely flammable, so take extra precautions when you work on any part of the fuel system. See the Warning in Section 2.

1   Relieve the fuel system pressure (see Section 2). Disconnect the negative battery cable.

2   Remove the fuel pump/fuel level sending unit from the fuel tank (see Section 5). On 1998 to 2000 models, remove the fuel filter retaining screw (see illustration 5.9b). Remove the fuel filter from the fuel pump/sending unit assembly.

3   On 1998 to 2000 models, remove the fuel pressure regulator from the pump/sender mounting plate (see illustration).

4   Remove the fuel pressure regulator on 2001 through 2003 models by pulling it from the assembly. On 2004 and later models, remove the clip and pull the fuel pressure regulator out of the fuel tube joint (see illustration 5.4c).

5   Installation is the reverse of removal. Be sure to install new O-rings on the fuel pressure regulator and fuel filter.

6.3 Remove the fuel pressure regulator mounting screw and remove the pressure regulator from the fuel pump/sending unit assembly - 1998 to 2000 models

7   Fuel level sending unit - check and replacement

❊❊ **WARNING:**

Gasoline is extremely flammable, so take extra precautions when you work on any part of the fuel system. See the Warning in Section 2.

CHECK

▶ **Refer to illustration 7.3**

1   Relieve the fuel system pressure (see Section 2). Disconnect the negative battery cable.

7.3 An accurate check of the sending unit can be made by removing the fuel pump/fuel level sending unit assembly from the fuel tank and checking the sending unit resistance

2 Remove the fuel pump/fuel level sending unit from the fuel tank (see Section 5).

3 Disconnect the sending unit connector and connect the probes of an ohmmeter to terminals 2 and 3 (see illustration). Check the resistance of the sending unit as you move the float arm.

4 With the float arm down (tank empty), the resistance of the sending unit should be approximately 110 to 115 ohms.

5 With the float arm up (tank full), the resistance should be approximately 2 to 3 ohms.

6 The resistance should change smoothly from empty to full. If the readings are incorrect, replace the sending unit.

8   Fuel tank - removal and installation

▶ **Refer to illustrations 8.8 and 8.10**

❊❊ **WARNING:**

Gasoline is extremely flammable, so take extra precautions when you work on any part of the fuel system. See the Warning in Section 2.

1 Relieve the fuel system pressure (see Section 2).
2 Remove the fuel filler cap to relieve fuel tank pressure.
3 Detach the cable from the negative terminal of the battery.
4 If the tank is full or nearly full, siphon the fuel into an approved container using a siphoning kit (available at most auto parts stores).

❊❊ **WARNING:**

Do not start the siphoning action by mouth!

5 Raise the vehicle and support it securely on jackstands. Remove the interfering braces and covers from the canister and the filler hose areas. On 2006 and earlier models, remove the rear section of the exhaust system.

6 Disconnect the fuel tank vent and supply tubes by pushing in the tabs, then pulling them apart.

7 Support the fuel tank with a floor jack. Place a sturdy plank between the jack head and the fuel tank to protect the tank. Remove the bolts and the plastic fuel tank shield.

8 Remove the bolts from the fuel tank retaining straps (see illustration).

7.10 Remove the mounting screws and push down on Tab A while pushing UP to separate the sending unit from the bracket - 1998 to 2000 models

REPLACEMENT

▶ **Refer to illustration 7.10**

7 Remove the fuel pump/fuel level sending unit assembly from the fuel tank (see Section 5).

8 Carefully angle the sending unit out of the opening without damaging the fuel level float located at the bottom of the assembly.

9 Disconnect the electrical connectors from the sending unit.

10 Separate the sending unit from the fuel pump assembly (see accompanying illustration and illustration 5.4b).

11 Installation is the reverse of removal.

8.8 Remove the tank strap bolts (arrows) from the body (early model shown)

9 Lower the tank enough to disconnect the electrical connector from the fuel pump/fuel gauge sending unit.

10 Disconnect the fuel lines, the vapor return line and the fuel inlet pipe from the fuel tank fittings (see illustration).

➡**Note: Be sure to plug the hoses to prevent leakage and contamination of the fuel system.**

11 Remove the tank from the vehicle.
12 Installation is the reverse of removal.

Fuel Tank Vent Tube Set Plate

Fuel Pump

Gasket

Fuel Tank Evaporation Vent Tube

Fuel Cut Off Valve

Fuel Tank

Drain Plug

Fuel Tank Band

Fuel Inlet Pipe Protector

Fuel Tank Protector

Fuel Tank Cap

Gasket

Fuel Inlet Pipe Shield

Fuel Tank Main Tube

Fuel Inlet Hose

Fuel Inlet Pipe

8.10 Typical fuel tank and related components

9 Fuel tank cleaning and repair - general information

1   Any repairs to the fuel tank or filler neck should be carried out by a professional who has experience in this critical and potentially dangerous work. Even after cleaning and flushing of the fuel system, explosive fumes can remain and ignite during repair of the tank.

2   If the fuel tank is removed from the vehicle, it should not be placed in an area where sparks or open flames could ignite the fumes coming out of the tank. Be especially careful inside garages where a gas-type appliance is located.

10 Air cleaner assembly - removal and installation

▶ **Refer to illustrations 10.2 and 10.3**

1   Disconnect the MAF sensor electrical connector. Detach the clips, lift up the air cleaner cover and remove the filter element (see Chapter 1). Disconnect the interfering vacuum hoses. Label them to avoid confusion later.

2   Disconnect the air intake hose from the cover (see illustration).
3   Remove the three bolts and remove the air cleaner assembly from the engine compartment (see illustration).
4   Installation is the reverse of removal.

10.2 To remove the air intake duct and resonator, detach the PCV hose from the resonator, then loosen the two intake duct hose clamps

10.3 Remove the three bolts from the air cleaner assembly and lift the assembly from the engine compartment

11 Accelerator cable - removal, installation and adjustment

➡**Note: This Section applies only to 2006 and earlier models. Later models have an electrically-controlled throttle body that does not have a cable.**

REMOVAL AND INSTALLATION

▶ **Refer to illustrations 11.2, 11.3 and 11.4**

1   Detach the cable from the negative terminal of the battery.
2   Loosen the locknut on the threaded portion of the accelerator

cable at the throttle body (see illustration).
3   Rotate the throttle lever, then slip the accelerator cable end out of the slot in the lever (see illustration).
4   Detach the accelerator cable from the accelerator pedal (see illustration).
5   Pull the cable and casing out of the firewall into the engine compartment.
6   Installation is the reverse of removal. Make sure the grommet seats properly in the firewall.

11.2 Loosen the locknuts on the accelerator cable using two wrenches

11.3 Rotate the throttle lever and remove the cable end from the slot

11.4 Detach the cable from the accelerator pedal arm and slide the cable end out of the slot

ADJUSTMENT

7   To adjust the cable:

a) *Lift up on the cable to remove any slack.*

b) *Turn the adjusting nut until it is 1/8-inch (3 mm) away from the cable bracket.*

c) *Tighten the locknut and check cable deflection between the throttle lever and the cable casing. Deflection should be 3/8 to 1/2-* *inch. If deflection is not within specifications, loosen the locknut and turn the adjusting nut until the deflection is as specified.*

d) *After you have adjusted the accelerator cable, have an assistant help you verify that the throttle valve opens all the way when you depress the accelerator pedal to the floor and that it returns to the idle position when you release the accelerator. Verify the cable operates smoothly. It must not bind or stick.*

12 Electronic fuel injection system - general information

The Electronic Fuel Injection (EFI) system consists of three subsystems: air intake, electronic control and fuel delivery. The system uses an Powertrain Control Module (PCM) along with several sensors to determine the proper air/fuel ratio under all operating conditions. Refer to illustration 1.1 for component locations.

The fuel injection system and the emissions control system are closely linked in function and design. For additional information, refer to Chapter 6.

AIR INTAKE SYSTEM

The air intake system consists of the air cleaner, the air intake ducts, the throttle bodies, the idle control system and the intake manifold. These models are equipped with an intake manifold (lower) and an intake air plenum (upper). Refer to Chapter 2A or 2B for the replacement procedures.

On early models covered by this manual, there are two throttle bodies, which function like a two-barrel unit. The lower portion of the throttle body is heated by engine coolant to prevent icing in cold weather. The idle adjusting screw is located on top of the throttle body. A throttle position sensor is attached to the throttle shaft to monitor changes in the throttle opening.

On early models, when the engine is idling, the air/fuel ratio is controlled by the idle air control system, which consists of the Powertrain Control Module (PCM), the Idle Air Control (IAC) valve and the various other sensors (ECT, IAT, TPS, MAP, MAF etc.) working in conjunction with the EFI system. The IAC valve is activated by the PCM depending upon the running conditions of the engine (air conditioning on, power steering demand, cold or warm temperature etc.). This valve regulates the amount of airflow bypassing the throttle plate and into the intake manifold. The PCM receives information from the sensors and adjusts the idle according to the demands of the engine and driver. Finally, to prevent rough running after the engine starts, the starting valve is opened during cranking and immediately after starting to provide additional air into the intake manifold. Later models have a simplified system that doesn't use a separate IAC circuit or a starting valve. These later models have all of the sensors used in earlier vehicles (see Chapter 6 for more information).

ELECTRONIC CONTROL SYSTEM

The electronic control system, Powertrain Control Module and sensors are described in detail in Chapter 6.

FUEL DELIVERY SYSTEM

The fuel delivery system consists of these components: The fuel pump, fuel pressure regulator, fuel filter, fuel lines, fuel rail and the fuel injectors.

The fuel pump is an electric in-line type. Fuel is drawn through an inlet strainer into the pump, flows through the fuel pressure regulator, passes through the fuel filter and is delivered to the injectors. The fuel pressure regulator maintains a constant fuel pressure to the injectors.

The injectors are solenoid-actuated, constant stroke, pintle types consisting of a solenoid, plunger, needle valve and housing. When current is applied to the solenoid coil, the needle valve raises and pressurized fuel fills the injector housing and squirts out the nozzle. The injection quantity is determined by the length of time the valve is open (the length of time during which current is supplied to the solenoid coils). Because it determines opening and closing intervals - which in turn determines the air-fuel mixture ratio - injector timing must be quite accurate.

The EFI main relay, located in the engine compartment relay/fuse box, supplies power to the fuel pump relay (circuit opening relay) from the ignition key. The PCM controls the grounding signal to the fuel pump in response to the starting and camshaft position signals at start-up.

13 Electronic fuel injection system - check

▶ **Refer to illustrations 13.7, 13.8 and 13.9**

✳✳ WARNING:

Gasoline is extremely flammable, so take extra precautions when you work on any part of the fuel system. See the Warning in Section 2.

1   Check all electrical connectors, especially ground connections, for the system. Loose connectors and poor grounds can cause many engine control system problems.

2   Verify that the battery is fully charged because the Powertrain Control Module (PCM) and sensors cannot operate properly without adequate supply voltage.

3   Refer to Chapter 1 and check the air filter element. A dirty or partially blocked filter will reduce performance and economy.

4   Check fuel pump operation (see Section 3). If the fuel pump fuse is blown, replace it and see if it blows again. If it does, refer to Chapter 12 and the wiring diagrams and look for a short in the wiring harness to the fuel pump.

5   Inspect the vacuum hoses connected to the intake manifold for damage, deterioration and leakage.

13.7 Use a stethoscope or a screwdriver to determine if the injectors are working properly - they should make a steady clicking sound that rises and falls with engine speed changes

13.8 Install the "noid" light into the fuel injector electrical connector and check to see that it blinks with the engine running

6   Remove the air intake duct from the throttle body and check for dirt, carbon, varnish, or other residue in the throttle body, particularly around the throttle plate. If it's dirty, refer to Chapter 6 and troubleshoot the PCV system for the cause of excessive varnish buildup.

7   With the engine running, place an automotive stethoscope against each injector, one at a time, and listen for a clicking sound that indicates operation (see illustration). If you don't have a stethoscope, you can place the tip of a long screwdriver against the injector and listen through the handle.

8   If an injector does not seem to be operating electrically (not clicking), purchase a special injector test light (sometimes called a "noid" light) and install it into the injector wiring harness connector (see illustration). Start the engine and see if the noid light flashes. If it does, the injector is receiving proper voltage. If it doesn't flash, further diagnosis is necessary. You might want to have it checked by a dealership service department or other qualified repair shop.

9   With the engine off and the fuel injector electrical connectors disconnected, measure the resistance of each injector with an ohmmeter (see illustration). Refer to the Specifications at the end of this chapter for the correct resistance.

10   Refer to Chapter 6 for other system checks.

13.9 Using an ohmmeter, measure the resistance across both terminals of the injector

14   Throttle body - check, removal and installation

✻✻ WARNING:

Gasoline is extremely flammable, so take extra precautions when you work on any part of the fuel system. See the Warning in Section 2.

CHECK

◆ **Refer to illustrations 14.2a and 14.2b**

1   Verify that the throttle linkage operates smoothly.

2   Remove the air intake duct from the throttle body and check for carbon and residue build-up. If it is dirty, clean it with aerosol carburetor cleaner (make sure the can specifically states that it is safe with oxygen sensor systems and catalytic converters) and a toothbrush (see illustrations).

✻✻ CAUTION:

Do not clean the Throttle Position Sensor (TPS) or Idle Air Control (IAC) valve with the solvent.

REMOVAL AND INSTALLATION

2006 and earlier models

◆ **Refer to illustrations 14.4, 14.7, 14.8 14.9a and 14.9b**

✻✻ WARNING:

Wait until the engine is completely cool before beginning this procedure.

14.2a The area inside the throttle body near the throttle plate suffers from sludge build-up because the PCV hose vents vapor from the crankcase here

14.2b With the engine off, use aerosol carburetor cleaner (make sure it is safe for use with catalytic converters and oxygen sensors), a toothbrush and a rag to clean the throttle body - open the throttle plate so you can clean behind it

14.4 Early model engine covers are secured with two screws - later models can be removed by pulling up at the front edge, then lifting the rear

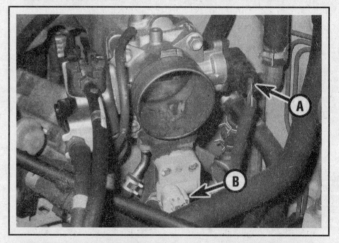

14.7 Disconnect the electrical connectors from the throttle position sensor (A) and from the idle air control valve (B) (early model shown)

➡Note: 2000 and earlier models, as well as 2004 through 2006 models, use a single throttle body. 2001 through 2003 models use two throttle bodies mounted to the "No. 1 Intake Air Control Valve."

3   After the engine is cool, slowly remove the cooling system pressure cap to verify that no pressure remains in the cooling system.

4   Remove the V-bank cover cap nuts and remove the V-bank cover (see illustration).

5   Remove the intake duct and resonator (see Section 10).

6   Disconnect the accelerator cable (see Section 11) and the Throttle Valve (TV) cable (see Chapter 7).

7   Remove the bolt which secures the throttle body to the throttle body bracket, disconnect the electrical connectors from the throttle position sensor and from the idle air control valve (see illustration). Detach any wire harness clamps.

8   Clamp off, then disconnect the coolant bypass hoses. Also detach the air assist hose, the fuel vapor feed hose and the vacuum hoses from the throttle body (see illustration).

9   On 2000 and earlier models and 2004 through 2006 models, remove the nuts and bolts that secure the throttle body to the intake plenum (see illustration). On 2001 and later models remove the three

14.8 Disconnect the coolant bypass hoses (A), and the air assist hose (B) from the throttle body

screws that secure each throttle body (see illustration).

10   Installation is otherwise the reverse of removal. Be sure to use

new gaskets between the throttle body and the intake plenum and tighten the retaining nuts/bolts to the torque listed in this Chapter's Specifications. Check the coolant level and add some, if necessary (see Chapter 1).

2007 and later models

11 Refer to Chapter 2B, Section 4 and remove the windshield wiper motor and the cowl assembly for access to the rear of the engine.

12 Remove the engine cover and both air inlet hoses.

13 Disconnect the hoses, then remove the air filter housing (see Section 10).

14 Make sure the engine is cool, then drain sufficient engine coolant (see Chapter 1). Disconnect the coolant hoses from the throttle body and plug them.

➡Note: The hoses can be temporarily pinched off rather than disconnected to avoid having to drain the system.

15 Disconnect the electrical connector and its clamp from the throttle body.

16 Remove the four throttle body mounting bolts, then lift off the throttle body. Discard the O-ring seal if it's hardened or damaged.

17 Installation is the reverse of removal. If you replace the O-ring,

14.9a Remove the two nuts and two bolts securing the throttle body to the intake plenum (2000 and earlier models/2004 and later models)

make sure to align its tab with the slot in the intake manifold. Tighten the bolts to the torque listed in this Chapter's Specifications.

No.1 Intake Air Control Valve

Protector

O-Ring

O-Ring

Gasket

Gasket

No.1 Throttle Body

No.2 Throttle Body

14.9b Throttle body mounting details - 2001 through 2003 models

15 Fuel rail and injectors - removal and installation

⁂ WARNING:

Gasoline is extremely flammable, so take extra precautions when you work on any part of the fuel system. See the Warning in Section 2.

REMOVAL

♦ **Refer to illustrations 15.4a, 15.4b, 15.10, 15.11, 15.12 and 15.13**

1   Relieve the fuel pressure (see Section 2).
2   Detach the cable from the negative terminal of the battery. Remove the V-bank cover.

2006 and earlier models

3   Remove the PCV hose.
4   Remove the assembly that retains the Vacuum Switching Valve (VSV) control solenoids (see illustrations). Remove the air intake plenum to gain access to the rear (right bank) fuel rail (see Chapter 2A).
5   Disconnect the fuel injector electrical connectors and set the injector wire harness aside.
6   Disconnect the fuel inlet hose from the fuel pump (2000 and ear-

15.4a Remove the two nuts ...

lier models) (see Chapter 1) or the fuel line (2001 and later models) (see illustrations 4.12c and 4.12d).

2007 and later models

7   Remove the upper intake manifold (see Chapter 2B).

15.4b ... and position the VSV assembly off to the side (2006 and earlier model shown)

15.10 Location of the fuel rail mounting bolts

15.11 Carefully pull up on the fuel rail while rocking back and forth to work the injectors out of their bores

15.12 Simultaneously twist and pull the injector to remove it from the fuel rail

8   Pinch the tabs on the fuel inlet tube connector and disconnect it.

9   Disconnect the fuel injector wire harness and set it aside.

All models

10 Remove the fuel rail mounting bolts (see illustration).

11 Remove the fuel rail with the fuel injectors attached (see illustration).

12 Remove the fuel injector(s) from the fuel rail (see illustration) and set them aside in a clearly labeled storage container.

13 If you intend to re-use the same injectors, replace the grommets and O-rings (see illustration).

INSTALLATION

14 Installation of the fuel injectors is the reverse of removal. Make sure the spacers are in place between the intake manifold and the fuel rails.

15 Tighten the fuel rail mounting bolts to the torque listed in this Chapter's Specifications.

15.13 If you plan to reinstall the original injectors, remove and discard the O-rings and grommets and replace them with new ones

16 Exhaust system servicing - general information

▶ **Refer to illustrations 16.1a, 16.1b, 16.1c and 16.4**

✴✴ WARNING:

Inspection and repair of exhaust system components should be done only after the system components have cooled completely.

1   The exhaust system consists of the exhaust manifolds, catalytic converter, the muffler, the tailpipe and all connecting pipes, brackets, hangers and clamps. The exhaust system is attached to the body with mounting brackets and rubber hangers (see illustrations). If any of these parts are damaged or deteriorated, excessive noise and vibration will be transmitted to the body.

2   Conducting regular inspections of the exhaust system will keep it safe and quiet. Look for any damaged or bent parts, open seams, holes, loose connections, excessive corrosion or other defects which could allow exhaust fumes to enter the vehicle. Deteriorated exhaust system components should not be repaired - they should be replaced with new parts.

3   If the exhaust system components are extremely corroded or rusted together, they will probably have to be cut from the exhaust system. The convenient way to accomplish this is to have a muffler repair shop remove the corroded sections with a cutting torch or reciprocating saw. If, however, you want to save money by doing it yourself and you don't have a cutting torch or reciprocating saw, simply cut off the old components with a hack-saw. If you have compressed air, special pneumatic cutting chisels can also be used. If you do decide to tackle the job at home, be sure to wear eye protection to protect your eyes from rust and metal chips, and wear work gloves to protect your hands.

4   Here are some simple guidelines to apply when repairing the exhaust system:

a) *Work from the back to the front when removing exhaust system components.*

b) *Apply penetrating oil to the exhaust system component fasteners to make them easier to remove* (see illustration).

c) *Use new gaskets, hangers and clamps when installing exhaust system components.*

16.1a The exhaust pipe is retained to the catalytic converter with two flange nuts

16.1b The front exhaust pipe and shield are retained to the body with two bracket mounting bolts

16.1c Inspect the muffler hanger for cracks and deterioration of the rubber

16.4 Lubricate the exhaust system fasteners with penetrating oil before attempting to loosen them

d) *Apply anti-seize compound to the threads of all exhaust system fasteners during reassembly. Be sure to allow sufficient clearance between newly installed parts and all points on the underbody to avoid overheating the floor pan and possibly damaging the interior carpet and insulation. Pay particularly close attention to the catalytic converter and its heat shield.*

✳✳ WARNING:

The catalytic converter operates at very high temperatures and takes a long time to cool. Wait until it's completely cool before attempting to remove the converter. Failure to do so could result in serious burns.

Specifications

Fuel system

Fuel system pressure	44 to 50 psi
Fuel system hold pressure (after five minutes)	21 psi minimum
Fuel injector resistance (approximate)	
2006 and earlier models	13.4 to 14.2 ohms
2007 and later models	11.6 to 12.4 ohms

Torque specifications   Ft-lbs (unless otherwise indicated)

➡ **Note: One foot-pound (ft-lb) of torque is equivalent to 12 inch-pounds (in-lbs) of torque. Torque values below approximately 15 ft-lbs are expressed in inch-pounds, since most foot-pound torque wrenches are not accurate at these smaller values.**

Throttle body mounting nuts/bolts	
(2000 and earlier models)	168 in-lbs
No. 1 intake air control valve-to-intake	
plenum nuts (2001 through 2003 models)	22
Throttle body-to-No. 1 intake air control	
valve screws (2001 through 2003 models)	61 in-lbs
Throttle body mounting bolts	
2004 through 2006 models	96 in-lbs
2007 and later models	84 in-lbs
Fuel rail mounting bolts	
2006 and earlier models	
Long bolts	84 in-lbs
Short bolts	168 in-lbs
2007 and later models	15

Section

Reference to other Chapters

5

**ENGINE
ELECTRICAL
SYSTEMS**

1   General information

▶ Refer to illustration 1.1

The engine electrical systems include all ignition, charging and starting components (see illustration). Because of their engine-related functions, these components are considered separately from chassis electrical devices like the lights, instruments, etc.

Be very careful when working on the engine electrical components. They are easily damaged if checked, connected or handled improperly. The alternator is driven by an engine drivebelt that could cause serious injury if your hands, hair or clothes become entangled in it with the engine running. Both the starter and alternator are connected directly to the battery and could arc or even cause a fire if mishandled, overloaded or shorted out.

Never leave the ignition switch on for long periods of time with the engine off. Don't disconnect the battery cables while the engine is running. Correct polarity must be maintained when connecting battery cables from another source, such as another vehicle, during jump starting. Always disconnect the negative cable first and hook it up last or the battery may be shorted by the tool being used to loosen the cable clamps.

Additional safety related information on the engine electrical systems can be found in Safety first near the front of this manual. It should be referred to before beginning any operation included in this Chapter.

1.1 Charging and ignition system components (earlier model shown)

1	Alternator	3	Starter	5	Battery
2	Ignition coils	4	Igniter (close to firewall)		

2   Battery - emergency jump starting

Refer to the Booster battery (jump) starting procedure at the front of this manual.

3   Battery - check and replacement

CHECK

▶ Refer to illustrations 3.2 and 3.3

1   Disconnect the negative battery cable, then the positive cable from the battery.

✳✳ CAUTION:

If the radio in your vehicle is equipped with an anti-theft system, make sure you have the correct activation code before disconnecting the battery.

2   Check the battery state of charge. Visually inspect the indicator eye on the top of the battery; if the indicator eye is black in color charge the battery as described in Chapter 1. Next perform an open voltage circuit test using a digital voltmeter (see illustration).

➡Note: The battery's surface charge must be removed before accurate voltage measurements can be made. Turn On the high beams for ten seconds, then turn them Off, and let the vehicle stand for two minutes.

With the engine and all accessories Off, touch the negative probe of the voltmeter to the negative terminal of the battery and the positive probe to the positive terminal of the battery. The battery voltage should

3.2 To test the open circuit voltage of the battery, simply touch the black probe of the voltmeter to the negative terminal and the red probe to the positive terminal of the battery - a fully charged battery should read between 12.6 to 13.2 volts depending on the outside air temperature

be 12.6 volts or slightly above. If the battery is less than the specified voltage, charge the battery before proceeding to the next test. Do not proceed with the battery load test unless the battery charge is correct.

3   Perform a battery load test. An accurate check of the battery condition can only be performed with a load tester (available at most auto parts stores). This test evaluates the ability of the battery to operate the starter and other accessories during periods of heavy amperage draw (load). Install a special battery load-testing tool onto the terminals (see illustration). Load test the battery according to the manufacturer's instructions for the particular tool. This tool utilizes a carbon pile to increase the load demand (amperage draw) on the battery. Maintain the load on the battery for 15 seconds or less and observe that the battery

3.5 Remove the two nuts (arrows) and detach the hold-down clamps

4   Battery cables - check and replacement

▶ **Refer to illustrations 4.4a and 4.4b**

1   Periodically inspect the entire length of each battery cable for damage, cracked or burned insulation and corrosion. Poor battery cable connections can cause starting problems and decreased engine performance.

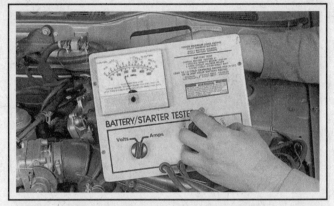

3.3 Some battery load testers are equipped with an ammeter which enables the battery load to be precisely dialed in, as shown - less expensive testers have a load switch and voltmeter only

voltage does not drop below 9.6 volts. If the battery condition is weak or defective, the tool will indicate this condition immediately.

➡**Note: Cold temperatures will cause the minimum voltage reading to drop slightly. Follow the chart given in the manufacturer's instructions to compensate for cold climates. Minimum load voltage for freezing temperatures (32 degrees F) should be approximately 9.1 volts.**

REPLACEMENT

▶ **Refer to illustration 3.5**

4   Disconnect the negative battery cable, then the positive cable from the battery.

✱✱ CAUTION:

Always disconnect the negative cable first and hook it up last or the battery may be shorted by the tool being used to loosen the cable clamps.

5   Remove the battery hold-down clamp (see illustration).
6   Lift out the battery. Be careful - it's heavy.

➡**Note: Battery straps and handlers are available at most auto parts stores for a reasonable price. They make it easier to remove and carry the battery.**

7   While the battery is out, inspect the battery tray for corrosion.
8   If corrosion exists on the battery tray, detach the bolts and remove the tray from the engine compartment. Clean the deposits from the metal to prevent the battery tray from further corrosion.
9   If you are replacing the battery, make sure you get one that's identical, with the same dimensions, amperage rating, cold cranking rating, etc.
10   Installation is the reverse of removal.

2   Check the cable-to-terminal connections at the ends of the cables for cracks, loose wire strands and corrosion (see Chapter 1). The presence of white, fluffy deposits under the insulation at the cable terminal connection is a sign that the cable is corroded and should be replaced. Check the terminals for distortion, missing mounting bolts and corrosion.

4.4a The negative battery cable is attached to the chassis as well as the engine to ensure a proper ground

4.4b Note the routing of the cable and replace it as originally installed

3   When removing the cables, always disconnect the negative cable first and hook it up last or the battery may be shorted by the tool used to loosen the cable clamps. Even if only the positive cable is being replaced, be sure to disconnect the negative cable from the battery first.

4   Disconnect the old cables from the battery, then trace each of them to their opposite ends and detach them from the starter solenoid and ground terminals. Note the routing of each cable to ensure correct installation (see illustrations).

5   If you are replacing either or both of the old cables, take them with you when buying new cables. It is vitally important that you replace the cables with identical parts. Cables have characteristics that make them easy to identify: positive cables are usually red and larger

in cross-section; ground cables are usually black and smaller in cross section.

6   Clean the threads of the solenoid or ground connection with a wire brush to remove rust and corrosion. Apply a light coat of battery terminal corrosion inhibitor, or petroleum jelly, to the threads to prevent future corrosion.

7   Attach the cable to the solenoid or ground connection and tighten the mounting nut/bolt securely.

8   Before connecting a new cable to the battery, make sure that it reaches the battery post without having to be stretched.

9   Connect the positive cable first, followed by the negative cable.

5   Ignition system - general information and precautions

▶ **Refer to illustration 5.1**

1   All models covered by this manual are equipped with a Distributorless Ignition System (DIS) (see illustration).

2   The DIS system includes the camshaft position sensor, the

crankshaft position sensor, coils, igniter and the PCM (computer). The PCM generates cylinder identification signals that allow the igniter to trigger the correct coil. The igniter distributes the signal to the proper coil driver circuit and determines dwell period based on coil primary

5.1 Typical ignition system electrical schematic (1998 to 2000 models)

current flow. Each coil is fired independently and in the proper sequence.

→Note: On 2001 and later models, the igniters are part of the individual ignition coils.

3 On 1998 to 2000 models, the front (left bank) spark plug connectors are integrated into the three ignition coils. Spark plug wires connect the rear (right bank) spark plugs to these coils. On 2001 and later models, there are six individual coils, one mounted over each spark plug, and there are no secondary spark plug wires.

4 Each coil has its own integral igniter.

5 When working on the ignition system, take the following precautions:

a) *Do not keep the ignition switch on for more than 10 seconds if the engine will not start.*

b) *Always connect a tachometer in accordance with the manufacturer's instructions. Some tachometers may be incompatible with this ignition system. Consult an auto parts counterperson before buying a tachometer for use with this vehicle.*

c) *Never allow the ignition coil terminals to touch ground. Grounding the coil could result in damage to the igniter and/or the ignition coil.*

d) *Do not disconnect the battery when the engine is running.*

e) *Make sure that the igniter is properly grounded.*

6   Ignition system - check

▶ Refer to illustrations 6.1, 6.4a, 6.4b, 6.6a, 6.6b and 6.7

✳✳ WARNING:

Because of the high voltage generated by the ignition system, extreme care should be taken whenever an operation is performed involving ignition components. This not only includes the igniter, coil and spark plug wires, but related components such as plug connectors, tachometer and other test equipment as well.

1 If the engine turns over but won't start, disconnect the spark plug wire from any spark plug and attach it to a calibrated ignition tester (available at most auto parts stores) (see illustration). Make sure the tester is designed for a distributorless ignition system if a universal tester isn't available. On 2001 and later models, remove one coil at a time and plug the tester into the plug socket.

2 Connect the clip on the tester to a bolt or metal bracket on the engine, crank the engine and watch the end of the tester to see if bright blue, well-defined sparks occur.

✳✳ CAUTION:

Do not crank the engine for longer than it takes to observe the spark tester. Longer cranking with one or more spark plugs out could cause too much unburned fuel to collect in the engine.

3 If sparks occur, sufficient voltage is reaching the spark plug to fire it (repeat the check at the remaining spark plug wires or coils to verify that all the ignition coils are functioning). However, the plugs themselves may be fouled, so remove and check them as described in Chapter 1 or install new ones.

→Note: On 1998 to 2000 models, use the spark plug wires leading to the rear bank spark plugs to check the coils. Since the waste spark system is used, it can be assumed the coils are firing the front bank spark plugs if the rear bank plug wires are firing.

4 If no sparks or intermittent sparks occur, check for battery voltage to the ignition coils (see illustrations). If battery voltage is present, check the coil resistance (see Section 7).

6.1 To use a calibrated ignition tester, simply disconnect a coil or spark plug wire, connect it to the tester, clip the tester to a convenient ground and operate the starter with the ignition ON - if there is enough power to fire the plug, sparks will be visible between the electrode tip and the tester body

6.4a On 1998 through 2000 models, disconnect the electrical connector at each ignition coil and check for battery voltage at terminal no. 1 with the ignition key turned to ON (engine not running)

6.4b On 2001 through 2006 models, unplug the black four-pin electrical connector at each ignition coil/igniter and check for battery voltage at terminal no. 1 with the key turned to ON (engine not running)

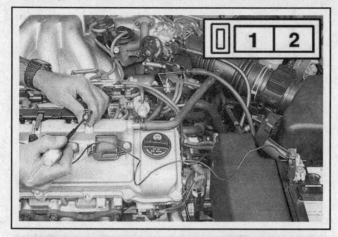

6.6a On 1998 through 2000 models, use an LED test light to check for a trigger signal from the igniter on terminal no. 2 as an assistant cranks the engine

5   Check the camshaft and crankshaft position sensors (see Chapter 6).

6   Check for a coil trigger signal to the coil packs from the PCM or igniter as follows:

   a) *On 1998 through 2000 models, disconnect the electrical connector from each coil pack and attach a 12-volt test light to the battery positive terminal. Make sure it is a light emitting diode (LED) type test light. Touch the test light probe to terminal no. 2 (see illustration). Have an assistant crank the engine over - the test light should blink on and off as the igniter completes the circuit to ground. Make this test for each coil pack. If the test results are incorrect, check the igniter (see Section 10).*

   b) *On 2001 through 2006 models, disconnect the black four-terminal electrical connector from each of the six ignition coil/igniter units and measure the voltage between terminal no. 3 (see illustration) and ground. It should be more than 0.1 and less than 4.5 volts. If it's out of range, troubleshoot the wiring harness between the ECM and the ignition coil/igniter unit. If the wiring is okay, the ECM may be defective. Have the ECM checked by a Toyota service department.*

6.6b On 2001 through 2006 models, unplug the black four-pin electrical connector at each ignition coil/igniter and, using a digital voltmeter, measure the trigger signal from the PCM at terminal no. 3 while an assistant cranks the engine; it should be more than 0.1 volts and less than 4.5 volts

6.7 On 2001 through 2006 models, unplug the black four-pin electrical connector at each ignition coil/igniter unit and measure the ignition confirmation voltage between terminal no. 2 and ground; it should be between 4.5 and 5.5 volts

7   On 2001 and later models, the igniter units also send an ignition confirmation signal (IGF) as a fail-safe measure to the ECM. To verify that this signal is present and correct, unplug the black four-pin electrical connector at each of the six ignition coil/igniter units and measure the voltage between terminal no. 2 (see illustration) and ground. It should be between 4.5 and 5.5 volts. If it isn't within this range, replace the ignition coil/igniter unit.

7   Ignition coil(s) - check and replacement

CHECK

Refer to illustrations 7.1 and 7.2

➡**Note 1: The following coil primary and secondary resistance checks do not apply to the ignition coil/igniter units used on 2001 and later models. The manufacturer does not publish primary or secondary resistance specifications for the ignition coil/igniter units used on these models. The only way to check them is to substitute a known good unit. But this option isn't feasible for a home mechanic because you can't return electrical components to a parts department once you have purchased them. If you have already eliminated all other possible causes of an ignition malfunction, a defective ignition coil/igniter unit is the likely cause of the problem, but the only way to verify this is to have a dealer substitute a known good unit.**

➡**Note 2: The following checks should be made with the engine cold. If the engine is hot the resistance will be greater.**

1   Check the primary resistance of each ignition coil on 1998 through 2000 models. With the ignition key OFF, disconnect the electrical harness connector(s) from each coil. Connect an ohmmeter across the coil primary terminals (see illustration). The resistance should be as listed in this Chapter's Specifications. If not, replace the coil.

2   Check the secondary resistance of each ignition coil. With the ignition key OFF, label and detach the spark plug wires from each coil. On 1998 through 2000 models, remove the coil for this test. Connect an ohmmeter across the two secondary terminals of each coil (see illustration). The resistance should be as listed in this Chapter's Specifications. If not, replace the coil. If no specifications are available, compare the readings of several coils or swap coils between cylinders to test.

REPLACEMENT

3   Disconnect the negative cable from the battery.

7.1 On 1998 through 2000 models, disconnect the electrical connectors and measure the coil primary resistance across the two terminals at each coil; to remove a coil, remove the retaining bolt

❋❋ CAUTION:

If the stereo in your vehicle is equipped with an anti-theft system, make sure you have the correct activation code before disconnecting the battery.

7.2 Remove the coils and measure the secondary resistance across the two spark plug wire terminals (1998 through 2000 models)

4   Remove the V-bank cover (see Chapter 1). On 2007 and later models, remove the upper intake manifold (see Chapter 2B).
5   Disconnect the ignition coil harness electrical connector(s) from each individual coil pack. Label each connector so they don't get mixed up. Label and detach the spark plug wires for the rear cylinder bank spark plugs.
6   Remove the bolt(s) securing the ignition coil to the engine (see illustration 7.1) and remove the coil.
7   Installation is the reverse of the removal procedure.

8   Ignition timing - check

▶ Refer to illustrations 8.2a, 8.2b and 8.4

➡Note: The following ignition timing procedure should apply to most 2003 and earlier models covered by this manual. However, if the procedure specified on the VECI label of your vehicle differs from this one, use the procedure found on the VECI label. The ignition timing cannot be adjusted on these models. The distributorless ignition system is controlled by the PCM (computer) during operation. If the ignition timing is incorrect, diagnose the ignition system components (see Section 6).

1   Remove the V-bank cover (see Chapter 1).
2   Locate the diagnostic electrical connector and insert a jumper wire (see illustrations). On 1998 through 2000 models, connect between terminal TE1 and E1, and on 2001 through 2003 models, connect between TC and E1.
3   With the ignition switch off, connect a timing light and a tachometer according to the tool manufacturer's instructions.
4   Locate the timing marks on the timing belt cover and the crankshaft pulley (see illustration).

8.2a Attach a jumper wire between terminals E1 and TE1 on the test connector (1998 through 2000 models)

8.2b Attach a jumper wire between terminals E1 and TC on the test connector (2001 through 2003 models)

8.4 The timing marks are clearly molded into the timing belt cover

5   Start the engine and allow it to warm up to normal operating temperature (upper radiator hose hot). Verify that the engine idle is correct (refer to the Specifications listed at the end of this Chapter).

6   Idle speed cannot be adjusted. If the idle speed is incorrect, inspect the intake system (see Chapter 4) for an air leak and check the operation of the idle air control valve (see Chapter 6). If the intake system and the idle air control valve are okay, the PCM might be defective. Have the vehicle diagnosed by a dealer service department or a qualified repair shop.

7   Aim the timing light at the timing scale on the front engine cover. The notch on the crankshaft pulley should line up with the pointer on the scale on the timing cover. Refer to the Specifications listed at the

end of this Chapter.

8   Ignition timing cannot be adjusted. If the timing is incorrect, the PCM might be defective. Have the vehicle diagnosed by a dealer service department or other qualified repair shop.

9   Remove the jumper wire from the diagnostic connector and recheck the ignition timing. Refer to the Specifications listed at the end of this Chapter. Again, if the timing is incorrect, have the vehicle diagnosed by a dealer or shop.

10   Turn off the engine and remove the tachometer and the timing light.

9   Igniter (1998 through 2000 models) - check and replacement

▶ Refer to illustration 9.1

➡Note 1: The following procedure does not apply to the integral ignition coil/igniter units used on 2001 and later models. Testing the igniter function of these units is beyond the scope of the home mechanic. You can check the ignition confirmation signal of each igniter (see Section 6, Step 7), but other than that, identifying a bad igniter is simply a process of elimination. If you suspect a bad igniter on one of these models, have the ignition coil/igniter unit tested by a dealer service department or a qualified repair shop.

➡Note 2: Refer to the wiring diagrams at the end of Chapter 12 when performing the following checks.

1   Disconnect the electrical connector from the igniter and perform the following electrical checks at the igniter harness connector with the ignition switch On (see illustration):

   a) Check for battery voltage on terminal no. 9. If battery voltage is not present check the circuit from the igniter to the battery.
   b) Check for approximately 5.0 volts at terminal no. 4. If 5.0 volts are not present, have the PCM checked by a dealership service department or other properly equipped repair facility.
   c) Check for a fluctuating 0.1 to 4.5 volt signal at terminal no. 5, 6 and 7 in turn, as an assistant cranks the engine. If a 0.1 to 4.5 volt signal at terminal no. 5, 6 and 7 is not present as an assistant cranks the engine, have the PCM checked by a dealership service department or other properly equipped repair facility.
   d) Check for continuity to a good chassis ground at terminal no. 3.

2   If the above checks are good, turn the ignition switch Off and

9.1 The igniter on 1998 through 2000 models is located close to the firewall, near the coolant filler cap

reconnect the electrical connector to the igniter.

3   Disconnect the electrical connectors at each ignition coil. Using an LED test light, check for an ignition coil trigger signal at each ignition coil connector as an assistant cranks the engine (see Section 6, Step 6). If no ignition coil trigger signal is present, check the circuits from the igniter to the ignition coils for continuity. If the circuits are good, replace the igniter.

10   Charging system - general information and precautions

The charging system includes the alternator, an internal voltage regulator, a charge indicator, the battery, a fusible link and the wiring between all the components. The charging system supplies electrical power for the ignition system, the lights, the radio, etc. The alternator is driven by a drivebelt at the front of the engine.

The purpose of the voltage regulator is to limit the alternator's voltage to a preset value. This prevents power surges, circuit overloads, etc., during peak voltage output.

The charging system doesn't ordinarily require periodic maintenance. However, the drivebelt, battery and wires and connections

should be inspected at the intervals outlined in Chapter 1.

The dashboard warning light should come on when the ignition key is turned to Start, then should go off immediately. If it remains on, there is a malfunction in the charging system. Some vehicles are also equipped with a voltage gauge. If the voltage gauge indicates abnormally high or low voltage, check the charging system (see Section 11).

Be very careful when making electrical circuit connections to a vehicle equipped with an alternator and note the following:

   a) When reconnecting wires to the alternator from the battery, be sure to note the polarity.

b) Before using arc-welding equipment to repair any part of the vehicle, disconnect the wires from the alternator and the battery terminals.

c) Never start the engine with a battery charger connected.

d) Always disconnect both battery leads before using a battery charger.

e) The alternator is driven by an engine drivebelt that could cause serious injury if your hand, hair or clothes become entangled in it with the engine running.

f) Because the alternator is connected directly to the battery, it could arc or cause a fire if overloaded or shorted out.

g) Wrap a plastic bag over the alternator and secure it with rubber bands before steam cleaning the engine.

11 Charging system - check

▶ **Refer to illustrations 11.3 and 11.6**

1   If a malfunction occurs in the charging circuit, do not immediately assume that the alternator is causing the problem. First, check the following items:

a) Make sure the battery cable clamps, where they connect to the battery, are clean and tight.

b) Test the condition of the battery (see Section 2). If it does not pass all the tests, replace it with a new battery.

c) Check the external alternator wiring and connections.

d) Check the drivebelt condition and tension (see Chapter 1).

e) Check the alternator mounting bolts for tightness.

f) Run the engine and check the alternator for abnormal noise.

g) Check the fusible links (if equipped) in the engine compartment fuse box (see Chapter 12). If they're burned, determine the cause and repair the circuit.

h) Check the charge light on the dash. It should illuminate when the ignition key is turned ON (engine not running). If it does not, check the circuit from the alternator to the charge light on the dash.

i) Check all the fuses that are in series with the charging system circuit. The location of these fuses and fusible links may vary from year and model but the designations are generally the same. Refer to the wiring schematics at the end of Chapter 12 for additional information.

2   With the ignition key off, check the battery voltage with no accessories operating. It should be approximately 12.6 volts. It may be slightly higher if the engine had been operating within the last hour.

3   Connect an ammeter to the charging system following the tool manufacturer's instructions. Start the engine, and check the battery voltage and amperage. It should now be approximately 13.2 to 15.0 volts at 10 amps or less (see illustration).

4   Load the battery by turning on the high beam headlights and the air conditioning (if equipped) and place the blower fan on HIGH. Raise the engine speed to 2,000 rpm and check the voltage and amperage. If the charging system is working properly the voltage should stay above 13.5 volts and the amperage should be 30 amps or more (depending on the condition of the battery - it could be less than 30 amps).

5   If the voltage rises above 15.0 volts in either test, the regulator is defective.

6   If the charging voltage is below the minimum charging voltage, turn the accessories and the engine off and use a small screwdriver to full field the alternator circuit (see illustration). Start the engine and check the charging voltage. If the charging voltage is now within the specified range, the voltage regulator is defective. If the charging voltage is still low, the alternator is defective.

11.3 Connect a voltmeter to the battery terminals and check the battery voltage with the engine Off and again with the engine running

11.6 If the alternator is not charging, ground terminal F to the alternator body, start the engine and check the voltage at the battery - if the reading is now within the specified range, replace the regulator; if the reading is less than the minimum charging voltage, replace the alternator

12 Alternator - removal and installation

REMOVAL

2006 and earlier models

♦ **Refer to illustrations 12.3 and 12.4**

1   Detach the cable from the negative terminal of the battery.

2   Detach the electrical connectors from the alternator.

3   Loosen the alternator adjustment and pivot bolts (see illustration) and detach the drivebelt.

4   Remove the adjustment and pivot bolts and remove the alternator from the engine bracket and the adjustment bracket (see illustration).

2007 and later models

5   Remove the engine cover by pulling up at the front edge, then lifting the rear.

6   Loosen the lug nuts of the right front wheel. Raise the vehicle and support it securely on jackstands. Remove the right front wheel.

7   Remove the engine lower splash shield and the right inner fender splash shield.

8   Drain the engine coolant (see Chapter 1).

✳✳ WARNING:

Make sure the engine is completely cool first.

9   Remove both air filter inlet tubes. Remove the battery (see Section 3).

10 Remove the front bumper and the energy absorber (see Chapter 11).

11 Remove the radiator and the cooling fan unit (see Chapter 3).

12 Remove the serpentine drivebelt (see Chapter 1).

13 Disconnect the wiring from the alternator and the air conditioning compressor. Disconnect the wiring harness clamps.

12.3 First loosen the pivot bolt (A), loosen the lock bolt (B) and then turn the adjustment bolt (C) counterclockwise to release the tension on the drivebelt (2006 and earlier shown)

14 Remove the bolts from the front of the alternator and the bolt from the rear bracket. Disconnect the remaining wiring harness clamp and lift off the alternator.

INSTALLATION

15 If you are replacing the alternator, take the old alternator with you when purchasing a replacement unit. Make sure that the new/rebuilt unit is identical to the old alternator. Look at the terminals - they should be the same in number, size and locations as the terminals on the old alternator. Finally, look at the identification markings - they will be stamped in the housing or printed on a tag or plaque affixed to the housing. Make sure that these numbers are the same on both alternators.

12.4 Typical early alternator mounting details

Plate Washer — Generator Wire — Generator Connector — Pivot Bolt — Adjusting Bolt — Generator — Adjusting Lock Bolt — Drive Belt

16 Many new/rebuilt alternators do not have a pulley installed, so you may have to switch the pulley from the old unit to the new/rebuilt one. When buying an alternator, find out the shop's policy regarding installation of pulleys - some shops will perform this service free of charge.

17 Installation is the reverse of removal.
18 After the alternator is installed, adjust the drivebelt tension (see Chapter 1).
19 Check the charging voltage to verify proper operation of the alternator (see Section 11).

13 Voltage regulator and alternator brushes - replacement

▶ **Refer to illustrations 13.2, 13.3, 13.5, 13.6 and 13.9**

1 Remove the alternator (see Section 12) and place it on a clean workbench.
2 Remove the output terminal nut and insulator. Remove the rear cover nuts and remove the rear cover (see Illustration).
3 Remove the two brush holder retaining screws (see illustration).
4 Remove the brush holder.
5 Remove the three voltage regulator retaining screws and remove the voltage regulator (see illustration).
➥**Note: 2007 and later models do not have voltage regulators as described here.**
6 Measure the exposed length of each brush (see illustration) and compare it to the specified minimum length. If the length of the brush is less than the minimum listed in this Chapter's Specifications, replace the brush assembly.

7 Make sure that each brush moves smoothly in the brush holder.
8 Install the voltage regulator.
9 Install the brush holder by depressing the brush with a small screwdriver to clear the shaft (see illustration).
10 Install the brush holder screws into the rear frame.
11 Install the rear cover and tighten the nuts securely.
12 Install the output terminal insulator and tighten it with the nut.
13 Install the alternator.

13.2 Remove the nut, washer and insulator from the output terminal, then the three nuts securing the end cover

13.3 Remove the two screws (arrows) that retain the brush holder

13.5 Remove the three screws (arrows) that retain the voltage regulator

13.6 Measure the exposed length of the brushes and compare your measurements to the specified minimum length to determine if they should be replaced

13.9 When installing the brush holder, depress each brush with a small screwdriver to clear the shaft

14 Starting system - general information and precautions

▶ **Refer to illustration 14.2**

The starting system consists of the battery, the starter motor, the starter solenoid and the electrical circuit connecting the components (see illustration). The solenoid is mounted directly on the starter motor.

The solenoid/starter motor assembly is installed on the upper part of the engine, next to the transaxle bellhousing.

When the ignition key is turned to the START position, the starter solenoid is actuated through the starter control circuit. The starter solenoid then connects the battery to the starter. The battery supplies the electrical energy to the starter motor, which does the actual work of cranking the engine.

The starter motor on a vehicle equipped with a manual transaxle

14.2 Exploded view of a typical starter assembly

can be operated only when the clutch pedal is depressed; the starter on a vehicle equipped with an automatic transaxle can be operated only when the transaxle selector lever is in Park or Neutral.

Always observe the following precautions when working on the starting system:

a) *Excessive cranking of the starter motor can overheat it and cause serious damage. Never operate the starter motor for more than 15 seconds at a time without pausing to allow it to cool for at least two minutes.*

b) *The starter is connected directly to the battery and could arc or*

c) *cause a fire if mishandled, overloaded or short-circuited.*

c) *Always detach the cable from the negative terminal of the battery before working on the starting system.*

✳✳ CAUTION:

If the stereo in your vehicle is equipped with an anti-theft system, make sure you have the correct activation code before disconnecting the battery.

15   Starter motor and circuit - check

♦ **Refer to illustration 15.4**

1   If a malfunction occurs in the starting circuit, do not immediately assume that the starter is causing the problem. First, check the following items:

a) *Make sure the battery cable clamps, where they connect to the battery, are clean and tight.*

b) *Check the condition of the battery cables (see Section 4). Replace any defective battery cables with new parts.*

c) *Test the condition of the battery (see Section 3). If it does not pass all the tests, replace it with a new battery.*

d) *Check the starter solenoid wiring and connections. Refer to the wiring diagrams at the end of Chapter 12.*

e) *Check the starter mounting bolts for tightness.*

f) *Check the fusible links (if equipped) exiting the engine compartment fuse box (see Chapter 12). If they're burned, determine the cause and repair the circuit. Also, check the ignition switch circuit for correct operation (see Chapter 12).*

g) *Check the operation of the Park/Neutral switch. Make sure the shift lever is in PARK or NEUTRAL. Refer to Chapter 7 for the Park/Neutral switch check and adjustment procedure. Refer to Chapter 12 wiring diagrams, if necessary, when performing circuit checks. These systems must operate correctly to provide battery voltage to the ignition solenoid.*

h) *Check the operation of the starter relay. The starter relay is located in the fuse/relay box inside the engine compartment. Refer to Chapter 12 for the testing procedure.*

2   If the starter does not actuate when the ignition switch is turned to the start position, check for battery voltage to the solenoid. This will determine if the solenoid is receiving the correct voltage signal from the ignition switch. Connect a test light or voltmeter to the starter solenoid positive terminal and while an assistant turns the ignition switch to the start position. If voltage is not available, refer to the wiring diagrams in Chapter 12 and check all the fuses and relays in series with the starting system. If voltage is available but the starter motor does not operate, remove the starter from the engine compartment (see Section 16) and bench test the starter (see Step 4).

3   If the starter turns over slowly, check the starter cranking voltage and the current draw from the battery. This test must be performed with the starter assembly on the engine. Crank the engine over (for 10 seconds or less) and observe the battery voltage. It should not drop below 8.0 volts on manual transaxle models or 8.5 volts on automatic transaxle models. Also, observe the current draw using an amp meter. It should not exceed 400 amps or drop below 250 amps. If the starter

15.4 Starter motor bench testing details

motor cranking amp values are not within the correct range, replace it with a new unit. There are several conditions that may affect the starter cranking potential. The battery must be in good condition and the battery cold-cranking rating must not be under-rated for the particular application. Be sure to check the battery specifications carefully. The battery terminals and cables must be clean and not corroded. Also, in cases of extreme cold temperatures, make sure the battery and/or engine block is warmed before performing the tests.

4   If the starter is receiving voltage but does not activate, remove and check the starter/solenoid assembly on the bench. Most likely the solenoid is defective. In some rare cases, the engine may be seized so be sure to try and rotate the crankshaft pulley (see Chapter 2A or 2B) before proceeding. With the starter/solenoid assembly mounted in a vise on the bench, install one jumper cable from the negative battery terminal to the body of the starter (see illustration). Install the other jumper cable from the positive battery terminal to the B+ terminal on the starter. Install a starter switch and apply battery voltage to the solenoid S terminal (for 10 seconds or less) and see if the solenoid plunger, shift lever and overrunning clutch extends and rotates the pinion drive. If the pinion drive extends but does not rotate, the solenoid is operating but the starter motor is defective. If there is no movement but the solenoid clicks, the solenoid and/or the starter motor is defective. If the solenoid plunger extends and rotates the pinion drive, the starter/solenoid assembly is working properly.

16 Starter motor - removal and installation

1   Detach the cable from the negative terminal of the battery.

2006 AND EARLIER MODELS

▶ **Refer to illustration 16.5**

2   Remove the battery and battery tray from the engine compartment.

Starter Connector

Starter

16.5 Starter motor installation details

Starter Wire

3   Disconnect and remove the cruise control actuator from the engine compartment, if equipped. Refer to Chapter 7 and disconnect the transaxle shift control cable.

4   Detach the electrical connectors from the starter/solenoid assembly.

5   Remove the starter motor mounting bolts (see illustration).

6   Remove the bracket from the upper section of the starter/solenoid assembly.

➡**Note: It is necessary to loosen one or two of the bracket bolts to allow the starter/solenoid assembly to partially drop down to gain access to the remaining bracket assembly bolts and hardware.**

7   Installation is the reverse of removal.

2007 AND LATER MODELS

8   Remove the battery (see Section 3).

9   Remove the air filter housing assembly; the air inlet tubes and the filter housing support bracket (see Chapter 4).

10 Disconnect the wiring from the starter.

11 Remove the mounting bolts and lift out the starter.

12 Installation is the reverse of removal.

17 Starter solenoid - removal and installation

17.2 Before disassembling the starter motor, solenoid and gear reduction assembly, scribe or paint an alignment mark across the starter motor and the gear reduction assembly

▶ **Refer to illustrations 17.2, 17.3, 17.4, 17.5, 17.6a and 17.6b**

1   Remove the starter motor (see Section 16).

2   Scribe or paint a mark across the starter motor and gear reduction assembly (see illustration).

3   Disconnect the strap from the solenoid to the starter motor terminal (see illustration).

4   Remove the screws that secure the gear reduction assembly to the solenoid (see illustration).

5   Remove the through-bolts that secure the starter motor to the gear reduction assembly (see illustration).

6   Separate the motor from the gear reduction and solenoid assembly then remove the solenoid from the gear reduction assembly (see illustrations).

7   Installation is the reverse of removal. Be sure to align the paint or scribe mark.

17.3 To disconnect the strap that connects the starter to the solenoid, remove this nut

17.4 To detach the solenoid from the starter motor, remove the screws that secure the gear reduction assembly to the solenoid . . .

17.5 . . . and remove the through-bolts that secure the starter motor to the gear reduction assembly (typical unit shown)

17.6a Separate the starter from the gear reduction assembly . . .

17.6b . . . and separate the solenoid from the gear reduction assembly (note the return spring protruding from the solenoid assembly - make sure that this spring is installed before reassembling the solenoid and the gear reduction assembly)

Specifications

Idle speed (cooling fan and all accessories off)*   650 to 750 rpm
If the idle speed specified on the VECI label is different, it supersedes the information provided here.

Ignition timing (transmission in Neutral) (2006 and earlier models)

Test terminals TC and E1 connected	8 to 12 degrees BTDC
Test terminals not connected	7 to 24 degrees BTDC

Ignition coil

1998 to 2000 models	
Primary resistance	
Cold	0.70 to 0.94 ohms
Hot	0.85 to 1.10 ohms
Secondary resistance	
Aisan coils	
Cold	10.8 to 14.9 k-ohms
Hot	13.1 to 17.5 k-ohms
Diamond coils	
Cold	6.8 to 11.7 k-ohms
Hot	8.6 to 13.7 k-ohms
2001 and later models	Specifications not available

Charging system

Charging voltage	13.5 to 14.8 volts
Standard current	
No load	10 amps or less
With load	30 amps or more
Alternator brush length	
Standard	0.413 inch
Minimum	0.059 inch

Section

6

EMISSIONS AND ENGINE CONTROL SYSTEMS

1 General information

▶ **Refer to illustrations 1.1, 1.6a and 1.6b**

To prevent pollution of the atmosphere from incompletely burned and evaporating gases, and to maintain good driveability and fuel economy, a number of emission control systems are incorporated (see illustration). They include the:

On-Board Diagnostic (OBD) system
Electronic engine controls (EFI) system
Evaporative Emissions Control (EVAP) system
Positive Crankcase Ventilation (PCV) system
Acoustic Control Induction System (ACIS)
Catalytic converter

The Sections in this Chapter include general descriptions, checking procedures within the scope of the home mechanic and component replacement procedures (when possible) for each of the systems listed above.

Before assuming that an emissions control system is malfunction-ing, check the fuel and ignition systems carefully. The diagnosis of some emission control devices requires specialized tools, equipment and training. If checking and servicing become too difficult or if a procedure is beyond your ability, consult a dealer service department or other repair shop. Remember, the most frequent cause of emissions problems is simply a loose or broken wire or vacuum hose, so always check the hose and wiring connections first.

This doesn't mean, however, that emissions control systems are particularly difficult to maintain and repair. You can quickly and easily perform many checks and do most of the regular maintenance at home with common tune-up and hand tools.

➡**Note: Because of a Federally mandated warranty which covers the emissions control system components, check with your dealer about warranty coverage before working on any emissions-related systems. Once the warranty has expired, you may wish to perform some of the component checks and/or replacement procedures in this Chapter to save money.**

1.1 Typical emission and engine control system components

1	*Diagnostic test connector*	*3*	*Throttle Position Sensor (TPS) (on other side of throttle body)*	*5*	*Oxygen sensor*
2	*Idle Air Control (IAC) valve (under throttle body)*	*4*	*Mass Airflow (MAF) sensor*	*6*	*Coils*
				7	*Coolant temperature sensor (on thermostat housing)*

1.6a The Vehicle Emission Control Information (VECI) label contains such essential information as the types of emission control systems installed on the engine and the idle speed and ignition timing specifications

1.6b The vacuum hose routing diagram is also located on the underside of the hood

Pay close attention to any special precautions outlined in this Chapter. It should be noted that the illustrations of the various systems may not exactly match the system installed on your vehicle because of changes made by the manufacturer during production or from year-to-year.

A Vehicle Emissions Control Information (VECI) label is attached to the underside of the hood (see illustration). This label contains important emissions specifications and adjustment information. Another

label, the Vacuum Hose Routing Diagram (see illustration), provides a vacuum hose schematic with emissions components identified. When servicing the engine or emissions systems, the VECI label and the vacuum hose routing diagram in your particular vehicle should always be checked for up-to-date information.

➡**Note: Specifications printed on your VECI label pertain to your vehicle exactly, and supercede specifications provided in this Chapter.**

2   On-Board Diagnostic (OBD) system and trouble codes

DIAGNOSTIC TOOL INFORMATION

◗ **Refer to illustrations 2.1 and 2.3**

1   A digital multimeter is necessary for checking fuel injection and emission related components (see illustration). A digital volt-ohmmeter is preferred over the older style analog multimeter for several reasons. The analog multimeter cannot display the volts-ohms or amps measurement in hundredths and thousandths increments. When working with electronic circuits that are often very low voltage, this accurate reading is most important.

2   Another good reason for the digital multimeter is the high impedance circuit. The digital multimeter is equipped with a high resistance internal circuitry (10 million ohms). Because a voltmeter is hooked up in parallel with the circuit when testing, it is vital that none of the voltage being measured should be allowed to travel the parallel path set up by the meter itself. This dilemma does not show itself when measuring larger amounts of voltage (9 to 12 volt circuits) but if you are measuring a low voltage circuit such as the oxygen sensor signal voltage, a fraction of a volt may be a significant amount when diagnosing a problem.

2.1 Digital multimeters can be used for testing all types of circuits; because of their high impedance, they are much more accurate than analog meters for measuring low-voltage computer circuits

2.3 Scanners like these from Actron and AutoXray are powerful diagnostic aids - they can tell you just about anything that you want to know about your engine management system

3   Hand-held scanners are handy for analyzing the engine management systems used on late-model vehicles. Because extracting the Diagnostic Trouble Codes (DTCs) from an engine management system is now the first step in troubleshooting many computer-controlled systems and components, even the most basic generic code readers are capable of accessing a computer's DTCs (see illustration). More powerful scan tools can also perform many of the diagnostics once associated with expensive factory scan tools.

➡**Note: An aftermarket generic scanner should work with any model covered by this manual. Before purchasing a generic scan tool, verify that it will work properly with the OBD-II system you want to scan. If necessary, of course, you can always have the codes extracted by a dealer service department or an independent repair shop with a professional scan tool. Some auto parts stores even provide this service.**

OBD SYSTEM GENERAL DESCRIPTION

4   As specified by CARB and EPA regulations, automobile manufacturers have designed a second generation self diagnosis system called On-Board Diagnosis-II (OBD-II). This system incorporates a series of diagnostic monitors that detect and identify emissions systems faults and store the information in the computer memory. This updated system also tests sensors and output actuators, diagnoses drive cycles, freezes data and clears codes.

5   This powerful diagnostic computer must be accessed using an OBD-II SCAN tool and 16 pin Data Link Connector (DLC) located under the driver's dash area. All engines and powertrain combinations described in this manual are equipped with the On-Board Diagnosis-II (OBD-II) system. This system consists of an onboard computer, known as the Powertrain Control Module (PCM), and information sensors, which monitor various functions of the engine and send data to the PCM. Based on the data and the information programmed into the computer's memory, the PCM generates output signals to control various engine functions via control relays, solenoids and other output actuators.

6   The PCM is the "brain" of the electronically controlled fuel and emissions system. It receives data from a number of sensors and other electronic components (switches, relays, etc.). Based on the information it receives, the PCM generates output signals to control various relays, solenoids and other actuators. The PCM is specifically calibrated to

optimize the emissions, fuel economy and driveability of the vehicle.

7   Because of a Federally mandated warranty which covers the emissions system components and because any owner-induced damage to the PCM, the sensors and/or the control devices may void the warranty, it isn't a good idea to attempt diagnosis or replacement of the PCM at home while the vehicle is under warranty. Take the vehicle to a dealer service department if the PCM or a system component malfunctions.

INFORMATION SENSORS

8   **Oxygen sensors (O2S)** - The O2S generates a voltage signal that varies with the difference between the oxygen content of the exhaust and the oxygen in the surrounding air.

9   **Crankshaft Position (CKP) sensor** - The CKP sensor provides information on crankshaft position and the engine speed signal to the PCM.

10   **Camshaft Position (CMP) sensor** - The CMP sensor produces a signal which the PCM uses to identify number 1 cylinder and to time the sequential fuel injection.

11   **Air/Fuel Sensor (California models)** - California models with an automatic transaxle are equipped with an air/fuel ratio sensor mounted upstream of the catalytic converter. These sensors work similar to the O2 sensors.

12   **Engine Coolant Temperature (ECT) sensor** - The ECT sensor monitors engine coolant temperature and sends the PCM a voltage signal that affects PCM control of the fuel mixture, ignition timing, and EGR operation.

13   **Intake Air Temperature (IAT) sensor** - The IAT provides the PCM with intake air temperature information. The PCM uses this information to control fuel flow, ignition timing, and EGR system operation.

14   **Throttle Position Sensor (TPS)** - The TPS senses throttle movement and position, then transmits a voltage signal to the PCM. This signal enables the PCM to determine when the throttle is closed, in a cruise position, or wide open.

15   **Mass Airflow Meter (MAF)** - The MAF sensor measures the mass of the intake air by detecting volume and weight of the air from samples passing over the hot wire element.

16   **Knock sensors** - A knock sensor is a piezoelectric crystal that oscillates in proportion to engine vibration. The term piezoelectric refers to the property of certain crystals that produce a voltage when subjected to a mechanical stress. The oscillation of the piezoelectric crystal produces a voltage output that is monitored by the PCM, which retards the ignition timing when the oscillation exceeds a certain threshold. When the engine is operating normally, the knock sensor oscillates consistently and its voltage signal is steady. When detonation occurs, engine vibration increases, and the oscillation of the knock sensor exceeds a design threshold. Detonation is an uncontrolled explosion, after the spark occurs at the spark plug, which spontaneously combusts the remaining air/fuel mixture, resulting in a pinging or slapping sound. If allowed to continue, the engine could be damaged. The knock sensors are located on top of the block, in the valley between the cylinder heads, under the intake manifold.

17   **EGR valve position sensor** - The EGR valve position sensor monitors the position of the EGR pintle in relation to the operating conditions of the EGR system.

18   **Vapor pressure sensor** - The fuel tank pressure sensor is part of the evaporative emission control system and is used to monitor vapor pressure in the fuel tank. The PCM uses this information to turn on and off the vacuum switching valves (VSV) of the evaporative emission system.

19 **Power Steering Pressure (PSP) switch** - The PSP sensor is used to increase engine idle speed during low-speed vehicle maneuvers.

20 **Transaxle/vehicle speed sensors** - In addition to the vehicle speed sensor, the PCM receives input signals from the following sensors inside the transaxle or connected to it: (a) the direct clutch speed sensor (b) the vehicle speed sensor.

21 **Accelerator pedal position sensor** - This sensor is used in 2007 and later models and is part of the accelerator pedal assembly. It consists of main and a back-up sensors that inform the PCM of the requested throttle opening. The throttle body is operated by the PCM, not a cable, on these models.

22 **Variable valve timing sensors** - One of these sensors takes information about the timing of each of the four camshafts used in 2007 and later engines. The PCM makes adjustments to the camshaft timing positions using this information.

OUTPUT ACTUATORS

23 **EFI main relay** - The EFI main relay activates power to the fuel pump relay (circuit opening relay). It is activated by the ignition switch and supplies battery power to the PCM and the EFI system when the switch is in the Start or Run position. Refer to Chapter 4 or your owner's manual for more information on relay location.

24 **Fuel injectors** - The PCM opens the fuel injectors individually in firing order sequence. The PCM also controls the time the injector is open, called the pulse width. The pulse width of the injector (measured in milliseconds) determines the amount of fuel delivered. For more information on the fuel delivery system and the fuel injectors, including injector replacement, refer to Chapter 4.

25 **Igniter** - The igniter triggers the ignition coil and determines proper spark advance based on inputs from the PCM. On 1998 to 2000 models, the igniter below the relay housing next to the brake master cylinder. Refer to Chapter 5 for more information.

26 **Idle air control (IAC) valve** - The IAC valve controls the amount of air to bypass the throttle plate when the throttle valve is closed or at idle position. The IAC valve opening and the resulting airflow is controlled by the PCM. Refer to Chapter 4 for more information on the IAC valve.

27 **EVAP vacuum switching valve (VSV)** - The EVAP vacuum switching valve is a solenoid valve, operated by the PCM to purge the fuel vapor canister and route fuel vapor to the intake manifold for combustion.

28 **Vapor Pressure Sensor vacuum switching valve (VSV)** - The Vapor Pressure Sensor vacuum switching valve is operated by the PCM during the OBD-II evaporative emission monitor and during an emission test of the evaporative system.

29 **Camshaft timing oil control valves** - One of these actuators is mounted at each of the four camshafts used on 2007 and later engines. The PCM operates them to change the timing of the camshafts for peak performance.

OBTAINING OBD-II SYSTEM TROUBLE CODES

▶ **Refer to illustration 2.31**

30 The PCM will illuminate the CHECK ENGINE light (also called the Malfunction Indicator Light) on the dash if it recognizes a component fault for two consecutive drive cycles. It will continue to set the light until the PCM does not detect any malfunction for three or more consecutive drive cycles.

31 The diagnostic codes for the OBD-II system can be extracted from the PCM by plugging a generic OBD-II scan tool (see illustration 2.3) into the PCM's data link connector (see illustration), which is located under the left end of the dash. A second diagnostic connector is located in the engine compartment, just in front of the timing cover. This connector is used by technicians to check certain aspects of the following systems: ABS braking, ignition timing, tire-pressure warning system, supplemental restraint system and the cruise control.

➡**Note: An aftermarket generic scanner should work with most models covered by this manual. However, before purchasing a generic scan tool, contact the manufacturer of the scanner you're planning to buy and verify that it will work properly with the OBD-II system you want to scan. If necessary, of course, you can always have the codes extracted by a dealer service department or an independent repair shop with a professional scan tool that's capable of extracting the codes on all Toyota models.**

32 Plug the scan tool into the 16-pin data link connector (DLC), and then turn the ignition key ON (engine not running) and make sure the CHECK ENGINE light on the instrument panel is on. If the light is off, either the bulb is burned out or there is a problem with the PCM or related circuit. Using the instructions included with the scan tool, extract any code(s) stored in the PCM.

CLEARING THE CODES

33 After you have extracted the diagnostic trouble codes and made any necessary repairs, make sure that you clear (erase) them before operating the vehicle. Also, always clear any stored codes from the PCM before replacing any electronic emission control component (information sensor or output actuator) that is part of the engine management system, i.e. computer controlled. Because the PCM stores trouble codes during sensor malfunctions, it will also store a code if a new sensor is installed before any codes regarding the old sensor have been erased. Clearing the old codes allows the computer to relearn the new operating parameters relayed by the new component. During the computer relearning process, the engine may experience a rough idle or slight driveability changes. This period of time, however, should last no longer than 15 to 20 minutes.

34 Plug the scan tool into the 16-pin DLC, scroll the menu for the "CLEARING CODES" mode and follow the manufacturer's instructions.

2.31 Data Link Connector (DLC) under the right side of the driver's knee bolster

DIAGNOSTIC TROUBLE CODES

➡ Note: The following table lists all trouble codes used on 1998 through 2002 models. But not all codes apply to all models. Some codes apply only to models with an automatic transaxle, others only to models with a manual transaxle; etc. Also, some of the following codes apply to all model years, while others apply only to some model years. But a generic scan tool can only extract those codes which have been stored in the PCM of the vehicle that it's scanning, so it's impossible to access a code that's doesn't apply to the vehicle you're diagnosing.

Code	Identification
P0010	Intake camshaft position actuator circuit open (bank 1)
P0011	"A" Camshaft position - timing - over-advanced (bank 1)
P0012	"A" Camshaft position - timing over-retarded (bank 1)
P0013	"B" Camshaft position - actuator circuit malfunction (bank 1)
P0014	"B" Camshaft position - timing over-advanced (bank 1)
P0015	"B" Camshaft position -timing over-retarded (bank 1)
P0016	Crankshaft position/camshaft position, bank 1, sensor A - correlation
P0017	Crankshaft position/camshaft position, bank 1, sensor B - correlation
P0018	Crankshaft position/camshaft position, bank 2, sensor A - correlation
P0020	Intake camshaft position actuator circuit open (bank 2)
P0021	Intake camshaft position timing - over-advanced (bank 2)
P0022	Intake camshaft position timing - over-retarded (bank 2)
P0023	"B" Camshaft position - actuator circuit (bank 2)
P0024	"B" Camshaft position - timing over-advanced or system performance (bank 2)
P0025	"B" Camshaft position - timing over-retarded (bank 2)
P0031	HO2S heater control circuit low (bank 1, sensor 1)
P0032	HO2S heater control circuit high (bank 1, sensor 1)
P0037	HO2S heater control circuit low (bank 1, sensor 2)
P0038	HO2S heater control circuit high (bank 1, sensor 2)
P0051	HO2S heater control circuit low (bank 2, sensor 1)

Code	Identification
P0052	HO2S heater control circuit high (bank 2, sensor 1)
P0057	HO2S heater control circuit low (bank 2, sensor 2)
P0058	HO2S heater control circuit high (bank 2, sensor 2)
P0100	Mass air flow or volume air flow circuit malfunction
P0101	Mass air flow or volume air flow circuit, range or performance problem
P0102	Mass air flow or volume air flow circuit, low input
P0103	Mass air flow or volume air flow circuit, high input
P011B	Engine coolant temperature/intake air temperature correlation
P0110	Intake air temperature circuit malfunction
P0112	Intake air temperature circuit, low input
P0113	Intake air temperature circuit, high input
P0115	Engine coolant temperature circuit
P0116	Engine coolant temperature circuit range/performance problem
P0117	Engine coolant temperature circuit, low input
P0118	Engine coolant temperature circuit, high input
P0120	Throttle position or pedal position sensor/switch circuit malfunction
P0121	Throttle position or pedal position sensor/switch circuit, range or performance problem
P0122	Throttle position or pedal position sensor/switch circuit, low input
P0123	Throttle position or pedal position sensor/switch circuit, high input

Code	Identification
P0125	Insufficient coolant temperature for closed loop fuel control
P0128	Coolant thermostat (coolant temperature below thermostat regulating temperature)
P0136	O2 sensor circuit malfunction (bank 1, sensor 2)
P0137	O2 sensor circuit, low voltage (bank 1, sensor 2)
P0138	O2 sensor circuit, high voltage (bank 1, sensor 2)
P0139	O2 sensor circuit, slow response (bank 1, sensor 2)
P0156	O2 sensor circuit malfunction (bank 2, sensor 2)
P0157	O2 sensor circuit, low voltage (bank 2, sensor 2)
P0158	O2 sensor circuit, high voltage (bank 2, sensor 2)
P0159	O2 sensor circuit, slow response (bank 2, sensor 2)
P0171	System too lean (bank 1)
P0172	System too rich (bank 1)
P0174	System too lean (bank 2)
P0175	System too rich (bank 2)
P0220	Throttle position or pedal position sensor/switch B circuit malfunction
P0222	Throttle position or pedal position sensor/switch B circuit, low input
P0223	Throttle position or pedal position sensor/switch B circuit, high input
P0300	Random/multiple cylinder misfire detected
P0301	Cylinder no. 1 misfire detected
P0302	Cylinder no. 2 misfire detected
P0303	Cylinder no. 3 misfire detected
P0304	Cylinder no. 4 misfire detected
P0305	Cylinder no. 5 misfire detected

Code	Identification
P0306	Cylinder no. 6 misfire detected
P0327	Knock sensor no. 1 circuit, low input (bank 1 or single sensor)
P0328	Knock sensor no. 1 circuit, high input (bank 1 or single sensor)
P0332	Knock sensor no. 2 circuit, low input (bank 2)
P0333	Knock sensor no. 2 circuit, high input (bank 2)
P0335	Crankshaft position sensor A circuit malfunction
P0339	Crankshaft position sensor A circuit - intermittent
P0340	Camshaft position sensor "A", circuit malfunction (bank 1)
P0341	Camshaft position sensor "A", circuit - range or performance problem
P0342	Camshaft position sensor "A", circuit - low input
P0343	Camshaft position sensor "A", circuit - high input
P0345	Camshaft position sensor "A", circuit malfunction (bank 2)
P0346	Camshaft position sensor "A", range/performance problem (bank 2)
P0347	Camshaft position sensor "A", circuit - low input (bank 2)
P0348	Camshaft position sensor "A", circuit - range/performance (bank 2)
P0350	Ignition coil primary or secondary circuit malfunction
P0351	Ignition coil A primary or secondary circuit malfunction
P0352	Ignition coil B primary or secondary circuit malfunction
P0353	Ignition coil C primary or secondary circuit malfunction
P0354	Ignition coil D primary or secondary circuit malfunction
P0355	Ignition coil E primary or secondary circuit malfunction
P0356	Ignition coil F primary or secondary circuit malfunction

Code	Identification
P0365	Camshaft position sensor "B" circuit (bank 1)
P0366	Camshaft position sensor "B" circuit range/performance (bank 1)
P0367	Camshaft position sensor "B" circuit low input (bank 1)
P0390	Camshaft position sensor "B" circuit
P0392	Camshaft position sensor "B" circuit low input (bank 2)
P0393	Camshaft position sensor "B" circuit high input (bank 2)
P0420	Catalyst system efficiency below threshold (bank 1)
P043E	Evaporative emissions orifice clog
P043F	Evaporative emissions orifice high flow
P0430	Catalyst system efficiency below threshold (bank 2)
P0441	Evaporative emission control system, incorrect purge flow
P0442	Evaporative emission control system, small leak detected
P0446	Evaporative emission control system, vent control circuit malfunction
P0450	Evaporative emission control system, pressure sensor malfunction
P0451	Evaporative emission control system, pressure sensor range or performance problem
P0452	Evaporative emission control system, pressure sensor low input
P0453	Evaporative emission control system, pressure sensor high input

Code	Identification
P0455	Evaporative emission (EVAP) control system leak detected (no purge flow or large leak)
P0456	Evaporative emission (EVAP) control system leak detected (very small leak)
P050A	Cold start idle air control system performance
P050B	Cold start ignition timing performance
P0500	Vehicle speed sensor malfunction
P0503	Vehicle speed sensor circuit, Intermittent, erratic or high input
P0504	Brake switch A/B correlation
P0505	Idle control system malfunction
P0560	System voltage malfunction
P0604	Internal control module, random access memory (RAM) error
P0606	PCM processor fault
P0607	Control module performance
P0617	Starter relay - circuit high
P0630	VIN not programmed or mismatch - ECM/PCM
P0657	Actuator supply voltage - circuit open
P0705	Transmission range sensor, circuit malfunction (PRNDL input)
P0724	Torque converter/brake switch B circuit, high

3 Powertrain Control Module (PCM) - removal and installation

▶ **Refer to illustration 3.1**

✳✳ WARNING:

The models covered by this manual are equipped with Supplemental Restraint systems (SRS), more commonly known as airbags. Always disable the airbag system before working in the vicinity of any airbag system components to avoid the possibility of accidental deployment of the airbag, which could cause personal injury (see Chapter 12).

✳✳ CAUTION:

To avoid electrostatic discharge damage to the PCM, handle the PCM only by its case. Do not touch the electrical terminals during removal and installation. If available, ground yourself to the vehicle with an anti-static ground strap, available at computer supply stores.

3.1 Typical PCM mounting details

ECM Connector

ECM

Cowl Side Trim

Front Door Inside Scuff Plate

No.2 Instrument Panel Finish Lower Panel

➡Note: Toyota refers to the PCM as the Electronic Control Module (ECM).

1   The Powertrain Control Module (PCM) is located inside the passenger compartment, near the glovebox (see illustration).

2   Disconnect the cable from the negative battery terminal.

3   On 2006 and earlier models, remove the panel beneath the glove box (see Chapter 11).

4   On 2007 and later models, remove the glove box door (see Chapter 11). Remove the instrument panel storage box by releasing the four clips and the two hooks using a plastic trim tool or a screwdriver wrapped with tape.

5   Unplug the electrical connectors from the PCM.

✴✴ CAUTION:

The ignition switch must be turned OFF when pulling out or plugging in the electrical connectors to prevent damage to the PCM.

6   Remove the retaining bolts from the PCM bracket.

7   Carefully remove the PCM.

➡Note: Avoid any static electricity damage to the computer by grounding yourself to the body before touching the PCM and using a special anti-static pad to store the PCM on once it is removed.

8   Installation is the reverse of removal.

4   Throttle Position Sensor (TPS) - replacement

▶ Refer to illustration 4.4

➡Note: On 2007 and later models, the TPS is an integral part of the throttle body. If it fails, the entire throttle body must be replaced.

1   The Throttle Position Sensor (TPS) is located on the end of the throttle shaft on the throttle body. By monitoring the output voltage from the TPS, the PCM can determine fuel delivery based on throttle valve angle (driver demand). A broken or loose TPS can cause intermittent bursts of fuel from the injectors and an unstable idle because the PCM thinks the throttle is moving. A problem with the TPS circuits will set a diagnostic trouble code (see Section 2).

2   Make sure the ignition key is in the OFF position.

3   Disconnect the electrical connector from the TPS.

4   Remove the screws that retain the TPS to the throttle body and remove the TPS (see illustration).

5   Installation is the reverse of removal.

4.4 Remove the screws and detach the TPS from the throttle body

5   Mass Airflow (MAF) sensor - replacement

▶ **Refer to illustration 5.3**

1   The Mass Airflow (MAF) sensor is located on the air intake duct. The MAF system circuit consists of a platinum hot wire, a thermistor and a control circuit inside a plastic housing. The platinum hot wire and the thermistor detect even the slightest change in the temperature of the intake air passing over them. As the throttle opens, more air passes over the hot wire, which cools the wire. The MAF sensor circuit is designed to maintain the hot wire at a constant preset temperature by controlling the current flow through the hot wire. So, as the wire cools, the PCM increases the flow of current through the hot wire in order to maintain the wire at a constant temperature. The output voltage signal of the MAF sensor varies in accordance with this current flow and is measured by the PCM, which converts this signal into a digital wave form, compares it to the map, calculates the requisite fuel injector pulse width (duration) and turns the injectors on and off accordingly. A problem in the MAF sensor circuit will set a diagnostic trouble code (see Section 2).

2   Make sure the ignition key is in the OFF position.

3   Disconnect the electrical connector from the MAF sensor and remove the mounting screws (see illustration).

5.3 Disconnect the MAF sensor connector and remove the two mounting screws (early model shown)

4   Twist the MAF sensor out of the air intake duct and remove the O-ring.

5   Installation is the reverse of removal. Be sure to install a new gasket or O-ring between the MAF sensor and the intake duct.

6   Intake Air Temperature (IAT) sensor - replacement

The intake air temperature (IAT) sensor is a thermistor (a resistor which varies the value of its resistance in accordance with temperature changes). The change in the resistance values will directly affect the voltage signal from the sensor to the PCM. As the sensor temperature DECREASES, the resistance values will INCREASE. As the sensor temperature INCREASES, the resistance values will DECREASE. A problem in any of the IAT sensor circuits will set a diagnostic trouble code. Refer to Section 2 for the code accessing procedure.

On the models covered by this manual, the IAT is part of the MAF sensor (see Section 5).

7   Engine Coolant Temperature (ECT) sensor - replacement

▶ **Refer to illustration 7.8**

✳✳ WARNING:

Wait until the engine has cooled completely before beginning this procedure.

1   The engine coolant temperature (ECT) sensor is a thermistor (a resistor which varies the value of its resistance in accordance with temperature changes). The change in the resistance values will directly affect the voltage signal from the sensor to the PCM. As the sensor temperature DECREASES, the resistance values will INCREASE. As the sensor temperature INCREASES, the resistance values will DECREASE. A problem in any of the ECT sensor circuits will set a diagnostic trouble code. Refer to Section 2 for the code accessing procedure.

2   Make sure the ignition key is in the OFF position.

3   Drain about 1 gallon of engine coolant (see Chapter 2).

7.8 The ECT sensor is located at the right end of the engine, below the cooling system pressure cap (it's the one with two wires) - 2006 and earlier model shown

4   On 2007 and later models, remove the engine top cover by pulling up at the front edge, then lifting the rear.

5   On 2007 and later models, remove both air filter housing inlet ducts.

6   On 2007 and later models, remove the air filter housing assembly (see Chapter 4).

7   Wrap the threads of the new sensor with Teflon sealing tape to prevent leakage and thread corrosion.

8   Disconnect the electrical connector and carefully unscrew the sensor (see illustration).

9   Installation is the reverse of removal.

10 Refill the cooling system (see Chapter 1).

8   Crankshaft Position (CKP) sensor - check and replacement

CHECK

1   The crankshaft position sensor (CKP) determines the timing for the fuel injection and ignition on each cylinder. A problem in the crankshaft sensor circuits will set a diagnostic trouble code (see Section 2).

2   To check the crankshaft sensor, remove the crankshaft sensor (see Steps 4 through 7) and probe the terminals with an ohmmeter. Because the crankshaft sensor is difficult to access using ohmmeter probes, it is best to remove the sensor and check it on the bench. Refer to the resistance values listed in this Chapter's Specifications.

3   This test checks only the crankshaft sensor. If the test results are correct, there may be a problem with the harness or the PCM. If necessary, have the PCM diagnosed by a dealer service department or other properly equipped repair facility.

REPLACEMENT

▶ **Refer to illustration 8.5**

4   Disconnect the cable from the negative battery terminal.

5   On 2006 and earlier models, refer to Chapter 11 and remove the right inner fender splash shield (see illustration).

8.5 Location of the crankshaft sensor

6   On 2007 and later models, remove the air conditioning compressor (see Chapter 3).

7   Disconnect the crankshaft position sensor electrical connector.

8   Remove the bolt and detach the sensor.

9   Installation is the reverse of removal.

9   Camshaft Position (CMP) sensor - check and replacement

➡ **Note: Two CMP sensors are only used on 2006 and earlier models. Four VVT sensors are used on 2007 and later models. See Section 18 for more information about VVT sensors and the variable valve timing system.**

CHECK

▶ **Refer to illustration 9.2**

1   The camshaft position sensor determines the position of the camshaft for sequential fuel injection to each cylinder. There are two camshaft position sensors, one at the end of each cylinder head. A problem in the camshaft sensor circuits will set a diagnostic trouble code. Refer to Section 2 for the code accessing procedure.

2   To check the camshaft sensor, disconnect the electrical connector at the sensor and probe the two terminals with an ohmmeter (see illustration). Refer to the resistance values listed in this Chapter's Specifications.

REPLACEMENT

▶ **Refer to illustration 9.5**

3　Make sure the ignition key is in the OFF position.

4　To access the sensor on the rear cylinder head, remove the fuel

injection V-bank cover (see Chapter 1) and remove the air cleaner hose (see Chapter 4).

5　Disconnect the harness connector, remove the mounting screws and remove the camshaft sensors from the cylinder heads (see illustration).

6　Installation is the reverse of the removal procedure.

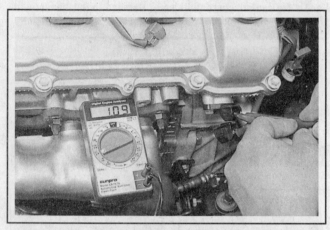

9.2 Check the resistance of the camshaft position sensor installed on the cylinder head

9.5 Remove the camshaft position sensor bolts

10　Oxygen sensor and air/fuel sensor - general information and precautions

GENERAL INFORMATION

1　All vehicles covered by this manual have On-Board Diagnostics-II (OBD-II) engine management systems, which means among other things that they have the ability to verify the accuracy of the basic feedback loop between the oxygen sensor and the PCM. They accomplish this by using an oxygen sensor or air/fuel sensor ahead of the catalytic converter and an oxygen sensor behind the catalyst. By sampling the exhaust gas before and after the catalytic converter, the PCM can determine the efficiency of the converter.

2　Models covered by this manual have three sensors. The primary (upstream) sensors are located in the exhaust manifolds and the secondary (downstream) sensor is located after the catalytic converter. On 1998 through 2000 California models, the upstream sensors are air/fuel sensors; on 1998 through 2000 non-California models, the upstream sensors are heated oxygen sensors. On all 2001 and later models, the upstream sensors are air/fuel sensors and the downstream sensor is a heated oxygen sensor.

3　Don't confuse oxygen sensors and air/fuel sensors. They're similar in appearance, but they operate differently and have different operating characteristics.

Oxygen sensor

4　An oxygen sensor is a galvanic battery that reacts to the oxygen content in the exhaust stream to produce a voltage output between 200 and 800 millivolts (mV) that the PCM monitors in order to determine the ratio of oxygen to fuel in the mixture and make the necessary correction.

5　The oxygen sensor produces no voltage when it is below its normal operating temperature of about 600-degrees F (most sensors begin to operate at about 482 to 572 degrees F). During this initial period before warm-up, the PCM operates in open loop mode. The oxygen

sensors used on the vehicles covered by this manual are equipped with small heating elements to ensure that they reach their normal operating temperature as quickly as possible. If the heater element in a sensor fails, the sensor must be replaced.

6　The operating voltage range of the typical oxygen sensor is between 0.1 volt and 0.9 volt. Once the oxygen sensor is warmed up, it produces a voltage signal that varies 200 to 450 mV (high oxygen, lean mixture) to 550 to 800 mV (low oxygen, rich mixture). A sensor in good condition responds so quickly to changes in the air/fuel ratio that it's constantly switching back and forth from lean to rich, rich to lean, etc. as the air-to-fuel mixture ratio varies from the ideal 14.7 to 1. Although this constantly switching voltage is, technically speaking, a variable output, it switches back and forth so quickly (many times a second) that it looks more like a digital signal, i.e. a switch turning on and off. The number of times that an oxygen sensor switches back and forth is known as its cross-count. The PCM responds to the cross-count by constantly altering the pulse width (open time) of the fuel injectors, which alters the air/fuel ratio. An air-to-fuel mixture ratio of 14.7 (air) to 1 (fuel) is the ideal mixture ratio for allowing the catalytic converter to operate at maximum efficiency, thus minimizing exhaust emissions. The PCM and the oxygen sensor(s) attempt to maintain this ratio of 14.7 to 1 at all times.

7　The oxygen sensor will operate correctly only under the following four conditions:

a)　*Electrical* - The low voltage generated by the sensor depends upon good, clean connections, which should be checked whenever a malfunction of the sensor is suspected or indicated.

b)　*Outside air supply* - The sensor is designed to allow air circulation to the internal portion of the sensor. Whenever the sensor is removed and installed or replaced, make sure the air passages are not restricted.

c)　*Correct operating temperature* - The PCM will not react to the sensor signal until the sensor reaches approximately 600-degrees F. This factor must be taken into consideration when evaluating the performance of the sensor.

   d) **Unleaded fuel** - The use of unleaded fuel is essential for proper operation of the sensor. Make sure the fuel you are using is of this type.

8 The PCM will set a diagnostic trouble code if the oxygen sensor continues to produce a steady signal voltage below 0.45-volts at 1,500 or more rpm after the engine reaches normal operating temperature and/or has been running for two or more minutes. The PCM will also set other codes if it detects any problem with the sensor's heater circuit (see Section 2).

9 When there is a problem with the oxygen sensor or its circuit, the PCM operates in the open loop mode - that is, it controls fuel delivery in accordance with a programmed default value instead of feedback information from the oxygen sensor. For help in diagnosing an oxygen sensor problem, refer to the next Section.

Air/fuel (A/F) sensor

10 The PCM uses the air/fuel (A/F) sensor as a feedback device to verify the accuracy of the alterations it makes to the injector pulse width in response to feedback from the oxygen sensor.

11 Like an oxygen sensor, the A/F sensor provides a variable voltage output to the PCM that's proportional to the air/fuel mixture ratio in the exhaust stream. But the A/F sensor doesn't "switch" back and forth like an oxygen sensor at the 14.7 to 1 stoichiometric threshold. Instead, it alters a PCM-controlled voltage between 3.3 volts (at the positive PCM terminal for the A/F sensor) and 3.0 volts (at the negative PCM terminal for the A/F sensor) in direct proportion to the amount of oxygen in the exhaust. In other words, as the air/fuel mixture in the exhaust becomes leaner, i.e. has a higher ratio of oxygen to fuel, the A/F sensor voltage increases (within its operating range of 3.0 to 3.3 volts).

12 Like an oxygen sensor, the A/F sensor doesn't operate correctly until it's warmed up. Also, like an oxygen sensor, the A/F sensor has a heating element that enables it to warm up quickly.

13 Because the operating voltage range of the A/F sensor is controlled by the PCM within such a narrow range (0.3 volt), it's impossible, according to the manufacturer, to check A/F sensor output accurately by backprobing the PCM terminals of the A/F sensor electrical connector. This information can only be accessed by a special OBD-II scan tool or hand-held tester. After eliminating other possible problem areas that might cause the PCM to display diagnostic trouble code P0125, P0171 or P0172 (see Section 2), take the vehicle to a dealer service department or other qualified repair shop to have the A/F sensor diagnosed. However, you can check the resistance of the heater element in the A/F sensor and you can replace the A/F sensor (see Section 12).

PRECAUTIONS

14 Special care must be taken whenever a sensor is serviced.

   a) Oxygen sensors and air/fuel sensors have a permanently attached pigtail and electrical connector that should not be removed from the sensor. Damage or removal of the pigtail or electrical connector can adversely affect operation of the sensor.

   b) Grease, dirt and other contaminants should be kept away from the electrical connector and the louvered end of the sensor.

   c) Do not use cleaning solvents of any kind on an oxygen sensor or air/fuel ratio sensor.

   d) Do not drop or roughly handle and oxygen sensor or air/fuel ratio sensor.

   e) The silicone boot must be installed in the correct position to prevent the boot from being melted and to allow the sensor to operate properly.

---

11 Oxygen sensor and air/fuel sensor - check and replacement

➡**Note: On 2007 and later models, the air/fuel sensors are mounted at the exhaust manifolds and the oxygen sensors are mounted downstream in the exhaust pipes.**

OXYGEN SENSOR

Check

▶ **Refer to illustrations 11.1 and 11.4**

1 Locate the oxygen sensor electrical connector and without disconnecting it, insert a long pin into the oxygen sensor connector signal terminal number 3 (+) and another pin into ground terminal number 4 (-) (see illustration). Install the positive and negative probes of a voltmeter onto the corresponding pins. Apply the parking brake, shift the transaxle into Park, raise the front of the vehicle and place it securely on jackstands. Primary O2 sensors are fairly easy to access because they are mounted in the front exhaust manifold; the secondary O2 sensors are difficult to access because they are mounted under the vehicle behind the catalytic converter. If you're checking the secondary O2 sensor, remove the passenger front seat and pull back the carpeting to access the harness connector.

11.1 Location of the upstream heated oxygen sensor (terminal guide shows the harness, i.e. PCM, side of the unplugged sensor connector)

2 Check the signal voltage from the oxygen sensor during operating conditions. Start the engine and monitor the voltage signal as the engine warms up.

❋❋ CAUTION:

Be extremely careful of hot exhaust components when performing this procedure.

➡Note: The secondary oxygen sensor will produce much slower fluctuating voltage values to reflect the results of the catalyzed exhaust gas.

3   The oxygen sensor will produce a steady voltage signal at first (open loop) of approximately 0.1 to 0.2 volts with the engine cold. After a period of approximately two minutes, the engine will reach operating temperature and the oxygen sensor should start to fluctuate between 0.1 to 0.9 volts (closed loop). If the oxygen sensor fails to reach the closed loop mode or there is a very long period of time until it does switch into closed loop mode, replace the oxygen sensor.

4   Also inspect the oxygen sensor heater. Disconnect the oxygen sensor electrical connector and connect an ohmmeter between the HT and B+ terminals (see illustration). Compare your measurement to the sensor heater resistance listed in this Chapter's Specifications. If the indicated heater resistance is incorrect, replace the sensor.

5   Verify that the heater is receiving battery voltage. Working on the PCM side of the connector, measure voltage between the B+ terminal and chassis ground. There should be battery voltage with the ignition key turned to ON (engine not running). If there is no voltage, check the circuit between the main relay, the PCM and the sensor. Refer to the wiring diagrams at the end of Chapter 12 for additional information.

6   If the oxygen sensor fails any of these tests, replace it with a new part.

Replacement

▸ Refer to illustrations 11.11a and 11.11b

➡Note: Because it is installed in the exhaust manifold or pipe, which contracts when cool, the oxygen sensor may be very difficult to loosen when the engine is cold. Rather than risk damage to the sensor (assuming you are planning to reuse it in another manifold or pipe), start and run the engine for a minute or two, then shut it off. Be careful not to burn yourself during the following procedure.

7   Disconnect the cable from the negative terminal of the battery.

8   If you're replacing the downstream sensor, remove the passenger seat and pull back the carpet, and then unplug the electrical connector.

9   If you're replacing the upstream sensor for the rear cylinder bank, or the downstream sensor on any model, raise the vehicle and place it securely on jackstands (the upstream sensor for the front cylinder bank can be replaced without raising the vehicle).

10   If you're replacing an upstream sensor, unplug the sensor electrical connector. If you're replacing a downstream sensor, carefully snake the connector and pigtail lead through the grommet in the floor.

11   Unscrew the sensor from the exhaust manifold or exhaust pipe (see illustrations).

➡Note: The best tool for removing an oxygen sensor is a special slotted socket, especially if you're planning to reuse a sensor. If you don't have this tool, and you plan to reuse the sensor, be extremely careful when unscrewing the sensor.

12   Apply anti-seize compound to the threads of the sensor to facilitate future removal. The threads of new sensors should already be

11.4 Ohmmeter hook-up for testing the oxygen sensor heater resistance

coated with this compound, but if you're planning to reuse an old sensor, re-coat the threads. Install the sensor and tighten it securely.

13   Reconnect the electrical connector of the pigtail lead to the main wiring harness.

14   Lower the vehicle (if it was raised), test drive the car and verify that no trouble codes have been set.

AIR/FUEL (A/F) SENSOR

Check

15   The air/fuel (A/F) sensor voltage cannot be checked without a special OBD-II scan tool or hand-held tester (see Section 11). However, the resistance of the heating element in the A/F sensor can be checked.

16   Unplug the electrical connector for the A/F sensor and, using an ohmmeter, measure the resistance between terminals B+ and HT (see illustration 11.4). Compare your measurement to the resistance listed in this Chapter's Specifications. If the indicated resistance is too low or too high, replace the A/F sensor.

Replacement

➡Note 1: Because it is installed in the exhaust manifold or pipe, which contracts when cool, the A/F sensor may be very difficult to loosen when the engine is cold. Rather than risk damage to the sensor (assuming you are planning to reuse it in another manifold or pipe), start and run the engine for a minute or two, then shut it off. Be careful not to burn yourself during the following procedure.

➡Note 2: Air/fuel sensors are installed in the same locations and look the same as oxygen sensors.

17   Disconnect the cable from the negative terminal of the battery.

18   If you're replacing the A/F sensor for the rear cylinder bank, raise the vehicle and place it securely on jackstands (the A/F sensor for the front cylinder bank can be replaced without raising the vehicle).

19   Unplug the sensor electrical connector from the sensor.

20   Carefully unscrew the sensor from the exhaust manifold.

21   Apply anti-seize compound to the threads of the sensor to facilitate future removal. The threads of new sensors should already be coated with this compound, but if you're planning to reuse an old sensor, re-coat the threads.

22   Install the sensor and tighten it securely.

23   Reconnect the electrical connector to the main wiring harness.

24   Lower the vehicle (if it was raised), test drive the car and verify that no trouble codes have been set.

11.11a Use a special slotted socket to remove an oxygen sensor

11.11b To replace the downstream heated oxygen sensor on early models, remove the seat, unplug the connector, raise the vehicle, snake the pigtail lead through the grommet in the floor and then unscrew the sensor

Connector for Seat

Heated Oxygen Sensor Downstream

Clamp

Heated Oxygen Sensor Connector Downstream

Grommet

12 Knock sensor - check and replacement

CHECK

▶ **Refer to illustration 12.2**

1   The knock control system is designed to reduce spark knock during periods of heavy detonation. This allows the engine to use opti- mal spark advance to improve driveability. The knock sensor detects abnormal vibration in the engine and produces a voltage output that increases with the severity of the knock. The voltage signal is moni- tored by the PCM, which retards ignition timing until the detonation ceases. The models covered by this manual use two knock sensors located under the intake manifold.

12.2 Verify that there is no continuity between the sensor terminal and the body of the sensor

2   To check a knock sensor, disconnect the electrical connector (see illustration) and use an ohmmeter to check continuity between the knock sensor terminal and the body of the sensor. Continuity should NOT exist. If continuity exists, replace it with a new sensor.

REPLACEMENT

◆ Refer to illustration 12.6

✳ WARNING:

Wait for the engine to cool completely before performing this procedure.

12.6 The knock sensors are located under the intake manifold (2006 and earlier model shown)

3   Disconnect the cable from the negative terminal of the battery.
4   Drain the cooling system (see Chapter 1).
5   Remove the lower intake manifold (see Chapter 2A or 2B).
6   Disconnect the electrical connector and remove the knock sensor (see illustration).
7   If you're going to reuse the old sensor, coat the threads with thread sealant (new sensors are pre-coated with thread sealant).
8   Install the knock sensor and tighten it securely (approximately 30 ft-lbs). Don't overtighten the sensor or damage may occur. Plug in the electrical connector, install the remaining components, then refill the cooling system (see Chapter 1) and check for leaks.

13 Idle Air Control (IAC) valve - check and replacement

➡ **Note 1: This procedure applies to 2003 and earlier models only.**

➡ **Note 2: The minimum idle speed is pre-set at the factory and should not require adjustment under normal operating conditions; however if the throttle body has been replaced or you suspect the minimum idle speed has been tampered with (for example, if the idle speed screw was removed from the throttle body) have the vehicle checked by a dealer service department or other qualified automotive repair shop.**

CHECK

◆ Refer to illustrations 13.2a, 13.2b and 13.6

1   The engine idle speed on 2003 and earlier models is controlled by the Idle Air Control (IAC) valve. The IAC valve controls the amount of air that bypasses the throttle plate into the intake manifold. The IAC valve is controlled by the PCM in accordance with the demands on the engine (air conditioning, power steering) and the operating conditions (cold or warmed up).

2   Apply the parking brake, shift the transaxle to Neutral (manual) or Park (automatic) and block the drive wheels. Install a tachometer in accordance with the manufacturer's instructions (see Chapter 1). Start the engine and allow it to reach normal operating temperature. Check the idle speed and compare it to the idle speed listed in the Chapter 1 Specifications. Using a jumper wire, bridge terminals TE1 and E1 (1998 through 2000 models) of the diagnostic test connector (see illustration). On 2001 through 2003 models, bridge terminals E1 and TC (see illustration).

13.2a Test terminal guide for TE1 and E1 (1997 through 2000 models)

13.2b Test terminal guide for E1 and TC (2001 through 2003 models)

3   The engine speed should increase to approximately 900 or 1000 rpm for five seconds then return to normal idle speed.

a)   *If the engine speed changes as described, the IAC valve is okay.*

b)   *If the engine speed does not change as described, measure the IAC valve resistance.*

4   Remove the jumper wire.

5   Disconnect the IAC valve electrical connector.

6   Measure the resistance between the middle terminal and each of the two outer terminals (see illustration). Compare your results to the IAC valve resistance in this Chapter's Specifications.

➡**Note: Specifications are not available for 2001 and later models.**

13.9 The IAC valve mounting screws are located under the throttle body

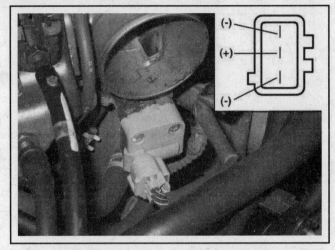

13.6 Using an ohmmeter, check the resistance between the middle terminal and each of the outer terminals

a)   *If the resistance is not as specified, replace the IAC valve.*

b)   *If the resistance is as specified, the IAC valve is okay, but there may be a problem with the wiring or the PCM.*

7   To determine whether there's a problem with the wiring or the PCM, remove the IAC valve (see below), and then apply battery voltage to the valve connector. Connect the positive battery terminal to the center terminal and ground each outer terminal, one at a time. The valve should open with one of the terminals grounded and close with the other terminal grounded.

a)   *If the IAC operates as described, check the wiring harness between the PCM and the IAC valve.*

b)   *f the wiring is okay, the PCM is probably defective. Have it checked by a dealer service department.*

REPLACEMENT

▶ **Refer to illustration 13.9**

8   Remove the throttle body (see Chapter 4).

9   Remove the mounting screws and detach the IAC valve and gasket (see illustration).

10 Installation is the reverse of removal. Be sure to use a new gasket when installing the IAC valve.

14 Acoustic Control Induction System (ACIS)

➡**Note: This system is only used on 2006 and earlier models.**

GENERAL INFORMATION

▶ **Refer to illustration 14.2**

1   The Acoustic Control Induction System (ACIS) diverts the path of intake air to one of two paths through the intake manifold in order to match the intake volume to the engine speed. Engine performance is enhanced by switching the intake air control valve to the closed posi-

tion for high torque at low rpm or to the open position for maximum horsepower at high rpm.

2   The ACIS actuator mechanism that opens and closes the butterfly valve inside the intake manifold is known as an "intake air control valve." On 1998 through 2000 models, there is one intake air control valve, located on the opposite end of the intake plenum from the throttle body. On 2001 and later models, there is an additional intake air control valve between the two throttle bodies and the other end of the air intake plenum. On these models, this other intake air control valve is referred to as the "No. 1 intake air control valve," because it's

Intake Air Control Valve

From Air Cleaner

14.2 Vacuum diagram of the Acoustic Control Induction System (ACIS)

Actuator

VSV

Vacuum Tank

14.3 Using a T-fitting, install a vacuum gauge between the vacuum actuator and the vacuum source and see if vacuum increases slightly with an increase in the engine rpm

14.5 When you depress the accelerator pedal to its wide open position, the vacuum actuator should pull the rod out, which opens the butterfly valve inside the plenum (mechanism removed for clarity)

Vacuum

upstream in relation to the intake air control valve, which is referred to as the "No. 2 intake air control valve." The actuator mechanism(s) is/are controlled by vacuum from the intake manifold (see illustration). A malfunction in the system can result in poor driveability. The following simple checks will help you diagnose any system defects.

➡**Note: There are no diagnostic trouble codes for this system.**

CHECK

1998 through 2000 models
▶ **Refer to illustrations 14.3, 14.5, 14.7, 14.8, 14.9, 14.11 and 14.12**

3   Install a T-fitting between the vacuum actuator and the vacuum hose and connect a vacuum gauge (see illustration) into the T-fitting.

4   Start the engine and allow it to idle. There should be no vacuum indicated by the gauge.

5   Quickly depress the accelerator pedal to its wide-open position and verify that the gauge indicates a vacuum of about 8 in-Hg. The actuator should pull the rod out (toward the actuator) (see illustration).

6   If no vacuum was indicated by the gauge, check for a blocked vacuum port, a collapsed or broken vacuum hose to the control valve or a defective vacuum switching valve (VSV) (see Step 9).

7   Inspect the vacuum tank. Locate the vacuum tank under the battery tray and apply pressure to port B. Air should pass through port B and out port A. Apply air pressure to port A and observe that air does not flow out port B (see illustration).

Air   Air

14.7 When air pressure is applied to port B, air should flow out of port A; when pressure is applied to port A, air should NOT flow out port B

14.8 Check the vacuum tank for a tight seal. Apply vacuum to port A while closing off port B with the tip of your finger. The tank should hold vacuum for at least one minute

8   Plug port B with the tip of your finger and apply vacuum to port A and observe that vacuum does not leak down after one minute (see illustration).

9   Check the VSV resistance. Touch the probes of an ohmmeter to the terminals and check the resistance (see illustration). It should be between 33 and 39 ohms. If the resistance is incorrect, replace the VSV.

10 Check the VSV ground. Using the ohmmeter, verify that there's no continuity between each terminal and the body of the valve.

14.9 Measure the resistance of the vacuum switching valve (VSV) - it should be between 33 and 39 ohms at 68-degrees F

11 Remove the V-bank cover (see illustration). Remove the emission control valve set retaining nuts and remove the emission control valve set. Remove the high-tension cord cover. Clearly mark the two vacuum hoses to the VSV and then detach them from the VSV, remove the VSV retaining screw and remove the VSV from the emission control valve set.

14.11 Typical ACIS system vacuum and electrical connections on 1998 through 2000 models - later models are similar but use two VSVs

Emission Control Valve Set

High–Tension Cord Cover

VSV Connector for EVAP

VSV Connector for EGR

VSV Connector for ACIS

Vacuum Hose

VSV for ACIS

14.12 Blow air through port E of the VSV and verify that it comes out the filter

14.16 Quickly depress the accelerator pedal to its wide-open position and verify that the gauge indicates a vacuum of about 8 in-Hg. - the actuator should pull the rod out (toward the actuator) (No. 1 intake air control valve assembly removed for clarity)

14.21 Intake air control valve installation details

12 Blow air through port E of the VSV and verify that it comes out the filter (see illustration).

13 Apply battery voltage across the electrical terminals of the VSV, blow through port E and verify that air comes out port F (the small port directly adjacent to Port E).

14 If the VSV fails any of the above tests, replace it.

15 Install the VSV on the emission control valve set and tighten the retaining screw securely. Reattach the vacuum hoses to the VSV (make sure you didn't accidentally switch them). Install the high-tension cord cover and install the emission control valve set. Tighten the emission control valve nuts securely. Install the V-bank cover.

2001 through 2006 models

♦ Refer to illustration 14.16

16 To check the No. 1 intake air control valve, follow Steps 3 through 6 but refer to the accompanying illustration (see illustration). To check the No. 2 intake air control valve, follow Steps 3 through 6 and refer to the illustrations accompanying those steps (see illustrations 14.3 and 14.5).

17 To check the vacuum tank, follow Step 7.

18 There are two vacuum switching valves (VSV) on these models, one for the No. 1 intake air control valve, another for the No. 2 intake air control valve. Both VSVs are identical - and they're identical to the single VSV used on earlier models. To check either one, follow Steps 8 through 15.

REPLACEMENT

1998 through 2000 models

Intake air control valve

♦ Refer to illustration 14.21

19 Disconnect the cable from the negative battery terminal.

20 Disconnect the vacuum hoses from the brake booster, the air conditioning idle-up valve and the intake air control valve vacuum hose.

21 Remove the intake air control valve retaining bolts (see illustration) and separate the assembly from the air intake plenum.

22 Scrape all remaining traces of the gasket material from the air intake plenum and valve body without damaging the aluminum material.

23 Installation is the reverse of removal. Be sure to coat the rubber O-ring seal with light engine oil and apply sealant to the ends of the rubber seal. Also, be sure to use a new gasket between the intake air control valve and the plenum.

Vacuum switching valve (VSV)

24 To replace the VSV, refer to Steps 11 and 15.

2001 through 2006 models

No. 1 intake air control valve

25 Remove the throttle body/No. 1 intake air control valve assembly (see Section 14 in Chapter 4). This section also includes the disassem-

bly procedure for separating the throttle bodies from the No. 1 intake air control valve.

26 Install the throttle body/No. 1 intake air control valve assembly (see Section 14 in Chapter 4). Be sure to use a new gasket and tighten the three mounting nuts to the torque listed in this Chapter's Specifications.

No. 2 intake air control valve

27 Follow Steps 19 through 23.

VSV for No. 1 intake air control valve/VSV for No. 2 intake air control valve

28 Refer to Step 11.

15 Positive Crankcase Ventilation (PCV) system

▶ **Refer to illustration 15.1**

1 The Positive Crankcase Ventilation (PCV) system (see illustration) reduces hydrocarbon emissions by scavenging crankcase vapors. It does this by circulating fresh air from the air cleaner through the crankcase, where it mixes with blow-by gases and is then rerouted through a PCV valve to the intake manifold.

2 The main components of the PCV system are the PCV valve, a blow-by filter and the vacuum hoses connecting these two components with the engine.

3 To maintain idle quality, the PCV valve restricts the flow when the intake manifold vacuum is high. If abnormal operating conditions (such as piston ring problems) arise, the system is designed to allow excessive amounts of blow-by gases to flow back through the crankcase vent tube into the air cleaner to be consumed by normal combustion.

4 Checking and replacement of the PCV valve is covered in Chapter 1.

15.1 Vapor flow diagram of a typical PCV system

16 Evaporative emissions control (EVAP) system - description, check and component replacement

GENERAL DESCRIPTION

▶ **Refer to illustrations 16.1a and 16.1b**

1 The fuel evaporative emissions control (EVAP) system absorbs

fuel vapors and, during engine operation, releases them into the engine intake where they mix with the incoming air-fuel mixture (see illustrations). On 1998 through 2000 models, the charcoal canister is mounted in the engine compartment, while on 2001 and later models, the charcoal canister is mounted behind the fuel tank.

16.1a EVAP system component locations (1998 through 2000 models)

16.1b EVAP system component locations (2001 through 2006 models)

2 The EVAP system employs a canister filled with activated charcoal to absorb fuel vapors. The following description of a typical system for the models covered by this manual should provide you enough information to understand the system on your vehicle.

3 The fuel filler cap is equipped with a two-way valve as a safety device. The valve vents fuel vapors to the atmosphere if the EVAP system fails.

4 When the engine is off, fuel vapors from the fuel tank and air cleaner housing are routed through hoses to the EVAP canister. The activated charcoal in the canister absorbs and stores these vapors.

5 When the engine is running and warmed up to a pre-set temperature, a vacuum switching valve (VSV) opens, allowing intake manifold vacuum to draw the fuel vapors from the canister to the intake manifold, where they're mixed with intake air before being burned with the air/fuel mixture inside the combustion chambers.

6 A fuel tank vapor pressure sensor monitors changes in pressure inside the tank and, when the pressure exceeds a preset threshold, opens a vacuum switching valve (VSV), which allows a purge port in the canister to admit fuel tank vapors into the canister.

16.10 Test 1 for canisters in 1998 through 2000 models

16.11a Plug the vent port with a cap, plug the purge port with a finger, blow air into the EVAP port and verify that air flows out the air drain port (2001 through 2006 models)

CHECK

Hoses

7   Always inspect the hoses first. A disconnected, damaged or missing hose is the most likely cause of a malfunctioning EVAP system. Refer to the Vacuum Hose Routing Diagram (attached to the underside of the hood) to determine whether the hoses are correctly routed and attached. Repair damaged hoses and replace missing hoses as necessary. If the diagram is missing, it can be ordered from a dealer service department.

Canister

▶ **Refer to illustrations 16.10, 16.11a and 16.11b**

8   Remove the canister from the vehicle (see Steps 42 through 44) and then check it as follows.

9   When the EVAP system is functioning, some parts of it, including the canister, are slightly pressurized, so inspect the canister and all ports for leaks, damage or cracks that could allow vapors to leak out during EVAP system operation. If the canister is obviously damaged, replace it. If the canister appears to be in satisfactory condition, leak test it as follows (these tests will also pinpoint a clogged filter or a stuck check valve or diaphragm).

10 On 1998 through 2000 models (rectangular canister in engine compartment): Plug port E and port B with your fingers (if that's awkward, plug one of the ports with a rubber plug), blow gently into port A and verify that air flows out port D (see illustration). Next, plug ports B and D, blow gently into port A and verify that no air flows out port C. Then, apply a 1.0 in-Hg vacuum to port B, and then verify that the vacuum does not decrease when port C is closed, and verify that vacuum decreases when port C is opened. Finally, plug port C, apply a vacuum of 1.0 in-Hg to port A and verify that air flows into port B. If the canister fails any of these four checks, replace it.

11 On 2001 and later models, plug the vent port with a cap, plug the purge port with a finger, blow gently into the EVAP port and verify that air flows out the air drain port (see illustration). Next, plug the purge port and the air drain port, blow gently into the EVAP port and verify that air does not flow out the air inlet port (see illustration). Then, apply a vacuum of 1.0 in-Hg vacuum to the purge port and verify that the vacuum doesn't decrease when the air inlet port is closed, and that the vacuum does decrease when the air inlet port is opened. Finally, plug the air inlet port, apply 1.0 in-Hg vacuum to the EVAP port and verify

16.11b Plug the purge port and the air drain port, blow air into the EVAP port and verify that air does not flow out the air inlet port (2000 and later models)

that air flows into the purge port. If the canister fails one or more of these tests, replace it.

Vacuum switching valve (VSV)

▶ **Refer to illustrations 16.12**

12 Remove the V-bank cover. Locate the VSV on the emission control valve set (see illustration on next page). Unplug the electrical connector, clearly label and then detach the EVAP hoses, remove the retaining bolt and detach the VSV from its mounting bracket.

13 Using an ohmmeter, measure the resistance of the VSV at the terminals. It should be between 27 and 33 ohms. If the resistance is incorrect, replace the VSV.

14 Verify that there is no continuity between either VSV terminal and ground. If there is, replace the VSV.

15 Blow some low-pressure air (no more than 13.5 psi) into the port closest to the electrical connector and verify that it doesn't flow out the other (outer) port. If it does, replace the VSV.

16 Apply battery voltage and ground to the VSV terminals, blow some low-pressure air into the port closest to the electrical connector and verify that it does flow out of the other (outer) port.

17 Installation is the reverse of removal.

16.12 Vacuum switching valve (VSV) for EVAP system

16.24 Vacuum switching valve (VSV) for canister closed valve (CCV) location, 1998 to 2000 models (air cleaner housing removed for clarity) - on 2001 through 2006 models, it is located between the air filter housing and the fender

Vacuum switching valve (VSV) for vapor pressure sensor (1998 through 2000 models)

18 Locate the VSV for the vapor pressure sensor (see illustration 16.1a). It's in the engine compartment, near the canister. Unplug the electrical connector from the VSV, clearly label the vacuum hoses connected to the VSV and then disconnect them. Remove the VSV retaining bolt and remove the VSV.

19 Using an ohmmeter, measure the resistance between the VSV terminals. It should be between 33 and 39 ohms. If it isn't, replace the VSV.

20 Verify that there is no continuity between either VSV terminal and the body of the valve. If there is, replace the VSV.

21 There are three ports on the VSV: a closely grouped pair of ports and another port at the other end of the VSV, near the electrical connector. Apply a small amount of low-pressure air to the inner of the closely-grouped pair of ports and verify it flows out the port closest to the electrical connector. If it doesn't, replace the VSV.

22 Apply battery voltage to the VSV terminals, blow a small amount of low-pressure air into the inner of the closely-grouped pair of ports

and verify that it comes out the other port of the pair. If it doesn't, replace the VSV.

23 Installation is the reverse of removal.

Vacuum switching valve (VSV) for canister closed valve (CCV) (2001 and later models)

▶ Refer to illustrations 16.24

24 Locate the VSV on a bracket near the air cleaner housing, unplug the electrical connector, detach the vacuum hose, remove the retaining bolts and remove the VSV (see illustration). Don't lose the O-ring.

16.30 Vacuum switching valve (VSV) for the pressure switching valve - installation details (2001 through 2006 models)

16.38 Vapor pressure sensor terminal guide

25 Using an ohmmeter, measure the resistance across the VSV terminals. At 68 degrees F, it should be between 25 and 30 ohms; at 248 degrees F, it should be between 33 and 42 ohms. If the resistance is incorrect, replace the VSV.

26 Verify that there is no continuity between either VSV terminal and the body of the valve. If there is, replace the VSV.

27 Apply some low-pressure compressed air into the outer port and verify that it flows out the inner port. If it doesn't, replace the VSV.

28 Apply battery voltage to the VSV terminals, blow some low-pressure air into the outer port and verify that it does not flow out the inner port. If it does, replace the VSV.

29 Installation is the reverse of removal.

Vacuum switching valve (VSV) for pressure switching valve (2001 through 2006 models)

▶ **Refer to illustration 16.30**

30 Raise the rear of the vehicle and place it securely on jackstands. Locate the VSV for the pressure-switching valve at the charcoal canister (see illustration). Unplug the electrical connector from the VSV, clearly label the vacuum hoses connected to the VSV and then disconnect them. Remove the VSV retaining bolt and remove the VSV.

31 Using an ohmmeter, measure the resistance between the VSV terminals. At 68 degrees F, it should be between 37 and 44 ohms; at 248 degrees F, it should be between 51 and 62 degrees. If the resistance is incorrect, replace the VSV.

32 Verify that there is no continuity between either VSV terminal and the body. If there is, replace the VSV.

33 Apply a small amount of low-pressure air into the inner port and verify that it does not flow out the outer port. If it does, replace the VSV.

34 Apply battery voltage to the VSV terminals, blow a small amount of low-pressure air into the inner port and verify that it comes out the outer port. If it doesn't, replace the VSV.

35 Installation is the reverse of removal.

Vapor pressure sensor

▶ **Refer to illustration 16.38 and 16.39**

36 The vapor pressure sensor is mounted in the engine compartment on 1998 to 2000 models, on the firewall or at the charcoal canister. On 2001 and later models, it's behind the fuel tank. Refer to illustrations 16.1a or 16.1b, if necessary.

37 If you're checking the vapor pressure sensor on a 2001 and later model, raise the rear of the vehicle and place it securely on jackstands.

38 Unplug the electrical connector from the vapor pressure sensor, touch the probes of a voltmeter to the indicated terminals, turn the ignition key to ON (engine not running) and measure the voltage supply to the vapor pressure sensor (see illustration). It should be between 4.5

16.39 To test the vapor pressure sensor output voltage on 1998 to 2000 models, detach this vacuum line and hook up a hand-operated vacuum pump in its place

and 5.5 volts. Reconnect the electrical connector. If the voltage supply is out of range, look for a short, open or bad connection in the wiring harness.

39 On 1998 to 2000 models, use a voltmeter and a pair of back-probes to measure the variation in voltage when vacuum is applied to the vapor pressure sensor (see illustration). Backprobe terminals PTNK and E2 (see illustration 16.38); connect the positive probe to terminal PTNK and the negative probe to terminal E2. Turn the ignition key ON (engine not running).

a) Using a hand-held vacuum pump, apply a vacuum of 0.5 in-Hg to the vapor pressure sensor; the voltage should be between 1.3 and 2.1 volts.

b) Release the vacuum and verify that the voltage is between 3.0 and 3.6 volts.

c) Apply a pressure of 0.2 psi to the vapor pressure sensor and verify that the voltage is between 4.2 and 4.8 volts.

Turn the ignition key to OFF and pull the probes out of the sensor connector.

40 On 2001 and later models, turn the key ON, remove the fuel filler cap and test the voltage between the middle terminal and VC. Voltage should be 3.0 to 3.6 volts.

41 If the vapor pressure sensor does not operate as described, replace it.

REPLACEMENT

Charcoal canister

42 Disconnect the cable from the negative battery terminal.

43 On 2001 and later models, raise the rear of the vehicle and support it securely on jackstands. Remove the canister shield from 2007 and later models

44 Unplug all electrical connectors and clearly label and disconnect the vent hoses to the charcoal canister, remove the bolts and separate the canister from the engine compartment or the underside of the vehicle. Refer to the illustrations at the beginning of this section if necessary.

45 Installation is the reverse of removal.

All other components

46 Refer to the appropriate checking procedure and the illustrations that accompany that procedure.

17 Catalytic converter

→Note: Because of a Federally mandated extended warranty which covers emissions-related components such as the catalytic converter, check with a dealer service department before replacing the converter at your own expense.

GENERAL DESCRIPTION

1 The catalytic converter is an emission control device added to the exhaust system to reduce pollutants from the exhaust gas stream. There are two types of converters. The conventional oxidation catalyst reduces the levels of hydrocarbon (HC) and carbon monoxide (CO). The three-way catalyst lowers the levels of oxides of nitrogen (Nox) as well as hydrocarbons (HC) and carbon monoxide (CO). On 2001 through 2006 models, there are three catalytic converters. A "warm-up" three-way catalytic converter (WU-TWC) is a part of the front exhaust manifold and another is part of the pipe coming from the rear manifold. The main exhaust pipe contains the final three-way converter.

CHECK

2 The test equipment for a catalytic converter is expensive and highly sophisticated. If you suspect that the converter on your vehicle is malfunctioning, take it to a dealer or authorized emissions inspection facility for diagnosis and repair.

3 Whenever the vehicle is raised for servicing of underbody components, check the converter for leaks, corrosion, dents and other damage. Check the welds/flange bolts that attach the front and rear ends of the converter to the exhaust system. If damage is discovered, the converter should be replaced.

4 Although catalytic converters don't break too often, they can become plugged. The easiest way to check for a restricted converter is to use a vacuum gauge to diagnose the effect of a blocked exhaust on intake vacuum.

a) Connect a vacuum gauge to an intake manifold vacuum source (see Chapter 2B).

b) Warm the engine to operating temperature, place the transaxle in Park and apply the parking brake.

c) Note and record the vacuum reading at idle.

d) Quickly open the throttle to near full throttle and release it shut. Note and record the vacuum reading.

e) Perform the test three more times, recording the reading after each test.

f) If the reading after the fourth test is more than one in-Hg lower than the reading recorded at idle, the exhaust system may be restricted (the catalytic converter could be plugged or an exhaust pipe or muffler could be restricted).

REPLACEMENT

♦ **Refer to illustration 17.5**

➡**Note: On 2001 and later models, the warm-up converters cannot be replaced separately. Refer to Chapter 2A for the exhaust manifold replacement procedure.**

5 Be sure to spray the nuts on the exhaust flange studs with penetrating oil before removing them from the catalytic converter (see illustration).

17.5 To remove the catalytic converter disconnect the flange at the rear of the converter - the front of the converter is welded to the pipe and must be cut for removal

6 Remove the nuts and separate the catalytic converter from the exhaust system.

7 Installation is the reverse of removal.

18 Variable Valve Timing (VVT) system - description and component replacement

DESCRIPTION

1 The Variable Valve Timing (VVT) system is used on 2001 and later models. The VVT system varies intake camshaft timing to produce valve timing that is optimized for the driving conditions. The VVT system achieves this by using engine oil pressure to advance or retard the controller on the front end of each camshaft.

2 The VVT system consists of four VVT sensors, the Powertrain Control Module (PCM), four VVT oil control valves and four camshaft sprocket/actuator assemblies.

3 Each controller consists of a timing rotor (for the VVT sensor), a housing with an impeller-type vane inside it, a lock pin and the actual timing chain sprocket for each camshaft. The vane is fixed on the end of the camshaft.

4 The camshaft timing oil control valve is a PCM-controlled device that controls and directs the flow of oil to the advance or retard passages leading to the controller. There are four oil control valves, one for each camshaft. A spring-loaded spool valve inside the oil control valve directs oil pumped into the valve toward either the advance outlet port or the retard outlet port, depending on the engine conditions.

COMPONENT REPLACEMENT

✳✳ WARNING:

Wait until the engine is completely cool before beginning this procedure.

VVT sensors

➡**Note: There are four VVT sensors. The sensors are located on top of the engine - one for each camshaft.**

5 Refer to Chapter 2B and remove the upper intake manifold for access to the rear two VVT sensors. The front sensors can be accessed by removing the engine cover.

6 Disconnect the electrical connector from the VVT sensor.

7 Remove the VVT sensor mounting bolt and remove the sensor.

8 Installation is the reverse of removal.

Camshaft timing oil control valves

9 Refer to Chapter 2B and remove the upper intake manifold for access to the rear two camshaft timing oil control valves. The front ones can be accessed by removing the engine cover.

10 Disconnect the electrical connector from the camshaft timing oil control valve.

11 Remove the camshaft timing oil control valve mounting bolt and remove the oil control valve.

12 Installation is the reverse of removal.

19 Accelerator Pedal Position (APP) sensor - replacement

1 Working under the left side of the instrument panel, disconnect the wiring from the accelerator pedal position sensor.
2 Remove the two mounting nuts and remove the pedal assembly from the floor.
3 Installation is the reverse of removal.

Specifications

Air/fuel sensor heater resistance	
1999 and later	
At 68 degrees F	0.8 to 1.4 ohms
At 1472 degrees F	1.8 to 3.2 ohms
Oxygen sensor heater resistance	11 to 16 ohms
Crankshaft position sensor resistance	
Cold	1,630 to 2,740 ohms
Hot	2,065 to 3,225 ohms
Camshaft position sensor resistance	
Nippondenso	
Cold	835 to 1,400 ohms
Hot	1,060 to 1,645 ohms
Wabash	
Cold	1,690 to 2,560 ohms
Hot	2,145 to 3,010 ohms
Idle Air Control valve resistance	
1998 through 2000	
Cold	17 to 24.5 ohms
Hot	21.5 to 28.5 ohms
2001 and later	N/A

Torque specifications

Ft-lbs (unless otherwise noted)

➡Note: One foot-pound (ft-lb) of torque is equivalent to 12 inch-pounds (in-lbs) of torque. Torque values below approximately 15 ft-lbs are expressed in inch-pounds, since most foot-pound torque wrenches are not accurate at these smaller values.

Intake air control valve/No. 2 intake air control valve retaining nuts	120 in-lbs
No. 1 intake air control valve-to-intake plenum retaining nuts	22
Knock sensor	
2003 and earlier models	29
2004 and later models	168 in-lbs

Section

Reference to other Chapters

7

AUTOMATIC
TRANSAXLE

1 General information

The transaxles covered by this manual are either automatic four-speed (early models) or five-speed units (late models).

Due to the complexity of the automatic transaxles covered in this manual and to the specialized equipment necessary to perform most service operations, this Chapter contains only those procedures related to general diagnosis, routine maintenance, adjustment and removal and installation.

If the transaxle requires major repair work, it should be left to a dealer service department or an automotive or transmission shop. You can, however, remove and install the transaxle yourself and save the expense, even if a transmission shop does the repair work.

2 Diagnosis - general

Automatic transaxle malfunctions may be caused by five general conditions:

a) *poor engine performance*
b) *improper adjustments*
c) *hydraulic malfunctions*
d) *mechanical malfunctions*
e) *malfunctions in the computer or its signal network*

Diagnosis of these problems should always begin with a check of the easily repaired items: fluid level and condition (see Chapter 1), shift linkage adjustment and throttle linkage adjustment. Next, perform a road test to determine if the problem has been corrected or if more diagnosis is necessary. If the problem persists after the preliminary tests and corrections are completed, additional diagnosis should be done by a dealer service department or transmission shop. Refer to the *Troubleshooting* section at the front of this manual for information on symptoms of transaxle problems.

PRELIMINARY CHECKS

1 Drive the vehicle to warm the transaxle to normal operating temperature.

2 Check the fluid level as described in Chapter 1:

a) *If the fluid level is unusually low, add enough fluid to bring the level within the designated area of the dipstick, then check for external leaks (see below).*

b) *If the fluid level is abnormally high, drain off the excess, then check the drained fluid for contamination by coolant. The presence of engine coolant in the automatic transaxle fluid indicates that a failure has occurred in the internal radiator walls that separate the coolant from the transaxle fluid (see Chapter 3).*

c) *If the fluid is foaming, drain it and refill the transaxle, then check for coolant in the fluid, or a high fluid level.*

3 Check the engine idle speed.

➡Note: If the engine is malfunctioning, do not proceed with the preliminary checks until it has been repaired and runs normally.

4 On early models, check the throttle valve cable for freedom of movement. Adjust it if necessary (see Section 4).

➡Note: The throttle cable may function properly when the engine is shut off and cold, but it may malfunction once the engine is hot. Check it cold and at normal engine operating temperature.

5 Inspect the shift control linkage (see Section 3). Make sure that it's properly adjusted and that the linkage operates smoothly.

FLUID LEAK DIAGNOSIS

6 Most fluid leaks are easy to locate visually. Repair usually consists of replacing a seal or gasket. If a leak is difficult to find, the following procedure may help.

7 Identify the fluid. Make sure it's transmission fluid and not engine oil or brake fluid (automatic transmission fluid is a deep red color).

8 Try to pinpoint the source of the leak. Drive the vehicle several miles, then park it over a large sheet of cardboard. After a minute or two, you should be able to locate the leak by determining the source of the fluid dripping onto the cardboard.

9 Make a careful visual inspection of the suspected component and the area immediately around it. Pay particular attention to gasket mating surfaces. A mirror is often helpful for finding leaks in areas that are hard to see.

10 If the leak still cannot be found, clean the suspected area thoroughly with a degreaser or solvent, then dry it.

11 Drive the vehicle for several miles at normal operating temperature and varying speeds. After driving the vehicle, visually inspect the suspected component again.

12 Once the leak has been located, the cause must be determined before it can be properly repaired. If a gasket is replaced but the sealing flange is bent, the new gasket will not stop the leak. The bent flange must be straightened.

13 Before attempting to repair a leak, check to make sure that the following conditions are corrected or they may cause another leak.

➡Note: Some of the following conditions cannot be fixed without highly specialized tools and expertise. Such problems must be referred to a transmission shop or a dealer service department.

Gasket leaks

14 Check the pan periodically. Make sure the bolts are tight, no bolts are missing, the gasket is in good condition and the pan is flat (dents in the pan may indicate damage to the valve body inside).

15 If the pan gasket is leaking, the fluid level or the fluid pressure may be too high, the vent may be plugged, the pan bolts may be too tight, the pan sealing flange may be warped, the sealing surface of the transaxle housing may be damaged, the gasket may be damaged or the transaxle casting may be cracked or porous. If sealant instead of gasket material has been used to form a seal between the pan and the transaxle housing, it may be the wrong sealant.

Seal leaks

16 If a transaxle seal is leaking, the fluid level or pressure may be too high, the vent may be plugged, the seal bore may be damaged, the seal itself may be damaged or improperly fitted, the surface of the shaft

protruding through the seal may be damaged or a loose bearing may be causing excessive shaft movement.

17 Make sure the dipstick tube seal is in good condition and the tube is properly seated. Periodically check the area around the speedometer gear or sensor for leakage. If fluid is evident, check the O-ring for damage.

Case leaks

18 If the case itself appears to be leaking, the casting is porous and will have to be repaired or replaced.

19 Make sure the oil cooler hose fittings are tight and in good condition.

Fluid comes out vent pipe or fill tube

20 If this condition occurs, the transaxle is overfilled, there is coolant in the fluid, the case is porous, the dipstick is incorrect, the vent is plugged or the drain-back holes are plugged.

---

3 Shift cable - adjustment and replacement

ADJUSTMENT

▶ **Refer to illustrations 3.3 and 3.4**

1 When the shift lever inside the vehicle is moved from the Neutral position to other positions, it should move smoothly and accurately to each position and the shift indicator should indicate the correct gear position. If the indicator isn't aligned with the correct position, adjust the shift cable as follows:

2 Raise the vehicle and support it securely on jackstands. Remove the splash shields that cover the area between the front of the vehicle and the lower crossmember (see Chapter 11).

3 Loosen the swivel nut on the manual shift lever at the transaxle (see illustration).

4 Place the manual lever in Park, then return it two notches to the Neutral position (see illustration).

5 Move the shift lever inside the vehicle to the Neutral position.

6 While holding the lever with a slight pressure toward the REVERSE position, tighten the swivel nut securely.

7 Check the operation of the transaxle in each shift lever position (try to start the engine in each gear - the starter should operate in the Park and Neutral positions only).

REPLACEMENT

▶ **Refer to illustrations 3.8, 3.9 and 3.12**

8 Disconnect the cable from the manual lever (see illustration 3.3) and remove the large C-clip cable retainer (see illustration) from the bracket above the manual lever.

Early models

9 Loosen the large grommet from around the cable housing at the firewall (see illustration).

3.3 Before adjusting the shift cable, loosen the swivel nut that connects the shift cable to the manual lever on the transaxle

3.4 To adjust the shift cable, push the manual lever all the way DOWN, return it two clicks to the Neutral position, place the shift lever inside the vehicle at the Neutral position and tighten the swivel nut

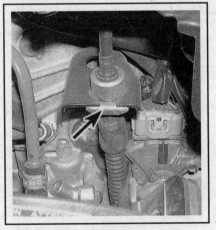

3.8 To disconnect the shift cable from the transaxle, remove the large C-clip retainer from the bracket on the front of the transaxle

3.9 Use a screwdriver and rubber lubricant to release the large cable grommet from the firewall

10 Remove the steering column upper and lower covers (see Chapter 11).

11 Remove the driver's knee bolster and the reinforcement panel behind it (see Chapter 11).

12 Remove the retaining clip (see illustration), pull out the clevis pin and disconnect the cable from the shift lever.

Later models

13 Remove the instrument cluster panel for access to the upper end of the cable (see Chapter 11).

14 Detach the secondary cable guide bracket, then remove the two nuts that secure the cable to the firewall.

15 Use a screwdriver to pry the cable end off of the shift lever. Use a small screwdriver to detach the cable outer housing from the shift lever bracket.

All models

16 Pull the cable through the firewall.

3.12 To disconnect the shift cable from the shift lever on early models, remove the retaining clip and pull out the clevis pin

17 Installation is the reverse of removal.
18 Adjust the cable at the transaxle end.

4   Throttle valve (TV) cable - check and adjustment

▶ **Refer to illustration 4.2**

➡**Note: This procedure applies only to early models with four-speed transaxles.**

1   Have an assistant hold the throttle pedal down while you verify that the throttle valve linkage opens all the way.

2   If the linkage does not open all the way, ask your assistant to hold the pedal down while you loosen the adjusting nuts and adjust the cable until the mark or stopper is the specified distance from the boot end (see illustration).

3   Tighten the adjusting nuts securely, recheck the clearance and make sure the link opens all the way when the throttle is depressed.

4.2 Throttle valve (TV) cable housing-to-stopper gap details

5   Park/Neutral position switch - check, replacement and adjustment

1   The Park/Neutral position switch prevents the engine from starting in any gear other than Park or Neutral. If the engine starts with the shift lever in any position other than Park or Neutral, adjust the switch. The Park/Neutral position switch is also a sensor for Electronic Controlled Transaxle information at the Engine Control Module (ECM, also called the PCM). When the shift lever is placed in position, the Park/Neutral position switch sends a voltage signal to the ECM.

CHECK

▶ **Refer to illustrations 5.4a and 5.4b**

2   Raise the front of the vehicle and place it securely on jackstands.

3   Disconnect the electrical connector from the Park/Neutral position switch.

4   Using an ohmmeter, check continuity between the indicated terminals for each switch position (see illustrations).

5   If the switch continuity isn't as specified, replace it.

REPLACEMENT

▶ **Refer to illustration 5.8**

6   Raise the front of the vehicle and place it securely on jackstands.

7   Disconnect the electrical connector.

8   Remove the manual-lever retaining nut (see illustration).
9   Remove the switch retaining bolts.

Shift Position	Terminal No. to continuity	
P	2 – 7	5 – 6
R	2 – 8	–
N	2 – 9	5 – 6
D	2 – 10	–
2	2 – 3	–
L	2 – 4	–

5.4a Park/Neutral position switch terminal guide and continuity table - 2003 and earlier models

5.8 **Remove the manual lever retaining nut (left), detach the manual lever and remove the switch retaining bolts (one bolt indicated at right)**

Shift Position	Terminal No. to continuity	
P	1 – 3	6 – 9
R	2 – 3	–
N	3 – 5	6 – 9
D, 4	3 – 7	–
3	3 – 4	–
2, L	3 – 8	–

5.4b **Park/Neutral position switch terminal guide and continuity table - 2004 through 2006 models**

10 Remove the switch.

11 Installation is the reverse of removal. Be sure to adjust the switch.

ADJUSTMENT

▶ **Refer to illustration 5.12**

12 Loosen the switch retaining bolts and rotate the switch until the groove and the neutral basic line are aligned (see illustration). Hold the switch in this position and tighten the bolts.

5.12 **Park/Neutral position switch alignment details**

---

6   Shift lock system - description, check and component replacement

DESCRIPTION

1   The shift lock system prevents the shift lever from being shifted out of Park until the brake pedal is applied. The system consists of a pair of mechanical cables, connecting the shiftlever assembly at the steering column with the shift control cable (to the transaxle) and controlled by a mechanical plunger that contacts the brake pedal. If the shift lock system doesn't perform as described, check the following components.

CHECK AND ADJUSTMENT

▶ **Refer to illustration 6.3**

➡ **Note: This procedure applies only to early models with a cable-operated interlock system. Later models use electric solenoids instead of cables.**

2   Refer to Chapter 11 and remove the driver's knee bolster and the reinforcement panel behind it.

3   Locate the shift-lock cable plunger at the brake pedal arm (see illustration).

4   The shift-lock plunger should be contacting the plate on the brake pedal.

5   With the ignition key On (engine off), try to move the shift lever from Park. It should not move out of Park unless the brake pedal is depressed. If it does move, adjust the plunger.

6   Loosen the two bolts securing the plunger to the steering column bracket (see illustration 6.3). Move the plunger assembly until the

6.3 **The two shift-lock cables end at this bracket bolted to a flange of the steering column (A) - the plunger tip (B) contacts the pedal**

6.9 Remove the four nuts to lower the steering column

6.10 Shift-lock cable system component mounting points

plunger contacts the pedal plate, then depress the plunger 0.28 inch and tighten the bolts. Check that shifting is possible only when the brake pedal is depressed.

COMPONENT REPLACEMENT

♦ Refer to illustrations 6.9 and 6.10

➡Note: This procedure applies only to early models with a cable-operated interlock system. Later models use electric solenoids instead of cables.

7   Refer to Chapter 12 and disable the airbag system.
8   Refer to Chapter 11 and remove the driver's knee bolster, the reinforcement panel behind it and the steering column covers.
9   Remove the four nuts securing the steering column and lower the column enough to access the shift control cable components (see illustration).
10 Remove the two Torx bolts securing Cable 1, the one Torx bolt at Cable 2, and the two bolts securing the plunger assembly (see illustration).
11 Remove the shift-lock cable assembly.
12 Installation is the reverse of the removal procedure. After installation, recheck the operation as in Step 5.

7   Oil seal replacement

1   Fluid leaks frequently occur due to wear of the driveaxle oil seals and/or speed sensor O-rings. Replacement of these seals is relatively easy, since the repairs can usually be performed without removing the transaxle from the vehicle.

DRIVEAXLE OIL SEALS

♦ Refer to illustrations 7.4 and 7.6

2   The driveaxle oil seals are located in each side of the transaxle, where the driveaxle shaft is splined into the differential. If leakage at the seal is suspected, raise the vehicle and support it securely on jackstands. If the seal is leaking, fluid will be found on the side of the transaxle.
3   Remove the driveaxle assembly (see Chapter 8). If you're replac-

ing the right side driveaxle seal, remove the intermediate shaft and the driveaxle assembly as a single unit.
4   Using a screwdriver or prybar, carefully pry the oil seal out of the transaxle bore (see illustration).
5   If the oil seal cannot be removed with a screwdriver or prybar, a special oil seal removal tool (available at auto parts stores) will be required.
6   Using a large section of pipe or a large deep socket as a drift, install the new oil seal. Drive it into the bore squarely and make sure that it is completely seated (see illustration). Lubricate the lip of the new seal with multi-purpose grease.
7   Install the driveaxle assembly (see Chapter 8). Be careful not to damage the lip of the new seal.

7.4 Carefully pry out the old driveaxle seal with a prybar, screwdriver or a special seal removal tool; make sure you don't gouge or nick the surface of the seal bore

7.6 Drive in the new driveaxle seal with a large socket or a special seal installer

DIRECT CLUTCH SPEED SENSOR SEAL

▶ **Refer to illustration 7.8**

8   The direct clutch speed sensor seal (2001 through 2006 models only) is located on the transaxle housing (see illustration). Look for lubricant around the sensor housing to determine if the O-ring is leaking.

9   Disconnect the electrical connector from the direct clutch speed sensor and remove the sensor from the transaxle.

10   Remove the O-ring.

11   Install a new O-ring on the sensor body and reinstall the direct clutch speed sensor. Tighten the hold-down bolt securely.

7.8   To remove the direct clutch speed sensor from the transaxle, disconnect the electrical connector and remove the sensor hold-down bolt (2001 and later models)

8   Automatic transaxle - removal and installation

REMOVAL

2006 and earlier models

▶ **Refer to illustrations 8.5, 8.8, 8.12, 8.28a, 8.28b, 8.31a, 8.31b, 8.32 and 8.33**

1   Place protective covers on the fenders and remove the cowl cover and hood (see Chapter 11).

2   Relieve the fuel system pressure (see Chapter 4).

3   Disconnect the negative cable from the battery.

4   Remove the battery and the battery tray (see Chapter 5).

5   If the vehicle is equipped with cruise control, unplug the electrical connector for the actuator and remove the actuator (see illustration).

6   Remove the starter (see Chapter 5).

7   Release the residual fuel pressure in the tank by removing the gas cap, then disconnect the fuel lines connecting the engine to the chassis (see Chapter 4). Plug or cap all open fittings.

8   Remove the fluid cooler lines from the transaxle (see illustration). Be sure to position a pan below the line connections to catch any residual fluid.

9   Disconnect the Park/Neutral position switch electrical connector

(see Section 5).

10   Disconnect the transaxle fluid temperature sensor and the direct clutch speed sensor, if applicable.

11   Disconnect the accelerator cable and the throttle valve (TV) cable from the throttle linkage (see Section 4).

12   Clearly label, then disconnect all vacuum lines, coolant and emissions hoses, wiring harness connectors (shift solenoid valve and Park/Neutral position switch) and ground straps (see illustration). Masking tape and/or a touch-up paint applicator works well for marking items. Take instant photos or sketch the locations of components and brackets.

13   Remove the cooling fan(s) and shroud(s). Drain the coolant and remove the radiator and all coolant and heater hoses (see Chapter 3).

14   Disconnect the shift cable (see Section 3) from the transaxle.

15   Loosen but do NOT remove the front wheel lug nuts. Raise the vehicle and support it securely on jackstands. Secure the engine using an engine support brace that is fitted above the engine compartment. If an engine support brace is not available, install an engine hoist and a lifting chain assembly. This will keep the engine stable during the entire transaxle removal procedure.

8.5   Location of the cruise control actuator

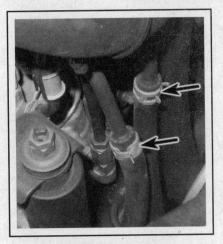

8.8   Disconnect the automatic transaxle cooler lines

8.12   Location of the ground strap bolt

8.28a Make subframe-to-chassis reference marks to insure correct reassembly

8.28b Location of the subframe mounting bolts and nuts - note the exact location of the various size fasteners to insure correct reassembly

❋❋ WARNING:

Be sure the engine/transaxle is securely supported by the brace or hoist. If it is not securely supported, it could fall during the removal procedure, causing injury or death. Remove the front wheels.

16 Remove the manifold brace that supports the exhaust manifold and the transaxle.

17 Detach the exhaust pipes from the manifolds (see Chapter 4). Detach the exhaust pipe from the catalytic converter and separate the pipe from the exhaust system.

➡**Note: On some models it will be necessary to remove the front pipe support bracket from the transaxle and chassis.**

18 Remove the splash shields (see Chapter 2).

19 Drain the transaxle fluid (see Chapter 1).

20 Remove the driveaxles (see Chapter 8).

21 Remove the two mounting bolts from the front engine mount (see Chapter 2A).

➡**Note: Vehicles equipped with the TMMK shift lock solenoid system will be equipped with a green colored bolt and a silver colored bolt. Refer to the Specifications listed in Chapters 2A or 2B for the correct torque specifications. Refer to Section 5 for additional details.**

22 Remove the mounting bolts from the front engine mount (see Chapter 2A).

23 Remove the left side transaxle mount nuts. Refer to Chapter 2A for engine mount information.

24 Remove the rear engine mount from the transaxle (see Chapter 2A).

25 Unbolt the power steering gear from the suspension. First, remove the two stabilizer bar mounting nuts and disconnect the stabilizer bar from the links (see Chapter 10).

26 Remove the four set bolts from the stabilizer bar bracket (see Chapter 10).

27 Use wire to tie the power steering gear to the chassis and remove the mounting bolts. The steering gear should remain suspended but out of the way during the transaxle removal procedure.

28 Remove the subframe mounting bolts from the chassis (see illustration). The front section of the subframe is attached with two bolts and two nuts while the rear section of the subframe is attached

with a combination of six nuts and bolts. Be sure to note exactly the size and location of each nut and bolt to insure correct reassembly (see illustration).

➡**Note: The transaxle should be supported by a transaxle jack immediately after the subframe is removed from the vehicle. The transaxle will tilt slightly but should remain steady if the engine is properly secured with the engine compartment brace.**

29 Support the transaxle with an approved transaxle jack and safety chains. Floor jacks are often not stable enough to support and lower the transaxle from the vehicle.

30 Remove the stiffener plate from the left side and right side of the transaxle.

➡**Note: TMC and TMMK use two different types of bolt arrangements for the engine. The TMMK system uses a mounting nut and two bolts while the TMC system uses three bolts.**

31 Remove the torque converter mounting bolts (see illustrations). Rotate the engine to gain access to each bolt.

32 Remove the transaxle housing bolts from the upper section in the engine compartment (see illustration).

33 Remove the transaxle housing bolts from the lower section of the transaxle housing (see illustration).

34 Recheck to be sure nothing is connecting the engine to the vehicle or to the transaxle. Disconnect and label anything still remaining.

35 Separate the transaxle from the engine, then slowly lower the transaxle assembly out of the vehicle. Keep the transaxle level as you're separating it from the engine to prevent damage to the input shaft. It may be necessary to pry the mounts away from the frame brackets.

❋❋ WARNING:

Do not place any part of your body under the transaxle assembly or engine when it's supported only by a hoist or other lifting device.

36 Move the transaxle assembly away from the vehicle and carefully place the transaxle assembly on the floor onto wood blocks. Leave enough room for a floor jack underneath the transaxle.

37 Check the engine and transaxle mounts and the transaxle shock absorber. If any of these components are worn or damaged, replace them.

8.31a Remove the torque converter cover mounting bolts

8.31b Remove the torque converter-to-driveplate bolts - rotate the engine to gain access to the other bolts

8.32 Locations of two of the upper transaxle-to-engine mounting bolts

2007 and later models

38 Remove the engine and transaxle assembly along with the subframe (see Chapter 2C). The entire assembly is removed from the bottom of the vehicle, so when you're finished, you'll have the subframe (with the engine and transaxle mounted on it) securely supported by blocks.

❋❋ **WARNING:**

The engine/transaxle assembly must be safely braced to avoid falling and possibly breaking components or injuring you.

39 If you haven't already removed them, refer to Chapter 10 and remove the driveaxles.

40 Label and then disconnect the wiring harnesses along with the retainers. Remove the shifter cable clamp and bracket.

41 Remove the starter (see Chapter 5).

42 Remove the transaxle dipstick tube and the transaxle fluid cooler tubes.

43 Remove the front engine mounting bracket.

44 Remove the cover from the bottom of the bellhousing, then remove the torque converter bolts. Rotate the crankshaft with a wrench for access to all the bolts.

45 Remove the ten transaxle-to-engine bolts.

46 Check to be certain there is nothing connecting the transaxle to the engine.

47 With the help of an assistant, separate the transaxle from the engine, keeping it level as you do so to prevent damage to the input shaft.

48 Move the transaxle away from the engine/subframe and the vehicle and carefully set it on wood blocks.

INSTALLATION

49 If removed, install the torque converter on the transaxle input shaft. Make sure the converter hub splines are properly engaged with the splines on the transaxle input shaft.

50 With the transaxle secured to the jack as on removal, and with an assistant holding the torque converter in place, raise the transaxle into position and turn the converter to align the bolt holes in the converter with the bolt holes in the driveplate. Do not use excessive force to

install the transaxle - if something binds and the transaxle won't mate with the engine, alter the angle of the transaxle slightly until it does mate.

❋❋ **CAUTION:**

Do NOT use transaxle-to-engine bolts to force the engine and transaxle into alignment. Doing so could crack or damage major components. If you experience difficulties, have an assistant help you line up the dowel pins on the block with the transaxle. Some wiggling of the engine and/or the transaxle will probably be necessary to secure proper alignment of the two.

51 Install the transaxle-to-engine bolts and the engine-to-transaxle bolt. Tighten the bolts to the torque listed in this Chapter's Specifications.

52 On 2006 and earlier models, lift the engine/transaxle assembly with the engine hoist and carefully lower the assembly into the engine compartment. Tighten all nuts and bolts securely.

53 On 2006 and earlier models, install the right engine mount, the front engine mount, the transaxle shock absorber, the left transaxle mount and the rear engine mount. Install the center bearing support on the rear of the block. Tighten all mounting bolts and nuts securely.

8.33 Locations of two of the lower transaxle-to-engine mounting bolts

54 On 2007 and later models, refer to Chapter 2C and install the engine transaxle assembly into the vehicle. On all models, install all of the removed components in the reverse order of removal.

55 Remove all jacks and hoists and lower the vehicle. Tighten the wheel nuts to the torque listed in the Chapter 1 Specifications.

56 Add the specified amounts of coolant and transaxle fluids (see Chapter 1).

57 Connect the negative battery cable. Road test the vehicle to check for proper transmission operation and check for leakage.

58 Run the engine and check for proper operation and leaks. Shut off the engine and recheck the fluid levels.

9   Electronic control system

TROUBLE CODES

1   The electronic control system for the transaxle has some self-diagnostic capabilities. If certain kinds of system malfunctions occur, the PCM stores the appropriate diagnostic trouble code in its memory and the CHECK ENGINE indicator light illuminates to inform the driver. The diagnostic trouble codes can only be extracted from the PCM using a SCAN tool that can be linked to the On Board Diagnostic (OBD II) computer via the 16-pin diagnostic link. Codes are listed below for reference, but can only be extracted with the correct SCAN tool (refer to Chapter 6 for additional information).

Trouble code	Trouble area
P0500	Defective speedometer gauge (number 1 speed sensor), open in wiring harness or short circuit
P0705	Transmission range sensor, circuit malfunction (PRNDL input)
P0710	Open or short in SL1 shift solenoid harness or short circuit, blocked or stuck valve body
P0711	Transmission fluid temperature sensor circuit, range or performance problem
P0712	Transmission fluid temperature sensor circuit, low input
P0713	Transmission fluid temperature sensor circuit, high input
P0717	Input/turbine speed sensor circuit, no signal
P0724	Torque converter/brake switch B circuit, high
P0741	Torque converter clutch, circuit performance or stuck in off position
P0746	Pressure control solenoid, performance problem or stuck in off position
P0748	Pressure control solenoid, electrical problem
P0750	Defective Shift Solenoid A (number 1 shift solenoid), valve stuck open or closed
P0753	Defective Shift Solenoid A (number 1 shift solenoid), open in wiring harness or short circuit
P0755	Defective Shift Solenoid B (number 2 shift solenoid), valve stuck open or closed
P0758	Defective Shift Solenoid B (number 2 shift solenoid), open in wiring harness or short circuit

Trouble code	Trouble area
P0765	Defective Shift Solenoid (number S4 shift solenoid), valve stuck open or closed
P0766	Shift solenoid D, performance problem or stuck in off position
P0768	Defective Shift Solenoid (number S4 shift solenoid), open in wiring harness or short circuit
P0770	Defective Shift Solenoid E, valve stuck open or closed
P0771	Shift solenoid E, performance problem or stuck in off position
P0773	Defective Shift Solenoid E, open in wiring harness or short circuit
P0776	Pressure control solenoid "B" performance or stuck off
P0778	Pressure control solenoid "B" electrical
P0793	Intermediate shaft speed sensor circuit no signal
P0796	Transmission fluid pressure (TFP) solenoid "C" - performance or stuck off
P0798	Transmission fluid pressure (TFP) solenoid "C" electrical malfunction
P0982	Shift solenoid (SS) D - control circuit low
P0983	Shift solenoid (SS) D - control circuit high
P0984	Shift solenoid (SS) E - control circuit range/performance
P0985	Shift solenoid (SS) E - control circuit low
P0986	Shift solenoid (SS) E - control circuit high
P1520	Defective stop light switch, an open or short in the stop light switch circuit or PCM malfunction
P1705	Defective Direct Clutch Speed sensor, an open or short in the direct clutch sensor circuit or PCM malfunction
P1725	Defective input turbine speed sensor, an open or short in the direct clutch sensor circuit or PCM malfunction
P1730	Defective counter gear speed sensor, an open or short in the counter gear speed sensor circuit or PCM malfunction
P1765	Defective Shift Solenoid Valve SLN, an open or short in the shift solenoid valve SLN circuit or PCM malfunction
P1780	Defective Park/Neutral switch, an open or short in the Park/Neutral switch circuit or PCM malfunction

OTHER ELECTRONIC CONTROL SYSTEM CHECKS

Preliminary checks

2   Check the fluid level and condition. If the fluid smells burned, replace it (see Chapter 1).

3   Check for fluid leaks (see Section 2).

4   Check and, if necessary, adjust the shift cable (see Section 3).

5   Check and, if necessary, adjust the throttle valve (TV) cable (see Section 4).

6   Check and, if necessary, adjust the Park/Neutral position switch (see Section 5).

O/D OFF indicator light check

7   Turn the ignition switch to ON.

8   Verify that the O/D OFF indicator light comes on when the O/D main switch is in the Off (up) position, and goes out when the O/D main switch is pushed to the On position.

9   If the O/D OFF indicator light does not light up, or remains on all the time, have the circuit checked out by a dealer service department.

Manual shifting test

♦ Refer to illustration 9.11

10   This test can determine whether a problem lies is in the electronic control system or is a mechanical problem inside the transaxle. This test should only be performed if a SCAN tool capable of resetting trouble codes is available (see Chapter 6).

11   Disconnect the solenoid connector (see illustration).

12   Drive the vehicle, shifting through the "L," "2" and "D" ranges manually and verify that the gear changes correspond to the shift lever positions.

13   If the transaxle does not perform as described above, the problem is in the transaxle itself and is not an electronic control system problem.

14   Connect the solenoid connectors.

15   Cancel the diagnostic trouble code using a special SCAN tool. Refer to Chapter 6 for additional information.

COMPONENT CHECK AND REPLACEMENT

➜Note: Most electronic control system tests are beyond the scope of this manual. The following procedures are tests you can do at home. Aside from these procedures, diagnosis of the electronic control system should be handled by a dealer service department.

Solenoids

♦ Refer to illustration 9.19

16   To check a solenoid, disconnect the electrical connector from the solenoid harness at the transaxle (see illustration 9.11). Measure the resistance on the transaxle-side of the connector with an ohmmeter. The resistance of each solenoid should be between 11 and 15 ohms. If the resistance is less than 8 ohms, there's a short circuit in the solenoid winding; if the resistance is more than 100 k-ohms, there's an open circuit in the solenoid windings. If the resistance of any solenoid is too high or too low, replace it.

> ✳✳ **CAUTION:**
>
> Do NOT contact any pins on the PCM side of this electrical connector with the ohmmeter leads. Most ohmmeters use a 9-volt battery that could damage the PCM circuitry.

17   The solenoids may also be bench tested for proper operation and obstructions, which would restrict fluid flow.

18   Remove the transaxle pan (see Chapter 1). Disconnect the solenoid from the harness and remove the solenoid from the valve body.

19   Apply battery voltage to each solenoid terminal and verify that the solenoids are working (see illustration). When energized, they should make a clicking sound.

20   Apply no more than 71 psi of compressed air to each solenoid and verify that it doesn't pass air. Now apply battery voltage to each solenoid and verify that the valve opens.

21   If a solenoid doesn't operate as described, replace it.

22   Installation is the reverse of removal.

9.11 The solenoid electrical connector is located off to the side of the Park/Neutral switch

No. 1 and No. 2 Solenoid Valves

Air

Battery

9.19 To check the solenoid valves, apply battery voltage to the terminals of each solenoid and verify that it makes a clicking sound; then apply about 65 psi of compressed air to each solenoid and verify that it doesn't pass air; finally, apply battery voltage to each solenoid and verify that the valve opens

Park/Neutral position switch

23 Refer to Section 5 and check the Park/Neutral position switch.

Throttle Position sensor

24 A malfunctioning TPS can cause shift-related problems. (A malfunctioning TPS should set a diagnostic trouble code).

Direct Clutch speed sensor

25 The number 2 speed sensor is also called the direct clutch speed sensor (see illustration 7.8). This sensor detects the rotation speed of the direct clutch drum and compares the speed signal with the vehicle speed sensor to arrive at the exact shift points for the transmission. Refer to Chapter 6 for the diagnostic and replacement procedures.

Specifications

Throttle valve outer cable end-to-stopper	0.040 inch

Torque specifications — Ft-lbs (unless otherwise indicated)

➡ **Note: One foot-pound (ft-lb) of torque is equivalent to 12 inch-pounds (in-lbs) of torque. Torque values below approximately 15 ft-lbs are expressed in inch-pounds, since most foot-pound torque wrenches are not accurate at these smaller values.**

Park-Neutral position switch bolts	
4-speed models	48 in-lbs
5-speed models	
Nut	61 in-lbs
Bolt	48 in-lbs
Exhaust manifold brace, 4-speed models	15
Subframe assembly (refer to Chapter 2C)	
4-speed models	
Bolt A	134
Bolt B	24
Nut C	27
Steering column nuts, 4-speed models	19
Transaxle-to-engine bolts	
4-speed models	48
5-speed models	
Topmost 7 bolts	47
Lowest 3 bolts	32
Transaxle fluid temperature sensor, 4-speed models	25
Torque converter-to-driveplate bolts	
4-speed models	30
5-speed models	35
Direct clutch speed sensor hold-down bolt,	
4-speed models	96 in-lbs

NOTES

Section

Reference to other Chapters

8

DRIVEAXLES

1 General information

The information in this Chapter deals with the components from the rear of the engine to the front wheels, except for the transaxle, which is dealt with in Chapter 7.

Since nearly all the procedures covered in this Chapter involve working under the vehicle, make sure it's securely supported on sturdy jackstands or a hoist where the vehicle can be easily raised and lowered.

2 Driveaxles - general information and inspection

1   Power is transmitted from the transaxle to the wheels through a pair of driveaxles. The inner end of each driveaxle is connected to the transaxle, directly splined to the differential side gears. The outer ends of the driveaxles are splined to the axle hubs and locked in place by a large nut. The left side driveaxle is shorter while the right side driveaxle is longer and equipped with an intermediate shaft that is supported in the middle by a bearing support.

2   The inner ends of the driveaxles are equipped with sliding constant velocity joints, which are capable of both angular and axial motion. Each inner joint assembly consists of either a tripod bearing and a joint tulip (housing) or a ball-and-cage type constant velocity joint in which the joint is free to slide in-and-out as the driveaxle moves up-and-down with the wheel. The joints can be disassembled and cleaned in the event of a boot failure, but if any parts are damaged, the joints must be replaced as a unit (see Section 11).

3   Each outer joint, which consists of ball bearings running between an inner race and an outer race (housing), is capable of angular but not axial movement.

4   The boots should be inspected periodically for damage and leaking lubricant. Torn CV joint boots must be replaced immediately or the joints can be damaged. Boot replacement involves removal of the driveaxle (see Section 10).

➡Note: Some auto parts stores carry "split" type replacement boots, which can be installed without removing the driveaxle from the vehicle. This is a convenient alternative; however, the driveaxle should be removed and the CV joint disassembled and cleaned to ensure the joint is free from contaminants such as moisture and dirt which will accelerate CV joint wear.

The most common symptom of worn or damaged CV joints, besides lubricant leaks, is a clicking noise in turns, a clunk when accelerating after coasting and vibration at highway speeds. To check for wear in the CV joints and driveaxle shafts, grasp each axle (one at a time) and rotate it in both directions while holding the CV joint housings, feeling for play indicating worn splines or sloppy CV joints. Also check the driveaxle shafts for cracks, dents and distortion.

3 Driveaxle - removal and installation

REMOVAL

▶ Refer to illustrations 3.3, 3.4, 3.8, 3.11, 3.13a, 3.13b, 3.13c, 3.14 and 3.15

❊❊ CAUTION:

This procedure applies to front-wheel drive vehicles, although it is very similar for all-wheel drive models. If you're doing this on an all-wheel drive vehicle, be sure to drain both the transfer case and the transaxle before starting. If this isn't done, the fluids will intermix and require replacement later to avoid damage.

➡Note: Not all of the steps in this procedure apply to all models. Read through the procedure carefully and determine which steps apply to the vehicle being worked on before beginning work.

1   Disconnect the cable from the negative terminal of the battery.
2   Set the parking brake.
3   Remove the wheel cover or hubcap. Remove the cotter pin and the bearing nut lock from the driveaxle/hub nut (see illustration).
4   Break loose the driveaxle/hub nut, but don't remove it yet (see illustration).
5   Loosen the front wheel lug nuts, raise the vehicle and support it securely on jackstands. Remove the wheel.
6   Remove any engine splash shields that are in the way (see Chapter 11). Remove the driveaxle/hub nut.

➡Note: Toyota recommends removing the entire right driveaxle assembly as a single unit before attempting to disassemble it because, although you could disassemble it, reattaching the outer driveaxle assembly to the intermediate shaft on the vehicle would be extremely difficult.

7   Remove the nuts and bolt securing the balljoint to the control arm, then pry the control arm down to separate the components (see Chapter 10).
8   To loosen the driveaxle from the hub splines, tap the end of the driveaxle with a soft-faced hammer or a hammer and a brass punch (see illustration). If the driveaxle is stuck in the hub splines and won't move, it may be necessary to remove the brake disc (see Chapter 9) and push it from the hub with a two-jaw puller.
9   Place a drain pan underneath the transaxle just in case lubricant leaks out.

3.3 Remove the cotter pin and the nut lock

3.4 You'll need a large breaker bar to loosen the driveaxle/hub nut

3.8 Using a hammer and a brass punch, sharply strike the end of the driveaxle - it should move noticeably (don't push it in too far, though; only until it's loose)

3.11 Pull the steering knuckle out and slide the end of the driveaxle out of the hub. There is a sharp ring around the CV joint just behind the stub axle - wrap a rag around it so you don't cut your hand

10 If the transaxle has a case protector (the small plastic cover bolted to the transaxle) over the inner CV joint, remove it.

11 Pull out on the steering knuckle and detach the driveaxle from the hub (see illustration).

3.13a To release the intermediate shaft bearing from the bearing support bracket, remove this lock bolt

12 On right driveaxle assemblies, the intermediate shaft and driveaxle assembly must be removed as a single unit.

13 If you're removing the right driveaxle on any model, remove the center bearing lock bolt (see illustration), remove the snap-ring (see illustration), grasp the intermediate shaft and pull the splined inner end of the shaft out of the differential side gear (see illustration).

3.13b To remove the snap-ring from the bearing support bracket, pinch the ends together as shown and pull it out of its groove in the bracket (driveaxle assembly and bearing support bracket removed from the vehicle for clarity)

3.13c To detach the intermediate shaft from the differential side gear, grasp the shaft firmly and pull

3.14 Pry the splined end of the driveaxle from the transaxle using a screwdriver or prybar

14 If you're removing the left driveaxle, carefully pry the inner CV joint out of the transaxle (see illustration).

15 Should it become necessary to move the vehicle while the drive-axle is out, place a large bolt with two large washers (one on each side of the hub) through the hub and tighten the nut securely (see illustration).

16 Refer to Chapter 7 for the driveaxle seal replacement procedure.

INSTALLATION

17 Installation is the reverse of the removal procedure, but with the following additional points:

a) *When installing the left driveaxle or when installing the intermediate shaft on any model, push the driveaxle sharply inward to seat the retaining ring on the inner CV joint in the groove in the differential side gear.*

b) *After installing the right driveaxle/intermediate shaft assembly, be sure to tighten the center bearing lock bolt to the torque listed in this Chapter's Specifications.*

c) *Install the wheel and lug nuts, lower the vehicle and tighten the lug nuts to the torque listed in the Chapter 1 Specifications.*

3.15 It isn't a good idea to move the vehicle with a driveaxle removed, but if you must, first install a bolt and a pair of washers through the hub and tighten them securely

1	2-inch (O.D.) washer	3	9/16-inch nut
2	1-3/4 inch (O.D.) washer	4	9/16-inch bolt

d) *Tighten the driveaxle/hub nut to the torque listed in this Chapter's Specifications, then install the nut lock and a new cotter pin.*

e) *Check the transaxle fluid and add some new fluid, if necessary, to bring it to the proper level (see Chapter 1).*

18 Check the intermediate shaft bearing for smooth operation. If it feels rough or sticky it should be replaced. Take it to a dealer service department or other repair shop, as special tools are needed to perform this job.

4 Driveaxle boot replacement

➡**Note: Complete rebuilt driveaxles are available on an exchange basis, which eliminates much time and work. Check on the cost and availability of parts before disassembling the vehicle.**

1 Remove the driveaxle (see Section 3).

2 Mount the driveaxle in a vise with wood lined jaws (to prevent damage to the axleshaft). Check the CV joint for excessive play in the radial direction, which indicates worn parts. Check for smooth operation throughout the full range of motion for each CV joint. If a boot is torn, the recommended procedure is to disassemble the joint, clean the components and inspect for damage due to loss of lubrication and possible contamination by foreign matter.

DISASSEMBLY

▶ **Refer to illustrations 4.3, 4.4, 4.6 and 4.7**

3 Using diagonal cutters, cut the boot clamps (see illustration), remove the clamps and discard them.

4 Using a screwdriver, carefully pry up on the edge of the outer boot and push it away from the CV joint. Old and worn boots can be cut off. Pull the inner CV joint boot back from the housing and slide the housing from the tripod (see illustration).

➡**Note: Right side driveaxles are equipped with an intermediate shaft attached to the inner driveaxle housing.**

4.3 Cut the old boot clamps off and discard them

4.4 Remove the boot from the inner CV joint and slide the tripod from the joint housing

4.6 Remove the snap-ring with a pair of snap-ring pliers

5   Mark the tripod and axleshaft to ensure that they are reassembled properly.

6   Remove the tripod joint snap-ring with a pair of snap-ring pliers (see illustration).

7   Use a hammer and a brass punch to drive the tripod joint from the driveaxle (see illustration).

➡**Note: The tripod joint must be removed from the driveaxle to be able to slide the inner and outer driveaxle boots over the driveaxle. Do not remove the outer CV joint from the driveaxle.**

8   If you haven't already cut them off, remove both boots.

CHECK

▶ **Refer to illustrations 4.9a and 4.9b**

9   Thoroughly clean all components, including the outer CV joint assembly, with solvent until the old CV joint grease is completely removed. Inspect the bearing surfaces of the inner tripods and housings for cracks, pitting, scoring and other signs of wear. It's not possible to inspect the bearing surfaces of the inner and outer races of the outer CV joint, but you can at least check the surfaces of the ball bearings themselves (see illustration). If they're in good shape, the races probably are,

4.7 Drive the tripod joint from the driveaxle with a brass punch and hammer; be careful not to damage the bearing surfaces or the splines on the shaft

too; if they're not, neither are the races. If the inner CV joint is worn, you can buy a new inner CV joint and install it on the old axleshaft; if the outer CV joint is worn, you'll have to purchase a new outer CV joint and axleshaft (they're sold preassembled). Check the condition of the

4.9a Clean the outer CV joint thoroughly with solvent and, working the joint through its entire range of motion, inspect the bearing surfaces of the balls; if they're worn or damaged, so are the bearing races

4.9b Check the condition of the center support bearing on the intermediate shaft. Make sure it turns freely, quietly and smoothly; if the bearing is hard to turn, is noisy or feels rough, have it replaced by an automotive machine shop (be sure to have a pair of new dust covers installed too)

bearing for the intermediate shaft (see illustration). It should turn freely and smoothly. If it's difficult to turn, or makes a grinding noise when rotated, take the intermediate shaft to an automotive machine shop and have a new bearing installed on the shaft.

REASSEMBLY

▶ **Refer to illustrations 4.10a, 4.10b, 4.10c, 4.10d, 4.10e, 4.12a, 4.12b and 4.12c**

10 Wrap the splines on the inner end of the axleshaft with electrical or duct tape to protect the boots from the sharp edges of the splines (see illustration). Slide the clamps and boots onto the axleshaft, outer boot first, then place the tripod on the shaft and install a new snap-ring. Apply grease to the tripod assembly and inside the housing. Insert the tripod into the housing and pack the remainder of the grease around the tripod (see illustrations). If you're repacking the outer joint, be sure to work the entire tube of CV joint grease (included with the boot kit) into the bearing assembly.

4.10a Wrap the splined area of the axleshaft with tape to prevent damage to the boots when removing or installing them

4.10b An exploded view of the driveaxle assemblies - typical

Drive Shaft (RH)

Rear Engine Mounting Insulator

Lock Bolt

Snap Ring

Snap Ring

Drive Shaft (LH)

Tie Rod End

Outboard Joint Shaft

Lower Suspension Arm

Boot Clamp

No.2 Dust Deflector

ABS Speed Sensor

Cotter pin

Lock Cap

Boot

Inboard Joint Shaft

Snap Ring

Dust Cover

LH

Inboard Joint Shaft

Center Bearing

Dust Cover

4.10c Install the tripod with the recessed portion of the splines facing the axleshaft, then install a new snap-ring

4.10d Place grease at the bottom of the CV joint housing

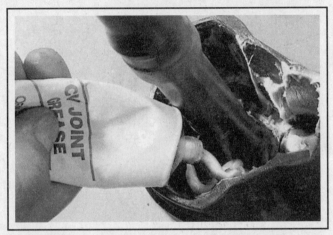

4.10e Install the boot and clamps onto the axleshaft, then insert the tripod into the housing, followed by the rest of the grease

4.12a Measure between the points indicated and move the inner CV joint in or out to set the driveaxle to the length listed in this Chapter's Specifications (right side driveaxle shown)

4.12b Equalize the pressure inside the boot by inserting a small, dull screwdriver between the boot and the outer race

4.12c You'll need a special boot clamp installation tool like this one to tighten the new clamps; follow the instructions provided by the tool manufacturer

11 Slide the boots into place, making sure the ends of both boots seat in their respective grooves in the axleshaft.

12 Adjust the driveaxle to the standard length listed in this Chapter's

Specifications, then equalize the pressure in the boot and tighten the boot clamps (see illustrations). The driveaxle is now ready for installation (see Section 3).

Specifications

Throttle valve outer cable end-to-stopper   0.040 inch

Torque specifications   Ft-lbs (unless otherwise indicated)

➡ **Note: One foot-pound (ft-lb) of torque is equivalent to 12 inch-pounds (in-lbs) of torque. Torque values below approximately 15 ft-lbs are expressed in inch-pounds, since most foot-pound torque wrenches are not accurate at these smaller values.**

Park-Neutral position switch bolts	48 in-lbs
Exhaust manifold brace	15
Subframe assembly (see Chapter 2A)	
Bolt A	134
Bolt B	24
Nut C	27
Steering column mounting nuts	19
Transaxle-to-engine bolts	48
Transaxle fluid temperature sensor	25
Torque converter to driveplate bolts	30
Direct clutch speed sensor hold-down bolt	96 in-lbs

Section

Reference to other Chapters

9
BRAKES

1 General information

The vehicles covered by this manual are equipped with hydraulically operated front and rear brake systems. The front brakes are disc type and the rear brakes are either disc or drum type. Both the front and rear brakes are self-adjusting. The disc brakes automatically compensate for pad wear, while the drum brakes incorporate an adjustment mechanism that is activated as the parking brake is applied.

HYDRAULIC SYSTEM

The hydraulic system consists of two separate circuits. The master cylinder has separate reservoirs for the two circuits, and, in the event of a leak or failure in one hydraulic circuit, the other circuit will remain operative. A dual proportioning valve on the firewall provides brake balance between the front and rear brakes.

POWER BRAKE BOOSTER

The power brake booster, utilizing engine manifold vacuum and atmospheric pressure to provide assistance to the hydraulically operated brakes, is mounted on the firewall in the engine compartment.

PARKING BRAKE

The parking brake operates the rear brakes only, through cable actuation. It's activated by a pedal mounted on the left side kick panel.

SERVICE

After completing any operation involving disassembly of any part of the brake system, always test-drive the vehicle to check for proper braking performance before resuming normal driving. When testing the brakes, perform the tests on a clean, dry, flat surface. Conditions other than these can lead to inaccurate test results.

Test the brakes at various speeds with both light and heavy pedal pressure. The vehicle should stop evenly without pulling to one side or the other. Avoid locking the brakes, because this slides the tires and diminishes braking efficiency and control of the vehicle.

Tires, vehicle load and wheel alignment are factors which also affect braking performance.

2 Anti-lock Brake System (ABS) - general information

♦ Refer to illustration 2.1

1 The Anti-lock Brake System (ABS) (see illustration), is designed to maintain vehicle steerability, directional stability and optimum deceleration under severe braking conditions and on most road surfaces. It does so by monitoring the rotational speed of each wheel and controlling the brake line pressure to each wheel during braking. This prevents the wheel from locking up. On the models covered by this manual, the ABS system also works with the Automatic Skid Control and tire pressure warning systems. The former helps to control skids by braking the outside wheels when "oversteering" is sensed by the wheel sensors. The tire pressure warning system alerts the driver through a light on the instrument panel that one or more tires is excessively low. Since a low tire rotates at a different speed than one fully-inflated, the ABS sensor can detect a low tire, though it can't sense a gradual loss of air.

COMPONENTS

Actuator assembly

2 The actuator assembly consists of the master cylinder, an electric hydraulic pump and four solenoid valves. The electric pump provides hydraulic pressure to charge the reservoirs in the actuator, which supplies pressure to the braking system. The pump and reservoirs are housed in the actuator assembly. The solenoid valves modulate brake line pressure during ABS operation. The body contains four valves - one for each wheel.

Speed sensors

3 These sensors are located at each wheel and generate small electrical pulsations when the toothed sensor rings are turning, sending a signal to the electronic controller indicating wheel rotational speed.

4 The front speed sensors are mounted to the front steering knuckle in close relationship to the toothed sensor rings, which are integral with the front driveaxle outer CV joints.

5 The rear wheel sensors are bolted to the axle carriers. The sensor rings are integral with the rear hub assemblies.

ABS computer (ECU)

6 The ABS computer is mounted within the ABS actuator and is the "brain" for the ABS system. The function of the computer is to accept and process information received from the wheel speed sensors to control the hydraulic line pressure, avoiding wheel lock up. The computer also constantly monitors the system, even under normal driving conditions, to find faults within the system.

7 If a problem develops within the system, an "ABS" light will glow on the dashboard. A diagnostic code will also be stored in the computer and, when retrieved, will indicate the problem area or component.

DIAGNOSTIC CODES

♦ Refer to illustration 2.10

8 The ABS system control unit (computer) has a built-in self-diagnosis system which detects malfunctions in the system sensors and alerts the driver by illuminating an ABS warning light in the instrument panel. The computer stores the failure code until the diagnostic system is cleared or malfunction is repaired.

9 The ABS warning light should come on for about three seconds when the ignition switch is placed in the ON position. When the engine is started, the warning light should go out. If the light remains on, the diagnostic system has detected a malfunction or abnormality in the system.

10 The codes for the ABS can be accessed by turning the ignition key to the OFF position (engine not running). On Nippondenso and Bosch systems, install a jumper wire or paper clip onto terminals E1

2.1 Anti-lock Brake System (ABS) component locations

and Tc of the DLC1 or DLC2 or Tc and CG of the DLC3 (see illustration) and turn the ignition key ON (engine not running). Observe the codes on the ABS warning light. Of course, the codes can also be read with a diagnostic scan tool.

11 The diagnostic code is the number of flashes indicated on the ABS light. If any malfunction has been detected, the light will blink the first digit(s) of the code, pause 1.5 seconds, then blink the second digit of the code. For example, a code 34 (left rear wheel sensor) will first blink three flashes, pause 1.5 seconds and blink four flashes. If there is more than one code stored in the ECM, the ECM will pause 2.5 seconds before flashing the next code. If the system is operating normally (no malfunctions), the warning light will blink once every 0.5 seconds.

12 The accompanying tables explain the code that will be flashed for each of the malfunctions. The accompanying charts indicate the diagnostic code - in blinks - along with the system, diagnosis and specific areas.

13 After the diagnosis check, clear the trouble codes. First, jump terminals E1 and Tc on the data link connector. Turn the ignition key ON (engine not running) and clear the codes by depressing the brake pedal eight or more times within five seconds. Remove the jumper wire and reinstall the cap on the data link connector. Check the indicated system or component or take the vehicle to a dealer service department to have the malfunction repaired.

2.10 There are three different types of data link connectors on these models

ABS TROUBLE CODES

Code number	Trouble area	Action to take
Code 11 (1 flash, pause, 1 flash)	Open circuit in solenoid relay circuit	Check the solenoid relay and the relay circuit
Code 12 (1 flash, pause, 2 flashes)	Short circuit in solenoid relay circuit	Check the solenoid relay and the relay circuit
Code 13 (1 flash, pause, 3 flashes)	Open circuit in ABS motor relay circuit	Check the pump motor relay and circuit
Code 14 (1 flash, pause, 4 flashes)	Short circuit in ABS motor relay circuit	Check the solenoid relay and the relay circuit
Code 21 (2 flashes, pause, 1 flash)	Problem in right front wheel solenoid circuit	Check the actuator solenoid and circuit
Code 22 (2 flashes, pause, 2 flashes)	Problem in left front wheel solenoid circuit	Check the actuator solenoid and circuit
Code 23 (2 flashes, pause, 3 flashes)	Problem in right rear wheel solenoid circuit	Check the actuator solenoid and circuit
Code 24 (2 flashes, pause, 4 flashes)	Problem in left rear wheel solenoid circuit	Check the actuator solenoid and circuit
Code 25 (2 flashes, pause, 5 flashes)	SMC1 circuit open or shorted	Check the ABS actuator and circuit
Code 26 (2 flashes, pause, 6 flashes)	SMC2 circuit open or shorted	Check the ABS actuator and circuit
Code 27 (2 flashes, pause, 7 flashes)	SRC1 circuit open or shorted	Check the ABS actuator and circuit
Code 28 (2 flashes, pause, 8 flashes)	SRC2 circuit open or shorted	Check the ABS actuator and circuit
Code 31 (3 flashes, pause, 1 flash)	Sensor signal problem - right front wheel	Check the speed sensor, sensor rotors, wire harness and connector of the speed sensor
Code 32 (3 flashes, pause, 2 flashes)	Sensor signal problem - left front wheel	Check the speed sensor, sensor rotors, wire harness and connector of the speed sensor
Code 33 (3 flashes, pause, 3 flashes)	Sensor signal problem - right rear wheel	Check the speed sensor, sensor rotors, wire harness and connector of the speed sensor
Code 34 (3 flashes, pause, 4 flashes)	Sensor signal problem - left rear wheel	Check the speed sensor, sensor rotors, wire harness and connector of the speed sensor
Code 35 (3 flashes, pause, 5 flashes)	Open circuit - right front speed sensor or circuit	Check the speed sensor, wire harness and electrical connector
Code 36 (3 flashes, pause, 6 flashes)	Open circuit - left front speed sensor or circuit	Check the speed sensor, wire harness and electrical connector
Code 37 (3 flashes, pause, 7 flashes)	Speed sensor rotor has incorrect number of teeth	Check for a damaged sensor rotor
Code 38 (3 flashes, pause, 8 flashes)	Open circuit - right rear speed sensor or circuit	Check the speed sensor, wire harness and electrical connector
Code 39 (3 flashes, pause, 9 flashes)	Open circuit - left rear speed sensor or circuit	Check the speed sensor, wire harness and electrical connector
Code 41 (4 flashes, pause, 1 flash)	Abnormally low battery positive voltage	Check the charging system (alternator, battery and voltage regulator) for any problems (see Chapter 5)

ABS TROUBLE CODES

Code number	Trouble area	Action to take
Code 43 (4 flashes, pause, 3 flashes)	ABS control system malfunction	Check all wiring and connections associated with the ABS system
Code 44 (4 flashes, pause, 4 flashes)	NE signal circuit open or shorted	Check wiring harness and connectors between ABS ECU and PCM
Code 45 (4 flashes, pause, 5 flashes)	Deceleration sensor malfunction	Check deceleration sensor and wiring harness connectors
Code 46 (4 flashes, pause, 6 flashes)	Master cylinder sensor malfunction	Check master cylinder sensor and wiring harness connectors
Code 49 (4 flashes, pause, 9 flashes)	Open circuit - brake light switch or circuit	Check the brake light switch or circuit
Code 51 (5 flashes, pause, 1 flash)	Pump motor locked	Check the pump motor, relay and battery for shorts or abnormalities
Code 53 (5 flashes, pause, 3 flashes)	PCM communication circuit malfunction	Check wiring harness and connectors between ABS ECU and PCM
Code 58 (5 flashes, pause, 8 flashes)	Open circuit - brake light switch or circuit	Check the brake light switch or circuit
Code 61 (6 flashes, pause, 1 flash)	Engine control system malfunction	Check for engine control system trouble codes (see Chapter 6)
Code 62 (6 flashes, pause, 2 flashes)	ECU malfunction	ECU problem
Light always ON	ECU malfunction	ECU problem

3   Disc brake pads - replacement

♦ Refer to illustrations 3.5 and 3.6a through 3.6s

❋❋ WARNING:

Disc brake pads must be replaced on both front or rear wheels at the same time - never replace the pads on only one wheel. Also, the dust created by the brake system is harmful to your health. Never blow it out with compressed air and don't inhale any of it. An approved filtering mask should be worn when working on the brakes. Do not, under any circumstances, use petroleum-based solvents to clean brake parts. Use brake system cleaner only!

1   Remove the cap from the brake fluid reservoir.

2   Loosen the wheel lug nuts, raise the front or rear of the vehicle and support it securely on jackstands. Block the wheels at the opposite end.

3   Remove the wheels. Work on one brake assembly at a time, using the assembled brake for reference if necessary.

4   Inspect the brake disc carefully as outlined in Section 5. If machining is necessary, follow the information in that Section to remove the disc, at which time the pads can be removed as well.

5   Push the piston back into its bore to provide room for the new brake pads. A C-clamp can be used to accomplish this (see illustra-

3.5 Before removing the caliper, be sure to depress the piston into its bore in the caliper with a large C-clamp to make room for the new pads

tion). As the piston is depressed to the bottom of the caliper bore, the fluid in the master cylinder will rise. Make sure that it doesn't overflow. If necessary, siphon off some of the fluid.

3.6a Always wash the brakes with brake cleaner before disassembling anything

3.6b To remove the caliper, remove the bolts indicated by the upper and lower arrows (the center arrow points to the brake hose banjo bolt, which shouldn't be unscrewed unless the caliper is being completely removed)

3.6c Remove the caliper . . .

3.6d . . . and hang it from the strut coil spring with a piece of wire; do not allow the caliper to hang by the flexible brake hose

3.6e Remove the upper anti-squeal spring (models through 2000 only) . . .

3.6f . . . and the lower anti-squeal spring (models through 2000 only)

3.6g Remove the outer shim . . .

6   If you're replacing the front brake pads, follow the accompanying photos, beginning with illustration 3.6a. Be sure to stay in order and read the caption under each illustration.

➡ **Note: When removing the caliper mounting bolts for pad replacement, use a second wrench to hold the hex on the sliding pin while the caliper bolt is removed.**

7   When reinstalling the caliper, be sure to tighten the mounting bolts to the torque listed in this Chapter's Specifications. After the job has been completed, firmly depress the brake pedal a few times to bring the pads into contact with the disc. Check the level of the brake fluid, adding some if necessary. Check the operation of the brakes carefully before placing the vehicle into normal service.

3.6h . . . and the inner shim from the outer brake pad

3.6i Remove the outer brake pad

3.6j Remove the outer shim . . .

3.6k . . . and the inner shim from the inner brake pad

3.6l Remove the inner brake pad

3.6m Remove the pad support plates; inspect them for damage and replace as necessary (the plates should "snap" into place in the torque plate; if they're weak or distorted, they should be replaced)

3.6n Pry the wear indicator off the old brake pad(s) and transfer it/them to the new pad(s) (if the wear indicator is worn or bent, replace it)

3.6o Install the pad support plates, the new inner brake pad and the shims; make sure the ears on the pad are properly engaged with the pad support plates as shown

3.6p Install the pad support plates, the outer pad and the shims

3.6q Install the upper and lower anti-squeal springs (models through 2000 only); make sure both springs are properly engaged with the pads

3.6r Pull out the upper and lower sliding pins and clean them off (if either rubber boot is damaged, remove it by levering the flange of the metal bushing that retains the boot) . . .

3.6s . . . apply a coat of high-temperature grease to the pins and install them

3.6t Install the caliper and tighten the caliper bolts to the torque listed in this Chapter's Specifications

4 Disc brake caliper - removal and installation

☀☀ WARNING:

Dust created by the brake system is harmful to your health. Never blow it out with compressed air and don't inhale any of it. An approved filtering mask should be worn when working on the brakes. Do not, under any circumstances, use petroleum-based solvents to clean brake parts. Use brake system cleaner only!

➡Note: Always replace the calipers in pairs - never replace just one of them.

REMOVAL

◆ Refer to illustrations 4.2 and 4.3

1   Loosen the wheel lug nuts, raise the vehicle and support it securely on jackstands. Remove the wheels.

2   If you're removing a front caliper, remove the brake hose banjo bolt and disconnect the hose from the caliper. Plug the hose to keep contaminants out of the brake system and to prevent losing any more brake fluid than is necessary (see illustration). If you're removing a rear caliper, break loose the hose fitting from the caliper, but don't try to unscrew it yet.

4.2 Using a piece of rubber hose of the appropriate size, plug the brake line banjo fitting to prevent brake fluid from leaking out and to prevent dirt and moisture from contaminating the fluid in the hose

3   Remove the caliper mounting bolts (see illustration).

4   Remove the caliper. If you're removing a rear caliper, unscrew the caliper from the brake hose. If necessary, remove the caliper torque plate from the steering knuckle (see illustrations 5.2a and 5.2b).

4.3 Front disc brake details

INSTALLATION

5   Install the caliper by reversing the removal procedure.

→Note: If you're installing a rear caliper, thread the caliper onto the brake hose as far as possible before installing the caliper. After installing the caliper and tightening the mounting bolts to the torque listed in this Chapter's Specifications, tighten the brake hose fitting securely.

Remember to install new sealing washers on either side of the brake hose banjo fitting (they should be included with the rebuild kit). Tighten the caliper mounting bolts (and torque plate bolts, if removed) to the torque listed in this Chapter's Specifications.

6   Bleed the brake system (see Section 10).

7   Install the wheels and lug nuts. Lower the vehicle and tighten the lug nuts to the torque listed in the Chapter 1 Specifications.

5   Brake disc - inspection, removal and installation

INSPECTION

▶ Refer to illustrations 5.2, 5.3, 5.4a, 5.4b, 5.5a and 5.5b

1   Loosen the wheel lug nuts, raise the vehicle and support it securely on jackstands. Remove the wheel and install the lug nuts to hold the disc in place. If the rear brake disc is being worked on, release the parking brake.

2   Remove the brake caliper as outlined in Section 4. It isn't necessary to disconnect the brake hose. After removing the caliper bolts, suspend the caliper out of the way with a piece of wire (see illustration 3.6d). Remove the torque plate mounting bolts and detach the torque plate (see illustration).

3   Visually inspect the disc surface for score marks and other damage. Light scratches and shallow grooves are normal after use and may not always be detrimental to brake operation, but deep scoring - over 0.039-inch (1.0 mm) - requires disc removal and refinishing by an automotive machine shop. Be sure to check both sides of the disc (see illustration). If pulsating has been noticed during application of the brakes, suspect disc runout.

4   To check disc runout, place a dial indicator at a point about 1/2-inch from the outer edge of the disc (see illustration). Set the indicator to zero and turn the disc. The indicator reading should not exceed the specified allowable runout limit. If it does, the disc should be refinished by an automotive machine shop.

→Note: The discs should be resurfaced regardless of the dial indicator reading, as this will impart a smooth finish and ensure a perfectly flat surface, eliminating any brake pedal pulsation or other undesirable symptoms related to questionable

discs. At the very least, if you elect not to have the discs resurfaced, remove the glaze from the surface with sandpaper or emery cloth using a swirling motion (see illustration).

5   It's absolutely critical that the disc not be machined to a thickness under the specified minimum allowable refinish thickness. The minimum wear (or discard) thickness is cast into the inside of the disc (see illustration). The disc thickness can be checked with a micrometer (see illustration).

REMOVAL

6   Remove the lug nuts that were put on to hold the disc in place and remove the disc from the hub.

INSTALLATION

7   Place the disc in position over the threaded studs.

8   Install the torque plate, tightening the bolts to the torque listed in this Chapter's Specifications.

9   Install the caliper, tightening the bolts to the torque listed in this Chapter's Specifications. Bleeding won't be necessary unless the brake hose was disconnected from the caliper.

10   Install the wheel and lug nuts. Lower the vehicle and tighten the lug nuts to the torque listed in the Chapter 1 Specifications. Depress the brake pedal a few times to bring the brake pads into contact with the disc. Check the operation of the brakes carefully before driving the vehicle.

5.2 To remove the front caliper torque plate from the steering knuckle, remove these two bolts

5.3 The brake pads on this vehicle were obviously neglected, as they wore down completely and cut deep grooves into the disc - wear this severe means the disc must be replaced

5.4a Use a dial indicator to check disc runout; if the reading exceeds the maximum allowable runout limit, the disc will have to be machined or replaced

5.4b Using a swirling motion, remove the glaze from the disc surface with sandpaper or emery cloth

5.5a The minimum wear dimension is cast into the back side of the disc

5.5b Use a micrometer to measure disc thickness

6 Drum brake shoes - replacement

▶ Refer to illustrations 6.4a through 6.4x and 6.5

✳✳ WARNING:

Drum brake shoes must be replaced on both wheels at the same time - never replace the shoes on only one wheel. Also, the dust created by the brake system is harmful to your health. Never blow it out with compressed air and don't inhale any of it. An approved filtering mask should be worn when working on the brakes. Do not, under any circumstances, use petroleum-based solvents to clean brake parts. Use brake system cleaner only!

✳✳ CAUTION:

Whenever the brake shoes are replaced, the return and hold-down springs should also be replaced. Due to the continuous heating/cooling cycle the springs are subjected to, they lose tension over a period of time and may allow the shoes to drag on the drum and wear at a much faster rate than normal.

1   Loosen the wheel lug nuts, raise the rear of the vehicle and support it securely on jackstands. Block the front wheels to keep the vehicle from rolling.
2   Release the parking brake.
3   Remove the wheel.

➡ Note: All four rear brake shoes must be replaced at the same time, but to avoid mixing up parts, work on only one brake assembly at a time.

4   Follow the accompanying illustrations for the brake shoe replacement procedure (see illustrations 6.4a through 6.4x). Be sure to stay in order and read the caption under each illustration.

➡ Note: If the brake drum cannot be easily removed, make sure the parking brake is completely released. If the drum still cannot be pulled off, the brake shoes will have to be retracted. This is done by first removing the plug from the backing plate. With the plug removed, push the lever off the adjuster star wheel with a narrow screwdriver while turning the adjuster wheel with another screwdriver, moving the shoes away from the drum (see illustration 6.4b). The drum should now come off.

6.4a Mark the relationship of the drum to the hub to insure that the dynamic balance is unaltered

6.4b If the brake shoes hang up on the drum because of excessive wear, insert two screwdrivers through the hole in the backing plate to push the adjuster lever off the star wheel and turn the star wheel to retract the brake shoes

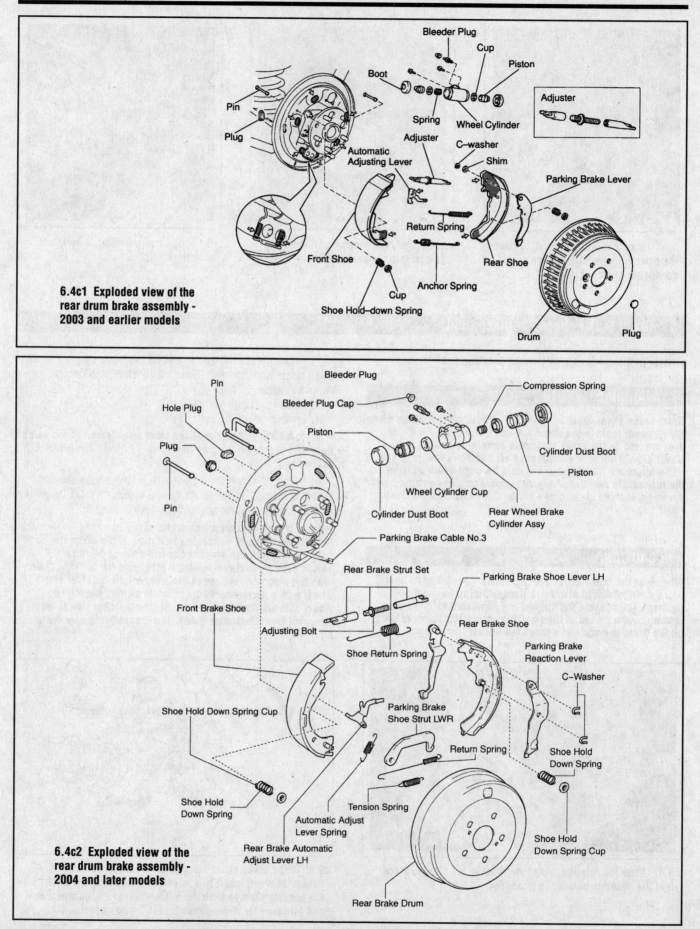

6.4c1 Exploded view of the rear drum brake assembly - 2003 and earlier models

Bleeder Plug

Cup

Piston

Boot

Spring

Wheel Cylinder

Pin

Plug

Adjuster

C-washer

Shim

Parking Brake Lever

Automatic Adjusting Lever

Return Spring

Rear Shoe

Front Shoe

Cup

Anchor Spring

Shoe Hold-down Spring

Drum

Plug

Adjuster

6.4c2 Exploded view of the rear drum brake assembly - 2004 and later models

Bleeder Plug

Compression Spring

Hole Plug

Bleeder Plug Cap

Pin

Cylinder Dust Boot

Plug

Piston

Piston

Pin

Wheel Cylinder Cup

Cylinder Dust Boot

Rear Wheel Brake Cylinder Assy

Parking Brake Cable No.3

Rear Brake Strut Set

Parking Brake Shoe Lever LH

Front Brake Shoe

Adjusting Bolt

Rear Brake Shoe

Shoe Return Spring

Parking Brake Reaction Lever

C-Washer

Shoe Hold Down Spring Cup

Parking Brake Shoe Strut LWR

Shoe Hold Down Spring

Shoe Hold Down Spring

Return Spring

Tension Spring

Automatic Adjust Lever Spring

Rear Brake Automatic Adjust Lever LH

Shoe Hold Down Spring Cup

Rear Brake Drum

6.4d Before removing anything, clean the brake assembly with brake cleaner and allow it to dry (position a drain pan under the brake to catch the fluid and residue); DO NOT USE COMPRESSED AIR TO BLOW OFF BRAKE DUST!

6.4e Unhook the return spring from the front brake shoe - use a pair of locking pliers to stretch the spring and pull the end out of the hole in the automatic adjuster

6.4f Remove the automatic adjuster from the pin on the front shoe

6.4g Depress the hold-down spring and turn the retainer 90-degrees, then release it; a pair of pliers will work, but a special hold-down spring removal tool makes the job easier (these inexpensive tools are available at most auto parts stores)

6.4h Once the tool has released the spring, remove the spring and its cup

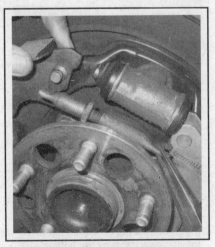

6.4i Move the front shoe away from the wheel cylinder and remove the adjuster with pliers

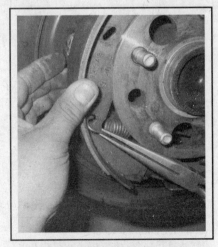

6.4j Unhook the anchor spring from the bottom of the front shoe, then remove the shoe from the backing plate

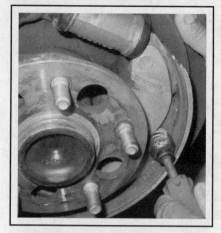

6.4k Remove the hold-down spring from the rear shoe

6.4l Use diagonal cutting pliers to pry the clip from the top of the rear shoe, on the backing plate side of the shoe

6.4m Use locking pliers to push the spring back on the cable, then clamp it in place and slip the cable end out of the parking brake lever

6.4n With the backing plate cleaned, apply light dabs of high-temperature grease to the shoe contact areas

6.4o Slip the parking brake cable end into the bottom of the lever and release the spring

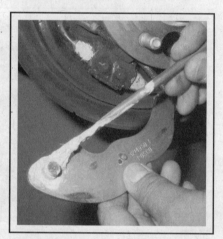

6.4p Lubricate the pin at the top of the parking brake lever

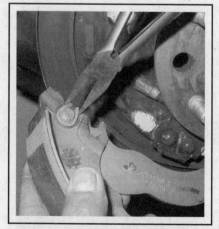

6.4q Assemble the parking brake lever to the new rear shoe, install the flat washer, then crimp the C-washer closed with a pair of pliers (always use a new C-washer)

6.4r Position the rear shoe against the stationary stop at the bottom, then insert the hold-down pin through from the back and hold it there

6.4s Install the cups (one on each end of the spring) and lock the outer cup to the pin by turning it 90-degrees after the spring has been compressed

6.4t Slip the (long, straight) end of the anchor spring into the hole in the rear shoe, then use pliers to insert the spring end into the front shoe

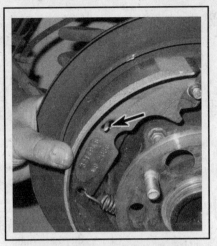

6.4u Position the front shoe at top and bottom and insert the hold-down pin

6.4v Lubricate the moving parts of the adjuster screw with a light coat of high-temperature grease; the screw portion of the adjuster will need to be threaded in further than before to allow the drum to fit over the new shoes

6.4w Install the adjuster assembly between the front and rear shoes with the star-wheel positioned as shown

6.4x Install the adjuster lever over the pin on the front shoe, with the bottom of the lever between the shoe and the adjuster

6.4y Use pliers to reinstall the return spring between the rear shoe and the slot in the adjuster lever

6.4z Wiggle the completed assembly to make sure it's seated properly against the backing plate

5   Before reinstalling the drum, it should be checked for cracks, score marks, deep scratches and hard spots, which will appear as small discolored areas. If the hard spots cannot be removed with fine emery cloth or if any of the other conditions listed above exist, the drum must be taken to an automotive machine shop to have it resurfaced.

➡Note: Professionals recommend resurfacing the drums each time a brake job is done. Resurfacing will eliminate the possibility of out-of-round drums. If the drums are worn so much that they can't be resurfaced without exceeding the maximum allowable diameter (stamped into the drum), then new drums will be required (see illustration). At the very least, if you elect not to have the drums resurfaced, remove the glaze from the surface with emery cloth using a swirling motion.

6   Install the brake drum on the axle flange.

7   Install the wheel and lug nuts, then lower the vehicle. Tighten the lug nuts to the torque listed in this Chapter's Specifications.

8   Make a number of forward and reverse stops and operate the parking brake to adjust the brakes until satisfactory pedal action is obtained.

6.5 The maximum drum diameter is cast into the inside of the rear drums

9   Check the operation of the brakes carefully before driving the vehicle.

7   Wheel cylinder - removal and installation

➡Note: If an overhaul is indicated (usually because of fluid leakage or sticking brakes) explore all options before beginning the job. New wheel cylinders are available, which makes this job quite easy. If the vehicle has high mileage, new wheel cylinders (not rebuilt) are highly recommended. Never replace only one wheel cylinder - always replace both of them at the same time.

REMOVAL

▸ **Refer to illustration 7.4**

1   Raise the rear of the vehicle and support it securely on jackstands. Block the front wheels to keep the vehicle from rolling.

2   Remove the brake shoe assembly (see Section 6).

3   Remove all dirt and foreign material from around the wheel cylinder.

4   Disconnect the brake line with a flare-nut wrench, if available (see illustration). Don't pull the brake line away from the wheel cylinder.

5   Remove the wheel cylinder mounting bolts.

6   Detach the wheel cylinder from the brake backing plate and place it on a clean workbench. Immediately plug the brake line to prevent fluid loss and contamination.

INSTALLATION

7   Place the wheel cylinder in position and install the bolts finger tight. Connect the brake line to the cylinder, being careful not to cross-thread the fitting. Tighten the wheel cylinder bolts to the torque listed in this Chapter's Specifications.

7.4 To remove the wheel cylinder, unscrew the hydraulic line-to-wheel cylinder threaded fitting, then remove the mounting bolts

8   Tighten the brake line fitting and install the brake shoes and drum.

9   Bleed the brakes (see Section 10). Install the wheel and lug nuts. Lower the vehicle to the ground and tighten the lug nuts to the torque listed in this Chapter's Specifications.

10 Check the operation of the brakes carefully before driving the vehicle.

8   Master cylinder - removal and installation

REMOVAL

▸ **Refer to illustrations 8.1, 8.2, 8.4 and 8.6**

1   Refer to Chapter 4 and remove the air cleaner assembly. Refer to Chapter 11 and remove the cowl cover. Unplug the electrical connector for the brake fluid level warning switch (see illustration).

➡Note: The fluid reservoir is remotely mounted, not directly attached to the master cylinder.

8.1 Unplug the electrical connectors for the brake-fluid-level warning switch

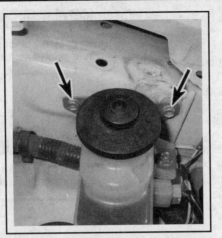

8.2 Remove the fluid from the remote reservoir, then unbolt the reservoir

8.4 Loosen the threaded fittings on the brake fluid hydraulic lines (A) - if needed, clamp off and disconnect the fluid hose (B)

8.6 Master cylinder mounting nuts

8.8 The best way to bleed air from the master cylinder before installing it on the vehicle is with a pair of bleed tubes - on models with remote reservoirs use hoses long enough to return the fluid to the reservoir

2   Remove as much fluid as possible from the reservoir with a syringe (see illustration).

3   Place rags under the fittings and prepare caps or plastic bags to cover the ends of the lines once they're disconnected. Use locking pliers to pinch off the fluid hose from the reservoir before disconnecting it at the master cylinder.

❊❊ CAUTION:

Brake fluid will damage paint. Cover all body parts and be careful not to spill fluid during this procedure.

4   Loosen the fittings at the ends of the brake lines where they enter the master cylinder (see illustration). To prevent rounding off the flats, use a flare-nut wrench, which wraps around the fitting hex.

5   Pull the brake lines away from the master cylinder and plug the ends to prevent contamination.

6   Remove the nuts attaching the master cylinder to the power booster (see illustration). Pull the master cylinder off the studs to remove it, with the remote reservoir and hoses attached. Again, be careful not to spill the fluid as this is done. The master cylinder can be removed with the remote reservoir and its hose still attached.

INSTALLATION

▶ **Refer to illustration 8.8**

7   Bench bleed the new master cylinder before installing it. Because it will be necessary to apply pressure to the master cylinder piston and, at the same time, control flow from the brake line outlets, it is recommended that the master cylinder be mounted in a vise, with the jaws of the vise clamping on the mounting flange.

8   Attach a pair of master cylinder bleeder tubes to the outlet ports of the master cylinder (see illustration).

9   Fill the reservoir with brake fluid of the recommended type (see Chapter 1).

10 Slowly push the pistons into the master cylinder (a large Phillips screwdriver can be used for this) - air will be expelled from the pressure chambers and into the reservoir. Because the tubes are submerged in fluid, air can't be drawn back into the master cylinder when you release the pistons.

11 Repeat the procedure until no more air bubbles are present.

12 Remove the bleed tubes, one at a time, and install plugs in the open ports to prevent fluid leakage and air from entering. Install the reservoir cover.

13 Install the master cylinder over the studs on the power brake booster and tighten the attaching nuts only finger tight at this time. Mount the fluid reservoir (see illustration 8.2).

14 Thread the brake line fittings into the master cylinder. Since the master cylinder is still a bit loose, it can be moved slightly in order for the fittings to thread in easily. Do not strip the threads as the fittings are tightened.

15 Fully tighten the mounting nuts, then the brake line fittings.

16 Fill the master cylinder reservoir with fluid, then bleed the master cylinder and the brake system as described in Section 10. To bleed the cylinder on the vehicle, have an assistant pump the brake pedal several times slowly and then hold the pedal to the floor. Loosen the fitting nut to allow air and fluid to escape. Repeat this procedure on both fittings until the fluid is clear of air bubbles.

✳✳ CAUTION:

Have plenty of rags on hand to catch the fluid - brake fluid will ruin painted surfaces.

17 Test the operation of the brake system carefully before placing the vehicle into normal service.

✳✳ WARNING:

Do not operate the vehicle if you are in doubt about the effectiveness of the brake system.

9   Brake hoses and lines - inspection and replacement

INSPECTION

1   About every six months, with the vehicle raised and supported securely on jackstands, the rubber hoses which connect the steel brake lines with the front and rear brake assemblies should be inspected for cracks, chafing of the outer cover, leaks, blisters and other damage. These are important and vulnerable parts of the brake system and inspection should be complete. A light and mirror will be helpful for a thorough check. If a hose exhibits any of the above conditions, replace it with a new one.

REPLACEMENT

Front brake hose

▶ **Refer to illustrations 9.3 and 9.4**

2   Loosen the wheel lug nuts, raise the vehicle and support it securely on jackstands. Remove the wheel.

3   At the frame bracket, unscrew the brake line fitting from the hose (see illustration). Use a flare-nut wrench to prevent rounding off the corners.

4   Remove the U-clip from the female fitting at the bracket with a pair of pliers (see illustration), then pass the hose through the bracket.

5   At the caliper end of the hose, remove the banjo fitting bolt (see illustration 3.6b), then separate the hose from the caliper. Note that there are two copper sealing washers on either side of the fitting - they should be replaced with new ones during installation.

6   Remove the U-clip from the strut bracket, then feed the hose through the bracket.

7   To install the hose, pass the caliper fitting end through the strut bracket, then connect the fitting to the caliper with the banjo bolt and copper washers. Make sure the locating lug on the fitting is engaged with the hole in the caliper, then tighten the bolt to the torque listed in this Chapter's Specifications.

8   Push the metal support into the strut bracket and install the U-clip. Make sure the hose isn't twisted between the caliper and the strut bracket.

9   Route the hose into the frame bracket, again making sure it isn't twisted, then connect the brake line fitting, starting the threads by hand. Install the clip and E-ring, if equipped, then tighten the fitting securely.

10 Bleed the caliper (see Section 10).

11 Install the wheel and lug nuts, lower the vehicle and tighten the lug nuts to the torque specified in Chapter 1.

9.3 Unscrew the brake line threaded fitting with a flare-nut wrench to protect the fitting corners from being rounded off

9.4 Remove the brake hose-to-brake line U-clip with a pair of pliers

Rear brake hose

12 Perform Steps 2, 3 and 4 above, then repeat Steps 3 and 4 at the other end of the hose. Be sure to bleed the wheel cylinder (see Section 10).

Metal brake lines

13 When replacing brake lines, be sure to use the correct parts. Don't use copper tubing for any brake system components. Purchase genuine steel brake lines from a dealer or auto parts store.

10 Brake hydraulic system - bleeding

▶ **Refer to illustration 10.8**

✳✳ WARNING:

Wear eye protection when bleeding the brake system. If the fluid comes in contact with your eyes, immediately rinse them with water and seek medical attention.

➡ **Note: Bleeding the hydraulic system is necessary to remove any air that manages to find its way into the system when it's been opened during removal and installation of a hose, line, caliper or master cylinder.**

1 You'll probably have to bleed the system at all four brakes if air has entered it due to low fluid level, or if the brake lines have been disconnected at the master cylinder.

2 If a brake line was disconnected only at one wheel, then only that caliper or wheel cylinder must be bled.

3 If a brake line is disconnected at a fitting located between the master cylinder and any of the brakes, that part of the system served by the disconnected line must be bled.

4 Remove any residual vacuum from the brake power booster by applying the brake several times with the engine off.

5 Remove the master cylinder reservoir cover and fill the reservoir with brake fluid. Reinstall the cover.

➡ **Note: Check the fluid level often during the bleeding operation and add fluid as necessary to prevent the fluid level from falling low enough to allow air bubbles into the master cylinder.**

6 Have an assistant on hand, as well as a supply of new brake fluid, a clear container partially filled with clean brake fluid, a length of tubing to fit over the bleeder valve and a wrench to open and close the bleeder valve.

7 Beginning at the right rear wheel, loosen the bleeder valve slightly, then tighten it to a point where it's snug but can still be loosened quickly and easily.

8 Place one end of the tubing over the bleeder valve and submerge the other end in brake fluid in the container (see illustration).

9 Have the assistant depress the brake pedal slowly, then hold the pedal down firmly.

10 While the pedal is held down, open the bleeder valve just enough to allow a flow of fluid to leave the valve. Watch for air bubbles to exit the submerged end of the tube. When the fluid flow slows after a couple of seconds, close the valve and have your assistant release the pedal.

11 Repeat Steps 9 and 10 until no more air is seen leaving the tube, then tighten the bleeder valve and proceed to the left rear wheel, the right front wheel and the left front wheel, in that order, and perform the same procedure. Be sure to check the fluid in the master cylinder reservoir frequently.

14 Prefabricated brake line, with the tube ends already flared and fittings installed, is available at auto parts stores and dealer parts departments.

15 When installing the new line, make sure it's securely supported in the brackets and has plenty of clearance between moving or hot components.

16 After installation, check the master cylinder fluid level and add fluid as necessary. Bleed the brake system (see Section 10) and test the brakes carefully before driving the vehicle in traffic.

10.8 When bleeding the brakes, a hose is connected to the bleeder valve at the caliper or wheel cylinder and then submerged in brake fluid. Air will be seen as bubbles in the tube and container. All air must be expelled before moving to the next wheel

12 If the master cylinder needs to be bled also, it must be done with the engine running. Open one of the wheel bleeder fittings and attach a hose to the fitting on top of the master cylinder. Submerge the other end of the hose in a container partially filled with brake fluid.

13 Push the brake pedal down several times, then hold it down. Open the master cylinder bleeder fitting, then close it and release the brake pedal.

14 Repeat this procedure until the master cylinder has no more air in it. Tighten the wheel bleeder fitting and top up the master cylinder.

15 Never use old brake fluid. It contains moisture, which will deteriorate the brake system components.

16 Refill the master cylinder with fluid at the end of the operation.

17 Check the operation of the brakes. The pedal should feel solid when depressed, with no sponginess. If necessary, repeat the entire process.

✳✳ WARNING:

Do not operate the vehicle if you are in doubt about the effectiveness of the brake system. It's possible for air to become trapped in the ABS hydraulic control unit, so, if the pedal continues to feel spongy after repeated bleedings or the BRAKE or ANTI-LOCK light stays on, have the vehicle towed to a dealer service department or other qualified shop to be bled with the aid of a scan tool.

11   Power brake booster - check, removal and installation

OPERATING CHECK

1   Depress the brake pedal several times with the engine off and make sure there's no change in the pedal reserve distance.

2   Depress the pedal and start the engine. If the pedal goes down slightly, operation is normal.

AIRTIGHTNESS CHECK

3   Start the engine and turn it off after one or two minutes. Depress the brake pedal slowly several times. If the pedal depresses less each time, the booster is airtight.

4   Depress the brake pedal while the engine is running, then stop the engine with the pedal depressed. If there's no change in the pedal reserve travel after holding the pedal for 30 seconds, the booster is airtight.

REMOVAL

▶ **Refer to illustration 11.11**

5   Power brake booster units shouldn't be disassembled. They require special tools not normally found in most automotive repair stations or shops. They're fairly complex and, because of their critical relationship to brake performance, should be replaced with a new or rebuilt one.

6   Refer to Chapter 11 and remove the cowl cover.

7   Remove the brake master cylinder with the remote reservoir and hoses (see Section 8).

8   Pull the ABS actuator and its mounting bracket out enough for brake booster removal.

9   Disconnect the vacuum hose from the brake booster. Be careful not to damage the hose when removing it from the booster fitting.

10   Inside the vehicle, remove the driver's knee bolster (see Chapter 11).

11   Using a flashlight or a droplight, locate the clevis which connects the booster pushrod to the top of the brake pedal. Remove the clevis-pin retaining clip with pliers and pull out the pin (see illustration).

11.14a On models with VSC, there should be no clearance between the booster pushrod and the master cylinder pushrod (clearance should be 0.014-inch on models without VSC), but no interference either; if there is interference between the two, the brakes may drag; if there is too much clearance, there will be excessive brake pedal travel

11.11 Power brake booster mounting nuts (three of four are visible here) and pushrod clevis pin

12   Remove the four nuts and washers holding the brake booster to the firewall (you may need a light to see them). Slide the booster straight out from the firewall until the studs clear the holes.

INSTALLATION

▶ **Refer to illustrations 11.14a, 11.14b, 11.14c, 11.14d and 11.14e**

13   Installation procedures are basically the reverse of removal. Tighten the clevis locknut securely and the booster mounting nuts to the torque listed in this Chapter's Specifications.

14   If a new power brake booster unit is being installed, check the pushrod clearance (see illustration) as follows:

a) *Measure the distance that the pushrod protrudes from the master cylinder mounting surface on the front of the power brake booster, including the gasket. Write down this measurement* (see illustration). *This is "dimension A."*

11.14b Measure the distance that the pushrod protrudes from the brake booster at the master cylinder mounting surface (including the gasket and the ABS bracket)

11.14c Measure the distance from the mounting flange to the end of the master cylinder

11.14d Measure the distance from the piston pocket to the end of the master cylinder

b) *Measure the distance from the mounting flange to the end of the master cylinder (see illustration). Write down this measurement. This is "dimension B."*

c) *Measure the distance from the end of the master cylinder to the bottom of the pocket in the piston (see illustration). Write down this measurement. This is "dimension C."*

d) *Subtract measurement B from measurement C, then subtract measurement A from the difference between B and C. This is the pushrod clearance.*

e) *Compare your calculated pushrod clearance to the pushrod clearance listed in this Chapter's Specifications. If necessary, adjust the pushrod length to achieve the correct clearance (see illustration).*

➡**Note: Clearance should be around zero (but with no interference) on models with VSC, and 0.014-inch on models without VSC.**

15 After the final installation of the master cylinder and brake hoses and lines, the brake pedal height and freeplay must be adjusted and the system must be bled. See the appropriate Sections of this Chapter for the procedures.

11.14e To adjust the length of the booster pushrod, hold the serrated portion of the rod with a pair of pliers and turn the adjusting screw in or out, as necessary, to achieve the desired setting

12 Parking brake - adjustment

◆ **Refer to illustration 12.7**

1 Slowly depress the parking brake pedal all the way and count the number of clicks. It should take about three to six clicks to apply the parking brake. If it travels less than three clicks, there's a chance the parking brake might not be releasing completely and might be dragging on the drum or disc. If it travels more than six clicks, the parking brake may not hold adequately on an incline, allowing the car to roll.

2 Raise the vehicle and support it suitably on jackstands.

3 Loosen the locknut at the equalizer while holding the adjusting nut with a wrench (see illustration). Tighten the adjusting nut until the desired travel is attained. Tighten the locknut.

12.7 Loosen the locknut at the parking brake cable equalizer, then rotate the inner nut to adjust the cable

13 Parking brake cables - replacement

EQUALIZER-TO-PARKING BRAKE CABLE

▶ **Refer to illustrations 13.4, 13.5 and 13.7**

1   Loosen the rear wheel lug nuts, raise the rear of the vehicle and support it securely on jackstands. Block the front wheels. Remove the rear wheels.

2   Make sure the parking brake is completely released, then remove the brake drum.

3   Remove the brake shoes and disconnect the cable from the parking brake lever at the rear shoe (see Section 6).

4   Disconnect the cable housing from the backing plate (see illustration).

5   Unbolt all cable brackets (see illustration).

6   Remove the two nuts and release the equalizer from the forward cable (see illustration 12.7).

7   Disconnect the cable ends from the equalizer by aligning the cable with the slot in the equalizer. Slide the cable end out of the hole (see illustration).

8   Installation is the reverse of removal.

9   Adjust the parking brake (see Section 12).

PARKING BRAKE PEDAL-TO-EQUALIZER

▶ **Refer to illustration 13.12**

10 Release the parking brake pedal.

11 Remove the knee bolster (see Chapter 11) to access the parking brake pedal bracket sub-assembly.

12 Remove the clip, pull out the clevis pin and disconnect the parking brake cable from the parking brake pedal assembly (see illustration).

13 Tie a wire to the end of the cable just released from the pedal assembly.

14 Remove the clip securing the front cable to the floor, just ahead of the equalizer (see illustration 12.7).

15 Pull the cable out through the floor, then remove the pull-wire and attach it to the new cable. Pull the new cable into position and secure it to the floor just ahead of the equalizer.

16 The remainder of the installation is the reverse of removal.

13.4 To detach a parking brake cable housing from the brake backing plate, use a small hose clamp or a tight-fitting wrench to compress the clips on the shoe side of the backing plate until the cable can be pushed through the backing plate

13.5 The parking brake cable bracket is located between the rear wheels and the equalizer

13.7 To detach either parking brake cable from the equalizer, align the cable with the slot in the equalizer and slide the cable end out of the hole

13.12 Pull the cable clip (A), then remove the cable end from the clevis (B)

14 Parking brake shoes (models with rear disc brakes) - inspection and replacement

▶ Refer to illustrations 14.3 and 14.4a through 14.4u

❉❉ WARNING 1:

Dust created by the brake system is hazardous to your health. Never blow it out with compressed air and don't inhale any of it. An approved filtering mask should be worn when working on the brakes. Do not, under any circumstances, use petroleum-based solvents to clean brake parts. Use brake system cleaner only!

❉❉ WARNING 2:

Parking brake shoes must be replaced on both wheels at the same time - never replace the shoes on only one wheel.

1 Remove the brake disc (see Section 5).
2 Inspect the thickness of the lining material on the shoes. If the lining has worn down to 1/32-inch or less, the shoes must be replaced.

3 Wash off the brake parts with brake system cleaner (see illustration).
4 Follow the accompanying illustrations for the brake shoe replacement procedure (see illustrations 14.4a through 14.4u). Be sure to stay in order and read the caption under each illustration.
5 Install the brake disc. Temporarily thread three of the wheel lug nuts onto the studs to hold the disc in place.
6 Remove the hole plug from the brake disc. Adjust the parking brake shoe clearance by turning the adjuster star wheel with a brake adjusting tool or screwdriver until the shoes contact the disc and the disc can't be turned (see illustrations 5.6a and 5.6b). Back off the adjuster eight notches, then install the hole plug.
7 Install the caliper bracket and brake caliper. Be sure to tighten the bolts to the torque listed in this Chapter's Specifications.
8 Install the wheel and tighten the lug nuts to the torque specified in Chapter 1.
9 Set the parking brake and count the number of clicks that it travels. It should be between about five to seven clicks - if it's not, adjust the parking brake as described in Section 12.

14.3 Before disassembling it, be sure to wash the parking brake assembly with brake cleaner

14.4a Remove the rear parking brake shoe return spring from the anchor pin . . .

14.4b . . . and unhook it from the rear shoe

14.4c Remove the front parking brake shoe return spring from the anchor pin . . .

14.4d ... and unhook it from the front shoe

14.4e Remove the rear shoe hold-down spring and pull out the pin

14.4f Remove the shoe strut from between the shoes

14.4g Remove the front shoe hold-down spring and pull out the pin

14.4h Remove the adjuster and the tension spring (the tension spring is not visible in this photo)

14.4i Pop the C-washer off the pivot pin on the back of the rear shoe . . .

14.4j . . . and pull the parking brake lever off the pivot pin

14.4k Apply a thin coat of high-temperature grease to the contact surfaces of the backing plate

14.4l Slide the parking brake lever onto the pivot pin and install a new C-washer

14.4m Attach the tension spring to the back side of the rear shoe . . .

14.4n . . . and to the back side of the front shoe

14.4o Flip the shoes around and install the adjuster; make sure both ends of the adjuster are properly engaged with the shoes as shown

14.4p Place the shoes in position and install the strut and spring as shown; make sure the ends of the strut are properly engaged with the shoes as shown

14.4q Install the front shoe return spring . . .

14.4r . . . and the rear shoe return spring

14.4s Install the rear shoe hold-down spring

14.4t . . . and the front shoe hold-down spring

14.4u This is how the parking brake assembly should look when you're done

15 Brake light switch - removal, installation and adjustment

REMOVAL AND INSTALLATION

▶ **Refer to illustration 15.1**

1   The brake light switch (see illustration) is located on a bracket at the top of the brake pedal.

2   Disconnect the wiring harness at the brake light switch.

3   Loosen the locknut and unscrew the switch from the pedal bracket.

4   Installation is the reverse of removal.

15.1 The brake light switch is located at the top of the brake pedal

ADJUSTMENT

▶ **Refer to illustration 15.6**

5   Check and, if necessary, adjust brake pedal height (see Chapter 1).

6   Loosen the switch locknut, adjust the switch so that the distance the plunger protrudes (see illustration) is within the range listed in this Chapter's Specifications. (If you're unable to measure this distance, adjust the plunger so that it lightly contacts the pedal stop.) Tighten the locknut.

7   Plug the electrical connector into the switch and reconnect the battery. Make sure the brake lights come on when the brake pedal is depressed and go off when the pedal is released. If not, repeat the adjustment procedure until the brake lights function properly.

8   Check and, if necessary, adjust brake pedal freeplay (see Chapter 1).

15.6 To adjust the brake light switch, loosen the locknut and rotate the switch until the plunger distance (dimension A) is within the range listed in this Chapter's Specifications, then tighten the locknut

Specifications

General

Brake fluid type	See Chapter 1
Brake pedal specifications	See Chapter 1
Power brake booster pushrod-to-master cylinder piston clearance	0.0 inch
Brake light switch plunger (dimension A)	0.20 to 0.60 inch

Disc brakes

Minimum brake pad thickness	See Chapter 1
Front disc thickness	
Standard	1.102 inches
Minimum*	1.024 inches
Rear disc thickness	
Standard	0.472 inch
Minimum*	0.413 inch
Disc runout limit	0.0020 inch
Parking brake shoe minimum thickness	1/32 inch

Drum brakes

Brake shoe minimum lining thickness	1/16 inch
Drum inside diameter	
2003 and earlier	
Standard	9.843 inches
Maximum*	9.921 inches
2004 and later	
Standard	10.00 inches
Maximum*	10.08 inches

* Note: If different specifications are cast into the disc or drum, they supersede information printed here.

Torque specifications   Ft-lbs (unless otherwise indicated)

➥Note: One foot-pound (ft-lb) of torque is equivalent to 12 inch-pounds (in-lbs) of torque. Torque values below approximately 15 ft-lbs are expressed in inch-pounds, since most foot-pound torque wrenches are not accurate at these smaller values.

Caliper mounting bolts	25
Caliper torque plate bolts	
Front	79
Rear	65
Brake hose-to-caliper banjo bolt	21
Wheel cylinder mounting bolts	
2003 and earlier	132 in-lbs
2004 and later	84 in-lbs
Master cylinder-to-brake booster nuts	108 in-lbs
Power brake booster mounting nuts	108 in-lbs
Wheel lug nuts	See Chapter 1

Section

10

SUSPENSION AND STEERING SYSTEMS

1 General information

▶ **Refer to illustrations 1.1 and 1.2**

The front suspension is a MacPherson strut design. The upper end of each strut is attached to the vehicle's body strut support. The lower end of the strut is connected to the upper end of the steering knuckle. The steering knuckle is attached to a balljoint mounted on the outer end of the suspension control arm (see illustration).

The rear suspension utilizes a beam axle with two integral rear arms that mount the hubs and brakes on each side. At the front, the beam is mounted to the chassis by two pivot bolts/nuts through bushings, while conventional coil springs and shock absorbers mount to the arms of the beam (see illustration). The axle pivots on the two front bolts. No separate stabilizer bar is used, as the axle itself acts like a stabilizer bar.

The power-assisted rack-and-pinion steering gear, which is located behind the engine/transaxle assembly, is mounted on the engine cradle. The steering gear actuates the tie-rods, which are attached to the steering knuckles. The steering column is designed to collapse in the event of an accident.

Frequently, when working on the suspension or steering system components, you may come across fasteners that seem impossible to loosen. These fasteners on the underside of the vehicle are continually subjected to water, road grime, mud, etc., and can become rusted or "frozen," making them extremely difficult to remove. In order to unscrew these stubborn fasteners without damaging them (or other components), be sure to use lots of penetrating oil and allow it to soak in for a while. Using a wire brush to clean exposed threads will also ease removal of the nut or bolt and prevent damage to the threads.

Sometimes a sharp blow with a hammer and punch will break the bond between a nut and bolt threads, but care must be taken to prevent the punch from slipping off the fastener and ruining the threads. Heating the stuck fastener and surrounding area with a torch sometimes helps too, but isn't recommended because of the obvious dangers associated with fire. Long breaker bars and extension, or "cheater," pipes will increase leverage, but never use an extension pipe on a ratchet - the ratcheting mechanism could be damaged. Sometimes tightening the nut or bolt first will help to break it loose. Fasteners that require drastic measures to remove should always be replaced with new ones.

Since most of the procedures dealt with in this Chapter involve jacking up the vehicle and working underneath it, a good pair of jack-stands will be needed. A hydraulic floor jack is the preferred type of jack to lift the vehicle, and it can also be used to support certain components during various operations.

❋❋ WARNING:

Never, under any circumstances, rely on a jack to support the vehicle while working on it.

Whenever any of the suspension or steering fasteners are loosened or removed they must be inspected and, if necessary, replaced with new ones of the same part number or of original equipment quality and design. Torque specifications must be followed for proper reassembly and component retention. Never attempt to heat or straighten any suspension or steering components. Instead, replace any bent or damaged part with a new one.

1.1 Steering and front suspension components

| 1 Steering gear assembly | 2 Control arm | 3 Balljoint fasteners | 4 Strut and spring assembly |

1.2 Rear suspension and related components

1 Rear axle beam	3 Coil spring	5 Parking brake cables
2 Shock absorber	4 Drum brake assembly	

2 Stabilizer bar and bushings (front) - removal and installation

REMOVAL

▸ **Refer to illustrations 2.4, 2.5 and 2.9**

1 Loosen the front wheel lug nuts. Raise the front of the vehicle and support it securely on jackstands. Apply the parking brake and block the rear wheels to keep the vehicle from rolling off the stands. Remove the front wheels.

2 Remove the left and right fender apron seals.

3 Disconnect the left and right tie-rod ends from the steering knuckles (see Section 14).

4 Disconnect the stabilizer bar links from the bar (see illustration). If the ballstud turns with the nut, use an Allen wrench to hold the stud.

5 Detach both stabilizer bar bushing retainers from the engine cradle (see illustration).

6 Remove the front exhaust pipe (see Chapter 4).

2.4 To detach the stabilizer bar link from the bar, remove the lower nut; if you're removing the strut, remove the upper nut

2.5 To detach the stabilizer bar from the engine cradle, remove these bushing retainer bolts and remove the retainer

2.9 To check the balljoint in the stabilizer bar link, flip the balljoint stud side-to-side five or six times as shown, install the nut and, using an inch-pound torque wrench, turn the nut continuously one turn every two to four seconds, then note the torque reading on the fifth turn. It should be about 0.4 to 8.7 in-lbs; if it isn't, replace the link

7   Remove the steering gear mounting bolts (see Section 16).
8   Lift the steering gear assembly and remove the stabilizer bar by working it out through the left wheel housing.
9   While the stabilizer bar is off the vehicle, slide off the retainer

bushings and inspect them. If they're cracked, worn or deteriorated, replace them. It's also a good idea to inspect the stabilizer bar link. To check it, flip the balljoint stud side-to-side five or six times as shown (see illustration), then install the nut. Using an inch-pound torque wrench, turn the nut continuously one turn every two to four seconds and note the torque reading on the fifth turn. It should be about 0.4 to 8.7 in-lbs. If it isn't, replace the link assembly.

10   Clean the bushing area of the stabilizer bar with a stiff wire brush to remove any rust or dirt.

INSTALLATION

11   Lubricate the inside and outside of the new bushings with vegetable oil (used in cooking) to simplify reassembly.

✳✳ CAUTION:

Don't use petroleum or mineral-based lubricants or brake fluid - they will lead to deterioration of the bushings.

12   Installation is the reverse of removal.
➡**Note: The right-side link is white, while the left-side link is green.**

3   Strut assembly (front) - removal, inspection and installation

REMOVAL

▶ **Refer to illustrations 3.2, 3.4, and 3.6**

1   Loosen the wheel lug nuts, raise the vehicle and support it securely on jackstands. Remove the wheel. Refer to Chapter 11 and remove the cowl cover.
2   Disconnect the stabilizer link from the strut, then remove the brake hose bracket from the strut (see illustration).
3   Detach the ABS speed sensor wiring harness from the strut by removing the clamp bracket bolt. If the strut is to be disassembled, loosen, but do not remove, the damper shaft (center) nut.
4   Remove the strut-to-knuckle nuts (see illustration) and knock the bolts out with a hammer and punch.
5   Separate the strut from the steering knuckle. Be careful not to

overextend the inner CV joint. Also, don't let the steering knuckle fall outward, as the brake hose could be damaged.
6   Support the strut and spring assembly with one hand and remove the three strut-mount-to-shock-tower nuts (see illustration). Remove the assembly from the fenderwell.

INSPECTION

7   Check the strut body for leaking fluid, dents, cracks and other obvious damage that would warrant repair or replacement.
8   Check the coil spring for chips or cracks in the spring coating (this can cause premature spring failure due to corrosion). Inspect the spring seat for cuts, hardness and general deterioration.
9   If any undesirable conditions exist, proceed to the strut disassembly procedure (see Section 4).

3.2 Detach nut (A) securing the brake hose bracket and ABS wire clamp from the strut - also remove the stabilizer bar link nut (B) and disconnect the link

3.4 To disconnect the lower end of the strut from the steering knuckle, remove these two nuts and knock out the bolts with a hammer and punch

INSTALLATION

10 Guide the strut assembly up into the fenderwell and insert the three upper mounting studs through the holes in the shock tower. Once the three studs protrude from the shock tower, install the nuts so the strut won't fall back through. This is most easily accomplished with the help of an assistant, as the strut is quite heavy and awkward.

11 Slide the steering knuckle into the strut flange and insert the two bolts. Install the nuts and tighten them to the torque listed in this Chapter's Specifications.

12 Reattach the brake hose bracket to the strut. Install the speed sensor wiring harness bracket, and reconnect the stabilizer link.

13 Install the wheel and lug nuts, then lower the vehicle and tighten the lug nuts to the torque listed in the Chapter 1 Specifications.

14 Tighten the three upper mounting nuts to the torque listed in this Chapter's Specifications.

15 Have the front wheel alignment checked and, if necessary, adjusted.

3.6 To disconnect the upper end of the strut from the vehicle body, remove these three nuts - mark the orientation of the strut to the body before removal

4   Strut/coil spring assembly - replacement

❄❄ WARNING:

Struts and/or coil springs must be replaced in pairs - never replace just one of them.

1   If the struts or coil springs exhibit the telltale signs of wear (leaking fluid, loss of damping capability, chipped, sagging or cracked coil springs) explore all options before beginning any work. The strut/shock absorber assemblies are not serviceable and must be replaced if a problem develops. However, strut assemblies complete with springs may be available on an exchange basis, which eliminates much time and work. Whichever route you choose to take, check on the cost and availability of parts before disassembling your vehicle.

❄❄ WARNING:

Disassembling a strut is potentially dangerous and utmost attention must be directed to the job, or serious injury may result. Use only a high-quality spring compressor and carefully follow the manufacturer's instructions furnished with the tool. After removing the coil spring from the strut assembly, set it aside in a safe, isolated area.

DISASSEMBLY

▶ **Refer to illustrations 4.3, 4.4, 4.5a, 4.5b, 4.6 and 4.7**

2   Remove the strut and spring assembly (see Section 3). Mount the strut assembly in a vise. Line the vise jaws with wood or rags to prevent damage to the unit and don't tighten the vise excessively.

3   Following the tool manufacturer's instructions, install the spring compressor (which can be obtained at most auto parts stores or equipment yards on a daily rental basis) on the spring and compress it sufficiently to relieve all pressure from the upper spring seat (see illustration). This can be verified by wiggling the spring.

4   Loosen the damper shaft nut (see illustration).

4.3 Install the spring compressor in accordance with the tool manufacturer's instructions and compress the spring until all pressure is relieved from the upper spring seat

4.4 Remove the damper shaft nut

4.5a An exploded view of the strut and spring assembly

5   Remove the nut and suspension support (see illustrations). Inspect the bearing in the suspension support for smooth operation. If it doesn't turn smoothly, replace the suspension support. Check the rubber portion of the suspension support for cracking and general deterioration. If there is any separation of the rubber, replace it.

6   Remove the upper spring seat from the damper shaft (see illustration). Check the spring seat for cracking and hardness; replace it if necessary. Remove the upper insulator from the damper shaft.

7   Carefully lift the compressed spring from the assembly (see illustration) and set it in a safe place.

⁂ WARNING:

Never place your head near the end of the spring!

8   Slide the rubber bumper off the damper shaft.

9   Check the lower insulator for wear, cracking and hardness and replace it if necessary.

REASSEMBLY

▶ **Refer to illustrations 4.11, 4.12, 4.13 and 4.14**

10 If the lower insulator is being replaced, set it into position with the dropped portion seated in the lowest part of the seat. Extend the damper rod to its full length and install the rubber bumper.

11 Carefully place the coil spring onto the lower insulator, with the end of the spring resting in the lowest part of the insulator (see illustration).

12 Install the upper insulator and spring seat, making sure that the flats in the hole in the seat match up with the flats on the damper shaft (see illustration).

13 Align the OUT mark of the spring upper seat with the mark of the

4.5b Lift the suspension support off the damper shaft

4.6 Remove the spring seat from the damper shaft

4.7 Remove the compressed spring assembly - keep the ends of the spring pointed away from your body

4.11 When installing the spring, make sure the end fits into the recessed portion of the lower seat

4.12 The flats on the damper shaft must match up with the flats in the spring seat

4.13 Align the OUT mark on the upper spring seat with the mark on the upper insulator

4.14 Make sure the arrow on the spring seat faces toward the lower bracket, where the steering knuckle fits

upper insulator (see illustration).

14 Make sure the arrow on the spring seat faces toward the lower bracket, where the steering knuckle fits (see illustration).

15 Install the dust seal and suspension support to the damper shaft.

16 Install the nut and tighten it to the torque listed in this Chapter's Specifications. Remove the spring compressor tool.

17 Install the strut/spring assembly (see Section 3).

5   Control arm - removal, inspection and installation

REMOVAL

▶ **Refer to illustrations 5.3a, 5.3b, 5.4 and 5.5**

1   Loosen the wheel lug nuts on the side to be disassembled.

2   Raise the front of the vehicle, support it securely on jackstands and remove the wheel.

3   Remove the balljoint retaining bolt and nuts (see illustration). Use a prybar to disconnect the control arm from the steering knuckle (see illustration).

4   Remove the two bolts that attach the front of the control arm to the engine cradle (see illustration).

5   Remove the bolt and nut that attach the rear of the control arm to the engine cradle (see illustration).

6   Remove the control arm.

INSPECTION

7   Make sure the control arm is straight. If it's bent, replace it. Do not attempt to straighten a bent control arm.

8   Inspect the bushings. If they're cracked, torn or worn out, replace the control arm.

INSTALLATION

9   Installation is the reverse of removal. Be sure to tighten all fasteners to the torque listed in this Chapter's Specifications.

10   Install the wheel and lug nuts, lower the vehicle and tighten the lug nuts to the torque listed in the Chapter 1 Specifications.

11   It's a good idea to have the front wheel alignment checked, and if necessary, adjusted after this job has been performed.

5.3a   Remove these nuts and this bolt to disconnect the control arm from the balljoint

5.3b   Separate the control arm from the steering knuckle with a prybar

5.4   To detach the front end of the control arm from the engine cradle, remove these two bolts

5.5   To detach the rear end of the control arm from the engine cradle, remove this nut and bolt

6 Balljoints - replacement

1   Loosen the wheel lug nuts, raise the vehicle and support it securely on jackstands. Remove the wheel.

➡Note: If you're going to remove the balljoint using a puller (as described in Steps 9 through 13), loosen the driveaxle/hub nut before removing the wheel (see Chapter 8).

PICKLEFORK METHOD

※※ CAUTION:

The following procedure is the quickest way to detach a balljoint from the steering knuckle, but it will very likely damage the balljoint boot. If you want to save the boot, proceed to Step 9.

2   Remove the cotter pin from the balljoint stud and loosen the nut (but don't remove it yet).

3   Separate the balljoint from the steering knuckle with a picklefork-type balljoint separator. Lubricate the rubber boot with grease and work carefully so as not to tear the boot. Remove the balljoint stud nut.

4   Remove the bolt and nuts securing the balljoint to the control arm (see illustration 5.3a). Separate the balljoint from the control arm with a prybar (see illustration 5.3b).

5   To install the balljoint, position it on the steering knuckle and install the nut, but don't tighten it yet.

6   Attach the balljoint to the control arm and install the bolt and nuts, tightening them to the torque listed in this Chapter's Specifications.

7   Tighten the balljoint stud nut to the torque listed in this Chapter's Specifications and install a new cotter pin. If the cotter pin hole doesn't line up with the slots on the nut, tighten the nut additionally until it does line up - don't loosen the nut to insert the cotter pin.

8   Install the wheel and lug nuts. Lower the vehicle and tighten the lug nuts to the torque listed in the Chapter 1 Specifications.

PULLER METHOD

▶ Refer to illustration 6.12

9   Separate the control arm from the balljoint (see Section 5).

6.12 To separate the balljoint from the steering knuckle, install a small puller and pop the balljoint stud loose

10 Pull the outer end of the driveaxle from the steering knuckle (see Chapter 8) and suspend the driveaxle with a piece of wire.

11 Remove the cotter pin from the balljoint stud and loosen the nut (but don't remove it yet).

12 Install a small puller (see illustration) and pop the balljoint stud from the steering knuckle.

13 Remove the nut and remove the balljoint.

14 Install the new balljoint into the steering knuckle and tighten the nut to the torque listed in this Chapter's Specifications. Install a new cotter pin. If the cotter pin hole doesn't line up with the slots on the nut, tighten the nut additionally until it does line up - don't loosen the nut to insert the cotter pin.

15 Insert the outer end of the driveaxle through the steering knuckle and install the nut. Tighten it securely, but don't attempt to tighten it completely yet.

16 Connect the balljoint to the lower arm and tighten the fasteners to the torque listed in this Chapter's Specifications.

17 Install the wheel and lug nuts, lower the vehicle and tighten the lug nuts to the torque listed in the Chapter 1 Specifications.

18 Tighten the driveaxle/hub nut to the torque listed in the Chapter 8 Specifications. Install the lock washer and cotter pin.

7 Steering knuckle and hub - removal and installation

※※ WARNING:

Dust created by the brake system is harmful to your health. Never blow it out with compressed air and don't inhale any of it. Do not, under any circumstances, use petroleum-based solvents to clean brake parts. Use brake system cleaner only.

REMOVAL

1   Loosen the driveaxle/hub nut (see Chapter 8). Loosen the wheel lug nuts, raise the vehicle and support it securely on jackstands. Remove the wheel.

2   Remove the brake caliper and support it with a piece of wire as described in Chapter 9. Remove the caliper torque plate and separate the brake disc from the hub.

3   Loosen, but do not remove the strut-to-steering knuckle bolts (see illustration 3.4).

4   Separate the tie-rod from the steering knuckle arm (see Section 14).

5   Remove the balljoint-to-lower arm bolt and nuts (see illustration 5.3a and 5.3b). The strut-to-knuckle bolts can now be removed.

6   Push the driveaxle from the hub as described in Chapter 8. Support the end of the driveaxle with a piece of wire.

7   Separate the steering knuckle from the strut. If necessary, detach the balljoint from the steering knuckle.

INSTALLATION

8 Guide the knuckle and hub assembly into position, inserting the driveaxle into the hub.

9 Push the knuckle into the strut flange and install the bolts and nuts, but don't tighten them yet.

10 Connect the balljoint to the control arm and install the bolt and nuts (don't tighten them yet).

11 Attach the tie-rod to the steering knuckle arm (see Section 14). Tighten the strut bolt nuts, the balljoint-to-control arm bolt and nuts and the tie-rod nut to the torque values listed in this Chapter's Specifications.

12 Place the brake disc on the hub and install the caliper as outlined in Chapter 9.

13 Install the driveaxle/hub nut and tighten it securely (final tightening will be carried out when the vehicle is lowered).

14 Install the wheel and lug nuts.

15 Lower the vehicle and tighten the lug nuts to the torque listed in the Chapter 1 Specifications. Tighten the driveaxle/hub nut to the torque listed in the Chapter 8 Specifications. Be sure to install a new cotter pin.

16 Have the front wheel alignment checked and, if necessary, adjusted.

---

8   Hub and bearing assembly - removal and installation

FRONT

Due to the special tools and expertise required to press the hub and bearing from the steering knuckle, this job should be left to a professional mechanic. However, the steering knuckle and hub may be removed and the assembly taken to a dealer service department or other repair shop. See Section 7 for the steering knuckle and hub removal procedure.

REAR

⁂ WARNING:

Dust created by the brake system is harmful to your health. Never blow it out with compressed air and don't inhale any of it. Do not, under any circumstances, use petroleum-based solvents to clean brake parts. Use brake system cleaner only.

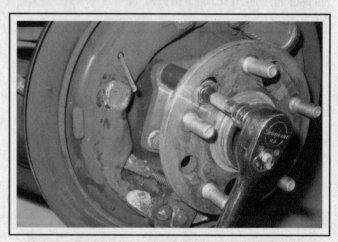

8.4 To remove the four bolts that attach the hub and bearing assembly to the rear axle carrier, rotate the hub flange and align one of the holes in the flange with each of the bolts

8.6 An exploded view of the rear hub and bearing assembly (drum brake model)

➡Note: The rear hub and bearing assembly is not serviceable. If found to be defective, it must be replaced as a unit.

Removal

▶ Refer to illustration 8.4

1   Loosen the wheel lug nuts, raise the vehicle and support it securely on jackstands. Remove the wheel.

2   Remove the brake drum from the hub (see Chapter 9).

3   Disconnect the ABS speed sensor.

4   Remove the four hub-to-axle carrier bolts, accessible by turning the hub flange so that the large circular cutout exposes each bolt (see illustration).

5   Remove the hub and bearing assembly from its seat, maneuvering it out through the brake assembly.

Installation

▶ Refer to illustration 8.6

6   Position the hub and bearing assembly on the axle carrier and align the holes in the backing plate (see illustration). Install the bolts. After all four bolts have been installed, tighten them to the torque listed in this Chapter's Specifications.

7   Install the brake drum and the wheel. Lower the vehicle and tighten the lug nuts to the torque listed in the Chapter 1 Specifications.

9   Shock absorber (rear) - removal and installation

▶ Refer to illustrations 9.2 and 9.3

※※ WARNING:

Shock absorbers must be replaced in pairs - never replace just one of them.

1   Loosen the rear wheel lug nuts, raise the rear of the vehicle and support it securely on jackstands. Block the front wheels to prevent the vehicle from rolling. Remove the wheels.

2   Remove the shock absorber lower mounting bolt (2003 and earlier models) or nut (2004 and later models) (see illustration).

3   Working inside the vehicle, remove the in access cover in the

9.2 Rear spring and shock absorber mounting details

rear quarter panel trim and remove the shock absorber upper mounting nut(s) (see illustration).

4   Place the lower retainer and rubber insulator onto the top of the shock absorber. Install the upper end of the shock absorber into its mounting hole and push the lower end onto its mounting stud. Install the lower mounting bolt or nut and tighten it to the torque listed in this Chapter's Specifications.

5   Install the upper retainers and insulator, followed by the upper mounting nut(s). Tighten the upper mounting nut(s) to the torque listed in this Chapter's Specifications. Install the access cover.

6   Install the wheel and lug nuts. Lower the vehicle and tighten the lug nuts to the torque listed in the Chapter 1 Specifications.

9.3 Pry out the shock mount cover with a trim tool, then use two wrenches to loosen and remove the upper shock absorber mounting nuts

10 Coil spring (rear) - removal, inspection and installation

REMOVAL

1   Loosen the rear wheel lug nuts, raise the rear of the vehicle and support it securely on jackstands. Block the front wheels to prevent the vehicle from rolling. Remove the wheels.

2   Support the rear axle beam with a floor jack on each side, under the lower spring mounts.

3   Remove the lower mounting bolt or nut from each rear shock absorber and pull the shocks from their studs (see illustration 9.2).

4   To remove the coil springs, slowly lower the two jacks until the coil springs are loose and there is room to remove them. Note how the bottom of the spring fits in its socket on the axle beam.

INSPECTION

5   If the rear of the vehicle does not sit evenly, side-to-side or front-to-rear, this may indicate the coil springs need replacing.

6   Inspect coil springs for chips, rust or cracks, and inspect the upper spring insulator for cracks or other signs the rubber is deteriorating.

✲✲ WARNING:

Coil springs must be replaced in pairs. If the spring on one side is defective, replace both sides with new ones.

INSTALLATION

7   Install the insulators on the top of the coil springs and insert the bottom of the springs into their sockets on the rear axle beam.

8   Raise both floor jacks until the upper part of the springs and insulators fit into the body and are secure.

9   Push the lower shock absorber eyes over their mounting studs and secure them with the mounting bolts.

10 Tighten the lower shock absorber mounting bolts to the torque listed in this Chapter's Specifications. Install the wheels and lug nuts. Raise the floorjacks until the jackstands can be removed, then lower the vehicle.

11 Tighten the lug nuts to the torque listed in this Chapter's Specifications.

11 Rear axle beam - removal and installation

✲✲ WARNING:

Dust created by the brake system is harmful to your health. Never blow it out with compressed air and don't inhale any of it. Do not, under any circumstances, use petroleum-based solvents to clean brake parts. Use brake system cleaner only.

REMOVAL

▶ **Refer to illustration 11.8**

1   Loosen the wheel lug nuts, raise the vehicle and support it on jackstands. Block the front wheels and remove the rear wheels.

2   Refer to Chapter 9 and remove the brake drums. Disconnect the ABS sensors and wire harnesses from each rear brake assembly.

3   Remove the rear hub and bearing assembly (see Section 8) on each side.

4   Disconnect the brake lines from the wheel cylinders. Also disconnect the flexible brake hoses from the hard lines and remove the lines, capping them immediately to prevent loss of fluid and entry of air or dirt.

5   It isn't necessary to disassemble the brake shoe assembly or disconnect the parking brake cables from the backing plates. Detach the backing plates and rear brake assemblies from the axle. Suspend the backing plates and brake assemblies from the body with a piece of wire. Disconnect any clips securing the parking brake cables to the axle beam.

6   Remove the two bolts and nuts and disconnect the exhaust tail-pipe at the joint just ahead of the rear suspension.

7   Refer to Section 10 and remove the coil springs.

8   Lower the axle beam all the way down. Remove the two pivot bolts/nuts securing the axle beam to the body (see illustration).

9   Lower the axle beam to the ground and remove it from under the vehicle.

INSTALLATION

10 Inspect the axle beam and the hub-mounting areas for cracks, deformation and signs of wear. If it is damaged, replace it. Do not attempt to repair it.

11 Use floor jacks and a helper to position the rear axle beam under the vehicle. Install the front pivot bolts/nuts. Raise the axle beam until ride height is approximated, then tighten the pivot bolts to this Chapter's Specifications.

12 Install the brake components (see Chapter 9).

13 Refer to Section 10 and install the coil springs. The remainder of installation is a reverse of the removal procedure.

14 Install the wheels and lug nuts.

11.8 Remove the rear axle beam pivot bolts/nuts (one side shown here)

15 Bleed the brake system (see Chapter 9).

16 Lower the vehicle and tighten the lug nuts to the torque listed in the Chapter 1 Specifications.

12 Steering system - general information

All models are equipped with rack-and-pinion steering. The steering gear is bolted to the engine cradle and operates the steering knuckles via tie-rods. The inner ends of the tie-rods are protected by rubber boots, which should be inspected periodically for secure attachment, tears and leaking lubricant. If lubricant is leaking from a boot, a faulty rack seal is indicated.

The power assist system consists of a belt-driven pump and the associated lines and hoses. The fluid level in the power steering pump reservoir should be checked periodically (see Chapter 1).

The steering wheel operates the steering shaft, which actuates the steering gear through universal joints. Looseness in the steering can be caused by wear in the steering shaft universal joints, the steering gear, the tie-rod ends and loose retaining bolts.

13 Steering wheel - removal and installation

☀☀ WARNING:

The models covered by this manual are equipped with Supplemental Restraint Systems (SRS), more commonly known as airbags. Always disable the airbag system before working in the vicinity of any airbag system components to avoid the possibility of accidental deployment of the airbag(s), which could cause personal injury (see Chapter 12).

REMOVAL

▶ **Refer to illustrations 13.2, 13.3a, 13.3b, 13.3c, 13.4 and 13.6**

1   Turn the ignition key to Off, then disconnect the cable from the negative terminal of the battery. Also disconnect the positive cable and wait at least two minutes before proceeding.

2   Turn the steering wheel so that the wheels are pointing straight ahead, then pry off the small covers on either side of the steering wheel and loosen the Torx screws that attach the airbag module to the steering wheel (see illustration). Loosen each screw until the groove in the circumference of the screw catches on the screw case.

➡ **Note: On some models, you may have to pry out the audio**

13.2 Pry off the small covers on either side of the steering wheel, then loosen the airbag module Torx screws

controller (at the steering wheel) to access the left-side airbag screw.

3   Pull the airbag module off the steering wheel (see illustration)

13.3a Remove the airbag module . . .

13.3b . . . flip up the lock for the module electrical connector . . .

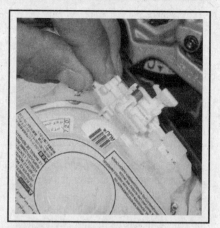

13.3c . . . and unplug the electrical connector

13.4 Unplug the electrical connector for the horn and cruise control

13.6 Use a steering wheel puller to remove the steering wheel

and disconnect the module electrical connector (see illustration).

> **※※ WARNING:**
>
> **Carry the airbag module with the trim side facing away from you and set it down in an isolated area with the trim side facing up.**

4   Unplug the electrical connector for the horn and cruise control system (see illustration).

5   Remove the steering wheel retaining nut, then mark the relationship of the steering shaft to the hub (if marks don't already exist or don't line up) to simplify installation and ensure steering wheel alignment.

6   Use a puller to disconnect the steering wheel from the shaft (see illustration).

> **※※ CAUTION:**
>
> **Don't hammer on the shaft in an attempt to remove the wheel.**

INSTALLATION

♦ Refer to illustration 13.7

7   Make sure that the front wheels are facing straight ahead. Turn the spiral cable counterclockwise by hand until it becomes harder to turn the cable. Rotate the cable clockwise about three turns and align the two red pointers (see illustration).

8   To install the wheel, align the mark on the steering wheel hub with the mark on the shaft and slip the wheel onto the shaft. Install the nut and tighten it to the torque listed in this Chapter's Specifications.

9   Plug in the horn and cruise control connector.

10 Plug in the electrical connector for the airbag module.

11 Install the airbag module and tighten the Torx retaining screws to the torque listed in this Chapter's Specifications.

12 Connect the battery cables (positive first, negative last).

13.7 To align the spiral cable, turn the cable counterclockwise until it's harder to turn, rotate the cable clockwise three turns and align the two red marks (the cable should be able to rotate about three turns in either direction when it's properly centered)

14 Tie-rod ends - removal and installation

REMOVAL

▶ **Refer to illustrations 14.2a, 14.2b and 14.4**

1   Loosen the wheel lug nuts. Raise the front of the vehicle, support it securely on jackstands, block the rear wheels and set the parking brake. Remove the front wheel.

2   Hold the tie-rod end with a pair of locking pliers or wrench and loosen the jam nut enough to mark the position of the tie-rod end in relation to the threads (see illustrations).

3   Remove the cotter pin and loosen the nut on the tie-rod end stud.

4   Disconnect the tie-rod from the steering knuckle arm with a puller (see illustration). Remove the nut and separate the tie-rod.

5   Unscrew the tie-rod end from the tie-rod.

INSTALLATION

6   Thread the tie-rod end on to the marked position and insert the tie-rod end stud into the steering knuckle arm. Tighten the jam nut securely.

7   Install the castle nut on the stud and tighten it to the torque listed in this Chapter's Specifications. Install a new cotter pin. If necessary, tighten the nut an additional amount to allow cotter pin insertion. Never loosen the nut to align a slot with the hole in the stud.

8   Install the wheel and lug nuts. Lower the vehicle and tighten the lug nuts to the torque listed in the Chapter 1 Specifications.

9   Have the front wheel alignment checked and, if necessary, adjusted.

14.2a Hold the tie-rod end with a wrench and break the jam nut loose with another wrench

14.2b Back off the jam nut and mark the exposed threads to ensure that the new tie-rod end is threaded on the same number of turns

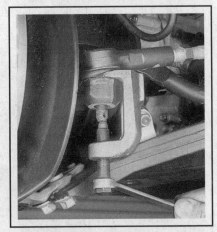

14.4 Install a small puller as shown to separate the tie-rod end from the steering knuckle

15 Steering gear boots - replacement

▶ **Refer to illustration 15.3**

1   Loosen the lug nuts, raise the vehicle and support it securely on jackstands. Remove the wheel.

2   Remove the tie-rod end and jam nut (see Section 14).

3   Remove the steering gear boot clamps (see illustration) and slide off the boot.

4   Before installing the new boot, wrap the threads and serrations on the end of the steering rod with a layer of tape so the small end of the new boot isn't damaged.

5   Slide the new boot into position on the steering gear until it seats in the groove in the steering rod and install new clamps.

6   Remove the tape and install the tie-rod end (see Section 14).

7   Install the wheel and lug nuts. Lower the vehicle and tighten the lug nuts to the torque listed in the Chapter 1 Specifications.

8   Have the front wheel alignment checked and, if necessary, adjusted.

15.3 Remove the outer clamp (arrow) from the steering gear boot with a pair of pliers; the inner clamp (not visible in this photo) must be cut or pried off

16   Steering gear - removal and installation

❈❈ WARNING:

Make sure the steering shaft is not turned while the steering gear is removed or you could damage the spiral cable for the airbag system. To prevent the shaft from turning, place the ignition key in the lock position or thread the seat belt through the steering wheel and clip it into place.

REMOVAL

▶ **Refer to illustrations 16.2, 16.3 and 16.6**

1   Park the vehicle with the front wheels pointing straight ahead. Loosen the front wheel lug nuts, raise the front of the vehicle and support it securely on jackstands. Apply the parking brake and remove the wheels. Remove the engine under-covers on models so equipped.

2   Place a drain pan under the steering gear. Detach the power steering pressure and return lines (see illustration) and cap the ends to prevent excessive fluid loss and contamination. Detach the bracket from the top of the steering gear assembly.

3   Mark the relationship of the lower universal joint to the steering gear input shaft. Remove the lower intermediate shaft pinch bolt (see illustration).

4   Separate the tie-rod ends from the steering knuckle arms (see Section 14).

5   Remove the stabilizer bar bushing retainer bolts (see Section 2). (You can't remove the steering gear mounting bolts until the stabilizer is lifted up out of the way.)

6   Remove the steering gear mounting nuts (see illustration), lift up the stabilizer bar and knock out the steering gear mounting bolts.

7   Separate the intermediate shaft from the steering gear input shaft and pull the steering gear assembly out from the left side.

8   Check the steering gear mounting grommets for excessive wear or deterioration, replacing them if necessary.

16.2 Disconnect the power steering fluid line fittings from the steering gear

16.3 Remove the U-joint pinch bolt and nut

16.6 Steering gear mounting details

INSTALLATION

9   Raise the steering gear into position and connect the U-joint, aligning the marks.

10 Install the mounting bolts and nuts and tighten them to the torque listed in this Chapter's Specifications.

11 Connect the tie-rod ends to the steering knuckle arms (see Section 14).

12 Install the U-joint pinch bolt and tighten it to the torque listed in this Chapter's Specifications.

13 Connect the power steering pressure and return hoses to the steering gear and fill the power steering pump reservoir with the recommended fluid (see Chapter 1). Reattach the bracket to the top of the steering gear assembly.

14 Install the stabilizer bar bushing retainer bolts and tighten them to the torque listed in this Chapter's Specifications.

15 Install the wheels and lug nuts. Lower the vehicle and bleed the steering system (see Section 19). Tighten the lug nuts to the torque listed in the Chapter 1 Specifications.

16 Have the front wheel alignment checked and, if necessary, adjusted.

17 Power steering pump - removal and installation

REMOVAL

▶ **Refer to illustration 17.5**

1   Disconnect the cable from the negative battery terminal.

✳✳ CAUTION:

If the stereo in your vehicle is equipped with an anti-theft system, make sure you have the correct activation code before disconnecting the battery.

2   Using a large syringe or suction gun, suck as much fluid out of the power steering fluid reservoir as possible. Place a drain pan under the vehicle to catch any fluid that spills out when the hoses are disconnected.

3   Loosen the right front wheel lug nuts, raise the vehicle and support it securely on jackstands. Remove the right front wheel.

4   Remove the right front fender apron seal.

5   Loosen the clamp and disconnect the fluid return hose from the pump (see illustration).

6   Remove the pressure line-to-pump union bolt and separate the line from the pump. Remove the sealing washers on each side of the

17.5 Installation details of the power steering pump assembly

fitting - these washers should be replaced with new ones when installing the pump.

7   Loosen the adjuster and pivot bolts and remove the drivebelt.
8   Remove the pivot and adjuster bolts, then remove the pump.

INSTALLATION

9   Installation is the reverse of removal. Be sure to tighten the fluid line banjo bolt and the adjuster and pivot bolts to the torque listed in this Chapter's Specifications. Adjust the drivebelt tension (see Chapter 1).
10 Top up the fluid level in the reservoir (see Chapter 1) and bleed the system (see Section 19).

18 Power Steering Pressure (PSP) switch - check and replacement

CHECK

▶ **Refer to illustration 18.4**

1   The power steering pressure (PSP) switch is located at the high pressure line outlet fitting of the power steering pump.
2   When steering system pressure reaches a high-pressure setpoint, the PSP switch closes and sends a signal to the PCM that the PCM uses to maintain engine idle speed during parking maneuvers.
3   Check the operation of the PSP switch if the engine stalls during parking or if the engine idles continuously at high rpm.
4   Disconnect the PSP switch connector and connect an ohmmeter to the terminals on the switch body (see illustration).
5   Start the engine and let it idle.
6   Turn the steering wheel to point the front wheels straight ahead and read the ohmmeter. It should indicate no continuity (infinite resistance).
7   Turn the steering wheel to either side and watch the ohmmeter. The PSP switch should close as the wheel nears the steering stop on either side, and the meter should indicate continuity (zero ohms).
8   If the switch fails either test, replace it.

REPLACEMENT

9   Raise the vehicle and support it securely on jackstands.
10 Disconnect the cable from the negative battery terminal.

18.4 Location of the Power Steering Pressure (PSP) switch

11 Disconnect the electrical connector from the switch and unscrew the switch from the fitting on the steering gear (see illustration 17.5).
12 Install and connect the new switch and lower the vehicle to the ground.
13 Refer to Section 19 and bleed air from the power steering system. Add fluid as required (see Chapter 1).

19 Power steering system - bleeding

1   Following any operation in which the power steering fluid lines have been disconnected, the power steering system must be bled to remove all air and obtain proper steering performance.
2   With the front wheels in the straight ahead position, check the power steering fluid level and, if low, add fluid until it reaches the Cold mark on the dipstick.
3   Start the engine and allow it to run at fast idle. Recheck the fluid level and add more if necessary to reach the Cold mark on the dipstick.
4   Bleed the system by turning the wheels from side to side, without hitting the stops. This will work the air out of the system. Keep the

reservoir full of fluid as this is done.
5   When the air is worked out of the system, return the wheels to the straight-ahead position and leave the vehicle running for several more minutes before shutting it off.
6   Road test the vehicle to be sure the steering system is functioning normally and noise free.
7   Recheck the fluid level to be sure it is up to the Hot mark on the dipstick while the engine is at normal operating temperature. Add fluid if necessary (see Chapter 1).

20 Wheels and tires - general information

▶ **Refer to illustration 20.1**

1   All vehicles covered by this manual are equipped with metric-sized fiberglass or steel belted radial tires (see illustration). Use of

other size or type of tires may affect the ride and handling of the vehicle. Don't mix different types of tires, such as radials and bias belted, on the same vehicle as handling may be seriously affected. It's recommended that tires be replaced in pairs on the same axle, but if only one

20.1 Metric tire size code

tire is being replaced, be sure it's the same size, structure and tread design as the other.

   2   Because tire pressure has a substantial effect on handling and wear, the pressure on all tires should be checked at least once a month or before any extended trips (see Chapter 1).

   3   Wheels must be replaced if they are bent, dented, leak air, have elongated bolt holes, are heavily rusted, out of vertical symmetry or if the lug nuts won't stay tight. Wheel repairs that use welding or peening are not recommended.

   4   Tire and wheel balance is important in the overall handling, braking and performance of the vehicle. Unbalanced wheels can adversely affect handling and ride characteristics as well as tire life. Whenever a tire is installed on a wheel, the tire and wheel should be balanced by a shop with the proper equipment.

21 Wheel alignment - general information

▶ **Refer to illustration 21.1**

     A wheel alignment refers to the adjustments made to the wheels so they are in proper angular relationship to the suspension and the ground. Wheels that are out of proper alignment not only affect vehicle control, but also increase tire wear. The alignment angles normally measured are camber, caster and toe-in (see illustration). Toe-in and camber are the only adjustable angles on the front. Caster should be measured to check for bent or worn suspension parts. Camber and toe-in should be measured on the rear to check for a bent axle.

     Getting the proper wheel alignment is a very exacting process, one in which complicated and expensive machines are necessary to perform the job properly. Because of this, you should have a technician with the proper equipment perform these tasks. We will, however, use this space to give you a basic idea of what is involved with a wheel alignment so you can better understand the process and deal intelligently with the shop that does the work.

     Toe-in is the turning in of the wheels. The purpose of a toe specification is to ensure parallel rolling of the wheels. In a vehicle with zero toe-in, the distance between the front edges of the wheels will be the same as the distance between the rear edges of the wheels. The actual amount of toe-in is normally only a fraction of an inch. On the front end, toe-in is controlled by the tie-rod end position on the tie-rod. On the rear end, it's not adjustable. Incorrect toe-in will cause the tires to wear improperly by making them scrub against the road surface.

     Camber is the tilting of the wheels from vertical when viewed from one end of the vehicle. When the wheels tilt out at the top, the camber is said to be positive (+). When the wheels tilt in at the top the camber is negative (-). The amount of tilt is measured in degrees from vertical and this measurement is called the camber angle. This angle affects the amount of tire tread which contacts the road and compensates for changes in the suspension geometry when the vehicle is cornering or traveling over an undulating surface. On the front end, camber is adjusted by altering the position of the steering knuckle in

21.1 Camber, caster and toe-in angles

the strut flange. If camber can't be adjusted within the specified range, special adjuster bolts, which replace the standard strut-to-knuckle bolts, are available. On the rear end, camber is not adjustable.

     Caster is the tilting of the front steering axis from vertical. A tilt toward the rear is positive caster and a tilt toward the front is negative caster. Caster is not adjustable on these vehicles.

Torque specifications	Ft-lbs (unless otherwise indicated)

➡Note: One foot-pound (ft-lb) of torque is equivalent to 12 inch-pounds (in-lbs) of torque. Torque values below approximately 15 ft-lbs are expressed in inch-pounds, since most foot-pound torque wrenches are not accurate at these smaller values.

Front suspension

Balljoint	
Balljoint-to-steering knuckle nut	90
Balljoint-to-control arm nuts and bolts	94
Control arm	
Front bolts	
2003 and earlier	152
2004 and later	148
Rear bolt	152
Stabilizer bar	
Stabilizer bar link nuts	
2003 and earlier	29
2004 and later	55
Stabilizer bushing/retainer bolts	
2003 and earlier	168 in-lbs
2004 and later	144 in-lbs
Strut	
Strut upper mounting nuts	59
Strut-to-suspension support (damper shaft) nut	36
Strut-to-steering knuckle bolts/nuts	155

Rear suspension

Hub and bearing assembly-to-axle bearing retainer nuts	
2003 and earlier	59
2004 and later	41
Shock absorber mounting	
2003 and earlier	
Lower bolt	27
Upper nuts	18
2004 and later	
Lower nut	85
Upper nut	22
Axle beam mounting nuts/bolts	
2003 and earlier	65
2004 and later	100

Steering system

Airbag module retaining screws	
Driver's	78 in-lbs
Passenger's	15
Steering wheel nut	
2000 and earlier models	25
2001 and later models	37
Steering gear mounting bolts/nuts	
2003 and earlier	134
2004 and later	52
Steering shaft universal joint pinch bolt	26
Tie-rod end-to-steering knuckle nut	36
Power steering pump	
Mounting fasteners	32
Pressure line union bolt	
2003 and earlier	38
2004 and later	61
Pulley nut (2003 and earlier)	32
Wheel lug nuts	See Chapter 1

Section

11

BODY

1 General information

These models feature a "unibody" layout, using a floor pan with front and rear frame side rails which support the body components, front and rear suspension systems and other mechanical components.

Certain components are particularly vulnerable to accident damage and can be unbolted and repaired or replaced. Among these parts are the body moldings, bumpers, front fenders, the hood and liftgate, doors and all glass.

Only general body maintenance practices and body panel repair procedures within the scope of the do-it-yourselfer are included in this Chapter.

2 Body - maintenance

1   The condition of your vehicle's body is very important, because the resale value depends a great deal on it. It's much more difficult to repair a neglected or damaged body than it is to repair mechanical components. The hidden areas of the body, such as the wheel wells, the frame and the engine compartment, are equally important, although they don't require as frequent attention as the rest of the body.

2   Once a year, or every 12,000 miles, it's a good idea to have the underside of the body steam-cleaned. All traces of dirt and oil will be removed and the area can then be inspected carefully for rust, damaged brake lines, frayed electrical wires, damaged cables and other problems.

3   At the same time, clean the engine and the engine compartment with a steam cleaner or water-soluble degreaser.

4   The wheel wells should be given close attention, since undercoating can peel away and stones and dirt thrown up by the tires can cause the paint to chip and flake, allowing rust to set in. If rust is found, clean down to the bare metal and apply an anti-rust paint.

5   The body should be washed about once a week. Wet the vehicle thoroughly to soften the dirt, then wash it down with a soft sponge and plenty of clean soapy water. If the surplus dirt is not washed off very carefully, it can wear down the paint.

6   Spots of tar or asphalt thrown up from the road should be removed with a cloth soaked in kerosene. Scented lamp oil is available in most hardware stores and the smell is easier to work with than straight kerosene.

7   Once every six months, wax the body and chrome trim. If a chrome cleaner is used to remove rust from any of the vehicle's plated parts, remember that the cleaner also removes part of the chrome, so use it sparingly. On any plated parts where chrome cleaner is used, use a good paste wax over the plating for extra protection.

3 Vinyl trim - maintenance

Don't clean vinyl trim with detergents, caustic soap or petroleum-based cleaners. Plain soap and water works just fine, with a soft brush to clean dirt that may be ingrained. Wash the vinyl as frequently as the rest of the vehicle.

After cleaning, application of a high quality rubber and vinyl protectant will help prevent oxidation and cracks. The protectant can also be applied to weather stripping, vacuum lines and rubber hoses, which often fail as a result of chemical degradation, and to the tires.

4 Upholstery and carpets - maintenance

1   Every three months remove the floormats and clean the interior of the vehicle (more frequently if necessary). Use a stiff whiskbroom to brush the carpeting and loosen dirt and dust, then vacuum the upholstery and carpets thoroughly, especially along seams and crevices.

2   Dirt and stains can be removed from carpeting with basic household or automotive carpet shampoos available in spray cans. Follow the directions and vacuum again, then use a stiff brush to bring back the "nap" of the carpet.

3   Most interiors have cloth or vinyl upholstery, either of which can be cleaned and maintained with a number of material-specific cleaners or shampoos available in auto supply stores. Follow the directions on the product for usage, and always spot-test any upholstery cleaner on an inconspicuous area (bottom edge of a backseat cushion) to ensure that it doesn't cause a color shift in the material.

4   After cleaning, vinyl upholstery should be treated with a protectant.

➡**Note: Make sure the protectant container indicates the product can be used on seats - some products may make a seat too slippery.**

✴✴ **CAUTION:**

Do not use protectant on steering wheels.

5   Leather upholstery requires special care. It should be cleaned regularly with saddlesoap or leather cleaner. Never use alcohol, gasoline, nail polish remover or thinner to clean leather upholstery.

6   After cleaning, regularly treat leather upholstery with a leather conditioner, rubbed in with a soft cotton cloth. Never use car wax on leather upholstery.

7   In areas where the interior of the vehicle is subject to bright sunlight, cover leather seating areas of the seats with a sheet if the vehicle is to be left out for any length of time.

FLEXIBLE PLASTIC BODY PANELS (FRONT AND REAR BUMPER FASCIA)

The following repair procedures are for minor scratches and gouges. Repair of more serious damage should be left to a dealer service department or qualified auto body shop. Below is a list of the equipment and materials necessary to perform the following repair procedures on plastic body panels. Although a specific brand of material may be mentioned, it should be noted that equivalent products from other manufacturers may be used instead.

Wax, grease and silicone removing solvent
Cloth-backed body tape
Sanding discs
Drill motor with three-inch disc holder
Hand sanding block
Rubber squeegees
Sandpaper
Non-porous mixing palette
Wood paddle or putty knife
Curved-tooth body file
Flexible parts repair material

1 Remove the damaged panel, if necessary or desirable. In most cases, repairs can be carried out with the panel installed.

2 Clean the area(s) to be repaired with a wax, grease and silicone removing solvent applied with a water-dampened cloth.

3 If the damage is structural, that is, if it extends through the panel, clean the backside of the panel area to be repaired as well. Wipe dry.

4 Sand the rear surface about 1-1/2 inches beyond the break.

5 Cut two pieces of fiberglass cloth large enough to overlap the break by about 1-1/2 inches. Cut only to the required length.

6 Mix the adhesive from the repair kit according to the instructions included with the kit, and apply a layer of the mixture approximately 1/8-inch thick on the backside of the panel. Overlap the break by at least 1-1/2 inches.

7 Apply one piece of fiberglass cloth to the adhesive and cover the cloth with additional adhesive. Apply a second piece of fiberglass cloth to the adhesive and immediately cover the cloth with additional adhesive in sufficient quantity to fill the weave.

8 Allow the repair to cure for 20 to 30 minutes at 60-degrees to 80-degrees F.

9 If necessary, trim the excess repair material at the edge.

10 Remove all of the paint film over and around the area(s) to be repaired. The repair material should not overlap the painted surface.

11 With a drill motor and a sanding disc (or a rotary file), cut a "V" along the break line approximately 1/2-inch wide. Remove all dust and loose particles from the repair area.

12 Mix and apply the repair material. Apply a light coat first over the damaged area; then continue applying material until it reaches a level slightly higher than the surrounding finish.

13 Cure the mixture for 20 to 30 minutes at 60-degrees to 80-degrees F.

14 Roughly establish the contour of the area being repaired with a body file. If low areas or pits remain, mix and apply additional adhesive.

15 Block sand the damaged area with sandpaper to establish the actual contour of the surrounding surface.

16 If desired, the repaired area can be temporarily protected with several light coats of primer. Because of the special paints and techniques required for flexible body panels, it is recommended that the vehicle be taken to a paint shop for completion of the body repair.

STEEL BODY PANELS

▶ **See photo sequence**

Repair of minor scratches

17 If the scratch is superficial and does not penetrate to the metal of the body, repair is very simple. Lightly rub the scratched area with a fine rubbing compound to remove loose paint and built up wax. Rinse the area with clean water.

18 Apply touch-up paint to the scratch, using a small brush. Continue to apply thin layers of paint until the surface of the paint in the scratch is level with the surrounding paint. Allow the new paint at least two weeks to harden, then blend it into the surrounding paint by rubbing with a very fine rubbing compound. Finally, apply a coat of wax to the scratch area.

19 If the scratch has penetrated the paint and exposed the metal of the body, causing the metal to rust, a different repair technique is required. Remove all loose rust from the bottom of the scratch with a pocketknife, then apply rust inhibiting paint to prevent the formation of rust in the future. Using a rubber or nylon applicator, coat the scratched area with glaze-type filler. If required, the filler can be mixed with thinner to provide a very thin paste, which is ideal for filling narrow scratches. Before the glaze filler in the scratch hardens, wrap a piece of smooth cotton cloth around the tip of a finger. Dip the cloth in thinner and then quickly wipe it along the surface of the scratch. This will ensure that the surface of the filler is slightly hollow. The scratch can now be painted over as described earlier in this Section.

REPAIR OF DENTS

20 When repairing dents, the first job is to pull the dent out until the affected area is as close as possible to its original shape. There is no point in trying to restore the original shape completely as the metal in the damaged area will have stretched on impact and cannot be restored to its original contours. It is better to bring the level of the dent up to a point that is about 1/8-inch below the level of the surrounding metal. In cases where the dent is very shallow, it is not worth trying to pull it out at all.

21 If the back side of the dent is accessible, it can be hammered out gently from behind using a soft-face hammer. While doing this, hold a block of wood firmly against the opposite side of the metal to absorb the hammer blows and prevent the metal from being stretched.

22 If the dent is in a section of the body which has double layers, or some other factor makes it inaccessible from behind, a different technique is required. Drill several small holes through the metal inside the damaged area, particularly in the deeper sections. Screw long, self-tapping screws into the holes just enough for them to get a good grip in the metal. Now the dent can be pulled out by pulling on the protruding heads of the screws with locking pliers.

23 The next stage of repair is the removal of paint from the damaged area and from an inch or so of the surrounding metal. This is easily done with a wire brush or sanding disk in a drill motor, although it can be done just as effectively by hand with sandpaper. To complete

These photos illustrate a method of repairing simple dents. They are intended to supplement Body repair - minor damage in this Chapter and should not be used as the sole instructions for body repair on these vehicles.

1 If you can't access the backside of the body panel to hammer out the dent, pull it out with a slide-hammer-type dent puller. In the deepest portion of the dent or along the crease line, drill or punch hole(s) at least one inch apart . . .

2 . . . then screw the slide-hammer into the hole and operate it. Tap with a hammer near the edge of the dent to help 'pop' the metal back to its original shape. When you're finished, the dent area should be close to its original contour and about 1/8-inch below the surface of the surrounding metal

3 Using coarse-grit sandpaper, remove the paint down to the bare metal. Hand sanding works fine, but the disc sander shown here makes the job faster. Use finer (about 320-grit) sandpaper to feather-edge the paint at least one inch around the dent area

4 When the paint is removed, touch will probably be more helpful than sight for telling if the metal is straight. Hammer down the high spots or raise the low spots as necessary. Clean the repair area with wax/silicone remover

5 Following label instructions, mix up a batch of plastic filler and hardener. The ratio of filler to hardener is critical, and, if you mix it incorrectly, it will either not cure properly or cure too quickly (you won't have time to file and sand it into shape)

6 Working quickly so the filler doesn't harden, use a plastic applicator to press the body filler firmly into the metal, assuring it bonds completely. Work the filler until it matches the original contour and is slightly above the surrounding metal

7　Let the filler harden until you can just dent it with your fingernail. Use a body file or Surform tool (shown here) to rough-shape the filler

8　Use coarse-grit sandpaper and a sanding board or block to work the filler down until it's smooth and even. Work down to finer grits of sandpaper - always using a board or block - ending up with 360 or 400 grit

9　You shouldn't be able to feel any ridge at the transition from the filler to the bare metal or from the bare metal to the old paint. As soon as the repair is flat and uniform, remove the dust and mask off the adjacent panels or trim pieces

10　Apply several layers of primer to the area. Don't spray the primer on too heavy, so it sags or runs, and make sure each coat is dry before you spray on the next one. A professional-type spray gun is being used here, but aerosol spray primer is available inexpensively from auto parts stores

11　The primer will help reveal imperfections or scratches. Fill these with glazing compound. Follow the label instructions and sand it with 360 or 400-grit sandpaper until it's smooth. Repeat the glazing, sanding and respraying until the primer reveals a perfectly smooth surface

12　Finish sand the primer with very fine sandpaper (400 or 600-grit) to remove the primer overspray. Clean the area with water and allow it to dry. Use a tack rag to remove any dust, then apply the finish coat. Don't attempt to rub out or wax the repair area until the paint has dried completely (at least two weeks)

the preparation for filling, score the surface of the bare metal with a screwdriver or the tang of a file or drill small holes in the affected area. This will provide a good grip for the filler material. To complete the repair, see the Section on filling and painting.

REPAIR OF RUST HOLES OR GASHES

24 Remove all paint from the affected area and from an inch or so of the surrounding metal using a sanding disk or wire brush mounted in a drill motor. If these are not available, a few sheets of sandpaper will do the job just as effectively.

25 With the paint removed, you will be able to determine the severity of the corrosion and decide whether to replace the whole panel, if possible, or repair the affected area. New body panels are not as expensive as most people think and it is often quicker to install a new panel than to repair large areas of rust.

26 Remove all trim pieces from the affected area except those which will act as a guide to the original shape of the damaged body, such as headlight shells, etc. Using metal snips or a hacksaw blade, remove all loose metal and any other metal that is badly affected by rust. Hammer the edges of the hole in to create a slight depression for the filler material.

27 Wire brush the affected area to remove the powdery rust from the surface of the metal. If the back of the rusted area is accessible, treat it with rust inhibiting paint.

28 Before filling is done, block the hole in some way. This can be done with sheet metal riveted or screwed into place, or by stuffing the hole with wire mesh.

29 Once the hole is blocked off, the affected area can be filled and painted. See the following subsection on filling and painting.

FILLING AND PAINTING

30 Many types of body fillers are available, but generally speaking, body repair kits which contain filler paste and a tube of resin hardener are best for this type of repair work. A wide, flexible plastic or nylon applicator will be necessary for imparting a smooth and contoured finish to the surface of the filler material. Mix up a small amount of filler on a clean piece of wood or cardboard (use the hardener sparingly). Follow the manufacturer's instructions on the package, otherwise the filler will set incorrectly.

31 Using the applicator, apply the filler paste to the prepared area. Draw the applicator across the surface of the filler to achieve the desired contour and to level the filler surface. As soon as a contour that approximates the original one is achieved, stop working the paste. If you continue, the paste will begin to stick to the applicator. Continue to add thin layers of paste at 20-minute intervals until the level of the filler

is just above the surrounding metal.

32 Once the filler has hardened, the excess can be removed with a body file. From then on, progressively finer grades of sandpaper should be used, starting with a 180-grit paper and finishing with 600-grit wet-or-dry paper. Always wrap the sandpaper around a flat rubber or wooden block, otherwise the surface of the filler will not be completely flat. During the sanding of the filler surface, the wet-or-dry paper should be periodically rinsed in water. This will ensure that a very smooth finish is produced in the final stage.

33 At this point, the repair area should be surrounded by a ring of bare metal, which in turn should be encircled by the finely feathered edge of good paint. Rinse the repair area with clean water until all of the dust produced by the sanding operation is gone.

34 Spray the entire area with a light coat of primer. This will reveal any imperfections in the surface of the filler. Repair the imperfections with fresh filler paste or glaze filler and once more smooth the surface with sandpaper. Repeat this spray-and-repair procedure until you are satisfied that the surface of the filler and the feathered edge of the paint are perfect. Rinse the area with clean water and allow it to dry completely.

35 The repair area is now ready for painting. Spray painting must be carried out in a warm, dry, windless and dust free atmosphere. These conditions can be created if you have access to a large indoor work area, but if you are forced to work in the open, you will have to pick the day very carefully. If you are working indoors, dousing the floor in the work area with water will help settle the dust that would otherwise be in the air. If the repair area is confined to one body panel, mask off the surrounding panels. This will help minimize the effects of a slight mismatch in paint color. Trim pieces such as chrome strips, door handles, etc., will also need to be masked off or removed. Use masking tape and several thickness of newspaper for the masking operations.

36 Before spraying, shake the paint can thoroughly, then spray a test area until the spray painting technique is mastered. Cover the repair area with a thick coat of primer. The thickness should be built up using several thin layers of primer rather than one thick one. Using 600-grit wet-or-dry sandpaper, rub down the surface of the primer until it is very smooth. While doing this, the work area should be thoroughly rinsed with water and the wet-or-dry sandpaper periodically rinsed as well. Allow the primer to dry before spraying additional coats.

37 Spray on the top coat, again building up the thickness by using several thin layers of paint. Begin spraying in the center of the repair area and then, using a circular motion, work out until the whole repair area and about two inches of the surrounding original paint is covered. Remove all masking material 10 to 15 minutes after spraying on the final coat of paint. Allow the new paint at least two weeks to harden, then use a very fine rubbing compound to blend the edges of the new paint into the existing paint. Finally, apply a coat of wax.

6 Body repair - major damage

1 Major damage must be repaired by an auto body shop specifically equipped to perform unibody repairs. These shops have the specialized equipment required to do the job properly.

2 If the damage is extensive, the body must be checked for proper alignment or the vehicle's handling characteristics may be adversely affected and other components may wear at an accelerated rate.

3 Due to the fact that some of the major body components (hood, fenders, doors, etc.) are separate and replaceable units, any seriously damaged components should be replaced rather than repaired. Sometimes the components can be found in a wrecking yard that specializes in used vehicle components, often at considerable savings over the cost of new parts.

7 Hinges and locks - maintenance

Once every 3000 miles, or every three months, the hinges and latch assemblies on the doors, hood and trunk (or liftgate) should be given a few drops of light oil or lock lubricant. The door latch strikers should also be lubricated with a thin coat of grease to reduce wear and ensure free movement. Lubricate the door and trunk (or liftgate) locks with spray-on graphite lubricant.

8 Windshield and fixed glass - replacement

Replacement of the windshield and fixed glass requires the use of special fast-setting adhesive/caulk materials and some specialized tools and techniques. These operations should be left to a dealer service department or a shop specializing in glass work.

9 Radiator grille - removal and installation

2006 AND EARLIER MODELS

◆ **Refer to illustrations 9.2a, 9.2b and 9.2c**

1 Open the hood and support it in the open position

2 Remove the four plastic pushpins (see illustrations). Turn the center of the pushpin with a Phillips screwdriver to unseat it, then pull the center up and pry the fastener out.

3 Once the pins are removed, release the clip in the center and lift the grille out. The grille has tabs that fit into brackets located under the headlights, but by careful wiggling of the grille, they will release and the grille can be removed without taking out the headlights.

4 Installation is the reverse of the removal procedure. To secure a pushpin, push the body of the fastener fully into the hole, then depress the center pin to lock it in place.

2007 AND LATER MODELS

5 Remove the front bumper cover (see Section 12).

6 Remove the four screws from the bottom of the grille.

7 Detach the four clips and separate the grille from the bumper cover. The outer trim cover can be removed by releasing the 10 clips.

8 Installation is the reverse of removal.

9.2a Remove the plastic pushpins at the top of the grille (2006 and earlier model)

9.2b Reach in to release this clip at the center of the grille, near the hood latch

9.2c The grille ends have tabs that fit into these notches on each side of the body (headlight removed for clarity)

10 Hood - removal, installation and adjustment

➥Note: The hood is somewhat awkward to remove and install, at least two people should perform this procedure.

REMOVAL AND INSTALLATION

▶ **Refer to illustration 10.3**

1   Open the hood, then place blankets or pads over the fenders and cowl area of the body. This will protect the body and paint as the hood is lifted off.

2   Disconnect any cables or wires that will interfere with removal. Disconnect the windshield washer tubing from the nozzles on the hood.

3   Make marks around the hood hinge to ensure proper alignment during installation (see illustration).

4   Have an assistant support the weight of the hood.

5   Remove the hinge-to-hood bolts and lift off the hood.

6   Installation is the reverse of removal. Align the hinge bolts with the marks made in Step 3.

ADJUSTMENT

▶ **Refer to illustrations 10.10 and 10.11**

7   Fore-and-aft and side-to-side adjustment of the hood is done by moving the hinge plate slot after loosening the bolts or nuts.

➥Note: The factory bolts are "centering" type that will not allow adjustment. To adjust the hood in relation to the hinges, these bolts must be replaced with standard bolts with flat washers and lock washers.

8   Mark around the entire hinge plate so you can determine the amount of movement.

9   Loosen the bolts and move the hood into correct alignment.

10.3 Draw alignment marks around the hood hinges to ensure proper alignment of the hood when it's reinstalled

Move it only a little at a time. Tighten the hinge bolts and carefully lower the hood to check the position.

10   If necessary after installation, the entire hood latch assembly can be adjusted up-and-down as well as from side-to-side on the radiator support so the hood closes securely and flush with the fenders. Scribe a line or mark around the hood latch mounting bolts to provide a reference point, then loosen them and reposition the latch assembly, as necessary (see illustration). Following adjustment, retighten the mounting bolts.

11   Finally, adjust the hood bumpers on the radiator support so the hood, when closed, is flush with the fenders (see illustration).

12   The hood latch assembly, as well as the hinges, should be periodically lubricated with white, lithium-base grease to prevent binding and wear.

10.10 To adjust the hood latch horizontally or vertically, loosen these bolts

10.11 To adjust the vertical height of the leading edge of the hood so that it's flush with the fenders, turn each edge cushion clockwise (to lower the hood) or counterclockwise (to raise the hood)

11 Hood latch and release cable - removal and installation

✱✱ WARNING:

The models covered by this manual are equipped with Supplemental Restraint systems (SRS), more commonly known as airbags. Always disconnect the negative battery cable, then the positive battery cable and wait two minutes before working in the vicinity of any airbag system component to avoid the possibility of accidental deployment of the airbag, which could cause personal injury (see Chapter 12).

LATCH

▶ **Refer to illustration 11.2**

1   Scribe a line around the latch to aid alignment when installing. Remove the retaining bolts securing the hood latch to the radiator sup-

11.2 Pry out the cable retainer from the backside of the hood latch assembly, then disengage the cable

port (see illustration 10.10). Remove the latch.

2   Disconnect the hood release cable by disengaging the cable from the latch assembly (see illustration).

3   Installation is the reverse of removal.

➡**Note: Adjust the latch so the hood engages securely when closed and the hood bumpers are slightly compressed.**

CABLE

▶ **Refer to illustrations 11.7a and 11.7b**

4   Disconnect the hood release cable from the latch assembly as described in step 1.

5   Attach a piece of thin wire or string to the end of the cable and unclip all remaining cable retaining clips. at the radiator support.

6   Refer to Section 13 and remove the plastic inner fenderwell.

7   Remove the two hood-release lever mounting bolts and detach the hood release lever from the bottom of the knee bolster (see illustrations).

8   Refer to Section 25 and remove the knee bolster.

9   Pull the cable and grommet rearward into the passenger compartment until you can see the wire or string. Ensure that the new cable has a grommet attached then remove the wire or string from the old cable and fasten it to the new cable.

10 With the new cable attached to the wire or string, pull the wire or string back through the firewall until the new cable reaches the latch assembly.

11 Working in the passenger compartment, reinstall the new cable into the hood release lever, making sure the cable housing fits snugly into the notch in the handle bracket.

12 The remainder of the installation is the reverse of removal.

➡**Note: Push on the grommet with your fingers from the passenger compartment to seat the grommet in the firewall correctly.**

11.7a Remove the two screws retaining the hood release lever to the lower dash sound panel

11.7b Release the cable end from the hood release lever

12 Bumper covers - removal and installation

✳✳ WARNING:

The models covered by this manual are equipped with Supplemental Restraint systems (SRS), more commonly known as airbags. Always disconnect the negative battery cable, then the positive battery cable and wait two minutes before working in the vicinity of any airbag system component to avoid the possibility of accidental deployment of the airbag, which could cause personal injury (see Chapter 12).

FRONT BUMPER

2006 and earlier models

▶ **Refer to illustrations 12.4a, 12.4b and 12.4c**

1   Apply the parking brake, raise the vehicle and support it securely on jackstands.

2   Disconnect the negative battery cable, then the positive battery cable and wait two minutes before proceeding any further.

3   Remove the radiator grille (see Section 9).

12.4a Remove the plastic pins retaining the front bumper cover in the grille opening area

12.4b From below, remove the two pushpins and two bolts securing the front bumper fascia

4   Detach the screws securing the top, bottom and sides of the bumper cover (see illustrations).

➡**Note: Use a small screwdriver to pop the center button up on the plastic fasteners, but do not try to remove the center buttons. They stay in the ferrules.**

5   Installation is the reverse of removal. Make sure the tabs on the back of the bumper cover fit into the corresponding clips on the body before attaching the bolts and screws. An assistant would be helpful at this point.

2007 and later models

6   Disconnect the cable from the negative battery terminal (see Chapter 5).

7   Raise the vehicle and support it securely on jackstands.

8   Detach the front fender inner splash shields from the bumper cover by removing the screws.

9   Remove the screws from the lower edge of the bumper cover to separate it from the lower engine splash shield.

10 Open the hood and remove the clips at the center upper section of the bumper cover.

11 Apply tape to the fenders (where they meet the bumper) to protect them from being scratched. With the help of an assistant, use a screwdriver wrapped with tape to carefully release the clips at each end of the bumper and pull it forward. Disconnect any wiring as you remove it.

REAR BUMPER

2006 and earlier models

▶ **Refer to illustrations 12.12, 12.13a, 12.13b, 12.13c and 12.14**

12 Working under the vehicle, detach the plastic clips and screws securing the lower edge of the bumper cover (see illustration).

13 With the rear fenderwell liner removed, remove the fasteners securing the bumper cover to the rear quarter panel (see illustrations).

14 Open the liftgate and remove the clips or pins securing the upper edge of the bumper cover (see illustration). Pull the bumper cover out and away from the vehicle.

12.4c Remove the fasteners on each side where the bumper cover attaches to the fender

➡️**Note: Use a small screwdriver to pop the center button up on the plastic fasteners, but do not try to remove the center buttons. They stay in the ferrules. Where studs/bolts stick through the body, use a plastic hammer to tap them out of the body.**

15 Installation is the reverse of removal.

2007 and later models

16 Remove the fasteners that connect the inner fender splash shields to the rear bumper cover.

17 Remove the two clips from each end of the lower edge of the bumper cover.

18 Open the hatch and remove the four clips from the top edge of the bumper. Also remove the screws from each end.

19 Apply tape to the quarter panels where they meet the bumper to protect them from being scratched. With the help of an assistant, use a screwdriver wrapped with tape to carefully release the clips at each end of the bumper and pull it forward to remove it.

20 Installation is the reverse of removal.

12.12 Remove the pins at the bottom of the rear bumper cover

12.13a Remove the fasteners securing the plastic fenderwell liner

12.13b Seen here from below, remove the one bumper cover bolt

12.13c Release the two clips at each end of the bumper cover (seen from below)

12.14 Remove the pins securing the top edge of the rear bumper cover to the liftgate opening

13 Front fender - removal and installation

▶ **Refer to illustrations 13.3a, 13.3b, 13.4a, 13.4b, 13.5, 13.6a and 13.6b**

1   Raise the vehicle, support it securely on jackstands and remove the front wheel.

2   Remove the front parking/turn signal light (see Chapter 12).

3   Detach the inner fenderwell screws and clips, then remove the inner fenderwell and mud shield (see illustrations).

4   Open the front door, and remove the upper fender-to-body bolt and the bolts in the door jamb (see illustrations).

5   Remove the lower fender-to-body bolt (see illustration).

6   Remove the fender-to-bumper cover fasteners (see Section 12), then remove the remaining fender mounting bolts (see illustrations).

7   Lift off the fender. It's a good idea to have an assistant support the fender while it's being moved away from the vehicle to prevent damage to the surrounding body panels.

8   Installation is the reverse of removal. Check the alignment of the fender to the hood and front edge of the door before final tightening of the fender fasteners.

13.3a Remove the bolts at the front lower portion of the inner fenderwell

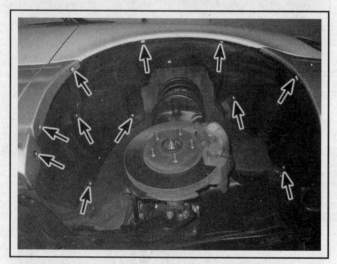

13.3b Detach the main portion of the inner fenderwell, secured by bolts, screws and plastic clips

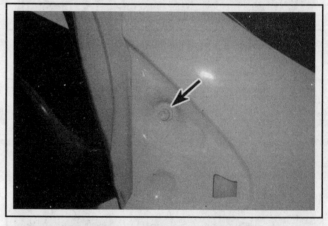

13.4a Remove the upper fender bolt with the door open . . .

13.4b . . . then remove these two bolts in the door jamb area

13.5 Remove the bottom bolt retaining the fender to the rocker panel area

13.6a With the parking/turn signal light housing removed (see Chapter 12), remove the front fender-to-brace bolt

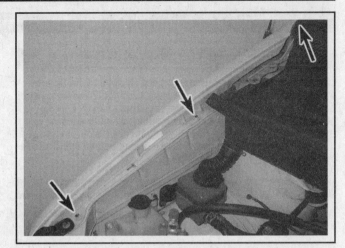

13.6b Remove the three bolts along the top of the fender

14 Fuel door cable - removal and installation

▶ Refer to illustrations 14.2, 14.5 and 14.6

1   Disconnect the negative battery cable.
2   Remove the rear fenderwell liner (see Section 13). Twist the fuel door latch cable end (white plastic part) one quarter-turn counterclockwise and pull it from the fuel door housing (see illustration).
3   Pry up the driver's side doorsill covers. Remove the center door pillar's lower trim panel.
4   Peel back the carpeting to access the release cable. Open all of the clips holding the cable to the body.
5   Remove the two screws holding the release handle assembly to the floor (see illustration).
6   Turn the housing over and remove the cable housings from the clips and the eyes from the levers (see illustration).
7   Attach a piece of thin wire to the end of the cable.
8   Working in the rear fenderwell, pull the cable towards the rear of the vehicle until you can see the wire.
9   Attach the wire to the front of the new cable and fish it back through the body until it can be attached to the lever. The remainder of the installation is the reverse of removal.

14.2 Twist the cable end to disconnect the cable from the fuel door latch

14.5 Remove the screw holding the fuel door release assembly to the floor

14.6 Remove the cable from the clip and detach the cable eye from the slot in the lever

15 Door trim panels - removal and installation

✳✳ WARNING:

The models covered by this manual are equipped with Supplemental Restraint systems (SRS), more commonly known as airbags. Always disconnect the negative battery cable, then the positive battery cable and wait two minutes before working in the vicinity of any airbag system component to avoid the possibility of accidental deployment of the airbag, which could cause personal injury (see Chapter 12).

✳✳ CAUTION:

Wear gloves when working inside the door openings to protect against cuts from sharp metal edges.

REMOVAL

Front door trim panels

2006 and earlier models

▶ **Refer to illustrations 15.1, 15.2, 15.3, 15.5 and 15.7**

1   On manual window models, remove the window crank handle (see illustration).

2   Remove the screw retaining the inside door handle trim and pry the trim bezel out with a taped screwdriver or trim tool (see illustration).

3   On power window/door lock models, disengage the spring clip at the front of the switch plate and unplug the electrical connectors (see illustration), then remove the plate and disconnect the electrical connectors.

15.1 On models equipped with manual windows, remove the window crank handle by working a cloth behind it to release the clip

15.2 Remove the screw in the inside handle trim bezel

15.3 Push a thin screwdriver into the front of the switch plate to disengage the spring clip, then pull the plate up and disconnect the electrical connectors

15.5 Remove the door panel screws, then carefully use a trim panel tool to pry all around the panel and release the clips

15.7 Carefully peel back the plastic watershield for access to the inner door

4 Remove the armrest by carefully pulling it straight up.
5 Remove the door trim panel retaining screws, then carefully pry the panel out until the clips disengage (see illustration). Work slowly and carefully around the outer edge of the trim panel until it's free.

➡Note: Most of the screws on the door panel are covered by small plastic discs, which must be pried out before removing the screws.

6 Once all of the clips are disengaged, pull the trim panel up from the door, unplug any wiring harness connectors and remove the panel.
7 For access to the door outside handle or the door window regulator inside the door, raise the window fully, then carefully peel back the plastic watershield (see illustration). Remove the power window control unit (if equipped), the door panel bracket and the speaker assembly as necessary (see Chapter 12).

2007 and later models

▶ Refer to illustrations 15.8, 15.9, 15.10a, 15.10b, 15.10c, 15.11, 15.12 and 15.14

8 Use a plastic trim tool or a screwdriver wrapped with tape to pry off the cover from the outside mirror. Start at the top, then lift it off (see illustration).
9 Use the same tool to release the inside door handle bezel and remove it (see illustration). Remove the screw under the bezel.
10 Remove the screws from the power window switch plate (see illustration). First use the trim tool to pry the plate up at the rear, then slide it rearward to disengage the clip at the front (see illustrations).
11 Disconnect the window switch wiring. Remove the switch from the armrest. Use pliers to remove the pins and the armrest. The armrest inner frame can be removed now (see illustration).

15.8 Use a plastic tool or a screwdriver wrapped with tape to carefully pry off the inside mirror trim

15.9 Pry out the handle trim bezel - there's a screw under it that must be removed

15.10a Remove the screws from the top of the arm rest

15.10b Carefully pry up the rear of the arm rest until it disengages . . .

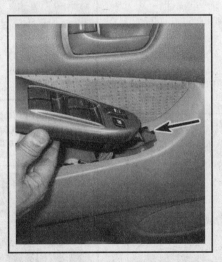

15.10c . . . then slide the arm rest to the rear until the front section is unclipped

15.11 Remove the inner arm rest brace

12 Remove the screw at each of the upper corners of the door panel (see illustration). Also remove the clip near the rear screw.

13 Use a plastic trim tool or a screwdriver wrapped with tape to release the 9 clips around the perimeter of the panel, then lift the panel upwards as you remove it and disconnect the remaining wiring.

14 Disconnect the cables from the inside handle (see illustration).

Sliding door trim panel

2006 and earlier models

▶ **Refer to illustration 15.16**

15 Remove the cupholder, using a trim tool to pry out the two clips, then remove the one screw located behind the cupholder.

16 The door panel is retained by ten clips. Carefully use a taped screwdriver or trim tool to pry all around the door panel, then pull the panel off (see illustration).

2007 and later models

17 Remove the screws from the window switch, then use a plastic trim tool or a screwdriver wrapped with tape to release the clips and remove the window switch.

18 Remove the screw from the bottom of the door panel.

19 Carefully pry the door panel off using the same trim tool.

20 Installation is the reverse of removal.

Liftgate trim panel

2006 and earlier models

▶ **Refer to illustration 15.21**

21 Remove the screws and the liftgate assist handle and pull strap (see illustration).

22 The liftgate panel is retained by eleven clips. Carefully use a taped screwdriver or trim tool to pry all around the panel, then pull the panel off.

2007 and later models

23 Use a plastic trim tool or a screwdriver wrapped with tape to carefully pry off the center and side door moldings.

24 Pry off the cover of the pull strap, then remove the strap bolt and remove the strap.

25 Use the same tool to carefully disengage the 14 clips that secure the door panel. Lift it off.

26 Installation is the reverse of removal.

INSTALLATION

27 Prior to installation of the door trim panel, be sure to reinstall any clips in the panel which may have come out when you removed the panel.

28 Plug in the wire harness connectors for the power door lock switch and the power window switch, if equipped, and place the panel in position in the door. Press the door panel into place until the clips are seated. Install the inner door handle and its screw. Install the power door lock switch assembly, if equipped, or the pull-pocket and its screw. Install the window regulator crank handle or power window switch assembly.

15.12 Upper door panel plastic fastener

15.14 After prying the door panel fasteners loose around its perimeter, lift it up and pull the cables out of their retainers - they can then be detached from the door handle

15.21 Remove the assist grip and door pull strap on the liftgate trim panel

15.16 Use a trim tool to pry out the clips for the sliding door trim panel - there is also one screw in the cupholder

16 Front door - removal, installation and adjustment

※※ WARNING:

The models covered by this manual are equipped with Supplemental Restraint systems (SRS), more commonly known as airbags. Always disconnect the negative battery cable, then the positive battery cable and wait two minutes before working in the vicinity of any airbag system component to avoid the possibility of accidental deployment of the airbag, which could cause personal injury (see Chapter 12).

※※ CAUTION:

Wear gloves when working inside the door openings to protect against cuts from sharp metal edges.

➡Note: The door is heavy and somewhat awkward to remove and install - at least two people should perform this procedure.

REMOVAL AND INSTALLATION

▶ **Refer to illustrations 16.6 and 16.8**

1 Lower the window completely in the door and then disconnect the negative cable from the battery.

2 Open the door all the way and support it from the ground on jacks or blocks covered with rags to prevent damaging the paint.

3 Remove the door trim panel and watershield as described in Section 15.

4 Disconnect all electrical connections, ground wires and harness retaining clips from the door.

➡Note: It is a good idea to label all connections to aid the reassembly process.

5 From the door side, detach the rubber conduit between the body and the door. Then pull the wiring harness through the conduit hole and remove it from the door.

6 Remove the door stop strut bolt (see illustration).

7 Mark around the door hinges with a pen or a scribe to facilitate realignment during reassembly.

8 With an assistant holding the door, remove the hinge-to-door bolts (see illustration) and lift the door off.

➡Note: Draw a reference line around the hinges before removing the bolts.

9 Installation is the reverse of removal.

ADJUSTMENT

▶ **Refer to illustration 16.13**

10 Having proper door-to-body alignment is a critical part of a well-functioning door assembly. First check the door hinge pins for excessive play. Fully open the door and lift up and down on the door without lifting the body. If a door has 1/16-inch or more excessive play, the hinges should be replaced.

11 Door-to-body alignment adjustments are made by loosening the hinge-to-body bolts or hinge-to-door bolts and moving the door. Proper body alignment is achieved when the top of the doors are parallel with the roof section, the front door is flush with the fender, the rear door is flush with the rear quarter panel and the bottom of the doors are aligned with the lower rocker panel. If these goals can't be reached by adjusting the hinge-to-body or hinge-to-door bolts, body alignment shims may have to be purchased and inserted behind the hinges to achieve correct alignment.

12 To adjust the door-closed position, scribe a line or mark around the striker plate to provide a reference point, then check that the door latch is contacting the center of the latch striker. If not adjust the up and down position first.

13 Finally adjust the latch striker sideways position, so that the door panel is flush with the center pillar or rear quarter panel and provides positive engagement with the latch mechanism (see illustration).

16.6 Remove the bolt retaining the door stop strut

16.8 Remove the door hinge bolts with the door supported (top hinge indicated, bottom hinge similar)

16.13 Adjust the door lock striker by loosening the mounting screws and gently tapping the striker in the desired direction

17 Door latch, lock cylinder and handle - removal and installation

✳✳ CAUTION:

Wear gloves when working inside the door openings to protect against cuts from sharp metal edges.

DOOR LATCH

▶ **Refer to illustrations 17.2 and 17.4**

1 Raise the window, then remove the door trim panel and watershield (see Section 15).

2006 and earlier models

2 Working through the large access hole, disengage the outside door handle-to-latch rod, outside door lock-to-latch rod, and the inside handle-to-latch rod (see illustration).

3 All door lock rods are attached by plastic clips. The plastic clips can be removed by unsnapping the portion engaging the connecting rod and then pulling the rod out of its locating hole. On models with power door locks, disconnect the electrical connectors at the latch.

17.2 Typical arrangement of actuating rods leading to the latch

17.4 The latch is secured to the end of the door with three screws

All models

4 Remove the screws securing the latch to the door (see illustration). Remove the latch assembly through the door opening.

5 Installation is the reverse of removal.

OUTSIDE HANDLE AND DOOR LOCK CYLINDER

6 To remove the outside handle and lock cylinder assembly, raise the window and remove the door trim panel and watershield (see Section 15).

✳✳ CAUTION:

Take care not to scratch the paint on the outside of the door. Wide masking tape applied around the handle opening before beginning the procedure can help avoid scratches.

2006 and earlier models

▶ **Refer to illustration 17.7**

7 Working through the access hole, disengage the plastic clips that secure the outside door lock-to-latch rod, and the bolts holding the lock and handle assembly (see illustration).

➡ **Note: The handle can be unbolted and pulled toward the outside of the door to make disconnecting the lock rod easier.**

2007 and later models

8 Remove the outside handle cover by pushing it rearward, then pulling it out.

9 Disconnect the bottom of the lock rod.

10 Remove the handle mounting bolt from inside the door, then slide the handle to remove it.

All models

11 Remove the handle and lock cylinder assembly from the vehicle. The lock cylinder can be removed from the handle assembly by removing a clip, or the electrical connector can be unbolted and the cylinder left on the handle assembly.

12 Installation is the reverse of removal.

17.7 From inside the door opening, detach the actuating rod and one of the retaining bolts - the second retaining bolt is at the jamb end of the door

INSIDE DOOR HANDLE

▶ **Refer to illustration 17.14**

➡**Note: This procedure applies only to 2007 and earlier models. The inside door handles on later models are removed when the door panel is removed.**

13 Raise the window and remove the door trim panel and watershield (see Section 15).

14 Remove the one bolt, then pull the handle out, allowing access to disconnect the two linkage rods (see illustration).

15 Installation is the reverse of removal.

17.14 Remove the inside door handle assembly from the door, then disconnect the two rods

18 Sliding door - removal, installation and adjustment

2006 AND EARLIER MODELS

▶ **Refer to illustrations 18.2, 18.3, 18.4 and 18.5**

➡**Note: The door is heavy and awkward. There should be at least two people to help.**

1 Refer to Section 15 and remove the door trim panel.

2 Remove the one screw, then use a screwdriver to pry the plastic molding covering the center door rail (see illustration).

3 Remove the quarter panel trim to access the mounting bolts for the center hinge. Remove the hinge (see illustration).

4 At the lower front of the door, remove the bolts and the lower roller assembly (see illustration).

5 At the top, remove the bolts and the upper roller, then lift the door from the vehicle (see illustration).

18.2 Remove the one screw at the rear of the sliding door, then carefully pry off the center rail molding

18.3 Remove the bolts and detach the hinge from the center rail

18.4 With the door supported, remove the bolts and the lower roller

18.5 Remove the upper roller mounting bolts to release the door

6 Installation is the reverse of removal.

7 Following installation of the door, check the alignment and, if necessary, adjust it as follows:

a) *Up and down and forward-and-backward adjustments for the rear of the door are made at the center hinge by removing the door trim panel and the rear lock striker, then loosening the hinge mounting bolts. Close the door and adjust the hinge to achieve the specified clearance.*

b) *The door can be adjusted up-and-down at the front by loosening the lower roller mounting bolts and moving the door as necessary (see illustration 18.4).*

c) *Adjust the top of the door in-or-out by loosening the upper roller adjusting bolts until the clearance between upper roller and the rails are as shown (see illustration 18.5).*

d) *Adjust the bottom of the door in-or-out by loosening the lower roller adjusting bolt and moving the door as necessary.*

2007 AND LATER MODELS

8 Use a plastic trim tool or a screwdriver wrapped with tape to carefully pry up the two foot scuff plates.

9 Remove the interior quarter trim panel with the same tool.

10 Remove the upper rail cushion from the guide rail.

11 Disconnect the wiring, then unscrew and remove the wiring harness.

12 Open the quarter glass. Use the trim tool to pry off the molding from the end of the rail.

13 Remove the two mounting bolts, then remove the center bracket and the white tensioner.

14 Remove the two mounting bolts, then remove the center bracket and the black tensioner. Remove both tensioners from the brackets.

15 Remove the two nuts and the open stop plate.

16 Turn the base of the door lower roller, then take the roller out through the cutout area of the lower rail.

❊❊ CAUTION:

The door is heavy and awkward to handle. There should be at least two people to help.

17 Open the slide door. Remove the roller from the cutout area in the rear of the upper door rail.

18 Slide the door farther to the rear, then remove the center hinge from the back of the center door rail. Carefully lift the door off.

19 Installation is the reverse of removal.

19 Liftgate support - removal and installation

▶ **Refer to illustrations 19.2a and 19.2b**

➡**Note: This procedure applies only to early models without a power liftgate.**

1 Open the liftgate and support it with a sturdy prop.

2 Remove the clips from each end of the support, then detach the support from the vehicle (see illustrations).

3 Installation is the reverse of removal. Always replace the supports in pairs.

19.2a Pry out this clip to detach the support from the door . . .

19.2b . . . and pry out this clip to release the support from the lower mount

20 Liftgate - removal, installation and adjustment

♦ **Refer to illustrations 20.5 and 20.9**

➡**Note: This procedure applies only to early models without a power liftgate.**

1   Open the liftgate and cover the upper body area around the opening with pads or cloths to protect the painted surfaces when the liftgate is removed.

2   Disconnect all cables and wire harness connectors that would interfere with removal of the liftgate.

3   Paint or scribe around the hinge flanges.

4   While an assistant (or two) supports the liftgate, detach the liftgate struts (see Section 19).

5   Remove the hinge bolts (see illustration) and detach the liftgate from the vehicle.

6   Installation is the reverse of removal.

7   After installation, close the liftgate and make sure it's aligned with the surrounding body panels.

8   Up-and-down adjustments are made by moving the position of the hinge bolts in the slots. To adjust it, loosen the hinge bolts and reposition the hinges either side-to-side or fore-and-aft the desired amount, then retighten the bolts.

9   The engagement of the liftgate can be adjusted by loosening the lock striker bolts, repositioning the striker and retightening the bolts (see illustration).

20.5 Remove the upper liftgate hinge bolts and remove the liftgate

20.9 Loosen the screws and move the striker to adjust the liftgate-closed position

21 Door window glass - removal and installation

⁕ CAUTION:

Wear gloves when working inside the door openings to protect against cuts from sharp metal edges.

21.3 Remove the two glass mounting bolts

FRONT DOOR GLASS

♦ **Refer to illustration 21.3**

1   Remove the door trim panel and the plastic watershield (see Section 15).

2   Lower the window glass all the way down into the door.

3   Raise the window just enough to access the window retaining bolts through the holes in the door frame (see illustrations).

4   Place a rag over the glass to help prevent scratching the glass and remove the two glass-mounting bolts.

5   Remove the glass by pulling it up and out.

6   Installation is the reverse of removal.

SLIDING SIDE DOOR AND LIFTGATE GLASS

7   Replacement of the sliding door and liftgate glass requires the use of special fast-setting adhesive/caulk materials and some specialized tools and techniques. These operations should be left to a dealer service department or a shop specializing in glass work.

22 Door window glass regulator - removal and installation

▶ Refer to illustration 22.4

✳✳ **CAUTION:**

Wear gloves when working inside the door openings to protect against cuts from sharp metal edges.

1 Remove the door trim panel and the plastic watershield (see Section 15).

2 Remove the window glass (see Section 21).

3 On power-operated windows, disconnect the electrical connector from the window regulator motor.

4 Remove the regulator assembly mounting bolts (see illustration). On models with power windows, the motor should come out with the regulator.

➡Note: On some models the regulator may be retained by rivets. Drill out the rivets to remove the regulator.

5 If the motor is to be removed from a power-window assembly, mark both the regulator gear and the motor bracket for alignment during installation.

6 Pull the equalizer arm and regulator assemblies through the service hole in the doorframe to remove it.

7 Installation is the reverse of removal. Lubricate the rollers, gears and wear points on the regulator with white grease before installation. Do not grease the regulator spring.

22.4 Remove the window regulator/motor assembly mounting bolts or rivets

23 Swing-out quarter-window glass - removal and installation

▶ Refer to illustrations 23.6 and 23.8

➡Note: This procedure applies only to 2006 and earlier models.

1 Remove the rear seats (see Section 29).

➡Note: To remove the right-side quarter-window glass requires the removal of the vehicle headliner, which in turn requires the removal of most of the interior panels. It is suggested that this job be handled at a dealer service department or other repair shop to avoid damage to the headliner.

2 To remove the left-side quarter-window glass, first remove the screws and the trim panel covering the bottom of the liftgate opening.

3 Pry the rear speaker cover from the quarter trim panel, then remove the speaker mounting screws, disconnect the electrical connector and remove the speaker.

4 Using a taped screwdriver or a trim tool, pry up the trim around the seat belt.

5 Remove and disconnect the courtesy lights.

6 Remove the screws, pry out the clips and remove the quarter trim panel (see illustration).

7 Remove the trim panels just ahead of and just behind the rear quarter glass.

8 Remove the two bolts at the lock end of the glass, then the two nuts at the hinged end and remove the glass. On models with power quarter glass, Remove the two bolts securing the motor to the body, and remove the clip to release the motor lever from the window, then remove the screw from the hinge end (see illustration).

9 Installation is the reverse of the removal procedure.

23.6 Rear quarter trim panel clip and screw locations (five-door model shown)

23.8 Remove the bolts and clip at the opening end on power quarter-glass models

24 Mirrors - removal and installation

OUTSIDE MIRRORS

♦ Refer to illustration 24.3

1   On power mirror equipped models, remove the door trim panel and the plastic watershield (see Section 15). Remove the access hole cover on 2007 and later models.

2   Disconnect the electrical connector from the mirror (if equipped).

3   Remove the three mirror retaining bolts and detach the mirror from the vehicle (see illustration).

4   Installation is the reverse of removal.

INSIDE MIRROR

2006 and earlier models

♦ Refer to illustration 24.5

5   Push a very thin screwdriver or a thick feeler gauge blade into the bottom of the mirror mount (see illustration). Wiggle the mirror upward to remove it from the mount.

6   To install the mirror, reinsert the spring if it was removed earlier. Slide the mirror base onto the mount, pushing downward until the mirror is secured.

2007 and later models

7   Disconnect the wiring from the mirror if so equipped. Remove the screw at the base of the mirror.

8   Slide the mirror upward to remove it. Installation is the reverse of removal.

All models

9   If the mount plate itself has come off the windshield, adhesive kits are available at auto parts stores to resecure it. Follow the instructions included with the kit.

24.3 Remove the three mirror mounting bolts - on electric mirrors, trace the electrical harness down into the door and disconnect the connector

24.5 While pulling up on the inside mirror, push a screwdriver into the slot in the bottom of the base to release it

25 Dashboard trim panels

✳✳ WARNING:

The models covered by this manual are equipped with Supplemental Restraint systems (SRS), more commonly known as airbags. Always disconnect the negative battery cable, then the positive battery cable and wait two minutes before working in the vicinity of any airbag system component to avoid the possibility of accidental deployment of the airbag, which could cause personal injury (see Chapter 12).

1   Disconnect the negative battery cable, then the positive cable.

INSTRUMENT CLUSTER BEZEL

2006 and earlier models

♦ Refer to illustrations 25.2a, 25.2b, 25.3a, 25.3b, 25.3c, 25.3d, 25.4a and 25.4b

2   If equipped with tilt steering, lower the column as far down as it will go. Refer to Section 26 and remove the steering column covers. Disconnect the shift lever from the column (see illustrations).

3   With the knee bolster removed (see below) remove the three

25.2a Remove the Torx bolt securing the shift lever to the steering column

25.2b Disconnect the electrical connector for the Overdrive switch on the shift lever, then remove the lever

25.3a Remove these two retaining screws at the bottom of the bezel to the right of the steering column . . .

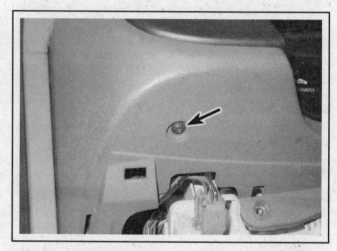

25.3b . . . and this screw to the left of the steering column

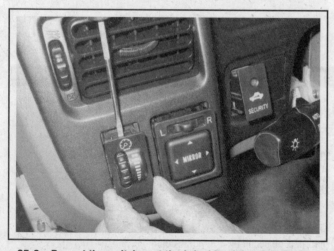

25.3c Pry out the switches at the left side of the cluster bezel and pull them out far enough to disconnect the electrical connectors

25.3d The switches at the right side of the bezel are mounted from behind - pull the bezel out far enough to disconnect these connectors from the back

screws at the bottom of the instrument cluster bezel (see illustrations). On 2001 and later models, remove the upper screws and the upper bezel trim before removing the instrument cluster bezel. Remove or disconnect the switches mounted to the instrument cluster bezel (see illustrations).

4   Using a screwdriver with the tip taped with masking tape, carefully pry the lower portion of the bezel away from the instrument panel until the clips are released. Take care not to scratch the surrounding trim on the instrument panel (see illustrations).

5   Installation is the reverse of the removal procedure. Make sure the clips are engaged properly before pushing the bezel firmly into place.

2007 and later models

6   Move the steering wheel to the down position.

7   Remove the two push-pin clips from the top of the bezel.

8   Pull the instrument cluster bezel to the rear to release the lower clips and remove it.

9   Installation is the reverse of removal.

KNEE BOLSTER

▶ **Refer to illustrations 25.11a, 25.11b, 25.11c and 25.12**

10 Remove the screws holding the hood-release lever to the knee bolster (see Section 11).

11 Remove the two lower bolts. There are clips and/or hooks that can be released by pulling the top of the panel rearward (see illustrations).

25.4a Before the bezel can be removed completely, disconnect the electrical connector for the ignition switch light

25.4b The instrument cluster bezel can be removed using a trim tool to separate the clips around the perimeter - the three top arrows here indicate hooks (2006 and earlier models)

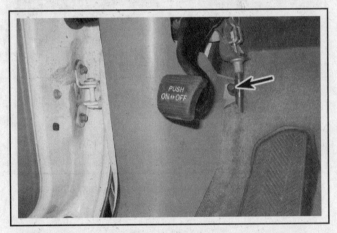

25.11a Remove the screw and pull out the driver's side kick panel

25.11b Remove the two knee bolster bolts

25.11c Pull the bolster away from the dash until the tabs clear the slots

25.12 Remove these two bolts and remove the reinforcement panel

12 Remove the retaining bolts securing the knee bolster reinforcement, if needed for access to components under the dashboard (see illustration). Pull outward on the lower edge of the knee bolster reinforcement panel and detach it from the vehicle.

13 Installation is the reverse of removal.

CENTER TRIM PANELS

2006 and earlier models

▶ Refer to illustrations 25.14a, 25.14b, 25.15a and 25.15b

14 Pry the center instrument panel trim bezel (trim that surrounds the radio) carefully from the dashboard with a taped screwdriver (see illustrations).

15 If the panel below the dash (that holds the radio and ashtray) is to be removed, remove the radio (see Chapter 12) and the ashtray, then remove the lower center trim panel screws (see illustrations).

16 Installation is the reverse of removal.

25.14a Pry the center bezel away from the clips (2006 and earlier models)

25.14b Pull the panel out far enough to disconnect the electrical connectors

25.15a Remove the four screws to remove the lower center trim panel

25.15b Pull the lower center trim panel forward and disconnect the electrical connectors

2007 and later models

♦ Refer to illustrations 25.17, 25.19, 25.20a, 25.20b, 25.21, 25,23a, 25.23b, 25.24a, 25.24b, 25.24c and 25.24d

17 The top trim panel above the radio can be removed by inserting a plastic trim tool or a screwdriver wrapped with tape at the top center of the curved panel. Pry the panel up to release the center hooks and the side clips (see illustration).

18 With the top and front of the panel loose, release the five hooks at the top of the radio. Remove the panel. Carefully pry off the side panel on each side of the radio.

19 To remove the sound system and heater control bezels, use a the trim tool to release the three clips at the left side of the bezel (see illustration). Disconnect the wiring as you detach the bezel from the right side.

20 To remove the center trim panel, first unscrew the shifter knob, then release the four hooks at the shift lever base cover. Remove the base cover. The trim cover can now be pried loose (see illustrations).

21 Remove the screw at the right top of the center panel that was concealed by the sound system bezel (see illustration). Release the five clips and the hook that retain the trim panel using a plastic trim tool or a screwdriver wrapped with tape.

22 Disconnect the wiring as you remove the panel.

25.17 Carefully pry the forward part of the radio top trim up enough to release the hooks at the rear edge

23 Remove the two clips from each side of the lower panel assembly (see illustration). Remove the six bolts and screws from the inner part of the assembly and slide it rearward (see illustration). Disconnect the wiring as you remove the panel assembly.

25.19 The panels on each side of the panel can be pried loose for access to the radio

25.20a The shifter knob unscrews by hand

25.20b The shifter bezel can be pried off using a plastic trim tool, but a screwdriver wrapped with electrical tape will also work

25.21 Remove the single screw (arrow) before prying off the center trim panel

25.23a The pins for the lower trim panel (A) and the inner kick panels (B)

25.23b The lower trim panel is secured by the side clips and 6 additional screws (3 shown)

25.24a The upper storage compartment can be pulled directly rearward to remove it

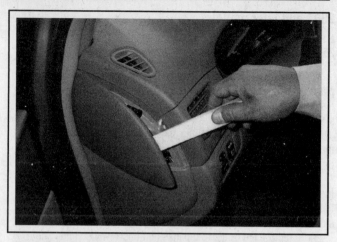

25.24b Both end caps are removed by prying with a plastic tool to avoid scratching them

25.24c The air registers on each end of the instrument panel pull straight to the rear for removal

25.24d Pry up on the rear portion of the speaker grilles, then release the hooks at the front

25.25a Remove the screw and pull the passenger kick panel out

25.25b Remove the two screws at the passenger lower sound panel . . .

25.25c . . . then pry panel off the clips at the top

24 The upper storage compartment, the air registers, speaker grilles and the instrument panel end caps can be removed by prying them off (see illustrations).

PASSENGER'S SIDE LOWER PANEL AND GLOVE BOX

2006 and earlier models

▸ **Refer to illustrations 25.25a, 25.25b, 25.25c and 25.26**

25 The passenger's side lower panel is held in place under the glove box area by bolts and clips (see illustrations). Remove the bolts and pry the panel away from the clips.

26 Disconnect the airbag connector inside the glove box (see the airbag Warning at the beginning of this Section). Remove the three nuts below the glove box door, then the screws inside and remove the door (see illustration).

27 Installation is the reverse of the removal procedure.

2007 and later models

▸ **Refer to illustrations 25.29 and 25.30**

28 Use a plastic trim tool or a screwdriver wrapped with tape to release the two hooks and four clips securing the panel beneath the glove box.

29 Open the glove box and push inward on both sides of it (see illustration).

30 Pull the glove box fully open and disconnect the arm on the right side, then pull it rearward to remove it (see illustration).

WINDSHIELD PILLAR COVERS

▸ **Refer to illustration 25.31**

31 On most models, the A-pillar (windshield) covers can be removed by prying them with a plastic trim tool or a screwdriver wrapped with tape. On models with airbags mounted in these locations, there is a cover that can be pried loose to reveal a screw beneath (see illustration).

25.26 Remove the lower glove box mounting nuts, then the two screws inside

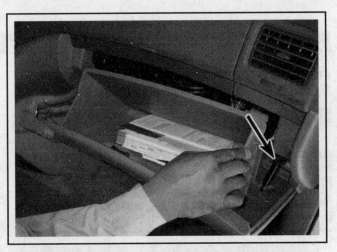

25.29 Press inward on each side of the glove box to allow it to open fully - the support (arrow) can then be disconnected

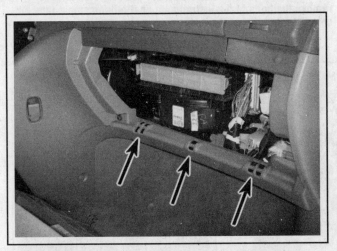

25.30 Pull the glove box rearward to detach it at these hinge points

25.31 The windshield pillar screws are under these covers; when the screws are removed, the covers can be carefully pried off - never touch the windshield with any metal tool

26 Steering column covers - removal and installation

♦ Refer to illustration 26.2

❊❊ WARNING:

The models covered by this manual are equipped with Supplemental Restraint systems (SRS), more commonly known as airbags. Always disconnect the negative battery cable, then the positive battery cable and wait two minutes before working in the vicinity of any airbag system component to avoid the possibility of accidental deployment of the airbag, which could cause personal injury (see Chapter 12).

1 On tilt steering columns, move the column to the lowest position. Refer to Chapter 10 and remove the steering wheel.

2 Remove the screws, then separate the halves and remove the upper and lower steering column covers (see illustration).

3 Installation is the reverse of the removal procedure.

26.2 Remove the screws, then remove the upper and lower steering column covers

27 Instrument panel - removal and installation

♦ Refer to illustrations 27.8a, 27.8b, 27.8c, 27.9a, 27.9b, 27.10a, 27.10b, 27.10c and 27.11

❊❊ WARNING:

The models covered by this manual are equipped with Supplemental Restraint systems (SRS), more commonly known as airbags. Always disconnect the negative battery cable, then the positive battery cable and wait two minutes before working in the vicinity of any airbag system component to avoid the possibility of accidental deployment of the airbag, which could cause personal injury (see Chapter 12).

1 Disconnect the negative battery cable, then the positive battery cable.

2 Remove the dashboard trim panels (see Section 25). Also remove the instrument cluster (see Chapter 12) and the glove box (see Section 25).

3 Disconnect the passenger's side air bag and remove it (see Chapter 12).

4 Remove the audio unit from the center of the dashboard (see Chapter 12).

5 Remove the air conditioning control panel (see Chapter 3).

6 Remove the driver's knee bolster and reinforcement panel (see Section 25).

7 Use a trim tool to pry off the windshield pillar trim panels and disconnect the small tweeter speakers, if equipped.

8 A number of electrical connectors must be disconnected in order to remove the instrument panel. Most are designed so that they will only fit on the matching male or female connector (see illustrations).

9 In the area where the instrument cluster had been mounted, disconnect the electrical connectors (see illustrations).

10 Remove all of the fasteners (bolts, screws and nuts) holding the instrument panel to the body (see illustrations).

11 Lift the panel then pull it away from the windshield and take it out through the driver's door opening (see illustration).

➡Note: This is a two-person job, and you may also have to remove the bolts to the instrument panel reinforcement tube for complete removal of the instrument panel.

12 Installation is the reverse of removal.

27.8a Label and disconnect the main instrument panel electrical connectors in the left kick panel area . . .

27.8b . . . and the right kick panel area

27.8c Disconnect the two largest connectors at the interior fuse panel

27.9a Disconnect this connector just above the fuse box . . .

27.9b . . . and these two connectors in the right side of the instrument cluster opening

27.10a Remove these bolts at the left side of the instrument panel (lower left bolt not visible in this photo) . . .

27.10b . . . two more at the right side of the panel . . .

27.10c . . . and these five bolts in the glove box area

27.11 Pull the instrument panel up and back, then have an assistant help you take it out of the car

28 Cowl covers - removal and installation

1   Remove the wiper arms (see Chapter 12).

2006 AND EARLIER MODELS

▶ **Refer to illustrations 28.2a, 28.2b, 28.3, 28.4a and 28.4b**

2   Remove the two pushpins, one at each end near the fender (see illustration). Carefully pry up the cowl rubber seal with a trim tool (see illustration).

3   Disconnect the washers hoses and nozzles from the grille panels and remove them (see illustration).

4   Remove the bolts, disconnect the electrical connector at the wiper motor, then lift out the cowl top panel (see illustrations).

2007 AND LATER MODELS

5   Release the six hooks, then pull off the upper plastic cowl.

6   Refer to Chapter 12 and remove the wiper motor assembly.

➡**Note: Refer to Chapter 2B, Section 4 for more information about the lower cowl assembly.**

7   Remove the inner cowl brace.

8   Remove the mounting nut from the fuel pump resistor bracket, then set the resistor aside.

9   Detach the wiring harness from the cowl.

10   Remove the seven mounting bolts from the front lower cowl section and lift it carefully out of the engine compartment.

ALL MODELS

11   Installation is the reverse of removal. Before installing a pushpin, raise the center part of the pin all the way up, then insert the pushpin. Lock it in place by pushing down on the center until it is flush with the body of the pin.

28.2a Depress the center then pry up the plastic push pins to remove the cowl cover vents . . .

28.2b . . . then remove the rubber sealing strip - squeeze the clips underneath and pull up as you go

28.3 Disconnect the hose(s) from the washer nozzles

28.4a Remove the bolts securing the cowl top panel to the cowl at the right . . .

28.4b . . . and the left sides of the cowl

29 Seats - removal and installation

FRONT SEAT

◆ **Refer to illustrations 29.2a and 29.2b**

⁂ **WARNING:**

The front seat belts on some models are equipped with pre-tensioners, which are pyrotechnic (explosive) devices designed to retract the seat belts in the event of a collision. On models equipped with pre-tensioners, do not remove the front seat belt retractor assemblies, and do not disconnect the electrical connectors leading to the assemblies. Problems with the pre-tensioners will turn on the SRS (airbag) warning light on the dash. If any pre-tensioner problems are suspected, take the vehicle to a dealer service department. The same models also have side-impact airbags that are located in the exterior side of the front seats. Do not remove the front seats without first disabling the airbag system (see Chapter 12) and do not disassemble the seats.

1   Pry off the plastic covers to access the rear mounting bolts. On 2007 and later models, remove the headrests.

2   Remove the retaining bolts (see illustrations).

3   Tilt the seat upward to access the underside, then disconnect any electrical connectors and lift the seat from the vehicle.

4   Installation is the reverse of removal.

REAR SEAT

2006 and earlier models

▶ Refer to illustration 29.7

5   Some models are equipped with bucket-type seats in the rear seat position. These are removed in much the same manner as the front seats.

6   On models with a bench-type rear seat, push the seatback lever and fold down the seatback.

7   Pull up the two seat-release levers at the bottom rear of the bench seat and pull the seat from the floor (see illustration).

8   Installation is the reverse of removal. Hook the front legs of the seat to the floor before inserting and locking the rear legs.

2007 and later models

9   Remove the headrest.

10   Remove the seat belt hold-down plate if necessary, then remove the seat. Installation is the reverse of removal.

THIRD SEAT

2006 and earlier models

▶ Refer to illustration 29.13

11   Third seat units are two individual seats mounted tightly side-by-side. Each can be moved forward or back independent of the other.

12   Tuck the center seat belt under the seat back of the right seat, then slide the left seat rearward.

13   Fold down the seatback. Pull up the left lever and hold it while pulling the center handle to release the seat from the floor (see illustration). The right seat can be removed in the same manner.

14   Installation is the reverse of removal. Hook the front legs of the seat to the floor before inserting and locking the rear legs.

29.2a Typical front seat track retaining bolts (the bolt covers have been removed)

29.2b Remove the rear bolts for the front seat (bolt covers have been removed)

⁂ CAUTION:

Make sure the center seat belt doesn't get trapped as the seat is reinstalled.

29.7 Pull up the two levers to release the rear seat from the floor

29.13 While holding up the lever (A), pull the center handles (B) and lift the seat out

2007 and later models

15 For manual seats, release the clips and remove the trim panel from the rear of the seat.

16 Remove the bolt and detach the cable, then remove the two mounting bolts and remove the seat. The procedure is the same for both sides.

17 For power seats, release the clips from the trim panels at the base of the rear of the seats.

18 Also remove the rear seat leg side trim panels and the hinge covers. The hinge covers are retained by hooks and can be pried off.

19 Disconnect the wiring harness, then remove the seat mounting bolts.

20 Operate the lever under the seat and remove the seat. Installation is the reverse of removal.

Section

12

CHASSIS ELECTRICAL SYSTEM

1 General information

The electrical system is a 12-volt, negative ground type. Power for the lights and all electrical accessories is supplied by a lead/acid-type battery that is charged by the alternator.

This Chapter covers repair and service procedures for the various electrical components not associated with the engine. Information on the battery, alternator and starter motor can be found in Chapter 5.

It should be noted that when portions of the electrical system are serviced, the cable should be disconnected from the negative battery terminal to prevent electrical shorts and/or fires.

2 Electrical troubleshooting - general information

♦ Refer to illustrations 2.5a, 2.5b, 2.6, 2.9 and 2.15

A typical electrical circuit consists of an electrical component, any switches, relays, motors, fuses, fusible links or circuit breakers related to that component and the wiring and electrical connectors that link the component to both the battery and the chassis. To help you pinpoint an electrical circuit problem, wiring diagrams are included at the end of this Chapter.

Before tackling any troublesome electrical circuit, first study the appropriate wiring diagrams to get a complete understanding of what makes up that individual circuit. Trouble spots, for instance, can often be narrowed down by noting if other components related to the circuit are operating properly. If several components or circuits fail at one time, chances are the problem is in a fuse or ground connection, because several circuits are often routed through the same fuse and ground connections.

Electrical problems usually stem from simple causes, such as loose or corroded connections, a blown fuse, a melted fusible link or a bad relay. Visually inspect the condition of all fuses, wires and connections in a problem circuit before troubleshooting it.

If testing instruments are going to be utilized, use the diagrams to plan ahead of time where you will make the necessary connections in order to accurately pinpoint the trouble spot.

The basic tools needed for electrical troubleshooting include a circuit tester or voltmeter (a 12-volt bulb with a set of test leads can also be used), a continuity tester, which includes a bulb, battery and set of test leads, and a jumper wire, preferably with a circuit breaker incorporated, which can be used to bypass electrical components (see illustrations). Before attempting to locate a problem with test instruments, use the wiring diagram(s) to decide where to make the connections.

VOLTAGE CHECKS

Voltage checks should be performed if a circuit is not functioning properly. Connect one lead of a circuit tester to either the negative battery terminal or a known good ground. Connect the other lead to an electrical connector in the circuit being tested, preferably nearest to the battery or fuse (see illustration). If the bulb of the tester lights, voltage is present, which means that the part of the circuit between the electrical connector and the battery is problem free. Continue checking the rest of the circuit in the same fashion. When you reach a point at which no voltage is present, the problem lies between that point and the last test point with voltage. Most of the time the problem can be traced to a loose connection.

➡Note: Keep in mind that some circuits receive voltage only when the ignition key is in the Accessory or Run position.

2.5a The most useful tool for electrical troubleshooting is a digital multimeter that can check volts, amps, and continuity

2.5b A test light is very handy for testing voltage

2.6 In use, a basic test light's lead is clipped to a known good ground, then the pointed probe can test connectors, wires or electrical sockets - if the bulb lights, the part being tested has battery voltage

2.9 With a multimeter set to the ohms scale, resistance can be checked across two terminals - when checking for continuity, a low reading indicates continuity, a high reading indicates lack of continuity

2.15 To backprobe a connector, insert a small, sharp probe (such as a straight-pin) into the back of the connector alongside the desired wire until it contacts the metal terminal inside; connect your meter leads to the probes - this allows you to test a circuit in operation

FINDING A SHORT

One method of finding shorts in a circuit is to remove the fuse and connect a test light or voltmeter in its place. There should be no voltage present in the circuit. Move the wiring harness from side to side while watching the test light. If the bulb goes on, there is a short to ground somewhere in that area, probably where the insulation has rubbed through. The same test can be performed on each component in the circuit, even a switch.

GROUND CHECK

Perform a ground test to check whether a component is properly grounded. Disconnect the battery and connect one lead of a self-powered test light, known as a continuity tester, to a known good ground. Connect the other lead to the wire or ground connection being tested. If the bulb goes on, the ground is good. If the bulb does not go on, the ground is not good.

CONTINUITY CHECK

A continuity check is done to determine if there are any breaks in a circuit - if it is passing electricity properly. With the circuit off (no power in the circuit), a self-powered continuity tester can be used to check the circuit. Connect the test leads to both ends of the circuit (or to the "power" end and a good ground), and if the test light comes on the circuit is passing current properly (see illustration). If the light doesn't come on, there is a break somewhere in the circuit. The same procedure can be used to test a switch, by connecting the continuity tester to the power in and power out sides of the switch. With the switch turned On, the test light should come on.

FINDING AN OPEN CIRCUIT

When diagnosing for possible open circuits, it is often difficult to locate them by sight because oxidation or terminal misalignment are hidden by the electrical connectors. Merely wiggling an electrical connector on a sensor or in the wiring harness may correct the open cir-

cuit condition. Remember this when an open circuit is indicated when troubleshooting a circuit. Intermittent problems may also be caused by oxidized or loose connections.

Electrical troubleshooting is simple if you keep in mind that all electrical circuits are basically electricity running from the battery, through the wires, switches, relays, fuses and fusible links to each electrical component (light bulb, motor, etc.) and to ground, from which it is passed back to the battery. Any electrical problem is an interruption in the flow of electricity to and from the battery.

CONNECTORS

Most electrical connections on these vehicles are made with multi-wire plastic connectors. The mating halves of many connectors are secured with locking clips molded into the plastic connector shells. The mating halves of large connectors, such as some of those under the instrument panel, are held together by a bolt through the center of the connector.

To separate a connector with locking clips, use a small screwdriver to pry the clips apart carefully, then separate the connector halves. Pull only on the shell, never pull on the wiring harness as you may damage the individual wires and terminals inside the connectors. Look at the connector closely before trying to separate the halves. Often the locking clips are engaged in a way that is not immediately clear. Additionally, many connectors have more than one set of clips.

Each pair of connector terminals has a male half and a female half. When you look at the end view of a connector in a diagram, be sure to understand whether the view shows the harness side or the component side of the connector. Connector halves are mirror images of each other, and a terminal shown on the right side end view of one half will be on the left side end view of the other half.

It is often necessary to take circuit voltage measurements with a connector connected. Whenever possible, carefully insert the test probes of your meter into the rear of the connector shell to contact the terminal inside. This kind of connection is called "backprobing" (see illustration). When inserting a test probe into a male terminal, be careful not to distort the terminal opening. Doing so can lead to a poor connection and corrosion at that terminal later.

3 Fuses - general information

▶ **Refer to illustrations 3.1a, 3.1b and 3.3**

The electrical circuits of the vehicle are protected by a combination of fuses, circuit breakers and fusible links. Fuse blocks are located under the instrument panel and in the engine compartment depending on the model year of the vehicle (see illustrations). Check your owner's manual for information on your specific model.

Each of the fuses is designed to protect a specific circuit, and the various circuits are identified on the fuse panel cover.

Miniaturized fuses are employed in the fuse blocks. These compact fuses, with blade terminal design, allow fingertip removal and replacement. If an electrical component fails, always check the fuse first. The best way to check a fuse is with a test light. Check for power at the exposed terminal tips of each fuse. If power is present on one side of the fuse but not the other, the fuse is blown. A blown fuse can also be confirmed by visually inspecting it (see illustration).

Be sure to replace blown fuses with the correct type. Fuses of different ratings are physically interchangeable, but only fuses of the proper rating should be used. Replacing a fuse with one of a higher or lower value than specified is not recommended. Each electrical circuit needs a specific amount of protection. The amperage value of each fuse is molded into the fuse body.

If the replacement fuse immediately fails, don't replace it again until the cause of the problem is isolated and corrected. In most cases, this will be a short circuit in the wiring caused by a broken or deteriorated wire.

3.1a The interior fuse box is located on the dashboard, to the left of the steering column (early model shown)

3.1b There are two separate fuse/relay boxes in the left-front area of the engine compartment on early models

3.3 When a fuse blows, the element between the terminals melts

4 Fusible links - general information

Some circuits are protected by fusible links. The links are used in circuits which are not ordinarily fused, such as the ignition circuit, or which carry high current.

Cartridge type fusible links are located in the engine compartment fuse/relay block and are similar to a large fuse and, after disconnecting the negative battery cable, are simply unplugged and replaced by a unit of the same amperage.

On models with Traction Control, a second fusible link box is located on the right side of the radiator support. Some fusible links are held in place by a screw that must be loosened before removing the link.

5 Circuit breakers - general information

Circuit breakers protect components such as power windows, power door locks and headlights.

On some models the circuit breaker resets itself automatically, so an electrical overload in a circuit-breaker-protected system will cause the circuit to fail momentarily, then come back on. If the circuit doesn't come back on, check it immediately. Once the condition is corrected, the circuit breaker will resume its normal function. Some circuit breakers must be reset manually.

6 Relays - general information and testing

GENERAL INFORMATION

1 Several electrical accessories in the vehicle, such as the fuel injection system, horns, starter, air conditioning/heating system and fog lights use relays to transmit the electrical signal to the component. Relays use a low-current circuit (the control circuit) to open and close

a high-current circuit (the power circuit). If the relay is defective, that component will not operate properly. The various relays are mounted in engine compartment fuse/relay boxes (see illustrations 3.1a and 3.1b). Some additional relays are mounted next to the interior fuse panel, but the driver's knee bolster must be removed for access to them (see Chapter 11). If a faulty relay is suspected, it can be removed and tested using the procedure below or by a dealer service department or a repair shop. Defective relays must be replaced as a unit.

➡Note: **Relay identifications are often found on the cover of the relay, and always on a decal on the inside of the fuse/relay box cover.**

TESTING

▶ **Refer to illustrations 6.4a, 6.4b and 6.4c**

2 It's best to refer to the wiring diagram for the circuit to determine the proper hook-ups for the relay you're testing. However, if you're not able to determine the correct hook-up from the wiring diagrams, you may be able to determine the test hook-ups from the information that follows.

3 On most relays, two of the terminals are the relay's control circuit (they connect to the relay coil which, when energized, closes the large contacts to complete the circuit). The other terminals are the power circuit (they are connected together within the relay when the control-circuit coil is energized).

4 The relays are usually marked as an aid to help you determine which terminals are the control circuit and which are the power circuit (see illustrations).

5 Connect a fused jumper wire between one of the two control circuit terminals and the positive battery terminal. Connect another jumper wire between the other control circuit terminal and ground. When the connections are made, the relay should click. On some relays, polarity may be critical, so, if the relay doesn't click, try swapping the jumper wires on the control circuit terminals.

6 With the jumper wires connected, check for continuity between the power circuit terminals as indicated by the markings on the relay.

7 If the relay fails any of the above tests, replace it.

6.4a Diagram and pin identification for a typical four-terminal relay

6.4b Some four-terminal relays are marked with 1, 2, 3 and 5, but they are four-terminal types tested the same as ones marked 1 through 4

6.4c Diagram and pin identification for a typical five-terminal relay

7   Turn signal and hazard flasher - check and replacement

▶ **Refer to illustration 7.1**

1 The turn signal/hazard flasher is contained in a small, canister-shaped unit located in the relay center under the dash near the steering column (see illustration). The knee bolster must be removed for access to the flasher, see Chapter 11.

2 When the flasher unit is functioning properly, an audible click can be heard during its operation. If the turn signal indicator (on the instrument panel) on one side of the vehicle flashes much more rapidly than normal, a faulty turn signal bulb on that side of the vehicle is indicated.

3 If both turn signals fail to blink, the problem may be due to a blown fuse, a faulty flasher unit, a broken switch or a loose or open connection. If a quick check of the fuse box indicates that the turn signal fuse has blown, check the wiring for a short before installing a new fuse.

4 To replace the flasher, simply pull it out of its holder and unplug it.

5 Make sure that the replacement unit is identical to the original. Compare the old one to the new one before installing it.

6 Installation is the reverse of removal.

7.1 Turn signal/hazard flasher location, near the interior fuse panel (shown with driver's knee bolster removed)

8   Steering column switches - check and replacement

☀ WARNING:

The models covered by this manual are equipped with Supplemental Restraint Systems (SRS), more commonly known as airbags. Always disable the airbag system before working in the vicinity of any airbag system components to avoid the possibility of accidental deployment of the airbag(s), which could cause personal injury (see Section 27).

CHECK

▶ **Refer to illustrations 8.3a and 8.3b**

1   There are two column-mounted switches. On the left side is the turn signal/headlight switch, while on the right side is the wiper/washer switch.

2   Trace the wire from the combination switch to the main wiring harness connector and disconnect the connectors.

3   Using an ohmmeter or self-powered test light and the accompanying diagrams, check for continuity between the indicated switch terminals with the switch in each of the indicated positions (see illustrations). If the continuity isn't as specified, replace the switch.

REPLACEMENT

▶ **Refer to illustration 8.8**

4   Disconnect the cable from the negative terminal of the battery.
5   Remove the steering wheel (see Chapter 10).

Combination switch position	Continuity between terminals
Headlight switch Off	None
Headlight switch - taillight	14 and 16
Headlight switch On	13, 14 and 16
Headlight dimmer: low beam	16 and 17
Headlight dimmer: high beam	7 and 16
Flash-to-pass	7, 8 and 16
Turn signal, Left	1 and 2
Turn signal, Neutral	None
Turn signal, Right	2 and 3

8.3a Combination switch connector terminal guide and continuity chart - early models

Washer/wiper switch position	Continuity between terminals
Off	7 and 16
Int	7 and 16
Lo	7 and 17
Hi	8 and 17
Washer On	2 and 11

8.3b Washer/wiper switch connector terminal guide and continuity chart - early models

6   Remove the steering column covers (see Chapter 11).

8.8 Combination switch retaining screws - both

2006 and earlier models

7   Unplug the wiring from the switch.

8   Remove the screws and pull the switch from the column (see illustration).

9   Individual switches can now be removed from the switch body and replaced as necessary. Detach the retaining screws or pins and remove the defective switch.

10 Installation is the reverse of removal.

2007 and later models

11 Detach the connector.

12 Use a plastic trim tool or a screwdriver wrapped with tape to release the plastic hook, then pull the switch out.

✳✳ CAUTION:

The hook can be easily broken.

13 Installation is the reverse of removal.

---

9   Ignition switch and lock cylinder - check and replacement

✳✳ WARNING:

The models covered by this manual are equipped with Supplemental Restraint Systems (SRS), more commonly known as airbags. Always disable the airbag system before working in the vicinity of any airbag system components to avoid the possibility of accidental deployment of the airbag(s), which could cause personal injury (see Section 27).

CHECK

◆ Refer to illustration 9.2

1   Trace the wire from the ignition switch to the main wiring harness connector and disconnect the connector.

2   Using an ohmmeter or self-powered test light and the accompanying diagrams, check for continuity between the indicated switch terminals with the switch in each of the indicated positions (see illustrations). If the continuity isn't as specified, replace the switch.

REPLACEMENT

◆ Refer to illustrations 9.9 and 9.12

3   Disconnect the cable from the negative terminal of the battery.

4   Place the ignition key in the ACC position.

5   Remove the steering wheel (see Chapter 10).

6   Remove the steering column covers (see Chapter 11).

7   Remove the steering column switches (see Section 8).

Ignition switch

8   Unplug the ignition switch wiring harness connectors.

Switch position	Tester connection	Specified condition
LOCK	—	No continuity
ACC	2 – 3	Continuity
ON	2 – 3 – 4 6 – 7	Continuity
START	1 – 2 – 4 6 – 7 – 8	Continuity

9.2 Ignition switch connector terminal guide and continuity chart

9.9 Detach the retaining screws to remove the ignition switch from the steering column housing

9   Detach the switch retaining screws (see illustration) remove the switch assembly from the steering column.
10   Installation is reverse of the removal.

Lock cylinder

11   Using a small screwdriver or punch to depress the lock cylinder retaining pin.
12   Pull straight out on the lock cylinder assembly to remove it from

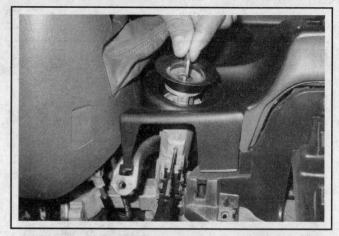

9.12 With the lock cylinder in the ACC position, depress the retaining pin with a small screwdriver, then pull straight out to remove the lock cylinder

the vehicle (see illustration).
13   To install the lock cylinder, depress the retaining pin and guide the lock cylinder into the steering column housing until the retaining pin extends itself back into the locating hole in the steering column housing.
14   The remainder of the installation is the reverse of removal.

---

10   Instrument panel switches - check and replacement

✳✳ WARNING:

The models covered by this manual are equipped with Supplemental Restraint Systems (SRS), more commonly known as airbags. Always disable the airbag system before working in the vicinity of any airbag system components to avoid the possibility of accidental deployment of the airbag(s), which could cause personal injury (see Section 27).

HAZARD WARNING SWITCH

Check

▶ **Refer to illustration 10.2**

1   To check the switch it must first be removed from the center dashboard trim bezel (see below).

2   Test for continuity between the terminals of the switch (see illustration). If the switch fails, replace it.

Replacement

▶ **Refer to illustration 10.4**

3   Carefully pry the upper cluster finish panel from the dashboard (see Chapter 11).
4   Pull the panel out until you can disconnect the electrical connector at the rear of the switch. Depress the tab and remove the switch from the bezel (see illustration).

POWER MIRROR CONTROL SWITCH

Check

▶ **Refer to illustrations 10.6a and 10.6b**

5   The power mirror control switch is mounted at the left end of the

Switch position	Tester connection	Specified condition
Switch OFF	5 – 7	Continuity
Switch ON	1 – 2 – 3 – 4 5 – 6	Continuity
Illumination circuit	8 – 9	Continuity

10.2 Hazard warning switch terminal guide and continuity chart

instrument panel, below the left dashboard vent. Remove the switch for testing (see Step 7).

6   Test for continuity between the terminals of the switch (see illustrations). If the continuity isn't as specified, replace the switch.

Replacement

7   Carefully pry the switch from the panel, using tape on the screwdriver tip to prevent scratching the instrument panel.

8   Disconnect the electrical connector and remove the switch.

9   Installation of the is the reverse of the removal procedure.

TRACTION CONTROL SWITCH

Check

10   The traction control switch works in conjunction with the ABS braking system to provide better traction in some driving conditions.

10.4 Carefully squeeze the clips retaining the hazard switch to the back of the upper cluster finish panel

Switch position	Tester connection	Specified condition
OFF	–	No continuity
UP	1 – 9, 6 – 10	Continuity
DOWN	1 – 10, 6 – 9	Continuity
LEFT	5 – 9, 6 – 10	Continuity
RIGHT	5 – 10, 6 – 9	Continuity

Switch position	Tester connection	Specified condition
OFF	–	No continuity
UP	6 – 10, 7 – 9	Continuity
DOWN	6 – 9, 7 – 10	Continuity
LEFT	6 – 10, 8 – 9	Continuity
RIGHT	6 – 9, 8 – 10	Continuity

10.6a Power mirror switch terminal guide and continuity charts - 1998 to 2000 models

Left side:

Switch position	Tester connection	Specified condition
OFF	–	No continuity
UP	4 – 8, 6 – 7	Continuity
DOWN	4 – 7, 6 – 8	Continuity
LEFT	5 – 8, 6 – 7	Continuity
RIGHT	5 – 7, 6 – 8	Continuity

Right side:

Switch position	Tester connection	Specified condition
OFF	–	No continuity
UP	3 – 8, 6 – 7	Continuity
DOWN	3 – 7, 6 – 8	Continuity
LEFT	5 – 8, 6 – 7	Continuity
RIGHT	5 – 7, 6 – 8	Continuity

10.6b Power mirror switch terminal identification and continuity charts - 2000 and later models

Remove the switch (see Step 12) to test it for proper operation.

11 Test for continuity between the two terminals at either end of the switch. There should be continuity with the switch pressed in, and no continuity with the switch released. If the continuity is not as described, replace the switch.

Replacement

12 Carefully pry the switch from the panel, using tape on the screwdriver tip to prevent scratching the instrument panel.

13 Disconnect the electrical connector and remove the switch.

14 Installation is the reverse of the removal procedure.

INSTRUMENT PANEL LIGHT CONTROL SWITCH

Check

▶ Refer to illustration 10.16

15 The functional unit is a rheostat that controls the voltage to the instrument panel lights. The following check applies only to 2006 and earlier models.

16 Remove the switch (see Step 17). Test the rheostat by applying battery voltage to terminal 1 and a ground jumper wire to terminal 3 (see illustration). Attach voltmeter leads (positive to terminal 3 and negative to terminal 2), and rotate the knob to see if voltage varies.

10.16 Test the dashboard light control rheostat with a voltmeter as shown - voltage should vary as the knob is turned (early models only)

Replacement

17 On models with the rheostat below the left vent, pry the switch panel out of the dashboard with a screwdriver (tape the tip to prevent scratches). On models with a thumbwheel, remove the instrument cluster to access the switch (see Section 12).

11 Instrument panel fuel and temperature gauges - check

▶ Refer to illustrations 11.3a and 11.3b

※ WARNING:

The models covered by this manual are equipped with Supplemental Restraint Systems (SRS), more commonly known as airbags. Always disable the airbag system before working in the vicinity of any airbag system components to avoid the possibility of accidental deployment of the airbag(s), which could cause personal injury (see Section 27).

1 Turn the ignition switch to the ON position.
2 If the gauge pointer does not move from the empty, low or cold

Tester connection	Resistance (Ω)
A – B	Approx. 261.5
A – C	Approx. 107.2
B – C	Approx. 154.3

11.3a Fuel gauge terminal guide and resistance chart - early models w/o Tachometer:

w/ Tachometer:

Tester connection	Resistance (Ω)
A – B	Approx. 175.7
A – C	Approx. 54.0
B – C	Approx. 229.7

11.3b Engine coolant gauge terminal guide and resistance chart - early models

positions, check the fuse. If the fuse is OK, locate the particular sending unit for the circuit you're working on (see Chapter 4 for fuel sending unit location or Chapter 3 for the temperature sending unit location). Connect the sending unit connector to ground. If the pointer goes to the full, high or hot position, replace the sending unit. If the pointer stays in same position, use a jumper wire to ground the sending unit terminal on the back of the gauge (if necessary, refer to the wiring diagrams at the end of this Chapter). If the pointer moves, the problem lies in the wire between the gauge and the sending unit. If the pointer does not move with the sending unit terminal on the back of the gauge grounded, check for voltage at the other terminal of the gauge. If voltage is present, replace the gauge.

3   To check the gauge units alone, remove the instrument cluster (see Section 12) and test the resistance on the terminals for the fuel and temperature gauges (see illustrations).

12 Instrument cluster - removal and installation

▶ **Refer to illustration 12.3**

✳✳ WARNING:

The models covered by this manual are equipped with Supplemental Restraint Systems (SRS), more commonly known as airbags. Always disable the airbag system before working in the vicinity of any airbag system components to avoid the possibility of accidental deployment of the airbag(s), which could cause personal injury (see Section 27).

1   Disconnect the negative battery cable.
2   Remove the instrument cluster bezel (see Chapter 11).
3   Remove the cluster mounting screws (see illustration) and pull the instrument cluster towards the steering wheel.
4   Disconnect any electrical connectors that interfere with removal, and remove the cluster.
5   Installation is the reverse of removal.

12.3 Remove the screws and pull out the instrument cluster

13 Wiper motor - check and replacement

CHECK

♦ **Refer to illustrations 13.2a and 13.2b**

➡Note: Refer to the wiring diagrams for wire colors and locations in the following checks. Keep in mind that power wires are generally larger in diameter and brighter colors, and ground wires are usually smaller in diameter and darker colors. When checking for voltage, probe a grounded 12-volt test light to each terminal at a connector until it lights; this verifies voltage (power) at the terminal.

13.2a Front wiper motor test: With a battery-power jumper on terminal 5 and a ground on terminal 1, the motor should operate at Low speed; with the power applied to terminal 4 and ground to terminal 1, the motor should operate at High speed (early models only)

13.2b Rear wiper motor test: With a battery-power jumper on terminal 3 and a ground on terminal 2, the motor should operate at Low speed - if the motor doesn't operate, replace it

1 **If the wipers work slowly**, make sure the battery is in good condition and has a strong charge (see Chapter 1). If the battery is in good condition, remove the wiper motor (see below) and operate the wiper arms by hand. Check for binding linkage and pivots. Lubricate or repair the linkage or pivots as necessary. Reinstall the wiper motor. If the wipers still operate slowly, check for loose or corroded connections, especially the ground connection. If all connections look OK, replace the motor.

2 **If the wipers fail to operate when activated**, check the fuse. If the fuse is OK, connect a jumper wire between the wiper motor and ground, then retest. If the motor works now, repair the ground connection. If the motor still doesn't work, turn on the wipers and check for voltage at the motor. If there's voltage at the motor, remove the motor and check it off the vehicle with fused jumper wires from the battery (see illustrations). If the motor now works, check for binding linkage (see Step 1 above). If the motor still doesn't work, replace it. If there's no voltage at the motor, check for voltage at the switch. If there's no voltage at the switch, check the wiring between the switch and fuse panel for continuity. If the wiring is OK, the switch is probably bad.

3 **If the wipers only work on one speed**, check the continuity of the wires between the switch and motor, and the continuity of the terminals on the motor. If the wires are OK, replace the switch.

4 **If the interval (delay) function is inoperative**, check the continuity of all the wiring between the switch and motor. If the wiring is OK, replace the interval module.

5 **If the wipers stop at the position they're in when the switch is turned off (fail to park)**, check for voltage at the wiper motor when the wiper switch is OFF but the ignition is ON. If voltage is present, the limit switch in the motor is malfunctioning. Replace the wiper motor. If no voltage is present, trace and repair the limit switch wiring between the fuse panel and wiper motor.

6 **If the wipers won't shut off unless the ignition is OFF**, disconnect the wiring from the wiper control switch. If the wipers stop, replace the switch. If the wipers keep running, there's a defective limit switch in the motor; replace the motor.

7 **If the wipers won't retract below the hoodline**, check for mechanical obstructions in the wiper linkage or on the vehicle's body that would prevent the wipers from parking. If there are no obstructions, check the wiring between the switch and motor for continuity. If the wiring is OK, replace the wiper motor.

13.9a Front wiper motor and linkage retaining bolts

13.9b Remove the liftgate trim panel, then pry the linkage arm from the ball-stud

REPLACEMENT

▶ **Refer to illustrations 13.9a, 13.9b and 13.9c**

8   Refer to Chapter 11 and remove the wiper arms and the cowl covers. The wiper motor and linkage come out with the cowl panel.

9   Remove the wiper linkage retaining bolts and remove the assembly with the motor (see illustration). To remove the rear wiper motor, remove the liftgate interior trim panel, remove the wiper arm and grommet from the outside of the liftgate, then remove the motor/linkage mounting bolts (see illustrations).

10   Remove the bolts and remove the motor from the linkage assembly.

11   Installation is the reverse of removal.

13.9c Remove the rear wiper motor/linkage mounting bolts

14 Radio and speakers - removal and installation

✳✳ WARNING:

The models covered by this manual are equipped with Supplemental Restraint Systems (SRS), more commonly known as airbags. Always disable the airbag system before working in the vicinity of any airbag system components to avoid the possibility of accidental deployment of the airbag(s), which could cause personal injury (see Section 27).

1   Disconnect the negative battery cable.

RADIO

▶ **Refer to illustrations 14.3a and 14.3b**

2   Remove the center dashboard trim bezel (see Chapter 11).

3   Remove the retaining screws and pull the radio outward to access the rear, then disconnect the electrical connectors and the antenna lead (see illustrations).

4   Installation is the reverse of removal.

DOOR SPEAKERS

▶ **Refer to illustration 14.6**

5   Remove the door trim panel (see Chapter 11). All models have

14.3a Remove the radio mounting screws

front door-mounted speakers, and speakers in the rear quarter panels.

6   Remove the speaker retaining screws. Disconnect the electrical connector and remove the speaker from the vehicle (see illustration).

7   Installation is the reverse of removal.

14.3b Pull the radio forward, then disconnect the antenna lead (A) and the electrical connector (B)

14.6 Remove the speaker retaining screws and disconnect the electrical connector to remove the speaker from the vehicle

TWEETERS

▶ **Refer to illustration 14.8**

8   In addition to the standard door and rear speakers, some models are equipped with tweeters for improved high-range sound. Mounted in the windshield pillar trim panels, they can be removed by simply prying under the edge of the tweeter with a screwdriver tip covered with tape. Pull the tweeter out and disconnect the electrical connector (see illustration).

9   Installation is the reverse of removal.

DASH MOUNTED SPEAKERS

10   Using a trim removal tool, carefully pry the speaker cover out from the instrument panel until the clips are released. Take care not to scratch the surrounding instrument panel. Remove the speaker cover

11   Remove the speaker mounting screws.

12   Lift the speaker from its mounting location, disconnect the elec-

trical connector and remove the speaker.

13   Installation is the reverse of the removal procedure. Make sure the speaker cover clips are engaged properly before pushing the panel firmly into place.

14.8 To remove the tweeter speaker from the windshield pillar trim, disconnect the electrical connector (A), then remove the two screws (B)

15 Antenna - check and repair

2006 AND EARLIER MODELS

1   These vehicles are equipped with a wire grid-type antenna attached to the rear window glass.

2   If there is a problem with radio reception, examine the antenna wires by checking for continuity with an ohmmeter.

3   Wrap small pieces of aluminum foil around the tips of your ohmmeter probes and touch them to the wires of the antenna grid. With one probe at one of the antenna terminals, move the other probe along the wire, checking for continuity until a break is found.

4   If a break is found, the wire can be repaired in the same manner as a rear window defogger wire (see Section 16).

2007 AND LATER MODELS

5   If there is a problem with radio reception, check the tightness of the antenna mast and the antenna cable connections at each end.

Antenna mast and trim bezel

6   The mast and the trim bezel can be removed by loosening and lifting upward. Installation is the reverse of removal.

Antenna base and primary cable

▶ **Refer to illustration 15.9**

7   Remove the fender inner splash shield enough to get working room at the antenna base, then remove the mounting nut.

8   Remove the antenna mast and trim bezel.

9   Remove the right A-pillar cover by prying it off with a plastic trim tool or a screwdriver wrapped with tape. Follow the antenna cable to the connector, then disconnect it from the lead-in cable (see illustration).

15.9 The antenna connector on 2007 and later models is under the windshield pillar trim

10   Tie a string to the antenna cable before removing it. Leave the string in place to aid in installing the new assembly. Installation is the reverse of removal.

Lead-in cable

11   Refer to Chapter 11 and remove the instrument panel outer cover to expose the cable.

12   Disconnect the cable at each end, then detach it from the five retainers. Installation is the reverse of removal.

Amplifier antenna (premium sound system)

13   This unit is mounted in the rear of the vehicle under the headliner. Removal of the headliner is a difficult procedure and should be done only by a qualified facility.

14   If the headliner is removed, the antenna can be removed by disconnecting the connectors, then removing the three mounting bolts and releasing the 16 clamps. Installation is the reverse of removal.

16 Rear window defogger - check and repair

1   The rear window defogger consists of a number of horizontal elements baked onto the glass surface.

2   Small breaks in the element can be repaired without removing the rear window.

CHECK

▶ **Refer to illustrations 16.4, 16.5 and 16.7**

3   Turn the ignition switch and defogger system switches to the ON

16.4 When measuring the voltage at the rear window defogger grid, wrap a piece of aluminum foil around the positive probe of the voltmeter and press the foil against the wire with your finger

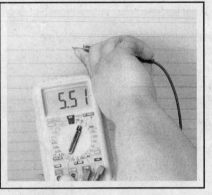

16.5 To determine if a heating element has broken, check the voltage at the center of each element - if the voltage is 5 or 6-volts, the element is unbroken - if the voltage is 10 or 12-volts, the element is broken between the center and the ground side - if there is no voltage, the element is broken between the center and the positive side

16.7 To find the break, place the voltmeter negative lead against the defogger ground terminal, place the voltmeter positive lead with the foil strip against the heating element at the positive terminal end and slide it toward the negative terminal end - the point at which the voltmeter reading changes abruptly is the point at which the element is broken

16.13 To use a defogger repair kit, apply masking tape to the inside of the window at the damaged area, then brush on the special conductive coating

6   Connect the negative lead to a good body ground. The reading should stay the same. If it doesn't, the ground connection is bad.

7   To find the break, place the voltmeter negative probe against the defogger ground terminal. Place the voltmeter positive probe with the foil strip against the heating element at the positive terminal end and slide it toward the negative terminal end. The point at which the voltmeter deflects from several volts to zero is the point at which the heating element is broken (see illustration).

REPAIR

▶ **Refer to illustration 16.13**

8   Repair the break in the element using a repair kit specifically recommended for this purpose, available at most auto parts stores. Included in this kit is plastic conductive epoxy.

9   Prior to repairing a break, turn off the system and allow it to cool off for a few minutes.

10 Lightly buff the element area with fine steel wool, then clean it thoroughly with rubbing alcohol.

11 Use masking tape to mask off the area being repaired.

12 Thoroughly mix the epoxy, following the instructions provided with the repair kit.

13 Apply the epoxy material to the slit in the masking tape, overlapping the undamaged area about 3/4-inch on either end (see illustration).

14 Allow the repair to cure for 24 hours before removing the tape and using the system.

position. Using a voltmeter, place the positive probe against the defogger grid positive terminal and the negative probe against the ground terminal. If battery voltage is not indicated, check the fuse, defogger switch and related wiring. If voltage is indicated, but all or part of the defogger doesn't heat, proceed with the following tests.

4   When measuring voltage during the next two tests, wrap a piece of aluminum foil around the tip of the voltmeter positive probe and press the foil against the heating element with your finger (see illustration). Place the negative probe on the defogger grid ground terminal.

5   Check the voltage at the center of each heating element (see illustration). If the voltage is 5 or 6-volts, the element is okay (there is no break). If the voltage is 0-volts, the element is broken between the center of the element and the positive end, If the voltage is 10 to 12-volts the element is broken between the center of the element and ground. Check each heating element.

17 Headlight bulbs - removal and installation

▶ **Refer to illustrations 17.1 and 17.2**

✳✳ WARNING:

Halogen gas filled bulbs are under pressure and may shatter if the surface is scratched or the bulb is dropped. Wear eye pro-

tection and handle the bulbs carefully, grasping only the base whenever possible. Do not touch the surface of the bulb with your fingers because the oil from your skin could cause it to overheat and fail prematurely. If you do touch the bulb surface, clean it with rubbing alcohol.

1 Reach behind the headlight assembly and unplug the electrical connector (see illustration).

2 Remove the rubber cover over the bulb. Release the spring securing the headlight bulb and remove the bulb (see illustration).

3 Without touching the glass with your bare fingers, insert the new bulb assembly into the headlight housing, and secure it with the spring.

4 Install the rubber cover, making sure the tab marked "Top Pull" is at the top.

5 Plug in the electrical connector.

17.1 Headlight bulb electrical connector

17.2 Release the bulb-retaining spring, then remove the bulb

18 Headlights - adjustment

◆ **Refer to illustrations 18.1 and 18.3**

➡ **Note: This procedure applies only to 2006 and earlier models with standard headlights. Later models have an electric headlight adjusting system that uses a driver-operated thumbwheel.**

➡ **Note: The headlights must be aimed correctly. If adjusted incorrectly they could blind the driver of an oncoming vehicle and cause a serious accident or seriously reduce your ability to see the road. The headlights should be checked for proper aim every 12 months and any time a new headlight is installed or front-end bodywork is performed. It should be emphasized that the following procedure is only an interim step, which will provide temporary adjustment until the headlights can be adjusted by a properly equipped shop.**

1 Halogen bulb type headlights have two adjustment screws located on the top of each headlight housing. Adjustments are made by turning two screws on the headlight housings (see illustration). The horizontal adjustment is made by turning both the lower headlight housing mounting nut and a bushing. Moving the bushing (on the housing stud) in or out changes the headlight aim, while the mounting nut secures it.

2 There are several methods of adjusting the headlights. The simplest method requires masking tape, a blank wall and a level floor.

3 Position masking tape vertically on the wall in reference to the vehicle centerline and the centerlines of both headlights (see illustration).

4 Position a horizontal tapeline in reference to the centerline of all the headlights.

➡ **Note: It may be easier to position the tape on the wall with the vehicle parked only a few inches away.**

5 Adjustment should be made with the vehicle parked 25 feet from the wall, sitting level, the gas tank half-full and no unusually heavy load in the vehicle.

6 Starting with the low beam adjustment, position the high intensity zone so it is two inches below the horizontal line and two inches to

18.1 Headlight adjustment screws

A   Horizontal adjustment   *B   Vertical adjustment*

18.3 Headlight adjustment details

the side of the headlight vertical line, away from oncoming traffic. Adjustment is made by turning the vertical adjusting screw to raise or lower the beam. The horizontal adjusting screw should be used in the same manner to move the beam left or right.

7   With the high beams on, the high intensity zone should be vertically centered with the exact center just below the horizontal line.

➡Note: It may not be possible to position the headlight aim exactly for both high and low beams. If a compromise must be made, keep in mind that the low beams are the most used and have the greatest effect on driver safety.

8   Have the headlights adjusted by a dealer service department or service station at the earliest opportunity.

19 Headlight housing - removal and installation

⬧ **Refer to illustration 19.3**

❊❊ WARNING:

These vehicles are equipped with halogen gas-filled headlight bulbs, which are under pressure and may shatter if the surface is damaged or the bulb is dropped. Wear eye protection and handle the bulbs carefully, grasping only the base whenever possible. Do not touch the surface of the bulb with your fingers because the oil from your skin could cause it to overheat and fail prematurely. If you do touch the bulb surface, clean it with rubbing alcohol.

1   Remove the headlight bulb (see Section 17). On 2007 and later models, remove the front bumper cover (see Chapter 11).
2   Remove the side marker light (see Section 21).
3   Remove the retaining bolts, detach the housing and withdraw it from the vehicle (see illustration).
4   Installation is the reverse of removal. Be sure to check headlight adjustment (see Section 18).

19.3 Headlight housing retaining bolts (2006 and earlier models)

20 Horn - check and replacement

CHECK

⬧ **Refer to illustration 20.3**

➡Note: Check the fuses before beginning electrical diagnosis.

1   Disconnect the electrical connector from the horn.

20.3 Check for power at the horn terminal (below) with the horn button depressed - at top is the mounting bolt

2   To test the horn, connect battery voltage to the terminal with a jumper wire. If the horn doesn't sound, replace it.
3   If the horn does sound, check for voltage at the terminal when the horn button is depressed (see illustration). If there's voltage at the terminal, check for a bad ground at the horn.
4   If there's no voltage at the horn, check the relay (see Section 6). Note that most horn relays are either the four-terminal or externally grounded, three-terminal type.
5   If the relay is OK, check for voltage to the relay power and control circuits. If either of the circuits is not receiving voltage, inspect the wiring between the relay and the fuse panel.
6   If both relay circuits are receiving voltage, depress the horn button and check the circuit from the relay to the horn button for continuity to ground. If there's no continuity, check the circuit for an open. If there's no open circuit, replace the horn button.
7   If there's continuity to ground through the horn button, check for an open or short in the circuit from the relay to the horn.

REPLACEMENT

8   On 2007 and later models, remove the front bumper cover (see Chapter 11). Disconnect the wiring and remove the bracket bolt (see illustration 20.3).
9   Installation is the reverse of removal.

21 Bulb replacement

FRONT PARK/TURN SIGNAL LIGHTS

▶ **Refer to illustrations 21.1a and 21.1b**

1   On 2006 and earlier models, remove the screw that secures the top of the park/turn signal light housing. Pull the side light housing outward to access the bulbs located in the backside. Rotate the bulb

21.1a Remove the screw on top of the park/turn housing, then rotate the housing outward to access the bulb

holder counterclockwise and pull the bulb out (see illustrations).

2   On 2007 and later models, these lights are located in the headlight housings. Twist the bulb holders to remove them from the rear of the housing. The bulbs can then be pulled straight out of the bulb holders.

3   Installation is the reverse of removal.

REAR TAIL LIGHT/BRAKE LIGHT/TURN SIGNAL

▶ **Refer to illustrations 21.4 and 21.5**

4   These vehicles have tail/brake/turn lights on both the rear corners of the body. To remove the lights for bulb replacement, remove the two screws and detach the taillight lens (see illustration).

5   Pull the taillight housing out from the body to access the rear bulbholders (see illustration). Use a trim tool to pry the taillight housing away from the body at the forward end, using a rag against the body to prevent scratches. Two plastic pins in body sockets secure the back of housing.

6   Rotate the bulb holders counterclockwise and pull the bulbs out to remove them.

7   Installation is the reverse of removal.

21.1b Rotate the bulb holder to pull it out for bulb replacement

21.4 Remove the two screws and push the taillight housing toward the side of the vehicle to release it from the body

21.5 Pry the light housing away from the body to release the two pins, there is access to replace the bulbs for the brake/tail light (top bulb) and the rear turn signal bulb (bottom bulb)

21.8 Remove the screws from the license light lens, then remove the lens to access the bulb

21.10 Remove the screws from the faceplate of the high-mounted brake light

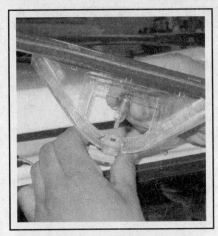

21.11 With the high-mounted brake light housing pulled away from the liftgate, the bulb holder can be removed and the bulb replaced

21.14 Remove the instrument cluster bulbs by rotating them 1/4-turn counterclockwise and pulling straight out

21.16 Pry out the interior light cover for access to the bulb

LICENSE PLATE LIGHT

▶ **Refer to illustration 21.8**

8   Remove the two screws in the license light lens, then pull the lens out (see illustration). Replace the bulbs.

9   Installation is the reverse of removal.

HIGH-MOUNTED BRAKE LIGHT

▶ **Refer to illustrations 21.10 and 21.11**

10 Remove the two screws securing the high-mounted brake light to the top exterior of the liftgate, then pull the housing out (see illustration).

11 On the back of the housing, twist the bulb holder counterclockwise to remove it, then pull the bulb straight out of the holder (see illustration).

12 Installation is the reverse of removal.

INSTRUMENT CLUSTER LIGHTS

▶ **Refer to illustration 21.14**

13 To gain access to the instrument cluster illumination bulbs, the instrument cluster will have to be removed (see Section 12). The bulbs can then be removed and replaced from the rear of the cluster.

14 Rotate the bulb counterclockwise to remove it (see illustration).

15 Installation is the reverse of removal.

INTERIOR LIGHTS

▶ **Refer to illustration 21.16**

16 Pry the interior lens off the interior light housing (see illustration).

17 Detach the bulb from the terminals. It may be necessary to pry the bulb out - if this is the case, pry only on the ends of the bulb (otherwise the glass may shatter). Do not get fingerprints on the glass of the bulb.

18 Installation is the reverse of removal.

22 Electric side view mirrors - description and check

1   Most electric rear view mirrors use two motors to move the glass; one for up and down adjustments and one for left-right adjustments.

2   The control switch has a selector portion that sends voltage to the left or right side mirror. With the ignition ON but the engine OFF, roll down the windows and operate the mirror control switch through all functions (left-right and up-down) for both the left and right side mirrors.

3   Listen carefully for the sound of the electric motors running in the mirrors.

4   If the motors can be heard but the mirror glass doesn't move, there's a problem with the drive mechanism inside the mirror. Remove and disassemble the mirror to locate the problem.

5   If the mirrors do not operate and no sound comes from the mirrors, check the fuse (see Chapter 1).

6   If the fuse is OK, remove the mirror control switch from the dashboard. Check the continuity of the switch (see Section 10).

7   Re-connect the switch. Locate the wire going from the switch to ground. Leaving the switch connected, connect a jumper wire between this wire and ground. If the mirror works normally with this wire in place, repair the faulty ground connection.

8   If the mirror still doesn't work, remove the mirror and check the wires at the mirror for voltage. Check with ignition ON and the mirror selector switch on the appropriate side. Operate the mirror switch in all its positions. There should be voltage at one of the switch-to-mirror wires in each switch position (except the neutral "off" position).

9   If there's not voltage in each switch position, check the circuit between the mirror and control switch for opens and shorts.

10 If there's voltage, remove the mirror and test it off the vehicle with jumper wires. Replace the mirror if it fails this test.

23 Cruise control system - description and check

1   The cruise control system maintains vehicle speed with a electrically-operated motor located in the engine compartment, which is connected to the accelerator pedal by a cable. The system consists of the cruise control unit, brake switch, control switches and vehicle speed sensor. Some features of the system require special testers and diagnostic procedures that are beyond the scope of this manual. Listed below are some general procedures that may be used to locate common problems.

2   Locate and check the fuse (see Section 3).

3   Have an assistant operate the brake lights while you check their operation (voltage from the brake light switch deactivates the cruise control).

4   If the brake lights don't come on or stay on all the time, correct the problem and retest the cruise control.

5   Visually inspect the control cable between cruise control motor and the throttle linkage for free movement, replace if necessary.

6   The cruise control system uses a speed-sensing input from the vehicle's ABS braking system. A scan tool may be necessary to look for diagnostic trouble codes to troubleshoot the cruise control system.

7   Test drive the vehicle to determine if the cruise control is now working. If it isn't, take it to a dealer service department or an automotive electrical specialist for further diagnosis.

24 Power window system - description and check

▶ **Refer to illustrations 24.10a, 24.10b, 24.10c and 24.10d**

1   The power window system operates electric motors, mounted in the doors, which lower and raise the windows. The system consists of the control switches, relays, the motors, regulators, glass mechanisms and associated wiring.

2   The power windows can be lowered and raised from the master control switch by the driver or by remote switches located at the individual windows. Each window has a separate motor that is reversible. The position of the control switch determines the polarity and therefore the direction of operation.

3   The circuit is protected by a fuse and a circuit breaker. Each motor is also equipped with an internal circuit breaker; this prevents one stuck window from disabling the whole system.

4   The power window system will only operate when the ignition switch is ON. In addition, many models have a window lockout switch at the master control switch that, when activated, disables the switches at the rear windows and, sometimes, the switch at the passenger's window also. Always check these items before troubleshooting a window problem.

5   These procedures are general in nature, so if you can't find the problem using them, take the vehicle to a dealer service department or other properly equipped repair facility.

6   If the power windows won't operate, always check the fuse and circuit breaker first.

7   If only the rear windows are inoperative, or if the windows only operate from the master control switch, check the rear window lockout switch for continuity in the unlocked position. Replace it if it doesn't have continuity.

Front Driver's Switch (Window unlock):

Switch position	Tester connection	Specified condition
UP	1 – 4, 3 – 9	Continuity
OFF	1 – 3 – 4	Continuity
DOWN	1 – 3, 4 – 9	Continuity

Front Driver's Switch (Window lock):

Switch position	Tester connection	Specified condition
UP	1 – 4, 3 – 9	Continuity
OFF	1 – 3 – 4	Continuity
DOWN	1 – 3, 4 – 9	Continuity

Front Passenger's Switch (Window unlock):

Switch position	Tester connection	Specified condition
UP	1 – 10, 8 – 9	Continuity
OFF	1 – 8 – 10	Continuity
DOWN	1 – 8, 9 – 10	Continuity

Front Passenger's Switch (Window lock):

Switch position	Tester connection	Specified condition
UP	8 – 9	Continuity
OFF	8 – 10	Continuity
DOWN	9 – 10	Continuity

24.10a Power window master control switch terminal guide and continuity chart - 1998 through 2000 models

Front Driver's Switch (Window unlock):

Switch position	Tester connection	Specified condition
AUTO UP	1 – 9, 4 – 7	Continuity
UP	1 – 9, 4 – 7	Continuity
OFF	1 – 4 – 9	Continuity
DOWN	1 – 4, 7 – 9	Continuity
AUTO DOWN	1 – 4, 7 – 9	Continuity

Front Passenger's Switch (Window unlock):

Switch position	Tester connection	Specified condition
UP	1 – 15, 6 – 13	Continuity
OFF	1 – 13 – 15	Continuity
DOWN	1 – 13, 6 – 15	Continuity

Front Passenger's Switch (Window lock):

Switch position	Tester connection	Specified condition
UP	6 – 13	Continuity
OFF	13 – 15	Continuity
DOWN	6 – 15	Continuity

9 — 1

18 — 10

24.10b Power window master control switch terminal guide and continuity chart - 2001 through 2006 models

8   Check the wiring between the switches and fuse panel for continuity. Repair the wiring, if necessary.

9   If only one window is inoperative from the master control switch, try the other control switch at the window.

➡ **Note: This doesn't apply to the drivers door window.**

10 If the same window works from one switch, but not the other, check the switch for continuity (see illustrations). If the continuity is not as specified replace the switch. Some models are equipped with power quarter-windows. The switch is located just below the radio. Check it for continuity if there is a problem with power quarter-window operation (see illustration).

5 4 3 2 1

Switch position	Tester connection	Specified condition
UP	1 – 2, 3 – 4	Continuity
OFF	1 – 2, 3 – 5	Continuity
DOWN	1 – 4, 3 – 5	Continuity

24.10c Passenger front power window switch terminal guide and continuity chart - early models

REAR VENT

4 3   2 1
10 9 8 7 6 5

Switch position	Tester connection	Specified condition
CLOSE	3 – 7, 8 – 9	Continuity
OFF	6 – 7, 8 – 9	Continuity
OPEN	3 – 8, 6 – 7	Continuity
Illumination Circuit	1 – 5	Continuity

24.10d Power quarter-window switch terminal guide and continuity chart - early models

11 If the switch tests OK, check for a short or open in the circuit between the affected switch and the window motor.

12 If one window is inoperative from both switches, remove the trim panel from the affected door and check for voltage at the switch and at the motor while the switch is operated.

13 If voltage is reaching the motor, disconnect the glass from the regulator (see Chapter 11). Move the window up and down by hand while checking for binding and damage. Also check for binding and damage to the regulator. If the regulator is not damaged and the window moves up and down smoothly, replace the motor. If there's binding or damage, lubricate, repair or replace parts, as necessary.

14 If voltage isn't reaching the motor, check the wiring in the circuit for continuity between the switches and motors. You'll need to consult the wiring diagram for the vehicle. If the circuit is equipped with a relay, check that the relay is grounded properly and receiving voltage.

15 Test the windows after you are done to confirm proper repairs.

25 Power door lock system - description and check

♦ Refer to illustrations 25.6a, 25.6b, 25.6c and 25.9

1 A power door lock system operates the door lock actuators mounted in each door. The system consists of the switches, actuators, a control unit and associated wiring. Diagnosis can usually be limited to simple checks of the wiring connections and actuators for minor faults that can be easily repaired. Since this system uses an electronic control unit in-depth diagnosis should be left to a dealership service department. The door lock control unit is located behind the instrument panel, to the right of the fuse box.

2 Power door lock systems are operated by bi-directional solenoids located in the doors. The lock switches have two operating positions: Lock and Unlock. When activated, the switch sends a ground signal to the door lock control unit to lock or unlock the doors. Depending on which way the switch is activated, the control unit reverses polarity to the solenoids, allowing the two sides of the circuit to be used alternately as the feed (positive) and ground side.

3 Some vehicles may have an anti-theft systems incorporated into the power locks. If you are unable to locate the trouble using the following general Steps, consult a dealer service department or other qualified repair shop.

4 Always check the circuit protection first. Some vehicles use a combination of circuit breakers and fuses.

5 Operate the door lock switches in both directions (Lock and Unlock) with the engine off. Listen for the click of the solenoids operating.

6 Test the switches for continuity (see illustrations). Replace the switch if there's not continuity in both switch positions.

7 Check the wiring between the switches, control unit and solenoids for continuity. Repair the wiring if there's no continuity.

25.6a Driver's power door lock switch terminal guide and continuity chart - 1998 through 2000 models

Switch position	Tester connection	Specified condition
LOCK	1 – 2	Continuity
OFF	–	No continuity
UNLOCK	1 – 5	Continuity

25.6b Driver's power door lock switch terminal guide and continuity chart - 2001 through 2006 models

Switch position	Tester connection	Specified condition
LOCK	1 – 10	Continuity
OFF	–	No continuity
UNLOCK	1 – 18	Continuity

25.6c Passenger's power door lock switch terminal guide and continuity chart - early models

Switch position	Tester connection	Specified condition
LOCK	3 – 6	Continuity
OFF	–	No continuity
UNLOCK	3 – 5	Continuity

8   Check for a bad ground at the switches or the control unit.

9   If all but one lock solenoids operate, remove the trim panel from the affected door (see Chapter 11) and check for voltage at the solenoid while the lock switch is operated. One of the wires should have voltage in the Lock position; the other should have voltage in the Unlock position (see illustration).

10 If the inoperative solenoid is receiving voltage, replace the solenoid.

11 If the inoperative solenoid isn't receiving voltage, check the relay for an open or short in the wire between the lock solenoid and the control unit.

➡ **Note: It's common for wires to break in the portion of the harness between the body and door (opening and closing the door fatigues and eventually breaks the wires).**

KEYLESS ENTRY SYSTEM

▶ **Refer to illustrations 25.14 and 25.15**

12 The keyless entry system consists of a remote control transmitter that sends a coded infrared signal to a receiver, which then operates the door lock system. On models so equipped, the transmitter may also engage the alarm system and provide a "panic" button that flashes the lights and blows the horn for emergencies.

13 Replace the transmitter batteries when the red LED light on the case doesn't light when the button is pushed. As the batteries deterio-

25.9 Check for voltage at the lock solenoid while the lock switch is operated

rate with age, the distance at which the remote transmitter operates will diminish.

14 Use a coin or small screwdriver to carefully separate the case halves for battery replacement (see illustration).

15 Replace the two lithium batteries with the same type as originally installed, observing the polarity diagram on the case (see illustration).

16 Snap the case halves together.

25.14 Use a small screwdriver or coin to separate the transmitter halves

25.15 Replace the lithium batteries with the same type as used originally - 1999 and later models have only one battery

26 Daytime Running Lights (DRL) - general information

The Daytime Running Lights (DRL) system used on Canadian models illuminates the headlights whenever the engine is running. The only exception is with the engine running and the parking brake engaged. Once the parking brake is released, the lights will remain on as long as the ignition switch is on, even if the parking brake is later applied.

The DRL system supplies reduced power to the headlights so they won't be too bright for daytime use, while prolonging headlight life.

27 Airbag - general information

▶ **Refer to illustration 27.1**

All models are equipped with a Supplemental Restraint System (SRS), more commonly known as an airbag (see illustration). This system is designed to protect the driver, and the front seat passenger, from serious injury in the event of a head-on or frontal collision. It consists of an airbag module in the center of the steering wheel and the right side of the instrument panel and a sensing/diagnostic module mounted in the center of the vehicle, ahead of the floor console. An impact sensor is bolted to the front of each unibody frame rail (near each side of the radiator). Seat belt pre-tensioners, which are explosive charges that retract the seat belts during an impact, are incorporated into the front seat retractor reels. 2001 and later models are equipped with side-impact airbags located in the backs of the front seats.

AIRBAG MODULES

Driver's side

The airbag inflator module contains a housing incorporating the cushion (airbag) and inflator unit, mounted in the center of the steering wheel. The inflator assembly is mounted on the back of the housing over a hole through which gas is expelled, inflating the bag almost instantaneously when an electrical signal is sent from the system. A coil assembly on the steering column under the module carries this signal to the module. This coil assembly can transmit an electrical signal regardless of steering wheel position.

Passenger's side

The airbag is mounted above the glove compartment and designated by the letters SRS (Supplemental Restraint System). It consists of an inflator containing an igniter, a bag assembly, a reaction housing and a trim cover.

The airbag is considerably larger that the steering wheel-mounted unit and is supported by the steel reaction housing. The trim cover is textured and painted to match the instrument panel and has a molded seam that splits when the bag inflates. As with the steering-wheel-mounted air bag, the igniter electrical signal converts to heat, which ignites the charge and inflates the bag.

Side-impact airbags

Extra protection is provided on 2001 and later models with the addition of side-impact airbags. These are smaller devices located in

27.1 Supplemental Restraint System (SRS) components

the seat backs on the side toward the exterior of the vehicle. The impact sensors for the side-impact airbags are located at the bottom of the door pillars in the body.

SENSING AND DIAGNOSTIC MODULE

The sensing and diagnostic module supplies the current to the airbag system in the event of the collision, even if battery power is cut off. It checks this system every time the vehicle is started, causing the "AIR BAG" light to go on then off, if the system is operating properly. If there is a fault in the system, the light will go on and stay on, flash, or the dash will make a beeping sound. If this happens, the vehicle should be taken to your dealer immediately for service.

PRECAUTIONS

✳✳ WARNING:

Failure to follow these precautions could result in accidental deployment of the airbag and personal injury.

Whenever working in the vicinity of the steering wheel, steering col-
umn or any of the other SRS system components, the system must be disarmed. To disarm the system:

a) Point the wheels straight ahead and turn the key to the Lock position.
b) Disconnect the cable from the negative battery terminal, then the positive cable.
c) Wait at least two minutes for the back-up power supply to be depleted.

Whenever handling an airbag module, always keep the airbag opening (the trim side) pointed away from your body. Never place the airbag module on a bench of other surface with the airbag opening facing the surface. Always place the airbag module in a safe location with the airbag opening facing up.

Never measure the resistance of any SRS component. An ohmmeter has a built-in battery supply that could accidentally deploy the airbag.

Never use electrical welding equipment on a vehicle equipped with an airbag without first disconnecting the yellow airbag connector, located under the steering column near the combination switch connector (driver's airbag) and behind the glove box (passenger's airbag).

Never dispose of a live airbag module. Return it to a dealer service department or other qualified repair shop for safe deployment and disposal.

28 Wiring diagrams - general information

Since it isn't possible to include all wiring diagrams for every year covered by this manual, the following diagrams are those that are typical and most commonly needed.

Prior to troubleshooting any circuits, check the fuse and circuit breakers (if equipped) to make sure they're in good condition. Make sure the battery is properly charged and check the cable connections (see Chapter 1).

When checking a circuit, make sure that all connectors are clean, with no broken or loose terminals. When unplugging a connector, do not pull on the wires. Pull only on the connector housings themselves.

Wire colors are indicated by an alphabetical code.

B	= Black	W	= White	BR	= Brown
L	= Blue	V	= Violet	SB	= Sky Blue
R	= Red	G	= Green	LG	= Light Green
P	= Pink	Y	= Yellow	GR	= Gray
O	= Orange				

The first letter indicates the basic wire color and the second letter indicates the color of the stripe.

Wiring diagram color code chart

Engine control system (1 of 2)

Engine control system (2 of 2)

Starting and charging systems

Headlight system (U.S. models)

Headlight system (Canadian models)

Interior lighting system

Turn signal, backup and tail lighting system

Vanity and courtesy lighting system (1 of 2)

Vanity and courtesy lighting system (2 of 2)

Tail and parking lighting system

Interior switch illumination

Front and rear window wiper/washer system

Power window system

Power door lock system (1 of 3)

Power door lock system (2 of 3)

Power door lock system (3 of 3)

Power moon roof and quarter window systems

Electronically controlled transaxle system

Antilock braking system

Cruise control system

Air bag system

Rear window defogger and power mirror system

Audio system

Instrument panel system

Radiator/condenser cooling fan system (towing package equipped)

Radiator/condenser cooling fan system (without towing package)

Front air conditioning system

Rear air conditioning system (5-door model) (1 of 2)

Rear air conditioning system (5-door model) (2 of 2)

Rear air conditioning system (4-door model)

Notes

MASTER INDEX